3D STUDIO MAX® 2
FUNDAMENTALS

Michael Todd Peterson

Contributing Author: Larry Minton

Cover Art by Steve Burke

New
Riders

New Riders Publishing   201 West 103rd Street
Indianapolis, IN 46290 USA

3D Studio MAX® 2 Fundamentals

By Michael Todd Peterson and Larry Minton

Published by:

New Riders Publishing

201 West 103rd Street

Indianapolis, IN 46290 USA

© 1998 by New Riders Publishing

Printed in the United States of America 1 2 3 4 5 6 7 8 9 0

Library of Congress Cataloging-in-Publication Data

```
***CIP data available upon request***
```

ISBN: 1-56205-839-8

Warning and Disclaimer

Publisher	Jordan Gold
Executive Editor	Alicia Buckley
Director of Editorial Services	Lisa Wilson
Managing Editor	Brice Gosnell
Brand Manager	Alan Bower

Development Editor
Laura Frey

Project Editor
Kevin Laseau

Copy Editors
Michael Brumitt
San Dee Phillips

Technical Editor
John Stetzer

Software Product Developer
David Garratt

Team Coordinator
Michelle Newcomb

Manufacturing Coordinator
Paul Gilchrist

Book Designer
Glenn Larsen

Cover Designer
Dan Armstrong

Cover Production
Casey Price

Director of Production
Larry Klein

Production Team Supervisor
Brad Chinn

Graphics Image Specialists
Steve Adams, Debi Bolhuis,
Kevin Cliburn, Sadie
Crawford, Wil Cruz,
Tammy Graham, Oliver
Jackson

Production Analysts
Dan Harris, Erich J. Richter

Production Team
Mona Brown, Carol
Bowers, Ayanna Lacey,
Gene Redding

Indexer
Bruce Clingaman

About the Authors

Michael Todd Peterson is the owner of MTP Graphics, an animation firm that specializes in Architectural, Forensics, and Multimedia. Todd also currently teaches 3D Studio MAX at Roane State Community College. In addition, Todd has also authored or co-authored Inside AutoCAD 14 and *Inside 3d Studio MAX* Vol II and III.

Larry Minton is the owner of Avguard Animations, located near Columbus, Ohio. Larry has been a 3D Studio user since 1991 and was a 3D Studio MAX R1 and R2 beta tester. After spending 15 years as a Chemical and Nuclear Safety Analyst figuring out how things blow up, he decided to limit the destruction to the virtual worlds. Larry was a contributing author and technical editor for New Rider's *Inside 3D Studio MAX* series and is currently performing the main character animations for a (hopefully) upcoming game.

Cover Artist

Steve Burke is currently the art director at a venerable computer company and has most recently founded Burke Studios. His personal ambition is to saturate the 3D market with humor and good taste.

steve@burkestudios.com

www.burkestudios.com

Trademark Acknowledgments

All terms mentioned in this book that are known to be trademarks or service marks have been appropriately capitalized. New Riders Publishing cannot attest to the accuracy of this information. Use of a term in this book should not be regarded as affecting the validity of any trademark or service mark.

Acknowledgments

I would like to take this opportunity to thank the people at New Riders for their patience and persistence with this book. I would also like to thank Gary Yost and the Yost group for providing and creating this wonderful software. Thanks to Paul Perrault at Kinetix for keeping me in the loop on many things related to MAX. Also thanks to the folks at Digimation for their help when I needed it. And, lastly a special thanks to Larry Minton for coming in at the last minute to help make sure this book got out on time.

—Michael Todd Peterson

I wish to thank my wife, Ann, for her patience and love, the virtual MAX community on CompuServe for their support of all MAX users, and the Kinetix and Yost Group development team for creating a grand new tool.

—Larry Minton

Contents at a Glance

Table of Contents

I NTRODUCTION

3D Studio MAX 2 is a major enhancement (over 1,000 new features) of the leading 3D animation software for a PC. This software, developed by Kinetix, works with Windows 95 or NT 3.51 or later and provides you with new levels of productivity, capability, and customizability. Some of the major new features of MAX 2 include:

- **NURBS (Non-Uniform Rational B-Splines) modeling:** Provides the best technology available for modeling objects with complex curves.

- **Dynamics:** Accurately creates real-world physics such as collisions, gravity, and friction in your animations.

- **Raytracing:** Provides great reflections and refractions implemented as a material that you can apply quickly to individual objects in the scene.

- **Scripting:** Gives you the power to create your own plug-ins without having to know C++ or how to program. Scripting can even be extended to make use of MAX plug-ins.

- **Interface Enhancement:** Includes a powerful, true 3D snap system, ghosting, support for OpenGL, and Direct3D, as well as a faster HEIDI engine for screen redraws and more keyboard shortcuts, all while keeping the same basic interface as version 1.2.

- **Material Editor Enhancements:** Preview more than six materials at a time, add bump maps to reflection maps, use Blinn shading instead of Gouraud, and have access to many types of procedural maps.

- **Enhanced particles:** Includes instanced geometry, meta-particles, and many other effects.

- **Optical Effects:** Provides you with lens flares, glows, highlights, and depth of field abilities.

3D Studio MAX 2 Fundamentals serves as an introduction to the basic functions of this powerful system. Within this book, you will explore 3D Studio MAX 2 and the concepts behind the technology with concise explanations and dozens of hands-on exercises. Each of the exercises is also included on the accompanying CD as an interactive demonstration.

Who Should Read This Book?

3D Studio MAX 2 Fundamentals is for individuals who have little or no practical experience with any 3D programs, or who are just starting or have limited experience with 3D Studio MAX.

Although it is geared toward the beginning user, advanced users will find the information in the book useful, too. This book focuses on the basics of modeling, rendering, and animating geometry in 3D Studio MAX 2. Each topic is introduced from a theoretical standpoint; then you dive into exercises and explanations of how to put that information to use.

For people who have never used any version of 3D Studio MAX, it is beneficial, but not required, to have some experience in the following areas:

♦ AutoCAD (or any CAD program for that matter)

♦ 3D drawing

♦ 3D Studio for DOS (or any rendering and animation package)

♦ Art or freehand drawing

Even if you do not have experience with one of these items, you can still learn and use 3D Studio MAX 2 by following along with the exercises in this book. It just might take you a little longer than someone who does have experience in these areas.

How This Book Is Organized

3D Studio MAX 2 Fundamentals gives you an overview of the MAX system and shows you how to work with it. To help provide you with a clear understanding of MAX, the book is divided into the following sections:

♦ **Section 1: Overview.** Provides you with an overview of 3D graphics terminology and concepts, followed by an introduction to the MAX 2 interface.

- **Section 2: Geometry Fundamentals.** Starts out by introducing the terms and technology behind modeling in the MAX system. This is followed by chapters on various modeling and editing techniques.

- **Section 3: Scene Composition Fundamentals.** Introduces the terminology and concepts behind scene composition, cameras, lights, materials, and rendering. Then, each chapter takes you through a different section of composition, while you develop a real-life bowling alley scene.

- **Section 4: Animation Fundamentals.** Introduces you to animation concepts and terminology, followed by a good grounding in the techniques used in MAX to create animation.

- **Section 5: Glossary.** A glossary of important 3D modeling, animation, and rendering terms.

In addition to the written text, this book contains a CD. The CD contains all of the data files necessary to complete each tutorial exercise, as well as Lotus ScreenCAM interactive versions of each exercise to help speed the learning process. CD installation instructions are printed on the CD label.

Notes, Tips, Warnings, and Upgrade Notes

3D Studio MAX 2 Fundamentals includes special sidebars, which are set apart from the normal text by icons. This book includes four distinct types of sidebars: Notes, Tips, Warnings, and Upgrade Notes. These passages have been given special treatment so that you can instantly recognize their significance and easily find them for future reference.

A *Note* includes extra information you should find useful. A Note might describe special situations that can arise when you use MAX under certain circumstances and might tell you what steps to take when such situations arise. **NOTE**

A *Tip* provides quick instructions for getting the most from your MAX setup. A Tip might show you how to speed up a procedure, or how to perform one of many time-saving and system-enhancing actions. **TIP**

WARNING

A *Warning* tells you when a procedure can be dangerous—that is, when you run the risk of a serious problem or error, even losing data or crashing your system. Warnings generally tell you how to avoid such problems or describe the steps you can take to remedy them.

UPGRADERS NOTE

Upgrade Notes provide information on features that have changed since MAX 1.2. Many MAX features and tools have different means of access in version 2. The Upgrade Note might tell you how a tool or feature was accessed in 1.2 and how it is now accessed in 2.

New Riders Publishing

The staff of New Riders Publishing is committed to bringing you the very best in computer reference material. Each New Riders book is the result of months of work by authors and staff who research and refine the information contained within its covers.

As part of this commitment to you, the NRP reader, New Riders invites your input. Please let us know if you enjoy this book, if you have trouble with the information and examples presented, or if you have a suggestion for the next edition.

Please note, though: New Riders staff cannot serve as a technical resource for 3D Studio MAX or for related questions about software- or hardware-related problems. Please refer to the documentation that accompanies 3D Studio MAX or to the application's Help systems.

If you have a question or comment about any New Riders book, there are several ways to contact New Riders Publishing. We will respond to as many readers as we can. Your name, address, or phone number will never become part of a mailing list or be used for any purpose other than to help us continue to bring you the best books possible. You can write us at the following address:

New Riders Publishing
Attn: Publisher Assistant
201 W. 103rd Street
Indianapolis, IN 46290

If you prefer, you can fax New Riders Publishing at (317) 817-7448.

You can send electronic mail to New Riders at the following Internet address:

abuckley@newriders.mcp.com

NRP is an imprint of Macmillan Computer Publishing. To obtain a catalog or information, or to purchase any Macmillan Computer Publishing book, call (800) 428-5331.

Thank you for selecting *3D Studio MAX 2 Fundamentals*!

PART

OVERVIEW OF 3D GRAPHICS AND 3D STUDIO MAX 2

1

3D Graphics and Animation Fundamentals

In today's world, computer generated imagery (CGI) is all around—on television, movie screens, and even in magazines and newspapers. The field of computer graphics has grown from a specialty area of study for computer scientists to a mainstream career that many people are striving towards. The foremost leading software package for use on a PC in this area is 3D Studio MAX.

In this book, you will learn how to create images and animations with 3D Studio MAX. Before you begin, however, you need to learn the basic terminology and concepts behind the CGI scenes and imagery you will create. This chapter explores the terminology and concepts behind computer graphics. In particular, this chapter covers:

♦ Defining 3D Graphics

♦ Moving from 2D to 3D Graphics

♦ Principles of 3D Computer Graphics

Defining 3D Graphics

Three-dimensional graphics means you are working with three dimensions; in other words, width, depth, and height. If you look around, everything you see is three-dimensional—the chair, the desk, the building, plants, and even yourself. However, the term 3D graphics is a distortion of the truth. In reality, 3D computer graphics are a two-dimensional representation of a virtual three-dimensional world.

To help illustrate this, imagine that you have a video camera and are filming the room around you. As you move around the room, you encounter various 3D objects, but when you play back the video on your VCR, you are looking at a flat, two-dimensional image representing the 3D world you filmed a minute ago. The scene appears realistic thanks to the lights, colors, and shadows, which give the scene life and three-dimensional depth, even though it is still 2D.

In computer graphics, objects exist only in the memory of the computer. They have no physical form; they are just mathematical formulas and little electrons running around. Because the objects don't exist outside the computer, the only way to record them is to add more formulas to represent lights and cameras. Fortunately, for you, 3D Studio MAX (often referred to as just MAX) takes care of the mathematical side of things, enabling you to explore the artistic side. Figure 1.1 shows 3D Studio MAX with a 3D scene loaded.

Figure 1.1

3D Studio MAX with a simple scene.

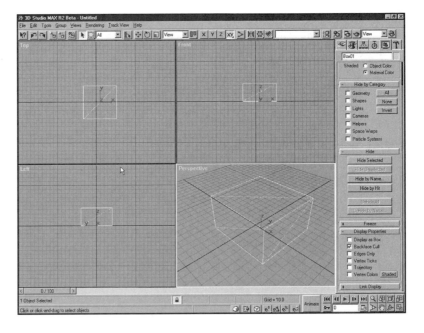

In many ways, using a program such as 3D Studio MAX is much like videotaping a room full of objects that you construct. MAX enables you to design the room and its contents using a variety of basic 3D objects such as cubes, spheres, cylinders, and cones that you can select and add to the scene. MAX also gives you the necessary tools needed to create more complex objects through a variety of other methods.

After all of the objects have been created and positioned in the scene, you can choose from a library of predefined materials such as plastic, wood, stone, or other materials and apply them to the objects. You can also create your own materials through 3D Studio MAX's materials editor, where you can control the color, shininess, and transparency, or even use painted or scanned images to make the surfaces appear any way you like.

After you have added materials to the scene, you can create cameras through which to record and view the scene. By adjusting the settings of the virtual camera, you can get wide-angle effects or zoom in on a small detail. Correct positioning of cameras in the scene always add to the drama or realism of the scene. MAX provides camera objects with real-world controls that you can use to create the views you are looking for in your scene.

To further the realism of the scene, you can add lighting. MAX enables you to add several different kinds of lights, as well as define the properties of these lights, such as the light color or brightness. By positioning the lights in the scene, you can control how the objects are illuminated.

The scene can then be brought to life by moving the objects, as well as the lights and cameras. You can make objects move mechanically, or make them appear to take on human characteristics. You can also use filmmaking techniques to tell a story with your animation, or simply create something cool and interesting.

Finally, you can render the animation to videotape, or a digital video file, enabling you to view the finished results and share it with others. Using 3D Studio MAX, you can create just about anything you can imagine, then use the result as a portfolio piece, a scene from a science fiction epic, or any number of other possibilities. There is no limit to the possibilities with MAX at your side.

Moving from 2D to 3D Graphics

Working with MAX can be frustrating if you don't have a solid handle on the principles and theories that are used. Although the theory is not as interesting as working with MAX, understanding theory now will save you a lot of time and trouble later on.

The easiest way to start is with a look at how 2D and 3D skills overlap. If you have any experience with programs such as AutoCAD or Illustrator, you can make good use of what you already know about making 2D objects (called shapes in MAX). The main difference between 2D and 3D is depth. Two-dimensional drawings have only height and width, no depth whatsoever. Although objects can be drawn so that the look like they are in 3D, if you want to change the perspective or viewpoint in any way, you have to redraw the object from scratch. Figure 1.2 illustrates this.

Figure 1.2

Two-dimensional drawing programs can be used to create images that look 3D, but if you want to view the object from a different perspective, you have to draw it over again.

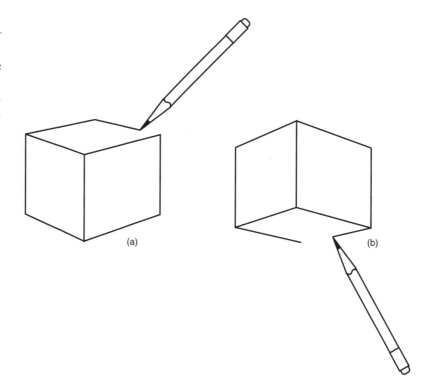

(a)   (b)

Because objects have depth (at least in the virtual world), you only have to "draw" them once; then you can view them from any angle or perspective without starting from scratch. After you have a view of the objects in the scene, you can apply materials and lighting. At this point, MAX automatically calculates highlight and shadow information for the scene based on how you arrange the objects and lighting, as shown in figure 1.3.

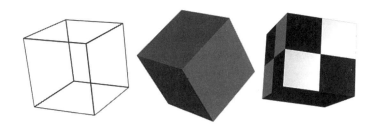

Figure 1.3

After an object has been constructed in 3D Studio MAX, it can be given color and texture, illuminated, and then rendered from any angle.

In a sense, when using MAX, you are not only able to redraw your subject from any angle you choose, but MAX can also create a painting (called a rendering in CG terms) of the scene based on the colors, textures, and lighting of the model. With all of these benefits, it's no wonder many artists rarely go back to traditional drawing and painting after they get into 3D.

Although major differences exist between 2D and 3D, many of the 2D drawing tools you may be familiar with are implemented in MAX as well. Tools such as line, arc, circle, and polygon are available and used in much the same way as in an illustration program. The difference is that instead of being used to create a finished shape in a 2D environment, these tools are used as a starting point for creating a 3D object. Some of the most common 3D forms that start with a 2D shape are lofts, sweeps, lathes, and extrudes. Objects such as wineglasses, bananas, phone handsets, and others are constructed with these methods. Actually constructing these types of objects is covered later in this book, but it is important at this time to remember that they rely upon 2D techniques.

Although 2D programs make use of "layers" to separate objects and organize their drawings, MAX makes use of a powerful object naming scheme where each object in the scene has a distinct name. Object naming in MAX applies to 2D objects as well as 3D. The object naming is combined with advanced display controls as well as groups to accomplish the same things. Grouping enables the user to choose a related collection of objects, then temporarily combine them into a single unit. This makes it much easier to move, scale, or perform other operations on the group as a whole because you don't have to choose each element individually every time you want to do something to them. Also, you can add, remove, or reassign objects from or to a group as you wish.

Principles of 3D Computer Graphics in 3D Studio MAX

When working with 3D Studio MAX, you must remember that you are dealing with a virtual computer world, and as such, you must understand how objects are represented and stored in this world.

Understanding 3D Space

3D space is a mathematically defined cube of cyberspace inside of your computer and controlled by MAX. Cyberspace differs from real physical space because it exists only inside of a piece of software.

Like real space, however, 3D space is infinitely large. Even with MAX, it's easy to get disoriented or to "lose" an object in cyberspace. Fortunately, this is made easier through the use of coordinates.

Coordinates

In 3D space, the smallest area that it is possible to "occupy" is a *point*. Each point is defined by a unique set of three numbers, called *coordinates*. An example would be the coordinate 0, 0, 0, which defines the center point of 3D space, also called the *origin point*. Other examples of coordinates include 12,96, 200 or 200, –349, –303.

Each point in cyberspace has three coordinates, one each representing the height, width, and depth position of the point. As such, each point represents a single axis in cyberspace.

Axes

An axis is an imaginary line in cyberspace that defines a direction. There are three standard axes in MAX, which are referred to as the X, Y, and Z axes, as shown in figure 1.4. In MAX, you can consider the X axis to be the width, the Y axis to be the depth, and the Z axis to be the height.

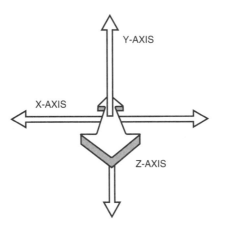

Figure 1.4

An axis is an imaginary line in 3D space that defines a direction. The standard axes used in MAX are called X, Y, and Z.

The intersection point of the three axes in MAX is the origin point 0, 0, 0. If you plot a point immediately adjacent to the origin along the "right" side of the X axis, that point would be 1,0,0. The next point in the same direction would be 2,0,0, and so on. On the other hand, if you moved to the left of the origin point, the first point would be –1,0,0, followed by –2,0,0, and so on.

The same holds true for the other axes. When you are traveling up the Y-axis, numbers are positive and while traveling down, they are negative. For example, 0, –1, 0 represents a point 1 step below the origin along the Y axis. The same rules apply for the Z axis as well.

Therefore, if you are trying to determine where the coordinate 128, –16, 25 is, you would find it 128 points to the right, 16 points below the X axis, and 25 points up in the Z direction.

Lines, Polylines, and Polygons

If you connect two points in cyberspace, you create what is called a *line*. For example, by connecting 0,0,0 to 5,5,0 (see figure 1.5) you will create a line. If you continue the line to 9,3,0 you create a *polyline*, which is a line with more than one segment. (In MAX, the terms line and polyline are interchangeable.) If you connect the last point back to the origin, you create a closed shape, which means the shape has an "inside" and an "outside." This is also a simple, three-sided *polygon* (also called a face) and is the basis of objects created in the 3D environment. The concept of a closed shape versus an open shape is very important in 3D Studio MAX. Many 2D objects cannot be converted to 3D shapes without being closed first, and you will see this in later chapters.

Figure 1.5

When a connection is made between two points, a line is formed. If that line is extended to additional points, it is a polyline. If the line is further extended to the starting point, it forms a polygon, or closed shape.

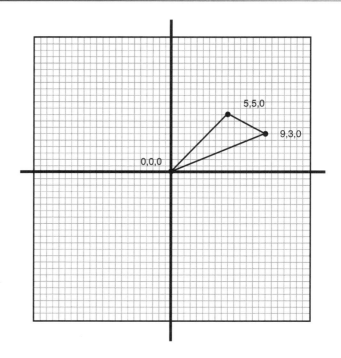

There are basic components of the polygon that you need to understand. These basic components, which can be manipulated by MAX, are vertices, edges, and faces. Figure 1.6 shows you a diagram of these components.

Figure 1.6

Polygons are composed of vertices, edges, and faces.

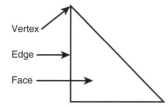

A *vertex* (plural vertices) is a point where any number of lines come together and connect to each other. In other words, it is an intersection point in 3D space.

In the previous example, each one of the points that were drawn became one of the vertices in the polygon. Similarly, each one of the lines that were drawn formed a boundary, or *edge*, of the polygon. Finally, when the shape was closed, it created an "inside" and an "outside" to the form. The area enclosed by the edges of the polygon, the "inside," is called a *face*.

Although three-sided polygons (also called *triangles*) are used a lot in 3D Studio MAX, they are by no means the only type. Four-sided polygons (called *quads*) are also common and most heavily used in MAX, but a polygon can have any number of sides, as shown in figure 1.7. Although these dull looking polygons are not much by themselves, when combined, they form complex objects.

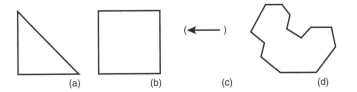

Figure 1.7

All polygons in 3D Studio MAX are either (a) triangles or (b) quads, but there is no limit to the number of sides a polygon can have.

NOTE

Even though polygons can have many sides, they are almost always comprised of triangles with one or more hidden edges. For example, in MAX, a quad is two triangles that share a hidden edge. This is true of more complex polygons as well. So even though the polygon may look simple, it probably has more detail than what is onscreen.

3D Objects

In 3D Studio MAX, objects are made up of polygons, patches, or NURBS surfaces, most of which are created with polygons arranged in a form your create. In some cases, only a few polygons are necessary to construct a convincing object. Most of the time, however, hundreds or thousands are needed, creating a massive amount of data. Thankfully, because computers are so good at handling reams of complex numbers, they are able to keep track of all the polygons, vertices, edges, and faces in the scene.

In the case of a simple cube, for example, MAX has to keep track of eight vertices, six faces, and 12 visible edges. For more complex objects, the number of polygon elements can soar into the tens of thousands.

Because these objects are made up of polygons, which are in turn defined by coordinates in cyberspace, the objects themselves take up spaces in our mathematical universe. For example, a cube may have one corner resting at the origin point and be 101 points wide in each direction, as shown in figure 1.8. That would mean that the corner of the cube immediately "above" the origin point would reside at coordinates 0, 100, 0, which should be considered the "upper-left front" of the cube. Because the cube is on the positive (right) side of the X axis (the horizontal one), the next set of corners is at 100, 0, 0 (lower-right front) and 100, 100, 0 (upper-right front). Finally, because the cube is positioned "behind" the origin point along the Z axis (depth), the final set of corners would be at 0, 0, –100 (lower-left rear), 0, 100, –100 (upper-left rear), 100, 0, –100 (lower-right rear), and 100, 100, –100 (upper-right rear).

Figure 1.8

The construction of a cube in cyberspace demonstrates how linking coordinates can form a 3D object out of polygons.

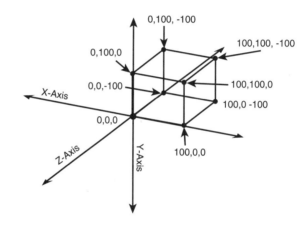

Understanding Viewpoints

Just as it would be challenging to drive your car if it didn't have windows, manipulating the objects in 3D space is much easier when you can define a viewpoint (see figure 1.9). A viewpoint is a position in or around cyberspace that represents the user's location. Viewpoints are analogous to the viewports in 3D Studio MAX, which provide you with the view into 3D space from the viewpoint.

MAX has a default set of four viewpoints: the Top, Left, Right, and Perspective views. By default, the top viewpoint has the X axis running horizontally, the Y axis vertical, and the Z axis coming out of the screen at you, indicating depth. The viewpoint in the Top view is centered on the origin. The other viewpoints are similarly configured but view the 3D space from different angles. Figure 1.9 shows you an example of how the Top viewpoint is configured.

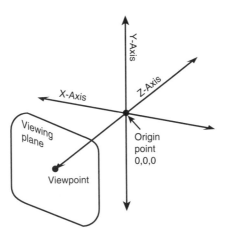

Figure 1.9

The viewpoint represents the current vantage point of the user. The viewing plane indicates the limits of the user's view because only objects in front of that plane are visible.

Surrounding the viewpoint at a perpendicular angle is the *viewing plane*, which is an imaginary flat panel that defines the limits of the user's "sight." In other words, the user can only see things that are in front of the viewing plane, and everything else is "clipped off." In fact, another name for the viewing plane is the *clipping plane*.

In order to see anything "behind" the viewing plane, the user's viewpoint must change. In a sense, the viewing plane is like the limits of your peripheral vision. If you want to see something that's in back of you, you either have to turn your head (in other words, rotate the viewing plane) or step backward until the object is in front of you (move the viewing plane).

In MAX, the windows that look into the 3D space are called viewports. The monitor screen itself is akin to the viewing plane because the user can only see what is "beyond" the monitor in cyberspace. This perspective is bound on the sides by the size of the viewport. In MAX, three of the four default views are orthographic, where objects are shown as orthographic projections, which may sound familiar if you have ever taken any mechanical drawing. Orthographic means that the viewer's location is infinitely distant from the object so that all lines along the same axis are parallel. The fourth default viewport in MAX, the Perspective viewport, is not orthographic and represents a more realistic view of 3D space where lines converge to vanishing points, as they do in real life.

Understanding Display Modes

So what do you see when peering into cyberspace from your chosen perspective? Because it takes time to convert all those polygons and data into a form that you can see, there are several different ways of viewing 3D objects to keep things moving along at a reasonable pace in MAX, as shown in figure 1.10.

Figure 1.10

*MAX is capable of
displaying
geometry in the
viewports in many
different ways. A
few are shown
here, left to right,
top to bottom.
(a) bounding box,
(b) wireframe,
(c) hidden line,
(d) flat shaded,
(e) smooth
shaded,
(f) smooth
textured.*

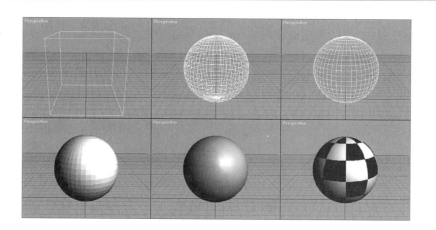

The fastest and simplest display format in MAX is the *bounding box*, which is a box that has the same overall dimensions as the object. This is a very fast way to indicate an object's position and rough shape, and it is frequently used in MAX when playing back animations, or when you are moving an object around in the scene.

Wireframe mode draws the object using lines to represent the visible edges of the polygons, which makes it resemble a sculpture made of wire mesh. This enables the user to see the true form of the object and have access to individual vertices for editing and modification.

For a higher level of realism, opt for a shaded display mode. In MAX, a shaded view is capable of displaying textures if the material definition is set to display the textures in the viewport. Flat shaded mode shows off the surface and color of the object in a course manner. The objects appear faceted, but the effects of lighting can be seen for the first time. Smooth shaded mode shows the surface of the object with color and smoothing, and provides the highest level of realism in MAX.

TIP   The more accurate or detailed the display mode, the longer it takes to redraw the viewport when something is changed. This can amount to quite a bit of time over the course of a project, especially with complex models or a scene with a lot of objects. If you find things bogging down, hide unneeded objects or switch to a simpler display mode. These topics are covered in full detail in Chapter 2, "Touring the MAX 2 Interface."

More on Coordinate Systems

Until now, the focus has been on the fundamental coordinate system of 3D space, called the world coordinate system, as shown in figure 1.11. Although world coordinates are used by MAX to keep track of everything in 3D space, you may want to switch to different coordinate systems for convenience and more precise control over objects. Two of the most common alternatives are view coordinates and local coordinates.

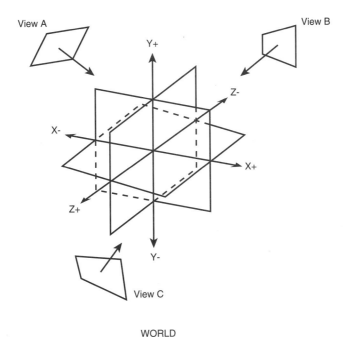

Figure 1.11

The fundamental coordinate system of 3D space is world coordinates. They remain the same, regardless of the viewpoint.

View coordinates use the viewport as the basis for the X, Y, and Z axes and remain the same, no matter how your viewpoint on the 3D scene changes (see figure 1.12). This can be convenient for repositioning objects. To move an object in your scene to the right, for example, you always know that you have to move it positively along the X axis when using view coordinates. Almost all of MAX's default transformations, such as Move, Rotate, and Scale, make use of view coordinates as their default coordinate system.

Figure 1.12

View coordinates are tied to the viewport and are always oriented in the same manner.

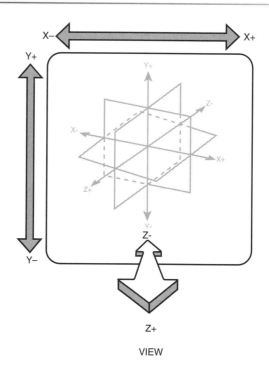

VIEW

Even though you have world coordinate systems, each object in MAX also maintains its own local coordinate system. When you rotate the object in world coordinates, the local coordinates rotate with the object, as shown in figure 1.13. This is desirable when you are rotating the object because using coordinate systems other than view or local may produce unexpected results.

Coordinate Systems and Rotation

When you rotate an object, three factors influence the way it turns:

♦ The coordinate system (world, view, local, or user) that is currently active.

♦ The location of the rotational center point. (The pivot point in MAX.)

♦ The axis you choose to rotate the object around.

As you know, the current coordinate system can have a big impact on how the axes are oriented, so this is the first thing that should be decided. In general, you will want to use the local coordinate system when rotating objects around one of its own axes.

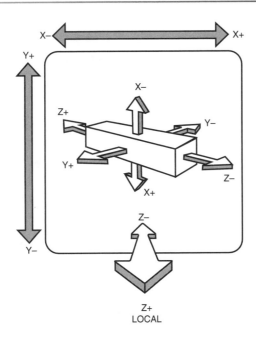

Figure 1.13

*Local coordinates
are assigned on
an object-by-object
basis. They make
it easier to rotate
objects
predictably.*

When local coordinates are selected, the center point is usually in the center of the object (unless it has been repositioned) and is located at the origin of the local coordinate system.

The final factor, the selected axis, determines which of the three axes to spin the object around, subject to the position of the center (pivot) point.

In order to illustrate why you must often switch to using the local coordinate system for rotation, imagine that you have created an elongated box, such as the one shown in figure 1.14.

By default, the box is created in alignment with the world coordinate system. At this point, then, you can rotate the object using world coordinates without any problems. After rotating the box at something other than a 90-, 180-, or 270-degree angle, however, the object's local axes are no longer aligned to the world coordinates, as shown in figure 1.15. Therefore, if you use anything except the local coordinates to rotate the object along its X axis, you are out of luck because the object's local X axis and the world X axis are not the same anymore. Indeed, the object would rotate at some oddball angle and it would take some effort to get it rotated in the proper manner.

Figure 1.14

When an object is in alignment with the world coordinates, coordinates can be used to manipulate it predictably.

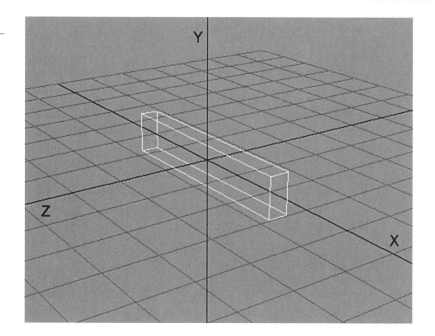

Figure 1.15

Once an object is no longer aligned with the world coordinate system, the user must switch to local or view coordinates to properly rotate the object around one of its axes.

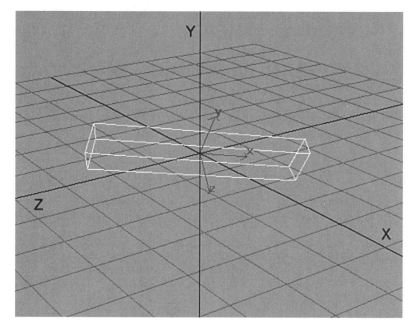

There are different ways to make a controlled rotation without relying on the local axis, however. One is to carefully position the viewpoint to make the view and local axes align, then rotate the object using the viewpoint coordinate system axes. A better method is to define a user coordinate system, as shown in figure 1.16. A *user axis* is just what it sounds like—an axis that you define. A user axis can be at any angle or it can be aligned to an existing axis. By creating one, you can define your axis along the same line as the object's local X axis. Then you can rotate the object around the user axis to accomplish the same result.

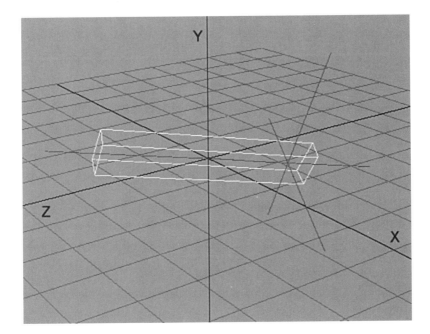

Figure 1.16

An alternative to using the local or view coordinates is to define a user axis, which is often used for defining joint rotation points in character animation.

Lights

So far, you've been wandering around in the 3D universe in MAX practically in the dark. You need some lights to illuminate the objects so that you can see them in the finished rendering. MAX actually creates two default lights to illuminate the scene, until you create your own, which makes life a little easier.

3D lights work much like photography studio lights, except that you can position them anywhere (including inside an object) and they don't fall down if objects bump into them. Each light type has its own set of configuration parameters in which features, such as light, color, and intensity, can be controlled. Also, most lights can cast some shadows, which add a great deal of realism to a scene. Four main kinds of lights are used in MAX:

♦ **Omni lights**, which are like bare bulbs and cast light in all directions.

♦ **Spot lights**, which are direction sources and are often used to highlight portions of an object or provide the main source of illumination for a scene.

♦ **Distant lights**, which are also directional but are used to simulate distant light sources such as the sun, which casts parallel shadows.

♦ **Ambient light** is present everywhere in the 3D space, illuminating all surfaces equally. Ambient lights generally are used to define a consistent brightness throughout the scene.

MAX enables you to use as many lights in a scene as you want, but adding more lights to a scene increases the rendering time. Lights are covered in full detail in Chapter 9, "Working with Lights and Cameras."

Cameras

Cameras are non-rendering objects that you can position in the 3D scene. They work like real cameras in that they provide a viewpoint on the scene that can be adjusted and animated. This camera viewpoint is different from most of the ones users employ for modeling because it enables the scene to be viewed in more realistic and natural perspective modes. Just as with real cameras, MAX cameras have different settings such as lens lengths and focal lengths that you can use to control the view of the scene.

In MAX, there exists two types of cameras: a target camera and a free camera. A target camera makes use of a target, which is a point in 3D space where the camera is aimed, making it easy to see where a camera is aimed in non-camera viewports. A free camera is a camera without a target that can easily be animated along a path or easily pointed by simply rotating the camera. Cameras are explored in further detail in Chapter 9.

Rendering

Rendering is the process wherein MAX interprets all the objects in the scene, in the context of lighting, materials, and viewpoint, to produce a finished image. The resulting image can be either a still or a frame in an animation sequence.

To understand how the 3D Studio MAX takes a bunch of polygons and turns them into a finished rendering, you have to examine how the computer interprets polygon surfaces. First of all, to be "seen" by the MAX as a surface, a polygon face must have a normal. A *normal* is an imaginary line sticking out of the center of the face; it indicates which side of the face is visible, and which direction it's facing, as shown in figure 1.17. If the normal faces away from the camera, the face is invisible. Just the opposite is true if the normal faces the camera. When MAX begins rendering, it calculates how much (and from which direction) lighting is striking a particular polygon face, based on the orientation of this normal.

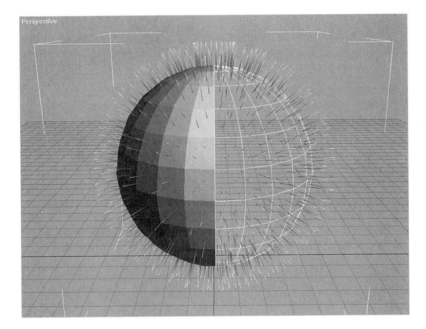

Figure 1.17

Normals are imaginary lines extending from polygon faces. They are used by the software to calculate the intensity and direction of light striking the face. They also determine the visibility of a face.

Most of the time, only one side of a polygon face has a normal, making it a *single-sided polygon*. Single-sided polygons can only be "seen" from the side with the normal, which can cause problems in some rendering situations (such as when a camera is moved to the inside of an object). Therefore, the MAX rendering engine can also be instructed to make the polygon double-sided so that it can be viewed from either side, as shown in figure 1.18.

Figure 1.18

Single-sided polygons have only one visible face, whereas double-sided polys are visible from either side.

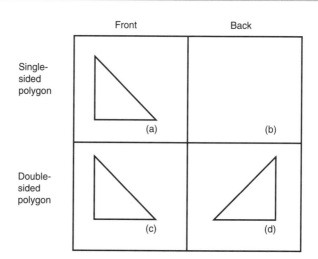

Rendering troubles, such as "invisible" polygons, can also arise if a polygon is non-planar. Using a four-sided polygon (quad) as an example, imagine that it's resting on a flat plane. If you take the right-front vertex and pull it up away from the rest, the polygon becomes "bent," or non-planar (see figure 1.19). Although it is still an acceptable polygon (remember, polygons can have any number of sides), part of it may not render properly because the normal won't be in the right position. One solution to this kind of problem is to convert all the objects to triangular polygons. Because they have only three sides, it is impossible for them to be "bent" or become non-planar.

Figure 1.19

Polygons with more than three vertices can become non-planar if one of the vertices is out of alignment with the others. This can result in rendering errors.

In addition to taking into account the position of normals, when the MAX rendering engine renders a scene, it considers any color or texture (material) that has been applied to a polygon, the light positions, intensity, and color, and many other factors. Then, the MAX "paints" the results of these calculations on the screen as an image. MAX supports several different rendering modes (either natively or through plug-ins).

The most basic, and fastest, rendering mode is *wireframe*, which is similar to the wireframe display mode discussed earlier. It is rarely used, except for animation tests or when a "computery" look is desired for the image.

For a *flat render*, the MAX calculates the color and value of a polygon face based on a single normal in the center of the face. The resulting image is a collection of sharply defined polygon surfaces, each with one solid color. This is a quick way to render a scene and is often used for making test renders of animation sequences.

The next level of quality is *phong*. In this mode, MAX calculates the color at each vertex of the face and then interpolates the result across the polygon face. The effect is smoothly blended object surfaces that are much more realistic than a flat rendering's surface. In addition, specular highlights are added for more realism. *Specular highlights* are the bright reflections of light seen on glossy objects.

Blinn mode is similar to phong but produces a more subtle highlight that tends to look a little more realistic.

Ray tracing is a method where the color and value of each pixel on the screen is calculated by casting an imaginary ray backward from the viewer's perspective into the model to determine what light and surface factors are influencing it. The difference between ray tracing and the other methods mentioned earlier (collectively called *scanline rendering* techniques) is that the ray can be bounced off surfaces and bent, just like real light, producing excellent shadows, reflections, and refractive effects. MAX actually implements ray tracing as a material instead of a completely different rendering mode. This gives you the advantage of selectively ray tracing objects in the scene, as well as just pure speed.

Beyond these basic shading modes, you can make use of other modes in MAX through plug-in rendering engines. Through plug-ins, you can add different ray tracing engines with advanced features, or even make use of advanced radiosity rendering techniques. Radiosity is capable of producing extremely accurate lighting for a scene but at the cost of very long render times. Rendering and the rendering process for MAX are discussed fully in Chapter 12, "Exploring Rendering Techniques."

Animation

MAX enables you to animate just about everything from the position of an object to the object creation parameters, such as length and width in the case of a box. You can move and change objects, pieces of objects, lights, cameras, and even materials. Although animation can be an involved process when working with complicated objects such as 3D figures of people, most of the time it is straightforward. You can choose how long you want a particular movement to take, then reposition the object, light, or camera to the new position at the correct time. MAX then interpolates the in-between animation. You can even view the interpolated animation as a time line or function curve in MAX's Track View utility. The last four chapters of the book deal with various animation techniques in MAX.

Conclusion

In this chapter, you explored the following topics:

♦ 3D Graphics Defined

♦ Moving from 2D to 3D Graphics

♦ Principles of 3D Computer Graphics

That's it for the basic 3D theory behind MAX. In other sections of the book, you will find more on 3D theory with in-depth explanations of specific aspects of 3D theory, where applicable. This chapter provided you with an overview to help familiarize you with the terminology and basic process.

Now, it is time to start becoming familiar with MAX. The next chapter gets you started by introducing you to the MAX 2 user interface and how to work with it.

2

Touring the MAX 2 Interface

Before exploring how to make the most out of 3D Studio MAX 2, you need to learn how to get around in the program. In other words, you need to get a little practical experience working with the MAX 2 interface and some of the features it presents to you.

At the end of this chapter, you will create a simple animation of a hedra that begins to pulse, before exploding. This exercise will help demonstrate the overall workflow process of MAX, as well as give you some practical experience in using the MAX interface.

This chapter focuses on the MAX 2 interface and how to use it. In particular, this chapter covers the following topics:

- Working with Files
- Working with Viewports
- Selecting Commands
- Working with Snaps, Grids, and Units
- Controlling the Display of Objects
- Naming Objects
- Working with Object Selection

♦ Using the Asset Manager

♦ Using Plug-Ins with MAX

The MAX 2 Interface

The 3D Studio MAX 2 interface is quite powerful and provides a highly streamlined workflow process. Thanks to this advanced interface, you will find working with MAX to be extremely intuitive, enabling you to learn the software quickly and progress with it in the future. Figure 2.1 shows the interface and the major areas, each of which is listed here and briefly described:

Figure 2.1

The MAX 2 Interface components, illustrating the easy access you have to commands and functions inside of MAX 2.

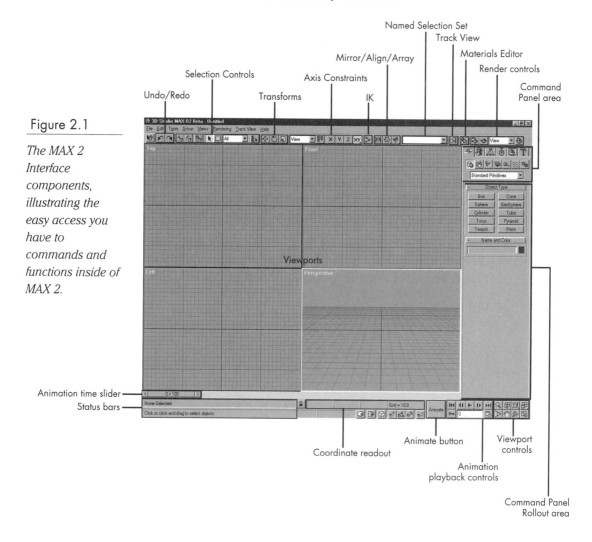

Working with Files

Before further exploring the interface, this is a good time to look at how MAX works with files. All 3D Studio MAX files are loaded and saved with a .MAX extension. By selecting File, Open or File, Save, you can use standard Windows file Open and Save dialog boxes to save your files. But MAX provides you with more file functionality than that. In MAX, you can also merge files, replace files, and import files.

UPGRADERS NOTE

MAX 2 does support the opening of MAX 1.x files by simply opening the file with File, Open. In most cases, the file will import fine, but fine-tuning on the lights and materials will be necessary due to changes in these systems. Unfortunately, MAX 2 files cannot be opened in MAX 1.x. In this case, you need to use File, Export in MAX 2 and export the file as a .3DS file.

Merging Files

One of the better file features of MAX is the ability to load a file and merge it with the current scene. This is handy anytime you want to bring an object in from another scene and use it in the current scene. Only 3D Studio MAX files can be merged. To merge other types of files, you must import them first. The following exercise merges a file into a scene.

MERGING A FILE INTO A SCENE

1. Select File, Merge. You will be presented with a File Open dialog box.

2. Select the file **MF02-01.MAX** from the accompanying CD. The Object Selection dialog box appears, where you can select the objects from the file that you want to merge into your scene. Select all the objects in the list and choose OK.

3. If you select any objects that have the same name as objects in your current scene, you will be prompted to rename them. At this point, a table with a teapot on it is merged into the scene.

A similar merge command available in MAX is Insert Tracks, which enables you to pull animation tracks from one file and insert them in another. This feature is covered in Chapter 15, "Exploring Other Animation Methods."

Replacing Files

As an alternative to merging files, you can replace objects in your scene with objects from another MAX file. You can select this option by choosing File, Replace. When you select a file to replace objects with, MAX searches the selected file for object names that match those in your current scene. Because object naming in MAX (discussed later in this chapter) is case sensitive, only exact matches will be processed. If it finds any, the objects are replaced. This command relies upon the naming of objects to perform the replacement. Make sure you do not have any objects with the same name in the scene.

If, for example, you are working on a complex animation, you may replace more complex objects with simple stand-in objects to make editing the animation quicker. Then, when it comes time to render the file image, replace the proxy objects with the real objects.

Importing Files

The last file operation to look at is MAX's capability to import files from other formats. You can import other file formats by selecting File, Import. You may export files by choosing File, Export as well. Natively, MAX supports 3D Studio 4 (3DS, PRJ, and SHP), Adobe Illustrator, StereoLithography (STL), and AutoCAD DXF for imports and 3D Studio 4, ASE, DXF, STL, and VRML WRL files for exporting. Additional file formats are supported through the use of plug-ins. This provides you with practically unlimited file exchange abilities, using the appropriate plug-ins.

After you have opened, imported, or merged your files into MAX, you can see the data in the MAX viewports. The viewports are a powerful tool for viewing your scene from a variety of different angles as you create and modify the geometry.

Working with Viewports

One of the most important user interface features is the MAX viewports. MAX viewports enable you to view your scene from a variety of different angles. Without the viewports, you cannot select objects, apply materials, or perform any other operation on the scene.

Hence, working with the MAX viewports is important. MAX has a default setting of four viewports: Top, Front, Left, and Perspective, as shown in figure 2.1. You can change, manipulate, and control these views in nearly every way you need. As a result, the ability to configure your viewports becomes important.

Configuring Viewports

MAX enables you to configure all of the features supported by the MAX viewports. You can configure options such as the shading level, layout, and view, or a variety of other options. You can configure the MAX viewports in one of two ways. The first method is to right-click the viewport name in the upper-left corner of each viewport window. This pops up a menu where you can adjust the most commonly used viewport settings. Figure 2.2 shows you this pop-up menu.

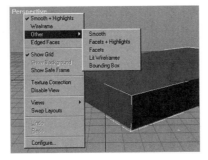

Figure 2.2

The viewport pop-up menu where you can select the shading level, view, or other viewport options with a right-click.

The second method of controlling viewports is through the Viewport Configuration dialog box, which can be accessed through the pop-up menu or by selecting Views, Viewport Configuration (see figure 2.3). The Viewport Configuration dialog box provides you with more options for the viewports than the pop-up menu. In general, you will use this dialog box to set viewport features permanently, or to apply the features to more than one viewport at the same time. The tabs on the Viewport Configuration dialog box include the following:

♦ **Rendering Method:** In this tab, you can set the Rendering Level, Apply To, Rendering Options, Fast View, and Perspective User View options. Figure 2.4 shows you the various rendering methods in MAX viewports.

♦ **Layout:** At the top of this tab, there are several predefined layouts that you can select from. You can change the viewports by clicking each shaded area. You should select the viewport layouts that you think will enable you to work with MAX most efficiently.

In addition, you can set up two different layouts (A and B) that you can switch between by selecting Swap Layouts from the viewport pop-up menu.

♦ **Safe Frames:** In this tab, you can set the Safe Frame parameters. Safe frames create a box in the viewport that indicates the safe area of the view. When you view your animations on a TV, parts of the image are chopped off to fit the TV screen format. Anything that appears within the safe frame will not be cropped on a TV. The default safe frame is 90% of the original frame.

♦ **Adaptive Degradation:** In this tab, you can set the General Degradation, Active Degradation, Degrade Parameters, and Interrupt Settings options. These control how MAX adjusts the shading level of the viewports to optimize speed.

♦ **Regions:** In this tab, you can set up a zoomed region within which to work for camera viewports. In other words, you can convert a camera view to a blowup of a portion of the camera view, temporarily, so you can work at a higher level of detail in the camera view. Regions are only available if you are using the OpenGL display driver. They are not available otherwise.

Figure 2.3

The Viewport Configuration dialog box where you can completely control the viewports in MAX from the shading level to the layout.

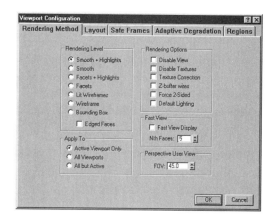

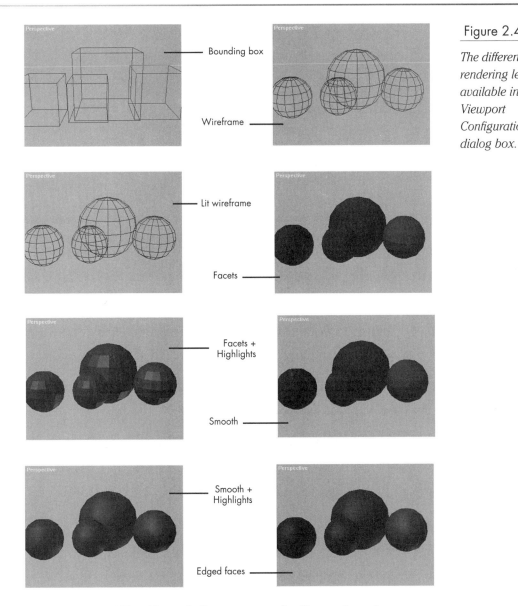

Figure 2.4

The different rendering levels available in the Viewport Configuration dialog box.

Bounding box

Wireframe

Lit wireframe

Facets

Facets + Highlights

Smooth

Smooth + Highlights

Edged faces

Working with the Viewport Controls

The viewport controls enable you to maneuver around in the scene. Operations such as zooming, panning, and rotating the view are handled through the viewport controls. Even views such as camera views, which are created as objects in MAX, can be controlled through these same controls.

The viewport controls are located in the lower-right corner of the MAX interface, as shown in figure 2.1. Depending upon the type of viewport that is active, the buttons shown here will change. You will see a totally different set of buttons for a Camera view, for example, than you will for a Top view. When you select a viewport control, the button will turn green to indicate it is active for the current viewport. Figure 2.5 shows what each of the standard MAX viewport controls represents.

Figure 2.5

The MAX viewport controls, where you can zoom, pan, or rotate your view of the scene.

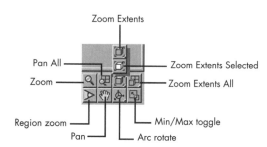

In addition to the selected button turning green, the MAX cursor will change to indicate the currently selected view control command. Almost all of the viewport controls work on a click and drag methodology. Zoom, which enables you to zoom in and out of your scene, works by clicking and dragging the mouse up and down in the current viewport.

In addition, MAX supports cursor wrapping. Cursor wrapping occurs when you use a command such as zoom. When you zoom in on a viewport, you move the cursor toward the top of the screen. When the cursor reaches the top, it automatically wraps to the bottom of the screen so that you can continue to zoom in further.

Several of the viewport controls have flyout toolbars that provide additional viewport controls. The Zoom Extents command has a sister command that performs the Zoom Extents command but limits it to the currently selected object.

Throughout this book, you will get plenty of practice using the various viewport controls as you work through the exercises.

Selecting Commands

MAX provides you several primary methods for selecting commands in its user interface. You can select commands from the following:

♦ **Pull-down menus:** There are a total of eight pull-down menus that you can use to access certain MAX commands such as File commands or Rendering commands. These pull-down menus work just like pull-down menus from other Windows programs.

♦ **Toolbars:** There are two toolbars at the top of the screen in MAX: a standard toolbar and a short toolbar for use on 800x600 screens such as laptops (see figure 2.6). At the bottom of the screen, you will find additional toolbars for accessing commands.

♦ **Command panels:** There are six command panels in MAX (Create, Modify, Hierarchy, Motion, Display, and Utility), each with its own set of commands and functionality. You switch between command panels by clicking the appropriate tab.

♦ **Floating command pallets:** These are replicas of specific commands found in certain command panels. Because they are floating, they are modeless dialog boxes, meaning they can be accessed at any time without canceling other commands.

♦ **Keyboard shortcuts:** These are quick methods of accessing commands by using key combinations on the keyboard. To create or adjust your own keyboard shortcuts, select File, Preferences from the pull-down menus. Then, select the Keyboard tab in the Preferences dialog box.

♦ **Strokes:** Strokes are intended to be used when you have a three button mouse. The idea being that you can hold down the middle button of the mouse and "stroke" the cursor in a particular direction over a specified portion of the current viewport. This action will then activate a command. Strokes are configured through the Strokes utility in the utility command panel.

In some cases, there are multiple methods for accessing the same commands, and in most cases, the command is only found in one place in the interface.

When you use MAX plug-ins, they integrate seamlessly into the interface. As such, plug-in commands are also accessed in the same way as the standard commands in MAX.

Figure 2.6

The short toolbar, which is a smaller version of the standard toolbar for use with laptop screens.

Command Panels

The next method for selecting commands is through the command panels. By far, you will use this method more than any other, especially if you do a lot of work with plug-ins in MAX. Figure 2.7 shows you the Create command panel and the various parts of the command panel.

Figure 2.7

The Create command panel, where you can create a variety of different objects for your scene.

In 3D Studio MAX, there are six command panels (Create, Modify, Hierarchy, Motion, Display, and Utility), each with its own set of commands and functionality. You can switch between command panels simply by clicking the appropriate tab, and the command panel will appear. Switching command panels cancels the currently selected command.

Take a close look at figure 2.7. Notice the layout of the Create command panel. Across the top of the command panel are seven buttons, below which is a drop-down menu. The seven buttons categorize different types of MAX objects that you can create, including Geometry, Shapes, Lights, Cameras, Helpers, Space Warps, and Systems.

When you a select a button such as Geometry, a drop-down list appears below the button. Here, the different types of geometry you can create are categorized. Figure 2.8 shows this drop-down list.

Figure 2.8

The Geometry drop-down list is where you can select the type of geometry you want to create.

The command panel is hierarchically organized to enable you to quickly and easily find the command you are looking for. After you select a set of commands, such as Standard Primitives under the Geometry button, a rollout will appear listing the types of standard primitives you can create. If you select any of these buttons, you are actually selecting a command in MAX. Upon doing so, further rollouts will appear below the Name and Color rollout.

The Box command has three rollouts, two of which are open. The Keyboard entry rollout is closed, indicated by the + symbol to the left of the rollout header. Clicking the header will expand the rollout. Clicking a rollout header that is already open will close the rollout.

As you can guess, sometimes the rollouts become much larger than the screen can accommodate. In these instances, you can use the mouse to scroll up and down the rollout by clicking and dragging vertically on any area of the rollout that does not have a spinner or text box.

If you have used MAX before, obviously you are used to scrolling up and down in the rollouts. You can speed this up in MAX 2 by holding down the Ctrl key while scrolling. This increases the scrolling speed substantially.

UPGRADERS NOTE

To help this even further, you can now right-click the command panel to access a pop-up menu with rollout controls (see figure 2.9). These controls enable you to maneuver around in the rollouts quickly and easily.

Figure 2.9

The command panel rollout pop-up menu where you can quickly manipulate a command panel.

At the top of the menu shown in figure 2.9, you can expand or collapse the current rollout or all of the rollouts. At the bottom of the menu, you can select open and close rollouts specific to the command you are working. As such, the bottom half of the menu is context sensitive to the command you are working with.

The rest of the command panels are similarly configured with command buttons at the top and rollouts at the bottom. Only the Modify and Utility command panels enable you to customize the buttons that appear at the top of the command panel.

As you progress through the rest of this book, you will become accustomed to using these command panels.

Keyboard Shortcuts

Another method of accessing commands in MAX is through the use of keyboard shortcuts. Keyboard shortcuts are simply quick methods of accessing commands by using key combinations on the keyboard. Often, this is the quickest method of accessing commands.

To create or adjust your own keyboard shortcuts, select File, Preferences from the pull-down menus. Then, select the Keyboard tab in the Preference Settings dialog box to get the screen shown in figure 2.10.

Figure 2.10

The keyboard shortcut controls in the Preference Settings dialog box. Here, you can create and customize your own keyboard shortcuts to enable quick access to MAX commands.

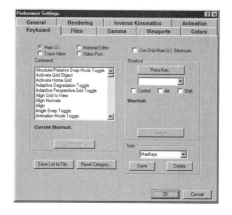

At the top of the dialog box, you will see four categories of keyboard shortcuts to work with: Main UI, Track View, Material Editor, and Video Post. When you select a category, the commands that can have keyboard shortcuts assigned to them appear in the command window.

To assign a keyboard shortcut, simply select the command from the list. Then, under the Shortcut section of the dialog box, select whether you want to use a Control, Alt, or Shift key modifier; then select the Press Key button. When you press a key on the keyboard, it is assigned to the command. If you select a key modifier such as Shift, you will need to hold down the Shift key when you select the key to make the command active.

You can even create your own keyboard shortcuts and save them to a file.

In MAX 2, plug-ins can now make use of keyboard shortcuts. You can use the plug-in keyboard shortcut toggle to override the MAX shortcuts and work with the plug-in shortcuts. Additionally, MAX now supports an Expert mode for working with keyboard shortcuts. In Expert mode, the entire MAX interface, except for viewports, is removed and you work completely with shortcuts. This provides you with much-needed screen real estate. Expert mode is activated by choosing Views, Expert mode from the pull-down menus. A Cancel button is provided to return to normal operation.

UPGRADERS NOTE

Floating Command Pallets

Another method for accessing commands in MAX is to make use of floating command pallets. These are replicas of specific commands found in certain command panels. Since they are floating, they are modeless dialog boxes, meaning they can be accessed at any time without canceling other commands. For the most part, the floating command pallets are intended to be used on machines with a dual screen setup where you can afford the screen real estate. Fortunately, they are handy enough that it also makes sense to use them, even on small monitors at lower resolutions, where it is difficult to give up even a small amount of screen space.

A good example of such a command pallet is the display pallet shown in figure 2.11. This pallet is activated by choosing Tools, Display floater from the pull-down menus. The display command pallet simply provides you with another method of accessing the commands found in the Display command panel, without having to leave another command panel such as the Modify command panel.

Another good example is the Object Selection floater. The Object Selection floater enables you to perform select by name operations at any given time, again without leaving the current command panel.

Figure 2.11

The Display Floater, which provides modeless access to display commands so you do not need to access the Display command panel.

If you remember from the earlier discussion on command panels, when you switch command panels, the current command is canceled. Using floaters avoids this problem and the associated waste of time. Otherwise, the commands found in the floaters are functionally the same as the commands found in the command panels.

NOTE   To get the stroke commands to work, you must configure your mouse to work with strokes. The default for MAX is to use the middle mouse button as a Zoom and Pan control. You can change this in the viewports section of the preferences dialog box.

Beyond the basic command access in MAX interface, you also have a set of drawing aids that you can use to help you create objects quickly, and very accurately. These drawings aids include unit setup and drawing snaps.

Working with Units, Snaps, and Other Drawing Aids

To accurately work in 3D Studio MAX when you are creating your drawings, you must make use of the several drawing aids in MAX, including units and snaps. These tools are important for various types of work in MAX, including architectural visualization, forensic animation, and mechanical modeling.

UPGRADERS   Under the General system preferences, you can now set an automatic unit
NOTE   conversion. This means if you merge a MAX file or objects that have a different unit setup, they will automatically be scaled to match the new environment.

Setting the Units

Units are the basis for understanding length and measurement in MAX. Without the use of units, you will not know how long one unit is. To accurately create models in MAX, you must set up a unit system that is appropriate for the type of model you are working with. A house, for example, might be modeled in feet and inches where a piston from an engine may be modeled in centimeters or millimeters.

3D Studio MAX supports several types of units including Metric, US Standard, Custom, and generic. The default unit type is generic. Metric units enable you to define 1 unit as a millimeter, centimeter, meter, or kilometer. US standard units are variations of feet and inches where you can select whether or not you want to use decimal or fractional units. You can have a dimension of 6'-5 1/2" or 6'-5.5", for example. Custom units enable you to define your own unit types. You can set a unit of CS (Column Spacing) to equal 10 feet, for example. MAX will then read coordinates back in CS units. Lastly, you have the default generic units. These are simply decimal units such as 1.100 and are treated as such. You can treat them as inches, feet, or any way you like.

Below the US standard drop-down list, you will see two radio buttons: Feet and Inches. These determine which unit to use if you type in a value without specifying whether it is feet or inches. If you type in a value of 5, for example, is it five feet or five inches. This setting determines the result.

NOTE

Units are defined through the use of a dialog box. You can access this dialog box by selecting View, Unit Setup from the pull-down menus. Figure 2.12 shows you the Units Setup dialog box. After you are done selecting your units and choose OK, the units are immediately put into effect. You can see this by watching your coordinate readout. After the units are selected, the entire MAX interface immediately makes use of them. When selecting different units, you must type in values with the correct units as well.

The coordinate readouts at the bottom of the MAX screen are extremely powerful in helping you to understand what is going on in MAX. They tell you the position of the cursor in the current viewport. They can also tell you how far you move an object when you use the Move command, or how many degrees you have rotated the object. When you work through the exercises, take the opportunity to watch the coordinate readout and make use of it.

TIP

Figure 2.12

The Units Setup dialog box is where you can select the type of units you are most comfortable working with in MAX.

After setting your units in your MAX file to the desired units you want to work with, you can set up your snaps to enable accurate drawing.

Setting Snaps

Snaps force the cursor to jump to a specific place in your scene when you are selecting a point such as the corner of a box (generally called a vertex). Snaps enable you to precisely position points that you select as you create or edit an object. You may create a stair in your scene, for example. You can use snaps to create each step in the correct position so that you don't have to move each step after you create it. You can accomplish this by setting a vertex snap so that you can accurately select the corner vertices of the previous step. You can snap to a wide variety of places, including parts of objects such as vertices, edges, and pivot points, or parts of the MAX interface such as the home grid or construction grid.

You access snap commands through the Views, Grid and Snap Settings dialog box (see figure 2.13).

Figure 2.13

The Grid and Snap Settings dialog box is where you can define the types of snaps that are active, as well as the grid spacing.

As you can see from the Grid and Snap Settings dialog box, there are three areas that you can configure through the tabbed sections of the dialog box. First is the Snaps. There are twelve snap types in MAX 2 that enable you to control placement or creation of objects. The basic snaps shown here are valid for all objects. But MAX also supports a second set of snaps specifically for use with the NURBS systems. You can access these through the drop-down list in the dialog box.

Next to each snap that you can select is a small symbol. When you activate snaps in MAX and try to pick a point, MAX will display the appropriate symbol for all active snaps. This gives you a clear indication of exactly what you are selecting and where it is in the scene.

Even though you may select one or more snaps in the Grid and Snap Settings dialog box, snaps are not active until you turn on the Snap Toggle. There are several snap toggles located at the bottom of the screen, as shown in figure 2.14. Once enabled, you may use any combination of snap modes to create very accurate models inside of 3D Studio MAX.

Figure 2.14

The Snap Toggle buttons for MAX. Snaps are not enabled until you enable one or more of the snap toggle buttons in MAX.

The Options tab of the Grid and Snap Settings dialog box enables you to define the settings for some of the other snap toggle buttons, including the angle snap toggle. By setting the Angle spinner under Snap Values, you can determine the degree increments MAX will use when rotating objects while the angle snap toggle is active. The default is 5 degrees, forcing you to rotate objects in five-degree increments when active.

The last tab of the Grid and Snap Settings dialog box, Home Grid, enables you to set the spacing, in units, of the grid that appears in your viewports. The default is 10 units with major lines, every 10 lines. An example of when you might want to change this is when you are working in US Standard units. Because you are working in feet and inches, it might be better to set the grid to 12 units so your grid is spaced 1 foot apart instead of 10 inches.

The entire snap system in MAX 2 has been rewritten to support much more accurate 3D snapping than was present in 1.2. In MAX 1.2, you could only snap to grid lines, intersections, vertices, or edges of objects. Now, you can snap to all parts of an object.

UPGRADERS NOTE

Along with snaps, construction grids are valuable drawings aids. You can use construction grids to work on different planes other than the home grids (XY, YZ, or XY planes) that are the default construction planes in MAX.

Working with Construction Grids

Construction grids are helper objects that enable you to work on a plane other than the home grid. Working on a different grid can sometimes be necessary when you are working with objects rotated in an unusual manner and you want an easy way to work with them. Construction grids are also helpful for creating a group of objects on a plane other than that of the home grid.

You might want to create a sloped table and place objects on the table, for example. You can work in the home grid and rotate and move each object into place on the table. Alternatively, you can create a construction grid on the surface of the sloped table and work directly on the slope as if it were flat.

You can create construction grids by selecting Helpers, Grids from the Create command panel. Construction grids are created by clicking and dragging out a square. After it is created, the grid must be activated to use it. In the following exercise, you will create a simple box on a construction plane that has been rotated out of alignment with the home grid.

WORKING ON A CONSTRUCTION PLANE

1. Open the file **MF02-02.MAX** from the accompanying CD. This file contains a single construction grid helper that has already been created.

2. Choose Views, Grids, Activate Grid Object. The home grid will disappear and a new smaller grid will appear on the helper object.

3. In the Create command panel, select the Box command and create a box in the Perspective view. Notice how the box is aligned with the new construction grid.

4. Choose Views, Grids, Activate Home Grid to return to the original construction plane.

By selecting View, Grids, Align to View after activating the grid object, you can align the current viewport to match the construction grid, essentially giving you a top view of the construction plane. This option is extremely powerful because it enables you to work on a different plane in 3D space, without becoming disoriented.

When put together, units, snaps, and construction grids enable you to work as accurately as you need to when modeling in MAX. Depending upon the type of scene, accuracy in your modeling can be very important. But even with all the accuracy you gain from snaps and grids, they do not help when the scene has many objects in it. This is where the ability to control the display of objects comes in.

Controlling the Display of Objects

One of the more important skills that helps speed the work process is the ability to control the display of objects in the viewport. In other words, you need to control whether or not an object displays. If, for example, you have a large complex scene, it is helpful to turn off the display of several objects to help you focus on one particular object.

First, take a look at hiding objects, which you will find useful when you start creating more complex scenes.

Hiding Objects

There are two methods of controlling the display in MAX. The first is to use the Display command panel and the second is to use the Display floater. The floater is easier to use because you can turn the display of objects on and off without ever leaving the command panel you are working in. (Remember, leaving a command panel cancels the command you are working with in that command panel.) The display floater is accessed under the Tools pull-down menu.

There are several display commands that you can make use of to hide objects in the scene:

♦ **Hide Selected:** Hides any selected objects in the scene.

♦ **Hide Unselected:** Hides any objects that are not selected. This command is particularly useful when you want to work on a single object. You can select that object and then choose Hide Unselected to hide all the other objects in the scene.

♦ **Hide By Name:** Makes use of the Select By Name dialog box to help you select objects to hide in a scene. This dialog box, which you will see in many other commands in MAX, enables you to select objects by their name. In figure 2.15, you can see the list of objects in the scene.

♦ **Hide by Color:** All objects have some sort of color assigned to them as they are created. MAX randomly assigns colors by default. You can, however, change the color of objects to anything you like. In such circumstances, you can use Hide by Color to hide all the objects that are the same color in the scene.

Figure 2.15

*The Hide Objects
dialog box, where
you can select
objects by name
or type and hide
them.*

♦ **Hide by Category:** All objects exist as a part of one or more categories of geometry. Objects are categorized, for example, as geometry, lights, helpers, particle systems, cameras, and so on. You can hide all the objects in a particular category in one command.

♦ **Hide by Hit:** Enables you to simply click objects to hide them. This feature is new to MAX 2.

Once you have hidden objects, you also have the ability to unhide objects. MAX provides two commands to accomplish this. You can unhide all the objects at once, or unhide them by name.

**UPGRADERS
NOTE**

The Hide by Hit and the Display floater introduced in this chapter are two new features to MAX 2 that greatly increase productivity. You will find that Hide by Hit is very useful.

TIP

When using Hide by Category, the Unhide All button is disabled. To unhide any objects that were hidden with Hide by Category, simply turn that option off.

By making use of the display controls in MAX, you can hide and unhide objects at will, making it easier for you to concentrate on specific objects in your scene.

Sometimes, however, you will want to have an object stay visible in your scene for reference but not to make changes to that object. This is where the ability to freeze an object comes in.

Freezing Objects

In both the Floater and the Command Panel rollout, you will find a Freeze command. This command works in the same way as the Hide command, but it freezes an object so it cannot be edited or even selected. When an object is frozen, it turns a different color (dark gray for geometry, blue for space warps) to indicate it is frozen. You cannot perform any operations on frozen objects until they are unfrozen.

If, for example, you want to model some hair for a human head, you will need the head as a reference for the hair. But, at the same time, you do not want to make changes to the head. So, by freezing the head, it stays in the scene for reference purposes but cannot be modified as you create the hair.

Hiding and freezing objects are valuable tools for working with objects in MAX. Another valuable tool is simply giving each object a distinct name.

Naming Objects

Of course, regardless of the modeling method you choose, you must develop good work habits to make your life easier. The most important of these is good object-naming skills. Each individual object in MAX has a name associated with it. When you create a box, for example, it is named Box01, Box02 and so on. Unfortunately, these object names are not particularly useful in scenes with hundreds of objects.

It's extremely helpful throughout the project if all objects follow a consistent naming convention, and it's practically vital when the scene is passed on to others for mapping or animation work. Naming conventions are a matter of personal taste. In MAX, you can name objects just about anything you want to practically any length. MAX objects names ARE case sensitive. In other words, Leftwheel and leftwheel are two different objects.

TIP

Be careful with your naming scheme in MAX. MAX does enable the use of duplicate object names, which can complicate and confuse the scene enormously. Don't use the same name for objects twice in the scene, even if you distinguish the difference with upper- or lowercase letter combinations.

Objects in MAX can be named when they are created or by renaming the object at any time. Whenever you select an object, the object name and color will appear on most command rollouts. You can change the name simply by selecting the object name and typing in a new one; there aren't any special commands.

An example of good object naming might be if you are planning an animation of a single jet fighter; names such as Nose, Right Wing, and Left Wing are OK. But if you are planning a dogfight, you will want to distinguish between the Left Wing objects for each plane. You can name the Right Wing objects J1Rwing to indicated Jet 1 right wing, for example. Because you can name objects just about anything, be creative with your names so that they are easily distinguishable by both you and others when they look at your scene.

Naming conventions easily become visibly important when you use the Select by Name functions where you select objects by their names only.

Working with Groups

Even when you have a good naming scheme in place, working in scenes with large numbers of objects can be difficult to deal with. Often, there will be related objects that you want to transform as one object but don't want to go through the hassle of selecting all of the objects in question. You can get around this by using the Groups function of MAX.

Groups are collections of objects treated as a single object when the group is closed, but they are accessible as individual objects when the group is open. The following steps show you how to create a group of objects:

1. Select the objects you want in the group.

2. Select Group, Group.

3. A dialog box will appear where you can name the group. Group names should be treated as object names.

After you have created the group, all the objects in the group are treated as one unless the group is open. You can also ungroup the objects, explode the group, detach objects from the group, or attach objects to the group.

Groups are very powerful and are a great way of organizing scenes with many objects. Get into the habit of using groups as early as possible to make your work a little easier.

Groups and object naming are handy when it comes to manipulating objects in your scene. But you can't manipulate objects without selecting them first.

Working with Object Selection

One of the most important features of MAX and the MAX interface is that of object selection. Many commands and operations in MAX require that you select one or more objects beforehand. If you want to move an object from one position to another in the scene, for example, you need to select the object to move it.

MAX provides you with many different ways to select one or more objects in your scene. These methods include:

♦ Select by Object

♦ Select by Region

♦ Select by Name

♦ Select by Color

♦ Named Selection Sets

One of the most common methods of selecting objects in MAX is to use the Select Object button from the main toolbar. Select object is most commonly used to select individual objects but can be used to select groups of objects through the use of regions.

Select by Object

Select by Object works by simply choosing the command and selecting a single object. But most of the time you will probably want to select more than one object in your scene to apply materials or perform other operations. In these cases, you can modify the Select Objects command to create additive selections. Additive selections enable you to click one object after another, and each is added to the current selection. You can do this in MAX by holding down the Ctrl key as you select. When you do, you will see a small + appear next to the cursor. Also, you can hold down the Alt key while using Select objects to subtract objects from the current selection. In this case, a small - appears next to the cursor.

Select by Objects is good for individual objects or a small number of objects. But a lot of times you will want to select a group of objects in an area in the scene quickly and easily. This is where Select by Region comes in.

Select by Region

Select by Region is actually an extension of the Select by Object command, but it makes use of "windowed" selection areas. Windowed selection areas work by defining a rectangle (or other shape) around the objects you want to select. This rectangle appears as a dashed black line in MAX. There are two different types of windowed selection areas in MAX: Window and Crossing.

A window region will select any objects that rest entirely within the region rectangle. If any portion of an object is outside the rectangle, it will not be selected. A crossing is the same as a window, except that a crossing will select any object that is inside or touches the rectangle. Figure 2.16 shows you an example of a region selection.

Figure 2.16

A rectangular region selection that crosses the area of a sphere. In this case, a window will not select the sphere where a crossing will.

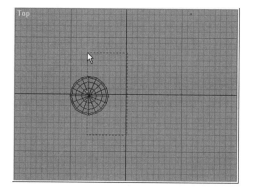

As you can imagine, region select is very powerful. But, being limited to a rectangular region can make selecting objects in a complex scene somewhat difficult. Fortunately, MAX enables you to use rectangular, circular, or polygonal shapes for your regions. You may select the type of shape by selecting the Flyout toolbar button to the right of Select objects on the main toolbar. Other than using a different shape, these select-by-region commands work exactly the same.

To take region selections a step further, you can even filter the selection set. In other words, select only objects of certain types that exist within the selection set. MAX enables you to do this through the drop-down list that is to the right of the region shape control. Figure 2.17 shows you this drop-down list.

If you select Warps from this list, for example, you can only select space warps. This filter applies to all select commands, except Select by Name. MAX 2 enables you to create combos of selection filters such as warps and shapes instead of just warps. This is done by selecting the Combos option, which brings up the Filter Combinations dialog box (new to 2). Each combo that you create receives a name such as SC (Shapes and Cameras) and appears in the drop-down list.

Figure 2.17

The selection filter drop-down list where you can choose the type of selection filter you want to use.

Although Select by Object is powerful and very intuitive, in large complex scenes, it can be very difficult to select a single object that you want to work on. You always end up selecting an object that is close by. This is where Select by Name comes in.

Select by Name

With Select by Name, you can select one or more objects based on the name you gave the object when you created it. Select by Name also has the advantage of restricting the list of objects to an object of a particular type, such as geometry or lights.

Select by Color

In addition to Select by Name, MAX also provides you with the ability to select one or more objects by the object color. This can be handy if you are careful about the colors you select for objects you create. You can access the Select by Color command through the Edit pull-down menu.

Selection Sets

As you can probably guess at this point, you may run across an object, or more appropriately, a group of objects that you select and deselect quite frequently during the course of creating your scene. There are two ways to handle selecting this group of objects quickly. The first way is to make a group out of them, which is effective but has its limitations. The other way is to make use of named selection sets (which can also include groups). A named selection set is a group of selected objects that have been given a name. Once named, you can select the same group over and over again quickly and easily.

Name selection sets are handled in the main toolbar in the blank drop-down list on the right side of the toolbar.

Although named selection sets are great, the ability to edit the sets is important. You may want to delete a named selection set when you are done with it, for example, or if you want to add or remove objects from the named set. MAX provides you with a dialog box for editing named selection sets. You may access this dialog box by choosing Edit, Edit Named Selections from the pull-down menus, as shown in Figure 2.18.

Figure 2.18

The Edit Named Selections dialog box where you can edit any named selections sets that you have already created.

 TIP   When working with named selections sets, an object can be a member of any or all selection sets you create. Objects are not restricted to one selection set.

At this point, you have seen two floating dialog boxes that are available in MAX 2: Display and Selection. Be careful when using these dialog boxes as they take up precious screen space. Consider running MAX at 1280x1024 or higher, or using a dual monitor setup if you plan on using these dialog boxes heavily. (They are excellent production tools, so you probably will make heavy use of them.) As an alternative, consider learning the keyboard shortcuts and running MAX in Expert mode.

Object selection, naming, groups, and drawing aids all combine to enable you to work quickly and accurately in your MAX scene. Now it is time to look at how these features and the MAX interface work together to provide you with a truly productive and efficient animation environment.

Bringing It All Together

Now that you have a basic idea of what MAX is and how its interface works, it is time to make use of it. In the following exercise, you will get a brief overview of the basic features of MAX from modeling a simple object all the way through applying materials and animating it.

CREATING A PULSATING, EXPLODING HEDRA

1. Load 3D Studio MAX.

2. In the Create command panel, click the drop-down list and choose Extended Primitives.

3. Click the Hedra button. In the Top viewport, click at approximately 0,0 and drag out until you reach a radius of 40. Then, let go of the mouse button. Watch your coordinate readouts to see when you are at the correct size. (The coordinate readouts will display the X, Y, and Z locations of the cursor. By selecting the radius at approximately 40,0 you will create the correct size hedra.)

4. In the Create command panel, set Family to Star1 and turn on Generate Mapping Coords at the bottom of the rollout. (You may need to scroll down the rollout to see the Mapping check box.)

5. Click the drop-down list again and choose Standard Primitives. Select the Box command.

6. In the Top viewport, click at −150,−150 and drag up and to the right until the coordinate readouts measure 150,150; then let go. Move the mouse down until the Height spinner in the rollout reads approximately −3 and click again to set the height of the box.

7. Choose Select and Move from the main toolbar.

8. In the Front viewport, select the Star object and drag it vertically until it sits on top of the box. Figure 2.19 shows the scene at this point.

9. Choose File, Save and save the file as **MF02-03.MAX**.

   For the purposes of this exercise, this is all the modeling you will do. Now, you need to create a camera to view the scene through and a light to illuminate it with.

10. Click the Lights button in the Create command panel.

11. Select Target Spot and click at −150,−150 in the Top viewport; drag to 0,0 and let go.

12. Choose Select and Move again. In the Front viewport, move the light source (the first point you picked when creating the light) vertically 200 units. Again, watch your coordinate readout.

13. While the light is still selected, go to the Modify command panel. Scroll down to the Shadow Parameters rollout. Turn on Cast shadows and set the Size spinner to 512.

Figure 2.19

The scene after creating two objects and transforming one of the objects.

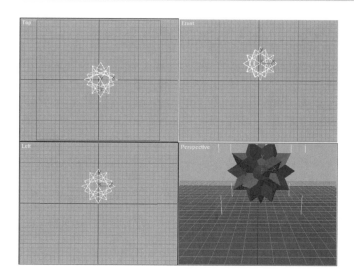

14. Return to the Create command panel and click the Camera button. Choose Target and click at 150,150 in the Top viewport and drag to 0,0 and let go.

15. In the Front viewport, again move the Camera object vertically 300 units. (You will probably need to use the Zoom command and zoom out in the viewport to move the camera that far.

16. Click in the Perspective view to activate the viewport. Press the C key to change the view to the Camera view. Figure 2.20 shows the scene at this point.

17. Save the file by choosing File, Save.

Figure 2.20

The scene after adding a light and a camera. Notice that both the light and camera appear in the scene as objects.

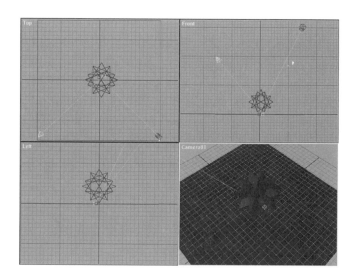

At this point, you have a very basic scene. All that is left is to apply two materials, create a bit of animation, and render the scene.

18. Open the Materials Editor by clicking the Materials Editor button on the main toolbar.

19. The material in the first slot should be active (indicated by a white outline). Click the button to the right of the Diffuse color swatch; this spawns a material/map browser.

20. Double-click Bitmap to select a bitmap map type. A new rollout appears in the Materials Editor. Under Bitmap parameters, choose the blank button next to Bitmap. This brings up a File, Open dialog box. Select **Benediti.tga** from your MAPS directory. (Note, this file should have been installed with MAX 2. If not, select a different map.) Choose OK.

21. Click the material in the preview window, and drag and drop it on the Hedra object in any window. This assigns the material to the object.

22. Click the second material window to activate it. Click the color swatch next to Diffuse. This spawns a Color Selector dialog box. In this dialog box you will see a Whiteness slider. Set this slider all the way to white. Choose Close.

23. Click and drag the white material and assign it to the box.

24. Save the file.

Now that you have applied materials to the scene, you will create two types of animation. First, you will animate one of the parameters of the Hedra; then you will animate the Hedra rotating. After that, you will explode the Hedra.

ANIMATING THE HEDRA

1. Choose Select objects and click the Hedra.

2. Open TrackView by clicking the TrackView button on the main toolbar. On the left side you will see a list of animatable objects in MAX. Expand the Objects list by clicking the + button next to Objects. Here, you will see Hedra01. Expand that list, and then expand the Object (Hedra) list. Here, you will find the Q Scale track.

3. Click Q Scale and select Assign controller from the TrackView toolbar. Select Noise Float and choose OK.

4. Right-click Q Scale and choose Properties. This opens the Noise controller panel. Set the Strength to 3000 and the Frequency to 0.15. Close the Noise Controller dialog box and TrackView.

5. Choose the Play button in the lower-right corner of the screen to see the results of the animation (which is a wildly pulsing Hedra). When satisfied, click the Play button again to stop the playback.

6. Drag the Time slider at the bottom of the screen to the right to frame 100. Click the Animate button to turn it on. It will turn red to indicate that it is active.

7. Choose Select and Rotate. In the Top viewport, rotate the Hedra 720 degree. (Watch your coordinate readouts again.) Turn Animate off when you are done.

8. Again, play back the animation to see the results.

9. Go to the Create command panel. Click the Space Warps buttons.

10. Choose the Bomb command and click at 0,0 in the Top viewport. This creates a bomb at the bottom center of the Hedra object.

11. Choose Bind to Space warp from the main toolbar. Click the space warp and drag out over the Hedra; let go when you see the cursor icon change. Almost immediately, the Hedra will explode.

12. With the Bomb object still selected, go to the Modify command panel again. Set the Strength to 3, Max to 3, Gravity to 0, Chaos to 4, and Detonation to 60. The last parameter, Detonation, sets the frame where the bomb goes off.

13. Activate the Camera viewport and click the Play button to see the animation. Click Play again to stop the animation when you are satisfied.

14. Choose File, Save and save the file as **MF02-03.MAX.**

Now, you are ready to render the scene.

15. Choose Render Scene from the main toolbar.

16. Set the time output to Active Time Segment. Set the Output size to 320x240. (You can do this by clicking the 320x240 button.)

17. Click the Files button. This gives you a File, Open dialog box. Under filename, type in **MAXfun1.avi** and then choose OK. A dialog box will appear asking for AVI compression options. Choose OK.

18. Choose Render to render the animation.

Depending on the speed of your system, it will take anywhere from a few minutes to up to 20 or 30 minutes to render the animation. You can play the animation back with the NT or 95 Media player or choose File, View File from the MAX pull-down menu. By default, the file was saved in your MAX Images directory. If you do not want to render the file, the animation is available on the accompanying CD as **MAXFUN1.AVI**.

As you can see from this exercise, even a simple animation requires heavy use of many of the features of the MAX interface. Don't worry if many of the commands you saw in the previous exercise were a little confusing. You will understand them better as you progress through the book.

Using the Asset Manager

The last item to look at before moving on to modeling is the MAX Asset Manager, a utility program that enables you to manage your MAX files, material bitmaps, and so on. You can select the Asset Manager by going to the Utility command panel, selecting the More button, and then selecting Asset Manager in the accompanying dialog box. When you launch the manager, the Asset Manager dialog box shown in figure 2.21 appears.

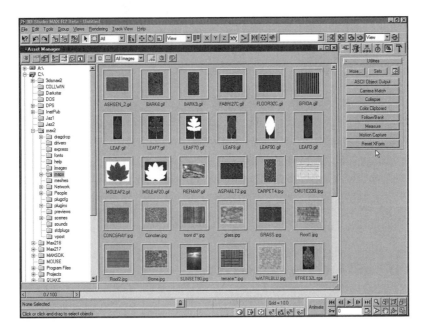

Figure 2.21

The Asset Manager interface showing you how easy it is to manage files.

On the left side of the interface is a directory tree of your machine, and the right side has bitmap previews of supported files in the current directory. The Asset Manager supports all bitmaps supported by MAX, as well as MAX files that have previews turned on. The drop-down list on the toolbar of the Asset Manager enables you to select the types of files that will appear. Figure 2.22 shows the Asset Manager with MAX files.

Figure 2.22

The Asset Manager demonstrating management of all the file types supported by MAX.

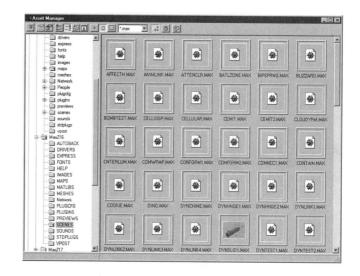

You can drag and drop files from the Asset Manager into the scene or materials editor. By double-clicking bitmap files, you can look at a blowup of the file.

Although technically not a user interface feature, the Asset Manager is handy to know and use early on while learning MAX. Future exercises in the book will use it.

Using Plug-Ins with MAX

Most plug-ins made for MAX integrate seamlessly into the environment and are almost transparent. As a matter of fact, all of the basic commands you use in MAX are essentially plug-ins.

In MAX 2, a plug-in can now take over the entire user interface and completely change all of the rules for working with MAX. Fortunately, to do this, the plug-in must create its own separate MAX icon because the interface takeover can only be activated as a command line option. Figure 2.23 shows an example of such an interface.

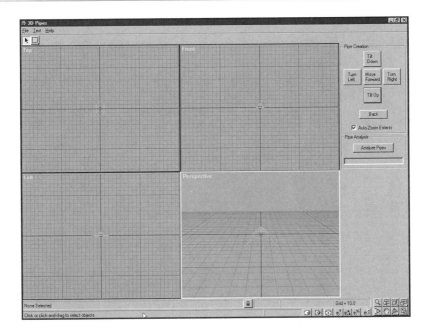

Figure 2.23

The MAX interface with a PipeMaker front end, showing how a MAX plug-in can now take over the entire interface.

Conclusion

The tools introduced in this chapter are very important to making efficient use of MAX. By the end of the book, these tools will be second nature to you. You may not feel exceptionally comfortable with the interface yet, but after a few minutes of practice with it, you will become comfortable very quickly.

This chapter introduced you to the basic concepts behind the MAX 2 interface including:

♦ The Interface Layout

♦ Viewport Controls

♦ Command Access

♦ Basic Drawing Aids Including Snaps and Grids

♦ Object Display, Naming, and Grouping

♦ Creating a Project from Start to Finish (The Exploding Hedra)

♦ The Asset Manager

Now it is time to start learning how to model. The next chapter covers the principles and theory behind the modeling methods used in MAX 2.

P A R T II

M O D E L I N G
F U N D A M E N T A L S

CHAPTER 3

Understanding Modeling Concepts

Before actually exploring the modeling techniques used in 3D Studio MAX, you need to develop a strong understanding of the underlying terminology and concepts behind the modeling process. Whereas in Chapter 1, "3D Graphics and Animation Fundamentals," you explored the overall concepts of 3D graphics, now you will focus on the modeling aspects.

When you look at modeling in 3D Studio MAX, there are many different methods that you can use to create the geometry in your scenes. Geometry is handled in MAX as an object, made up of smaller sub-objects. By manipulating the geometry at an object or sub-object level, you can create any model that you need.

Each modeling method handles objects and sub-objects differently and provides its own advantages and disadvantages. Some types of objects are easier to model in one method versus another. Over time, you will learn which method to use when. Then again, you may find one method is your favorite and use it all the time.

MAX 2 supports the following modeling methods:

♦ Spline-Based Modeling

♦ Polygonal or Mesh-based Modeling

♦ Parametric Modeling

♦ Patch Modeling

♦ NURBS Modeling

Spline-Based Modeling

Spline modeling creates 3D objects from straight or curved lines called splines. A *spline* is a line that is usually defined by control points or vertices and can be straight or curved. You can transform these splines into 3D objects through a variety of methods. The most common purposes for splines are related to modeling, but you can also use splines as motion paths for cameras and objects in a scene.

A spline is an object such as a line, circle, arc, or even text. Like all objects in MAX, a spline is composed of smaller parts (sub-objects) that make the complete spline. Figure 3.1 shows you a spline and the various parts of a spline.

Figure 3.1

A MAX spline and its parts. By understanding how MAX handles each part of the spline, you can understand how to manipulate the spline to obtain certain effects.

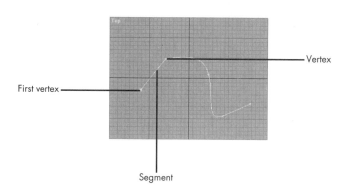

As you can see in figure 3.1, the spline is composed of vertices, segments, and an overall spline object. In terms of vertices, each spline has one special vertex, called the first vertex. A white box around the vertex indicates the first vertex when you are editing the spline. This vertex indicates the start of the spline and is generally the first vertex you select, unless you are using a prebuilt spline type such as rectangle where it is predefined. The first vertex becomes very important, especially in closed shapes, when you are creating 3D objects from the splines. This problem is discussed in Chapter 4, "Basic Modeling Methods."

When you create a spline, if you connect the last vertex you draw to the first vertex, you create a closed shape. A *closed shape* is a spline that has no breaks around its perimeter. Many of the spline editing and lofting commands require a closed shape to function correctly.

Tangent Controls

Each vertex in a spline also has a set of tangent controls (called handles) associated with it. The handles control how the curvature of the spline is interpreted as the spline enters and leaves the vertex. MAX supports four different types of vertex tangents: Smooth, Corner, Bézier, and Bézier Corner.

You apply tangent types during the creation process for lines only. Other spline types such as rectangles, ellipses, and so on, have the tangents predefined at creation time. You can edit these tangents anytime after creation.

Corner Tangent

The most basic type of tangent is the Corner tangent. Corner tangents are angular and do not have any curvature around them. This is the default when creating a line. In MAX, you create a line by clicking on two different points in a viewport. If you click and drag when you select a point, you will create a type of corner different than the default corner. The type of corner that is created is defined in the rollout for the line object. The default is a Bézier Corner.

Smooth Tangent

A Smooth tangent is an interpolated curve before and after the vertex. In other words, a Smooth tangent is very similar to an arc and is the same curvature before and after the vertex. Figure 3.2 shows you a spline and figure 3.3 shows you the same spline with a smooth vertex.

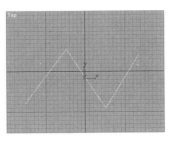

Figure 3.2

A spline with two Corner vertices.

Figure 3.3

The same spline after the corner has been converted to a Smooth tangent. Notice how the curvature was interpolated before and after the vertex to create a smooth curve.

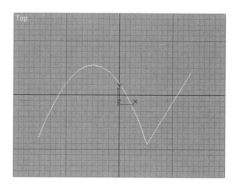

Bézier Tangent

A Bézier tangent type is similar to a smooth curve but enables you to control the curve of the spline as it enters and leaves the vertex. In a Smooth or Corner tangent, you cannot do this. Figure 3.4 shows you the same spline with a Bézier tangent applied. Notice the tangent line with the green handles. There are two handles here, one to handle the curvature entering the vertex and one to handle the curvature leaving the vertex. In a Bézier tangent type, the angle between the handles is locked but not the relative strengths.

By adjusting the position of the handles on the tangent line, you can adjust how strong a particular Bézier tangent is. The farther away from the vertex the handle is, the more it pulls the curvature of the spline away from the vertex. The closer the handles are to the vertex, the less they influence the direction of the tangent line.

Figure 3.4

The spline with a Bézier tangent applied. The Bézier tangent enables you to define the angle and exaggeration of the spline as it enters and leaves the vertex.

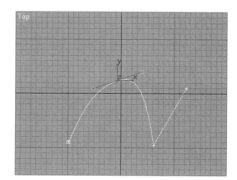

Bézier Corner Tangent

The last tangent type is a Bézier Corner tangent type. A Bézier Corner is the same as a Bézier tangent type, with one difference. In a Bézier tangent type, when you adjust the handles, both handles of the line adjust equally, except for their strength. In a Bézier corner, each end of the tangent line is independent of the other and can be adjusted as such. This makes it easy to create a spline that is almost angular on one side of a vertex and curved on the other, as shown in figure 3.5.

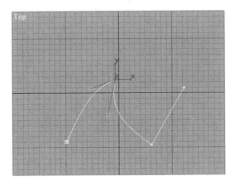

Figure 3.5

A Bézier Corner tangent showing how you can adjust the tangents independently of each other.

Segments and Steps

The next higher sub-object in a spline is a segment. A segment is simply the line that exists between two vertices. A segment is composed of smaller straight segments called steps. The more steps in a segment, the more accurate the curve but the more memory the spline takes up. In all of the splines available in MAX, you can set the number of steps.

MAX, by default, always tries to optimize the number of steps between vertices and reduce them to a minimum without losing clarity. This helps to make the models smaller without sacrificing detail. For the most part, the number of steps in a spline segment is not important until you try to create a 3D object from the shape. At that point, you may or may not need to adjust the number of steps.

When you combine vertices and segments, you get a spline. In MAX, a shape is a combination of one or more individual splines treated as a single object. For example, if you want to model a wall of a building, one approach is to model the wall as splines and extrude it into a 3D object. If the wall has any windows, you create them as separate splines. But, to extrude correctly, they must be a part of the same shape. When you create splines in MAX, you can set whether you are creating a new shape, or adding more splines to the same shape, by selecting the Start New Shape button in the Spline rollout.

After you create the shapes, you can convert them to 3D objects. This is called spline modeling. Spline modeling is the most commonly used method for creating objects such as bananas, flashlights, or beveled text.

The basic process of spline modeling is fairly simple. First, you create the outline of the object you want to model, as a shape. Then, you can either extrude, lathe, bevel, or bevel profile the shape, or loft it along another spline to create a more complex 3D object. Figure 3.6 shows you an object and the associated splines that created it.

Figure 3.6

A set of two splines and the resulting 3D lofted object. Here, a star shape has been lofted around a helical spline.

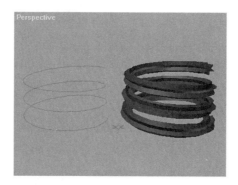

MAX 2 provides a new feature for spline modeling. When you create any splines, under the General rollout, you will find a rendering section where you can make a spline renderable. In essence, this makes the spline act as a wire object. Figure 3.7 shows you an example of this.

Figure 3.7

A text spline object that has been made renderable. You can use this feature to create many nice effects such as neon tubing for signs.

Mesh or Polygonal Modeling

Mesh modeling (also referred to as polygonal modeling) creates 3D objects from three- or four-sided polygons that have been joined together to form a more complex object. Mesh objects are generally created as a series of primitives that are combined, transformed, and modified to create the object you need. As a matter of fact, an extruded or lofted spline is a mesh object because they are created out of polygons during the extrusion or lofting process. Figure 3.8 shows you some examples of mesh objects.

Figure 3.8

Several mesh models, including a teapot, spindle, box, and a box that has had a cylinder subtracted out of it.

Mesh modeling is the most popular form of modeling in MAX. Here, you can take objects such as boxes and spheres and combine them using a variety of tools to create almost an infinite number of 3D objects.

Mesh Sub-Objects

Mesh objects, as with splines, are created out of a series of smaller sub-objects. All mesh objects are composed of vertices, edges, and faces. These sub-objects provide you with a high level of control over the object, especially when you begin to edit the object at sub-object levels. For example, by simply editing a box in various ways, you can create complex objects such as planes or hands.

Vertices

At the most basic level is the vertex. Unlike a spline, the vertices in a mesh do not have tangent controls. Hence, the vertices in a mesh can only be moved, scaled, added, or deleted. Editing at a vertex level provides precise control over individual points in the mesh, enabling you to refine your object as you need.

Edges

Between each vertex in a mesh model is an edge. An edge is the line between two vertices that forms the edge of a quad or tri. Quads and tris are smaller faces that are combined together to create the larger object. For example, a box has 6 quads and 12 tris, as well as 8 vertices. Edges may be visible or invisible. Figure 3.9 shows you the details of a simple box mesh object.

Figure 3.9

A box object that shows you vertices, edges, and faces. By manipulating one or more of these sub-objects, you can transform a simple box into a more complex object.

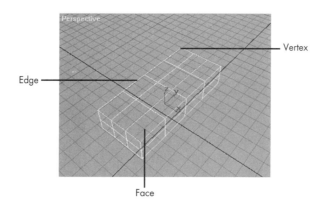

Faces

The edges and vertices combine to form faces. A face is the actual triangular surface rendered in MAX. Sometimes, a face is also called a polygon, hence the term polygonal modeling. MAX supports two types of faces, as mentioned earlier, quads and tris. A quad is a four-sided face and a tri is a three-sided face.

Each face has an associated surface normal, which is a vector perpendicular to the center of the face that determines which side of the face is visible. The normal is also used to handle the smoothing of the object. Because polygons are basically flat surfaces, creating smooth curved surfaces such as a sphere requires many polygons, unless you use smoothing.

Smoothing

Smoothing is the process where faceted surfaces are smoothed over during rendering, if the angle of their surface normals is within the defined range for smoothing. MAX automatically applies smoothing to most objects, but you can also apply smoothing to individual groups of faces. You can use the extra smoothing groups to refine the smoothing in areas of objects that are not perfectly smooth. For example, objects with a high degree of curvature such as a human face may need extra smoothing groups applied to smooth the transitions between the nose and cheek bones or other areas of the face. In other cases, you can apply smoothing to objects that do not yet have it applied to them. Usually, objects that do not have smoothing have been imported from other programs.

Segments

Mesh models, like splines, also have segments, which run between vertices. In mesh models, though, you use segments to increase the detail for a variety of purposes. With a box, for example, if you want to bend the box with the bend modifier, you cannot do so unless you increase the number of segments. There is simply not enough detail in the standard box to bend accurately. Figure 3.10 shows you an example of this. Of course, increasing the number of segments increases the vertices, edges, and faces in the object, making it more complex and time-consuming to work with. You should strive to keep the number of segments in an object as small as possible.

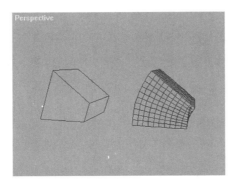

Figure 3.10

A box with 1 segment and a box with 10 segments. Both boxes have the bend modifier applied, but notice how the box with 10 segments is more accurate. Increasing the segments further results in a better bend.

In general, mesh modeling involves creating one or more objects, whether they are primitives, lofts, or some other type of mesh and modifying the mesh to match what you want. For example, you can create a chair out of six boxes. This makes for a fairly plain chair. But, with a little sub-object editing and some more detail, you can create a better version of the chair.

Mesh modeling is powerful and easy to use. But, it does have its downfalls. Mesh modeling becomes very difficult with highly organic shapes such as the human face, or just about any living creature for that matter. When mesh modeling can't handle the job, you must explore other modeling methods to accomplish the same tasks quickly and easily to produce acceptable results.

Parametric Modeling

Parametric modeling is a powerful modeling method where all the parameters for an object are parametric and can be adjusted or animated at any time. Instead of having to use a less precise method such as scaling, you can simply adjust the creation parameters as accurately as you need. Parametric modeling works with splines, meshes, and other types of models. MAX is a parametric modeler through and through, whereas many modeling and animation packages are not parametric.

In MAX, when you create a box, for example, you have length, width, and height parameters that you can animate. In addition, you have three segment spinners to control the detail of the box. In many packages, if you want to create a box that changes shape over time, you accomplish this by scaling the box over time. You can do this in MAX, but it is just as easy to simply animate the length, width, and height parameters.

In addition to modifying the box parameters, you can apply a variety of modifiers to the object to produce different shapes quickly and easily. This is another form of parametric modeling because the modifiers may be individually adjusted or animated, separate from each other. You can even apply different modifiers as tests and remove them from the object just as easily. Figure 3.11 shows you a box and the same box after some parametric modifications.

Overall, parametric modeling is extremely powerful if you want to animate the creation parameters of the object, including modifiers. In MAX, parametric modeling is not a separate modeling method, but rather the underlying methodology for all forms of modeling. But parametric modeling still does not solve any difficult modeling tasks such as human faces. This is where Patch and NURBS modeling come into play.

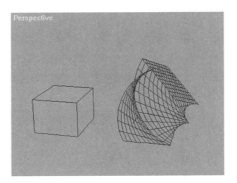

Two boxes, one unmodified, the other modified by changing the parametric height value, increasing the number of segments, and then applying a parametric twist and a parametric bend to the object, creating a complex object quickly and easily. Imagine trying to do this with standard mesh modeling or spline modeling techniques.

Patch Modeling

Patch modeling is a type of modeling that makes use of many of the principles found in splines with Bézier tangents. A patch surface is comprised of two parts: the surface and a deformation lattice. The deformation lattice is a series of connected points along the surface of the patch. Each point of the lattice is a control point that has control over the associated area of the patch. Adjusting a lattice point adjusts an area of the patch surface, not just a single point as you would see in mesh editing of a vertex. What is unique here is that the lattice acts as the vertices in a Bézier spline and deforms the surface along a Bézier curve, instead of creating a linear curve. Figure 3.12 shows you an example of this. If you take a section cut of the deformed surface shown in figure 3.12, it looks like a Bézier spline.

Figure 3.12

A single patch grid that has been adjusted by modifying a single control point. Notice how the surface was adjusted over a large area and how the surface still remains smooth.

Patch Sub-Objects

Like all objects in MAX, patches have objects and sub-objects, including points, edges, and patches. In addition, you have a lattice object that is part of the overall surface. When you edit a patch at a sub-object level, you are either editing the lattice or the surface directly. The points of a patch surface are the control points of the lattice. By adjusting these, you adjust the curvature of the surface. Like splines, the control points of the lattice have independent tangent handles to control the curvature of the surface as it enters and leaves the vertex, as shown in figure 3.13.

Figure 3.13

A patch lattice control point tangent handle. By adjusting these handles, you can control the curvature of the surface around the control point.

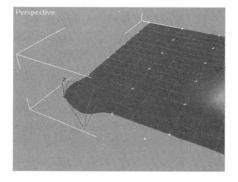

You also can edit the edges of a patch. The only editing that actually occurs at this sub-object level is the addition of more patches to the current surface. Any added patches automatically take on the curvature of the selected edge.

Segments

Patches, like splines and mesh objects, also have segments that you can use to increase the detail. This enables you to precisely control the surface with a more complex lattice or create a surface that deforms more smoothly through the use of a more complex surface. As you increase the number of segments in the surface, the lattice increases correspondingly. Again, you should try to keep the number of segments as small as possible to save memory in MAX.

Patch modeling works in a method similar to clay sculpture. You create one or more patch grids that will form the surface of the object. Then, you manipulate the control points to push and pull the surface into the form you want. Although this may seem tedious and time-consuming, you can create acceptable results quickly.

But, even with all this flexibility, patch modeling has its limitations. In patch modeling, it can be difficult to get the edges of patches to line up correctly to form larger patches. You also can't create a blended surface between two patches without help. This is where NURBS comes in.

NURBS Modeling

NURBS (Non-Uniform Rational B-Spline) modeling is probably the most powerful modeling method for creating complex surfaces available today. NURBS are completely new to MAX 2 and provide you with an entirely different modeling methodology. With NURBS, you have two basic approaches to modeling. One is to create NURBS splines and create surfaces between the splines. The other is to create NURBS surfaces and adjust the surfaces or create blends between surfaces.

NURBS Curves

NURBS curves are created out of either points or control vertices. The difference between the two is how the curve is interpreted around the vertices. When using points, the curve passes directly through the control points. When using control vertices (CV), the points act more as a deformation lattice. Figure 3.14 shows you the difference between the two point types when using NURBS curves.

Figure 3.14

Two NURBS curves, one created as a point curve, the other as a CV curve. Notice how the curve is interpreted around the control points.

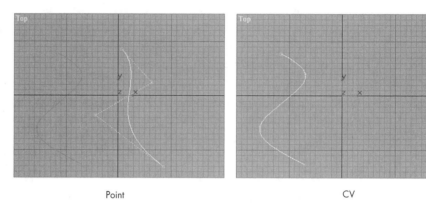

Point   CV

CV curves provide several advantages over point curves. A CV curve is interpreted between and around the CVs, making it easier to control the curve. In addition, you can assign a weight value to a particular CV. So if you assign a higher weight to a particular CV, the curve is pulled closer to the CV. Weights are relative to the others in the curve. So if each CV had a weight of 1 and you adjusted them all to 2, the curve would still be the same. But, if you adjust one to a different value than the others, the curve would change.

Like splines, NURBS curves also work as shapes where you can have multiple NURBS curves under the same NURBS shape. NURBS shapes are then used as the basis for creating NURBS surfaces. This process introduces two key concepts that you need to understand when working with NURBS. These concepts are independence and dependence.

Independent and Dependent NURBS Objects

Any NURBS points, curves, or surfaces can be categorized as either independent or dependent. An independent NURBS object is a standalone object such as a NURBS curve that does not rely upon other geometry to define its shape. A dependent NURBS object relies upon other NURBS objects to determine the shape and structure of the object. A NURBS surface created based on curves is a dependent surface. This is because it depends upon the location and orientation of the curves to derive its shape. At any time, dependent curves can be converted to independent curves for various operations. Many of the NURBS commands enable you to create objects as either dependent or independent curves.

NURBS Surface

The last type of NURBS object is a NURBS surface. As with NURBS curves, there are two types of surfaces: point and CV. Again, a point curve has control points at each vertex, whereas a CV surface makes use of a lattice, much like a patch model. The difference here is when you deform the surface by transforming a control point. A patch relies upon the principles of Bézier splines to deform the surface. Although this creates a nice smooth surface, it is still an approximation. NURBS surfaces, however, are extremely accurate and deform better. Figure 3.15 shows you a NURBS surface using CVs.

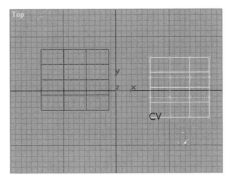

Figure 3.15

A CV NURBS surface that makes use of a lattice to distribute a smaller number of control points across the NURBS surface when compared to point surfaces where the control points exist at each and every vertex.

NURBS objects in MAX are a totally different way of handling surfaces. As such, they are not composed of quads and tris, but they are true NURBS surfaces. For MAX to render these surfaces, they must be converted to a mesh. This is called surface approximation. This works by creating as many triangles as necessary to approximate the surface. Fortunately, MAX handles this at render time. All you have to do is set the approximation method and values. This enables you to create more accurate approximations of the surface when you need to.

Overall, NURBS takes a different approach to modeling than found in mesh or spline modeling. In mesh and spline modeling, you create objects and deform them into other objects. In NURBS, you can create surfaces by blending or by creating surfaces between NURBS splines. It takes a while to get used to this methodology if you are used to mesh modeling, but once you get the hang of it, you will create complex models quickly and easily.

Working with Object Properties

All objects in MAX have a standard set of properties associated with them. Some of these properties you have control over, and others you do not. The easiest way to access the object properties of an object is to select the object, right click on it, and choose Properties from the pop-up menu that appears. Figure 3.16 shows you the Object Properties dialog box.

Figure 3.16

*The Object
Properties dialog
box. Here, you can
define features that
are common to all
objects in MAX.*

There are three sections of the Object Properties dialog box worth exploring at this point: Object Information, Rendering Control, and Display Properties. Motion Blur and G-Buffer are covered in later chapters.

The Object Information section of the Object Properties dialog boxes provides you with information about the currently selected object. When more than one object is selected before you access the Object Properties dialog box, this section will be grayed out and unavailable. Each of the Object Information sections is listed here and briefly described:

♦ **Name:** This text box displays the name of the object. If you want, you can change the name of the object here, or in the command panels. To the right of the Name box is a color swatch showing you the current color of the object. Clicking on the color swatch enables you to change the color.

♦ **Dimensions:** The X, Y, and Z dimensions of the object in world space units.

♦ **Vertices:** The number of vertices in the object.

♦ **Faces:** The number of faces in the object.

♦ **Polygons:** The number of polygons in the object.

> When modeling in MAX, you should strive to keep the number of vertices, faces, and polygons as low as possible. The more vertices and faces you have, the larger the object is and the longer it takes to manipulate, display, and render. **TIP**

♦ **Parent:** All objects in the scene are linked to a parent object of some sort. In most cases, this is the root of the scene. However, objects can be linked as children to other objects. You will see more on this in Chapter 15, "Exploring Other Animation Methods."

♦ **Material Name:** The name of the material currently assigned to the object.

♦ **Num. Children:** When the selected object is a parent, this displays the number of objects that are children of the selected object.

♦ **In Group:** If the object is a member of a group, the group name appears here.

The Rendering Control section controls various properties of the object at render time. Each option is listed here and briefly described:

♦ **Renderable:** When checked, the object is processed and rendered by MAX's rendering engine. When not checked, the object is ignored by the rendering engine. You can use this feature to create objects that are markers, spacers, or others that do not need to be rendered but help you with the modeling or animation.

♦ **Cast Shadows:** When checked, the object casts shadows if it is lit by a shadow-casting light. When not checked, the object does not cast shadows. When used in combination with exclude lists, you can accurately control when and where shadows appear in your scene.

♦ **Receive Shadows:** When checked, the object shows a shadow if a shadow is cast upon it. When not checked, the object will not display shadows that are cast on it.

The Display Properties section controls how the object appears in the scene and is very similar to the controls found in the Display command panel. Each option is listed here and briefly described:

♦ **Show as Boxes:** Enables you to display the object as a bounding box. This is independent of the shading mode that you select in the scene.

♦ **Backface Cull:** When objects are drawn in wireframe, all edges are drawn. Backface cull removes the edges that would normally be hidden in real life. This is on by default.

♦ **Edges Only:** Controls the display of edges. When not checked, any edges that are shared, but hidden, are shown as a dotted line.

♦ **Vertex Ticks:** Shows the vertices in the object, regardless of the display mode or sub-object selection.

♦ **Trajectory:** When the position of an object is animated, it creates a motion path called a trajectory. This checkbox enables the display of the motion path when it is present.

♦ **Vertex Colors:** Displays the object in the viewport according to the colors assigned to the vertices.

The controls found in the object properties are rarely needed, but they are very handy on occasion. By far, the rendering controls and information readouts are the most important.

Choosing a Modeling Approach

Overall, MAX provides you with many different modeling methods to support the many different uses of MAX. Because of these different approaches to modeling geometry, you may or may not need to make use of some modeling methods. The following list shows you some examples of where to use specific modeling types:

♦ **Spline Modeling:** This type of modeling is great for creating any type of object that has a profile or shape that can be lofted or extruded. Examples include bananas, bottles, phone handles, wine glasses, plates, and so on.

♦ **Mesh Modeling:** This type of modeling is great for objects that are somewhat planar in nature and are not particularly organic. Most of the objects you model will be mesh models. Examples include buildings, simple people, space stations, road intersections, and many others.

♦ **Patch Modeling:** Use this type of modeling to create somewhat organic surfaces that require fairly precise control over the curvature of the surface. Examples include faces, human bodies, animals, and so on.

♦ **NURBS Modeling:** Use this type of modeling to create highly organic surfaces, or any type of object that has a lot of curves or difficult curves in it. Examples include cars, humans, faces, or any other complex surface.

The exact choice as to which modeling method to use is up to you. For example, you can do architectural modeling with splines just about as easy as with meshes. By the same token, with a little work, you can create a human face with mesh modeling techniques, but it is probably easier with patches or NURBS.

In any case, the ultimate answer is to become well-versed in all modeling methods so that you may adequately handle any modeling task. Throughout this book, all of these modeling methods will be used in one form or another.

Conclusion

Modeling is sometimes a difficult task, even in a program such as MAX. This is especially true when you try to model an object with a method that is not ideally suited to that type of modeling. Fortunately, MAX provides many different types of modeling methods. Each modeling method creates objects out of various sub-objects such as vertices, faces, and edges. This chapter introduced several topics related to modeling in MAX. These topics included:

♦ Spline-Based Modeling

♦ Polygonal or Mesh-Based Modeling

♦ Working with Sub-Objects and Level Editing

♦ Parametric Modeling

♦ Patch Modeling

♦ NURBS Modeling

As you progress through this book, you will learn how to manipulate objects and sub-objects using the various modeling methods to create the objects you need. The next chapter introduces the basic modeling methods available to you in MAX.

4

Basic Modeling Methods

Now that you are well-grounded in the modeling theories and methods, it is time to look at the way the modeling methods are implemented in the MAX system. This chapter focuses on the basic modeling methods that are available. In particular, this chapter focuses on the following topics:

♦ Working with Splines

♦ Exploring Spline Lofting Methods

♦ Working with 3D Primitives

♦ Working with Compound Objects

♦ Creating Doors and Windows

Throughout this book, you will create small elements that you will combine into a larger scene, in this case, a bowling alley. By the end of the book, you will have created many elements of the bowling alley, applied materials, lighting, and cameras, as well as animated the scene. Most of the exercises in the book involve adding elements to this scene. This will provide you with a lot of practice in the main commands of MAX, as well provide you with a good sense of the workflow in MAX. If you elect not to complete a particular exercise, you will find the exercise completed on the accompanying CD, so you may complete exercises later in the book.

Working with Splines

To learn how to begin creating objects in 3D Studio MAX 2, you will start with the most basic object: the spline. If you remember from the previous chapter, splines in MAX are created out of vertices and segments, which form the splines. Each vertex can also be of a different type, enabling you to control the curvature, or tangent, of the spline around the vertices.

Combining and modifying splines in MAX can create many objects. Examples of such objects include phone cords, wine glasses, and so on. The trick is in how you create the splines and once created, how you transform the spline(s) into 3D objects.

MAX supports a variety of spline types, the most basic of which is the Line command. The Line command enables you to create almost any shape or form you want and is the most flexible of the splines. Other spline types include circles, arcs, text, and others. By creating and combining one or more of the spline types, you can create many shapes necessary for your modeling tasks.

You can find all of the spline commands in MAX in the Create command panel, under the Shapes button. Figure 4.1 shows the Splines rollout and all of the spline commands. Of course, when you select a particular spline, you will get the associated rollouts and controls for that command.

Figure 4.1

The spline commands in MAX enable you to create just about any kind of 2D or 3D line object that you need.

The Line Command

The Line command and its rollouts are shown in figure 4.2. Before you create a line, you can adjust these settings to match the type of line you want to draw.

Figure 4.2

The Line command rollouts showing you the type of controls that you have over a spline object.

Create a line in MAX by selecting the Line command and then choosing the locations of the vertices of the line. The line is drawn in the order that you selected the vertices. If you click and drag while placing a vertex, however, you can adjust the curvature of the spline around the vertex by holding the left mouse button down and moving around. When you have a curve that you like, you can let go of the mouse button and continue drawing the line.

Obviously, clicking and dragging to create the curvature of a spline is not an exact method. It can be difficult to create the exact curve that you need. Many times, you will need to modify the spline and its vertices after you have created it. This is called sub-object editing because you must edit the sub-objects of the spline. Sub-object editing is covered in the next two chapters. For now, you will create the splines as accurately as possible without sub-object editing and come back to edit them later.

When you are creating a line, you will see a white box appear around the first vertex you create. This indicates the presence of the first vertex. If, while you are still creating the shape, you place another vertex over the first vertex, MAX will ask if you want to close the shape. This creates a shape without any breaks in its boundaries, called a closed shape. Closed shapes are required for many 3D operations involving splines, such as a loft shape.

The ability to create a closed shape, as well as the knowledge of the location of the first vertex will become important in later spline operations. By default, many of the other spline commands, such as rectangle and circle, automatically create closed shapes and create a first vertex in a predefined location.

As you create the line, MAX will automatically create the minimum number of segments between the vertices to accurately portray the curve. The default setting is 6 segments between vertices, with MAX set to optimize this number. Optimization is the process where MAX removes as many segments as possible without compromising the curvature of the line. By reducing the segments, you reduce the amount of memory the line takes, as well as the complexity of the line and any geometry generated from that line.

Optimization can also be set to adaptive, which will adaptively add or remove segments from the spline as the curvature changes. Obviously, the more curvature that exists in the spline, the more segments needed to accurately represent the curve. Of course, you can override the optimization settings and set your own number of segments as well.

The other spline commands vary in how they work. Some make use of click-and-drag techniques to create the spline object, such as Circle and Ellipse. Others work more like the Line command by accepting simple clicks, without dragging the cursor. Arcs are created in this way. Still others require both techniques, such as the Helix command. Figure 4.3 shows you some of the spline shapes that you can create with these commands.

As you discovered in the last chapter, MAX handles splines as shapes. One or more splines can be combined to create more complex shapes for you to use. The Start New Shape button shown at the top of figure 4.1 enables you to create new shapes, or add splines to the currently selected shape. In this manner, you can refine and build all of the necessary shapes you might need.

Figure 4.3

*A set of spline
shapes created by
using different
spline commands.*

The following exercise shows you how to create a spline using MAX 2. The shape
is the profile of a bowling pin that you will use in the next chapter to create a true
3D pin.

CREATING A BOWLING PIN SHAPE

1. Start a new file and select Views, Grid and Snap Settings.

2. Select the Home Grid tab and set the grid spacing to 1.0. Close the Grid and Snap Settings
   dialog box.

3. In the Top viewport, use the Zoom tool to zoom in around the origin 0,0,0 so that you can see
   an area roughly 20 units in size. (This should be obvious when you are zooming in as you will
   see the density of the grid change about this point.)

4. Select the Shapes button under the Create command panel.

5. Select the Line command.

6. Turn on the 3D Snap toggle to enable you to draw accurately.

7. Click at 0,0 (watch your coordinate readout for exact coordinates).

8. Click at 2,0.

9. Click at 3,4. When you do, drag the mouse vertically to approximately 3,6 to add a curve to the
   spline, as shown in figure 4.4.

10. Click at 1,9 and drag to create the inner curve at the top of the shape.

11. Click at 2,11 and drag to create the top of the pin.

12. Click at 0,13 and drag to complete the shape. This creates a bowling pin that is roughly 13
    inches tall, if you take one unit to be one inch.

13. Once satisfied with the last curve, right-click to end the Line command. You should end up with
    a shape similar to the one shown in figure 4.5.

Figure 4.4

*The first of the
vertices in the
bowling pin that
has a tangent
curve associated
with it. Clicking
and dragging
while placing the
point enables you
to create this
curve.*

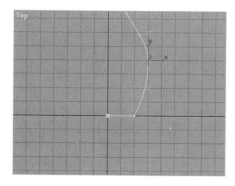

Figure 4.5

*The completed
bowling pin shape
can now be lathed
to create a three-
dimensional pin.
Later, you create a
3D bowling pin
out of this shape.*

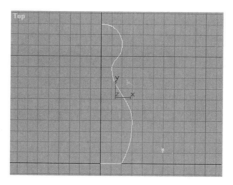

14. Save the file as **MF04-1.MAX** for use later in this chapter.

You might have found it difficult to create the curves of the bowling pin accurately the first time through. If you have difficulty, please keep trying until you do get it. You will gain a lot of experience working with the tangents. Later, in Chapter 6, "Exploring More Editing Methods," you will learn how to edit the tangents. For now, just keep trying until you get it right. You will get plenty of practice this way.

The Text Command

The last spline feature you look at in this chapter is the Text command. (In later chapters, you will get more practice with different spline commands.) The Text command is used to create 2D text that can then be converted to 3D. MAX enables you to use any TrueType font that is installed on the system to create text. If you are not familiar with fonts, a font determines the shape, size, orientation, and position of the letters. Different fonts provide you with different looks.

If you open the Text command in the Create command panel of MAX, you will see a variety of controls. If you have done any word processing, these controls should look familiar. At the top of the rollout, you can select the font. Then, you can select whether it is bold or italic and the type of justification you want to use. Below that are three spinners to set the size, kerning, and leading. Then, there is a large white box where you can type in the text you want.

As you can see, the Text command is not quite like other spline commands. It has many more options and is used for the specific task of creating text. Figure 4.3 shows you an example of the word Cool created with MAX text. The following short exercise shows you how to create a sign for the 3D bowling alley you are creating.

You may have noticed that the Text command now has additional options including justification, kerning, and leading. Justification enables you to set how the text is placed in multiline text objects. Kerning enables you to control the spacing between letters, and the leading spinner adjusts the amount of space between text lines.

UPGRADERS NOTE

CREATING A SIGN FOR THE BOWLING ALLEY

1. Start a new scene in MAX.

2. Go to the Create command panel and click the Shapes button. Select the Text command.

3. Set the font type to Arial, if it is not already set there. (Arial is an NT system font and should be present on your system. You may, of course, choose a different font if you want.)

4. Set the size to 24. This will create text lettering that is two feet tall for the bowling alley scene.

5. In the text box, enter **MAX Bowling**.

6. In the Top viewport, click close to the origin. This will create the text shape.

7. In the Create command panel, adjust the Kerning spinner to 5.0. This increases the spacing between the letters. Figure 4.6 shows you the text lettering.

8. Save the file as **MF04-02.MAX** for use later in this chapter.

Figure 4.6

The text object after creation. Notice how you have precise control over the lettering including size and spacing.

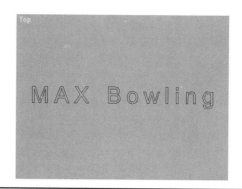

When you create splines, be sure to realize when you are adding splines to an existing shape and when you are creating new shapes. In Chapter 6, you will see more on how to edit and combine splines to make more complicated shapes than those introduced here.

Now that you have seen how to create some of the various splines, it is time to look at how to create some 3D objects from these shapes.

Exploring Spline Lofting Methods

You have seen how to create basic shapes out of splines. Now it is time to look at how to turn a shape into a 3D Object using several methods that are available in MAX 2. You can create 3D objects from 2D splines in four different ways:

♦ Extrusion

♦ Lathing (sometimes called Revolving)

♦ Beveling

♦ Lofting

The following sections discuss each of these methods.

Extruding Splines

An extruded spline is a spline that has been given a thickness in a particular direction. You can also think of extruding as making an exact copy of a spline at a certain distance away from the original and then creating a surface between the two.

Take, for example, a case where you want to create a wall for a house. This can easily be done in MAX by drawing the elevation of the wall in splines (or importing the splines from another drawing package such as AutoCAD or Adobe Illustrator) and then extruding the wall to a particular thickness. In many cases, this is easier than using 3D primitives and Boolean operations or other methods of creating the same object.

There are hundreds of examples where extrusions can be helpful in the modeling process. You can extrude text to create 3D text. You can extrude many shapes to create complex objects such as walls, CDs, cookie cutters, and even simple tires. In general, extrusion works great if the object has one profile and a consistent height.

Extrusion of a shape is handled by applying an Extrude modifier to the selected shape. (The actual use of modifiers is covered in the next chapter.) After extrusion is applied in the Modify command panel, you can adjust the height, as well as the axis along which the shape is extruded. The Z axis is the default axis for most extrusions. Figure 4.7 shows you the MAX Bowling text object that you created earlier as an extruded object with a thickness of 6 units.

Figure 4.7

The MAX Bowling text object after applying the Extrude modifier and adjusting the height to 6 units.

TIP

When you extrude text, you may find that the letters may not always extrude correctly. This is usually font dependent. Not all TrueType fonts will extrude correctly. If you run across this problem, try a different font.

Extruding a spline is a powerful method for creating 3D objects out of 2D shapes. There are many instances, however, where you cannot create a specific object using extrusions. In those cases, you must use other techniques such as lathing.

Lathing Splines

A lathed spline is a spline that has been rotated around a point in space, usually the center, left (minimum), or right (maximum) edge of the spline. As the spline is rotated, a surface is generated to create the 3D object.

When creating a lathed spline, you can control the number of degrees around which the object is created, as well as the number of segments to create smoother objects. In addition to controlling the amount of lathing, you can control in which world space axis the lathe will occur. The amount of detail in the resulting object is a combination of the detail in the original spline and the settings in the lathe process.

An example of a lathed spline is a wine glass. This would be impossible to create as an extrusion because of how the glass is shaped. It is an excellent candidate, however, for a revolved surface. All you need to do is create a profile or section cut of half the glass. Figure 4.8 shows you an example of a wine glass profile and the resulting lathed object.

Figure 4.8

A spline shape and the resulting lathed object.

As with the Extrude command, a spline is lathed by applying a Lathe modifier and then adjusting the number of degrees, the number of segments, and the center axis location. You can also set the type of geometry for the Lathe command to output, such as mesh, patch, or NURBS geometry.

In the following exercise, you will take the bowling pin shape that you created earlier in this chapter and create a 3D version of it using the Lathe command.

LATHING THE BOWLING PIN

1. Load the file **MF04-01.MAX** that you created earlier in this chapter. (If you did not complete that exercise, you may find the file on the accompanying CD.)

2. Choose Select Object and select the spline.

3. Open the Modify command panel and select the Lathe button. Figure 4.9 shows you the bowling pin at this point.

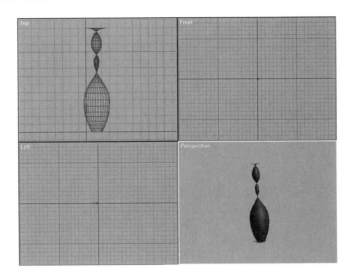

Figure 4.9

The bowling pin immediately after lathing. The pin looks incorrect because of the location of the center of rotation.

As you can see from figure 4.9, the pin is wrong. This occurs from incorrect alignment of the center point of the lathe. The spline is lathed around a center point, which can be defined as the minimum, center, or maximum point of the spline shape. The default is the center point, which is the geometry center of the bowling pin shape. What is needed here is to lathe the object around the left edge of the shape, which is the minimum point.

4. Click the Min button under Align to set the center point of the lathe to the correct edge of the bowling pin shape. The bowling pin is now correctly lathed.

5. Name the object **Bowling Pin1**.

6. Save the file as **MF04-01a.MAX** for use in the next chapter.

When using the Lathe command, the center point around which the spline is lathed is critical. There are three choices: Min, Center, and Max, with Center being the default. The center point is the geometric center of the shape to be lathed. The Min, or minimum, point is the farthest left point of the shape, whereas the Max, or maximum, point is the farthest right point in the shape. In addition to selecting the center of rotation, you can also select the axis about which the lathe occurs under Direction. The default is the Y axis.

Lathing is helpful for creating many types of objects that are circular in nature but have varying profiles. Wine glasses, plates, simple clocks, or even footballs are great examples of when to use the Lathe command. You can probably think of many more examples of objects that you might like to create with this command.

The Lathe command is very powerful, but it is limited to objects that can be revolved around a center point. Another command that converts shapes to 3D objects is the Bevel command.

Beveling Splines

Beveling splines is very similar to extruding splines. In a beveled spline, you can define a height for the extrusion and also a scale for the spline at each level of the bevel. So, if you extrude a spline to a height of 3, you have two spline shapes, one at the bottom and one at the top of the 3D object. When you create the bevel, you can define the scale of either spline. So, if you scale the top spline down to 0.9 (90%) of its original size, you will create a beveled look to the extruded spline. The angle of the bevel is defined by the difference in size between the top and bottom splines. Almost all of the uses for beveling splines involve text. But, you can also create objects such as plaques or even simple egg crates.

The actual process of beveling involves creating a shape (with one or more splines) and then applying a Bevel modifier to the shape to create the bevel. The Bevel modifier enables you to create three different levels of beveling. You can consider this to be three independent beveled objects laid on top of one another. For each level, you can control the height of the extrusion and the size of the outline. Creating an outline smaller than the base results in a bevel that gets smaller toward the top of the object. Additionally, you can create either straight or curved sides.

Of course, if you create too small an outline, the bevel may fail and create very unusual effects. Fortunately, you can turn on the keep lines from crossing option to control this. Unfortunately, using this option can take a few minutes.

In the following exercise, you will take the text you created earlier in this chapter and apply a bevel to it.

BEVELING THE MAX BOWLING TEXT

1. Load the file **MF04-02.MAX** that you created earlier. If you did not complete the previous exercise, you can load the file from the accompanying CD.

2. Choose Select Object from the main toolbar and Select the text object.

3. Click the Modify Command Panel.

4. Select the More button because the Bevel command is not normally in the Modify command panel. Figure 4.10 shows you the Modifiers dialog box where you can select modifiers that do not appear on the Modify command panel.

Figure 4.10

The Modifiers dialog box where you can select modifiers that do not appear on the Modify command panel.

5. Select Bevel and choose OK.

6. The Bevel rollout appears. Under the Bevel values rollout, set the height to 6.

7. Set the outline to –0.3. The result will be text similar to that shown in figure 4.11.

8. Name the object **Alley Text**.

9. Save the file as **MF04-02a.MAX** for use in the next chapter.

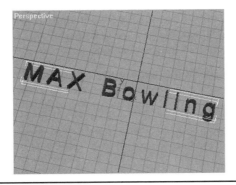

Figure 4.11

The object after applying two levels of beveling to create a chiseled look.

The Bevel tool is very powerful for creating the types of effects shown in the last exercise. You can quickly and easily create objects such as 3D text with one or more levels for use in your scenes and animations. In addition, MAX 2 provides a second Bevel tool, called bevel profile, that enables you to use a second spline as a profile along which to bevel the spline. This enables you to easily create extruded objects with curved edges.

But, although the Bevel tool is powerful, there is one more powerful method for converting splines to 3D objects. This method (lofting) is probably the most heavily used spline method.

Lofting Splines

The last method for converting splines to 3D objects is the Lofting method. Lofts are very similar to extrusions except for three key differences:

♦ Whereas an extrusion is straight and at a defined distance, a loft extrudes a shape along a loft path.

♦ As the shape is lofted along the path, it can be deformed using one or more of the five deformation tools available in MAX.

♦ You can loft an object along a path and also change profile shapes along the path as the loft is created.

These three items make lofting extremely powerful but a little confusing sometimes.

An example of a loft object might be a banana. A banana could not really be created as an extrusion, lathe, or bevel. But it can be created as a loft. Many other objects can be created as loft objects, such as phone cords and handsets; even the bowling pin that you created as a lathe can easily be created as a loft.

You create loft objects by first creating the profile shape and then the loft path, which is a separate shape. Then, you select either shape and go to the Create command panel. (This usually works better if you select the loft shape first because the loft object will be created at the location of the first object selected.) Under the Geometry drop-down list, you will find a Loft Object entry. Selecting this provides you with the Loft command. Figure 4.12 shows you the resulting rollout.

Figure 4.12

The loft object rollout where you can select the loft object and its loft path, which creates the three-dimensional object.

By default, when the loft object is created, the skin, or surface of the object, will not appear in a wireframe viewport but only in a shaded viewport. To change this, open the Skin Parameters rollout and select the Skin check box under the Display options. Most of the other options shown in the Create command panel are related to handling the smoothing and mapping of the final object.

TIP

If you are going to create a loft with more than one loft shape, make sure you line up the first vertex of each shape along the path, or the object will appear twisted. A white box indicates the location of the first vertex.

Many times, when you create a loft object, you will need to deform it, in one way or another, to create the object you are looking for. To do this, go to the Modify command panel while the loft object is selected. You will immediately see the standard loft rollouts. At the bottom of the rollouts, you will find the Deformations rollouts. Figure 4.13 shows the Deformations rollout.

Figure 4.13

The Deformations rollout, where you can apply deformations to a loft object.

There are five different deformations that you can apply to the loft object. Each may be activated or deactivated by clicking the button to the right of each deformation type. You may enable as many deformations of the same type as you like. Each deformation is listed here and briefly described:

♦ **Scale:** Applies a scale to the loft shape as it travels along the path. This is the most often used deformation.

♦ **Twist:** Twists the loft shape using the loft path as the center point of rotation. Objects such as twisted metal gates are easily created with this deformation.

♦ **Teeter:** In a normal deformation, the loft shape is always kept perpendicular to the loft path. With this deformation, you can rotate the loft shape off of perpendicular for subtle changes in the loft object.

♦ **Bevel:** Enables you to apply a bevel to the loft shape as it is extruded along the loft path. This is similar to the scale deformation but is much more exaggerated and difficult to control.

♦ **Fit:** The most difficult of the set to use. In a Fit deformation, you make use of two additional spline shapes: a top view of the object and a side view of the object.

When the loft shape is lofted, it is forced to conform to the two profiles. An example of this type of lofting is the creation of a telephone handset.

Deformations are applied through the use of a deformation grid. This grid provides you with a graphical representation of exactly how much deformation you are applying to specific points of the loft object. Figure 4.14 shows you the scale deformation grid and all of its parts.

Figure 4.14

The Scale Deformation grid dialog box, where you can adjust the scale of the loft shape as it travels along the loft path.

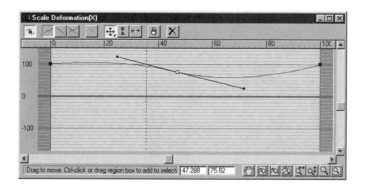

The horizontal axis of the deformation grid represents the length of the loft object. The vertical axis represents the strength of the deformation. By adding vertices to the deformation line and then repositioning them, you can apply the deformation precisely at any point. The deformation line is essentially a spline and can make use of corner points as well as Bézier tangent points to create and apply curvature to the line. You can also apply and control the deformation in the X or Y axis, or both, through the Deformation dialog box.

The following exercise shows you how to create a banana as a loft object.

LOFTING A BANANA

1. Load the file **MF04-03.MAX** from the accompanying CD. This file contains two shapes: a six-sided polygon representing the cross section of a banana, and a spline representing the length and curvature of the banana.

2. Click the Geometry button under the Create Command panel.

3. Choose Select Object and select the Line object.

4. Select Loft Object from the drop-down list.

5. Select the Loft button to access the loft controls.

6. Choose Get Shape in the Command panel rollout and click the six-sided polygon. Immediately, a shape appears in the Perspective viewport, as shown in figure 4.15.

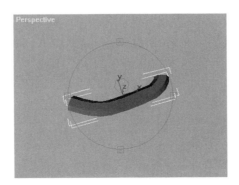

Figure 4.15

The Banana object in the Perspective viewport.

Before proceeding, you should note that the loft object will only appear in a shaded viewport unless you change the Skin Parameter display options. Also, because this object doesn't quite look like a banana yet, you will get a brief introduction to the loft editing tools that will be covered in Chapter 6.

7. With the banana still selected, go to the Modify command panel.

8. Scroll down to the bottom of the rollout and access the Deformations rollout. Here, you can apply a deformation to finish the banana. Select Scale and the Scale Deformation dialog box appears.

9. Click and hold the Insert Corner Point button until you get a flyout. Pick the bottom button off the flyout. This is the Bézier Corner point button.

10. Click at 20, 70, and 90 percent on the red line to create three new points.

11. Select the Move point button.

12. Click and drag and move the point at 0 to a positive 20 percent value.

13. Move the point at 20 vertically to 90.

14. Move the point at 70 vertically to 90.

15. Move the point at 90 vertically to 30.

16. Move the point at 100 vertically to 25. You should get a deformation chart similar to the one shown in figure 4.16. Figure 4.17 shows the resulting banana.

17. Name the object **Banana**.

18. Save the file as **MF04-03a.MAX** for use in a later chapter.

Figure 4.16

The Scale Deformation grid for the corrected banana. Notice how the red line looks very similar to the profile of a banana.

Figure 4.17

The final Banana object after applying a scale deformation.

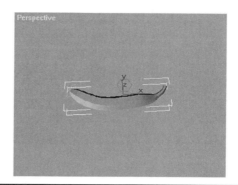

Overall, creating splines and converting them to 3D objects is a very intuitive and powerful method of modeling. After you have created your shapes (composed of one or more individual splines), you can convert the shapes to 3D objects by beveling, extruding, lathing, or lofting them. Because many of these operations are implemented as modifiers, you can adjust the parameters of the final 3D objects at any time.

Splines and spline modeling represent one of the most basic forms of modeling available to you in MAX. The next level of 3D modeling occurs when you work with 3D primitives in MAX.

Working with 3D Primitives

3D primitives are the basis of many modeling packages and provide you with a method for creating many simple objects. Many times, these objects are combined or modified to form other objects. MAX 2 provides you with two different sets of primitive objects: Standard and Extended. The standard primitives include Box, Sphere, Geosphere, Cone, Cylinder, Tube, Torus, Pyramid, Teapot, and Prism. The extended primitives include objects such as Hedra, Torus Knot, Chamfer Box, Chamfer Cylinder, Oil Tank, Capsule, Spindle, L Extrusion, C Extrusion, and Gengon.

When you model with primitives, you will almost always end up transforming or modifying the primitives to create other objects. You can create walls in a building with a series of long thin boxes, for example. You can place door and window openings by adding more boxes and creating compound objects out of them. Rarely will you ever use single primitives by themselves.

In the following exercise, you will use primitives to build a simple chair for use in the bowling alley scene.

BUILDING A CHAIR

1. Start a new file in MAX. In the Create command panel, select the Box object.

2. Click at 0,0 in the Top viewport and drag out to around 10,10 and let go. Move the mouse toward the top of the viewport and click to give the box a height.

3. With the box selected, go to the Create command panel and set the width and length to 1 and the height to 18. Name the object **Chair Leg1**.

4. Select Region zoom and zoom in on an area surrounding the Box object. Create three other boxes exactly the same but approximately 18 inches apart, forming a square. Name the objects **Chair Leg2** through **Chair Leg4**.

5. Select the Box command again. Create a box that is slightly larger than the four chair legs and is 1 inch thick. Name the object **Chair Seat**.

6. Choose Zoom Extents All. Choose Select and Move. In the Front viewport, click the box you just created and move it vertically in the viewport until it rests on top off the chair legs. Figure 4.18 shows the chair at this point.

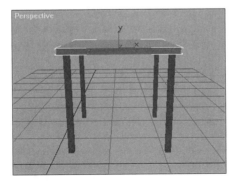

Figure 4.18

The chair approximately halfway through construction.

7. Select the Cylinder command from the Create command panel. Create six cylinders along the back edge of the chair, each with a radius of .5 and a height of 18. Name the objects **Chair Back1** through **Chair Back6**.

8. Use Select to move again in the Front viewport, and move each cylinder so it rests on top of the chair seat.

9. Select the Box command again and create a box in the Top viewport that outlines the top of the cylinders, with a height of 1. Name the object **Chair Back7**.

10. Use Select to move and position the last box at the top of the cylinders in the Front viewport. Figure 4.19 shows the finished chair.

Figure 4.19

A chair constructed solely out of 3D primitives. Although still a simple chair, further adjustments and additions can create a better chair.

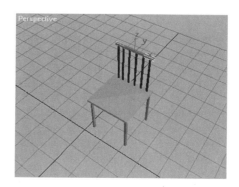

11. Select all of the chair objects and choose Group/Group from the pull-down menus. Name the group **Alley Chair**.

12. Save the file as **MF04-04.MAX** for use later.

For the most part, the primitives in MAX are straightforward and easy to generate. By combining one or more primitives, you can quickly and easily create more complex objects. In Chapter 5, "Basic Editing Methods," you will see how to modify primitives for even more power. Take some time at this point and create at least one of each primitive to get an idea of how they work.

Working with Compound Objects

Compound objects are objects created by combining two or more existing objects (usually primitives) to create a third. Compound objects are a powerful method of modeling many objects such as underwater mines, walls with door and window openings, or even liquid-like objects. MAX provides you with six different compound objects. Each is listed and briefly described:

♦ **Morph:** Enables you to animate one object transforming into another. This compound object is covered in Chapter 15.

♦ **Boolean:** Enables you to combine the volumes of two or more objects to create a third. This is used to create holes or openings in objects or to join two objects together as one. This type of compound object is great for architectural modeling or any time you need to subtract the volume of one object from another.

♦ **Scatter:** Enables you to copy one object over the surface of another. You can use this to create grass blades, dimples on a golf ball, or trees on a landscape.

♦ **Conform:** Enables you to force one object to conform to the surface of another. This is great for creating effects such as melting or slime.

♦ **Connect:** Enables you to connect open areas between two objects. To make use of this, you must have an opening in each object that has only one face on each side of the opening.

♦ **ShapeMerge:** Enables you to merge a spline shape onto the surface of an object. This essentially lets you draw splines on the surface of other objects.

Only the Boolean and Scatter compound objects are discussed in this chapter. Morph and Conform are covered in Chapter 15, "Exploring Other Animation Methods." Connect and ShapeMerge are left to you to explore on your own.

Boolean Objects

Boolean objects work on the principle of Boolean algebra and are used to create compound objects by combining two or more primitives. There are three types of Boolean objects you can create: a Union, an Intersection, and a Subtraction. Figure 4.20 shows you an example of two primitives and results of creating the three different types of Boolean with them.

Booleans are a powerful method of modeling in MAX. You can easily create many types of objects using Booleans. Most commonly, you can use Booleans to subtract the volume of one object from another. When you create the third object, the original two objects are considered *operands*. You can manipulate these operands, and even animate them over time in MAX, resulting in the ability to parametrically change your final Boolean objects.

The following exercise shows you how to create a few quick Boolean objects including a wall with a door opening and a bowling ball with finger holes.

Figure 4.20

*Two primitives
and what
happens to them
when they are
combined as
Boolean objects.*

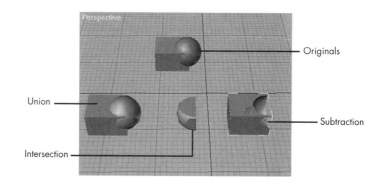

CREATING A WALL WITH A DOOR OPENING

1. Load the file **MF04-05.MAX** from the accompanying CD. This file has two boxes, one for the Wall object and one to be subtracted to create an opening.

2. Choose Select Object and select the Wall object.

3. Under the Create command panel drop-down list, select Compound Objects.

4. Choose the Boolean button.

5. Make sure Subtraction (A-B), under Operation, is selected. Then, choose Pick Operand B.

6. Click the door opening box. The Boolean is created. Rename the object **Long Wall** at this point. Save the result as **MF04-05b.MAX.**

7. Load the file **MF04-05a.max** from the accompanying CD.

8. Select the Sphere object, and then select the Boolean command again.

9. Set the operation type to Subtraction (A-B), and then choose the Pick Operand B button.

10. Click any one of the cylinders and it is subtracted from the sphere.

11. Restart the Boolean command again, by selecting the Boolean button in the command panel, and repeat steps 8 through 10, except select one of the remaining cylinders. Repeat until you have subtracted all cylinders from the sphere.

12. Name the object **Bowling Ball**.

13. Save the file as **MF04-05c.MAX**.

The Boolean command is simple to use. Select the first object (Operand A), select the type of Boolean operation you want to perform, and then select the second object (Operand B).

The Boolean compound object creates the compound object with adaptive **TIP** optimization turned on. Adaptive optimization reduces the number of polygons in the final shape. Unfortunately, this can create problems with the final Boolean. If you see problems such as missing faces, try turning off the Optimize Result checkbox at the bottom of the Boolean rollout.

Booleans represent one kind of compound object that performs a specific, yet powerful, function. Another powerful compound object is Scatter.

Scatter

The Scatter compound object enables you to make copies of one object across the surface of another. Some good examples of using this type of compound object include: creating hair, grass, or trees on a landscape.

To make use of Scatter, you simply need a source object and a distribution object. You select the source object, go to the Scatter command, and then choose the Select distribution object button. Scatter contains a variety of controls to manage the spacing, orientation, and size of the objects that are distributed across the surface. You can save your scatter settings and apply them to other source and distribution objects.

In the following exercise, you will see how to use the Scatter compound object to create a mine with proximity sensors.

CREATING A MINE OBJECT

1. Load the file **MF04-06.MAX** from the accompanying CD. This file contains two spheres, one large and one small.

2. Choose Select Object and select the smaller sphere.

3. Select Compound Object from the Create command panel drop-down list. Then select Scatter from the rollout that appears.

4. Choose the Pick Distribution Object button and select the larger sphere.

5. Under Source Object parameters, set the number of duplicates to 100 and the vertex chaos to 0.25. (The vertex chaos adds a little randomness to the vertices of the small sphere, making them look rough.)

6. Set the Distribution Object parameters to Perpendicular and Even. The result, shown in figure 4.21, is what an underwater mine looks like.

Figure 4.21

The sphere with distributed smaller spheres, creating an underwater mine.

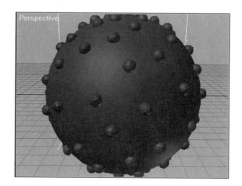

The Scatter objects compound object is an extremely powerful modeling tool. At this point, take a few moments to try different settings in the command panel to achieve different results. Just be aware that depending upon the type of parameters you choose, it may take a few minutes for the screen to update.

Creating Doors and Windows

Doors and Windows are some more complex 3D objects that have been added to MAX from the 3D Studio Viz product. You can create a series of basic doors and windows for use in architectural visualizations or in buildings used for backdrops in other animations.

Unfortunately, these door and window objects require a wall object that already has door and window openings in it. These objects do not automatically create openings in other objects to make room for them. But these door and window objects are parametric, meaning you can adjust any or all of their parameters at will.

MAX 2 contains three door objects (Pivot, Sliding, and Bi-fold) and six window types (Awning, Casement, Fixed, Pivoted, Projected, and Sliding). Through these types, you can create most of the doors and windows you will need.

In the following exercise, you will create a door and correctly position the door inside of a Wall object that has already been prepared for the doors and windows.

ADDING A DOOR TO A WALL

1. Load the file **MF04-05b.MAX** that you created earlier. If you skipped the exercise, you may load the file from the accompanying CD.

2. Choose Region zoom, and zoom in on the area of the wall object where the door opening exists in the Top viewport.

3. Select Doors from the Create command panel drop-down list.

4. Select Pivot Door.

5. Select Views, Grid and Snap Settings. Set the Snap mode to Vertex in addition to Grid Points. Close the Grid and Snap Settings dialog box.

6. Select 2D Snap toggle from the 3D Snap Toggle flyout. (The 2D toggle will force the system to select the vertices at the bottom of the door opening from the Top view.)

7. In the Top view, click and drag from one vertex of the door opening to the other and let go. Then you can select the depth. Select the vertex on the opposite side of the wall.

8. Move the mouse vertically to position the height of the jamb. Watch your other viewports and select a point that looks good. Name the object **Door1**. Figure 4.22 shows the wall at this point.

9. Save the file as **MF04-07.MAX** for use in a later exercise.

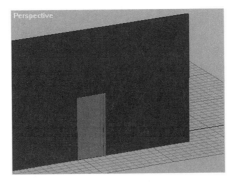

Figure 4.22

The Wall object with a door placed in the door opening.

The Door and Window objects both have many settings to control the appearance of the window. You may explore these settings on your own. If you know a little about building construction or architecture, they will be very easy to figure out.

Doors and windows are easy to use and create. But, unfortunately, you must have walls that are already prepared for the Door and Window objects. One method of preparing a Wall object is to use Boolean operations in a compound object.

Conclusion

This chapter showed you how to create several different basic object types in MAX. These included:

♦ Splines

♦ Extruded, Lathed, and Lofted Splines

♦ Primitives

♦ Compound Objects

In addition, the display commands showed you how to control the display of objects in the MAX viewport. Overall, creating objects in MAX is not a difficult task. In later chapters, you will learn how to manipulate these same objects into various other objects quickly and easily.

As mentioned several times in this chapter, especially when dealing with primitives, you can create more complex objects and combinations of objects by editing and transforming the geometry. The next chapter explores how to perform basic editing on objects in MAX.

CHAPTER 5

Basic Editing Methods

Although it is easy to create objects inside of 3D Studio MAX, they are not very helpful unless they can be transformed and manipulated. In other words, it doesn't do any good to create a wonderful dragon model unless you can correctly position it in the scene. To accomplish this, you need to learn how to edit objects that you create.

This chapter focuses on the basic editing methods available inside of 3D Studio MAX. In particular, this chapter focuses on the following:

♦ Editing Object Parameters

♦ Using Move, Scale, and Rotate

♦ Working with the MAX Reference System

♦ Using Align, Array, and Mirror

Editing Object Parameters

One of the most powerful aspects of 3D Studio MAX is the ability to go back and edit the creation parameters of an object at almost any time. The only time you cannot edit these parameters is when you have converted the object to a different type of geometry, such as an editable mesh or a NURBS object.

When you first create an object, you can access the object parameters in the Create command panel. After you create or edit another object, the parameters disappear. But you can access them again by selecting the object and going to the Modify command panel. Here you will see the object parameters and can freely adjust them. Figure 5.1 shows you the Modify command panel with a tube object loaded.

Figure 5.1

The Modify command panel with a single tube object loaded. Here you can adjust any of the creation parameters at any given time.

In addition to accessing the object creation parameters, you can also change the name or color of the selected object at the top of the Modify command panel. If you select more than one object, you cannot change the name, but you can change the color for all of the selected objects at once. When you select multiple objects, you will not have access to the creation parameters of any object until you select just one.

When you create objects such as Booleans, they convert standard primitives over to Boolean objects. When you access these in the Modify command panel, you will get the Boolean rollout, not any of the primitive rollouts.

Also, many types of objects that you create may have additional rollouts in the Modify command panel that do not appear in the Create command panel. Two examples of such objects are Loft objects and NURBS objects. Loft objects, if you remember from the last chapter, have an additional rollout of deformation tools in the Modify command panel. These types of objects enable you to further edit them without having to resort to using any modifiers. (Modifiers are covered in Chapter 6, "Exploring More Editing Methods.")

With MAX, you can literally be very carefree when creating your geometry because you can come back and edit the parameters at any time. This allows you to experiment with different modeling techniques, or experiment with different ideas, without losing the original geometry. This is the heart of parametric modeling.

Using Move, Scale, and Rotate

The most basic type of editing in MAX is transforming objects. There are three types of transforms that you can apply to objects in MAX: Move, Scale, and Rotate. Obviously, you will use these commands over and over again, so you need to become very familiar with them. Each transform is accessible in a variety of ways, the most common of which is to select the command from the main toolbar. The transform commands are shown on the main toolbar in figure 5.2.

Figure 5.2

The Move, Scale, and Rotate buttons on the main toolbar. These are some of the most used commands in MAX.

Besides the main toolbar, you can access the transform commands by right-clicking any selected object or group of selected objects. In the pop-up menu that appears, you will see the three transforms. Figure 5.3 shows an example of the pop-up menu.

There is a small difference between the toolbar and pop-up menu commands. The transform commands on the toolbar enable you to select one or more objects, whereas the pop-up menu relies upon an existing object selection. Because of this fact, the toolbar commands are selection and transformation commands at the same time.

Figure 5.3

By right-clicking a selected object, you can quickly access the Move, Scale, and Rotate MAX transform commands.

Transforms, Coordinate Systems, and Axis Restriction

All of the transforms such as Move, Rotate, and Scale base the transformation of the selected object on the currently selected coordinate system. The coordinate system determines how the object is actually transformed. MAX provides you with the ability to use alternate coordinate systems (called reference coordinate systems) to give you the flexibility needed to transform objects under just about any condition.

When you select an object to apply a transform to, a tripod appears that indicates the X, Y, and Z axes for the currently selected coordinate system. This tripod is your key to determining the location and orientation of the coordinate system and how the object will react when you transform it.

The default coordinate system for transforms, for example, is a view coordinate system that places the transform tripod in alignment with the current viewport. In this orientation, the X axis is always horizontal, Y is always vertical, and Z always comes out of the viewport toward you. This is true of most viewports. Camera, Perspective, and User views make use of the world coordinate system for transforms instead of screen coordinates. You may select different coordinate systems from the main toolbar by selecting the reference coordinate system drop-down list, shown in figure 5.4.

Figure 5.4

The reference coordinate system drop-down list. Here you can select the type of coordinate system you want to use when you transform an object.

The reason the type of coordinate system is so important is because of axis restriction. It is possible to restrict the transformation of an object to a single axis. The best example of this is the Rotate command. By default, when you rotate an object, you are rotating it around the Z axis, thus restricting the transform. But, the reference coordinate system determines the orientation of the Z axis within the object.

Axis restriction works along a single axis or along a plane such as the XY axis. For example, when you create objects in the Top viewport, by default you are creating them on the XY plane. In the front viewport, it is the XZ plane. You may select the type of axis restriction you want to use by selecting the Transform command and then selecting one of the axis restriction buttons shown in figure 5.5. The XY button shown in figure 5.5 contains a flyout where you can access the XZ and YZ planes as well.

Figure 5.5

The axis restriction controls, where you can restrict the application of a particular transform to an object.

New in MAX 2 is the ability to access the axis restriction controls in the pop-up menu. This provides you with an easy way to quickly select an axis restriction.

UPGRADERS NOTE

If you select the Move command and apply an X axis restriction to it, for example, you can move only the selected object or objects along the X axis of the reference coordinate system. This is made obvious by the presence of the coordinate system tripod that was mentioned earlier. When you set an axis restriction, that axis of the tripod will turn red to indicate it is active. The rest of the tripod remains gray. Figure 5.6 shows you an example of X axis restriction on a coordinate system tripod.

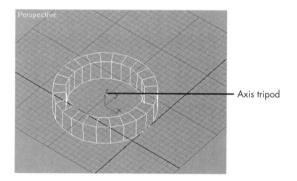

Figure 5.6

A tube object showing the axis tripod with X axis restriction active. In this case, you can move only the object in the direction indicated by the tripod.

MAX provides seven different reference coordinate systems that you can use to control the transformations of objects. Each is listed here and briefly described:

♦ **View:** The default transform coordinate system that relies upon the view to set the X, Y, and Z axes. Regardless of the view you take in MAX, the axis tripod will always appear with X to the right, Y to the top, and Z coming out of the screen toward you.

♦ **Screen:** Aligns the transform tripod to the screen. This appears best when viewing the scene from a Perspective view. In the Perspective viewport, a view-aligned coordinate system is still aligned to the top view, but a screen-aligned system is aligned to your viewport.

♦ **World:** The standard world space coordinate system. This is an absolute setting, where the X, Y, and Z axes are always aligned in the same direction. This is unlike view and screen, which change depending upon the viewport you are working in.

♦ **Parent:** Later in this book, you will see how to link one object to another creating a Parent-Child hierarchy. This coordinate system is used when you have a child object that is attached to a parent. The coordinate system derives itself from the parent object.

♦ **Local:** The local coordinate system for the object. When you rotate an object, you rotate its coordinate system as well. This is the most popular reference coordinate system to use when you are rotating objects.

♦ **Grid:** Aligns the axis tripod to the current construction grid helper object.

♦ **Pick:** A user coordinate system where you can pick an object to align the coordinate system to. Doing so adds the selected object's name to the bottom of the drop-down list, so you may pick it again later in the same session.

The following exercise enables you to see how to make use of these coordinate systems.

WORKING WITH ALTERNATE COORDINATE SYSTEMS

1. Load the file **MF05-01.MAX** from the accompanying CD.

2. Turn on the Angle Snap toggle at the bottom of the screen.

3. Choose Select and Rotate. In the Top viewport, click the box and drag it vertically to rotate it. Watch your coordinate readouts and rotate the box –45 degrees.

4. Repeat the Rotate command, but in the Front viewport this time. Rotate the box another –45 degrees. This box will look like the one shown in figure 5.7.

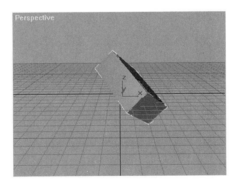

Figure 5.7

The box after applying to rotations in different viewports. Notice how the local grid of the box is no longer aligned with the world coordinate system.

At this point, the box has been rotated around two axes. Now, assume you want to rotate the box around the short end. How would you do that? No matter how hard you try, you cannot successfully accomplish this without using a reference coordinate system.

5. Click the reference coordinate system drop-down list and select Local. (Watch the tripod change in the Perspective viewport.)

6. Set the axis restriction to X.

7. Rotate the box another 45 degrees.

This exercise clearly illustrates the importance of using axis restriction in combination with the reference coordinate systems. The most important thing to remember here is that the reference coordinate system and the axis restriction settings are applied to specific transform commands. You must select the transform before you set the coordinate system and axis restriction. As such, these settings are independent for the Move, Scale, and Rotate commands. This means you need to be careful when setting up the coordinate system and axis restrictions so that you do not apply them to the wrong transform.

You can select the Move command and set the coordinate system to local and axis restriction to X, for example. When you go to the Rotate command, the settings will change to either the default settings, or the last setting they had. When you return back to the Move command, the settings will be restored to the local coordinate system and the X-axis restriction you set previously. This makes it easy to set an axis restriction and think that it is applied to all of the transform commands at once, which is not the case.

The reference coordinate system and the axis restriction controls are not the only methods you have for controlling how an object is transformed. You also have control over the location of the center point of the selected object or group of objects.

Changing the Center Point Location

Changing the location of the center point effects the transform commands by determining the location of the axis tripod, which is also indicative of the center point.

The center point controls are between the reference coordinate system drop-down list and the Axis restriction buttons on the main toolbar. Figure 5.8 shows this flyout toolbar.

Figure 5.8

*The center point
controls. These
commands enable
you to set the
location of the
center point of the
reference
coordinate system.*

There are three types of center point controls that you can use:

◆ **Use Pivot Point Center:** Each object in MAX has its own local coordinate system. The origin of this system is called the pivot point and is generally at the bottom of the object, in the center. This is the default location for the center point of the coordinate system. When you select different reference coordinate systems, they will always be located at the pivot point, just oriented differently.

◆ **Use Selection Center:** When you select more than one object, the pivot point option is not easy to use. This option sets the center point to the geometric center of the selection set. In this case, the center point may be located anywhere in 3D space and is not always restricted to the bottom of the geometry as is the case with the pivot center.

◆ **Use Transform Coordinate Center:** When you select a reference coordinate system, it may have its own center. For example, the world space option has a center at 0,0,0 or the origin of world space. Selecting this center enables you to transform objects around that point.

By selecting the appropriate center point, you can further refine how the transform is applied to the object.

The pivot point center option brings up another interesting feature. As mentioned, all objects have a center point, called the pivot point. When you select a different transform center point, you are doing so on a temporary basis. It is possible to permanently change the location of the pivot point of an object.

Changing the Pivot Point

To change the pivot point of an object permanently, select the object and go to the Hierarchy command panel. Here, you will find the pivot point controls shown in figure 5.9.

Figure 5.9

The pivot point controls in the Hierarchy command panel. These controls enable you to set, move, and rotate the center point of an object.

There are six buttons worth exploring at this point. Each is listed here and briefly described:

♦ **Affect Pivot Only:** This option enables you to transform the pivot point only. You cannot transform the geometry when this is active. When you select the Affect Pivot Only button, you can move, scale, or rotate the pivot point. A special icon will appear in MAX that you can perform the transform on. Figure 5.10 shows you this icon, which appears with Affect Object Only as well.

Figure 5.10

The Pivot Point icon when working in the Hierarchy command panel. You can apply standard transforms to this object.

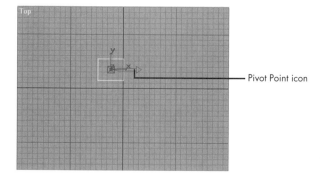

Pivot Point icon

♦ **Affect Object Only:** The opposite of Affect Pivot Only. Here, the pivot point is static, and you transform the object to adjust the pivot point.

♦ **Center to Object:** Aligns the pivot point to the center of the object. If you remember from earlier discussion, the default is centered but at the bottom of the geometry. This centers the pivot point completely.

♦ **Align to Object:** Aligns the X, Y, and Z axes of the pivot point with the local coordinate system of the selected object.

♦ **Align to World:** Aligns the pivot point with the world coordinate system.

♦ **Reset Pivot:** Resets the pivot point to its original setting. Be careful when using this with Affect Object Only. If you select Affect Object Only and move the object, when you reset the pivot point, the object does not return to its original position. Instead, the pivot point returns to its original location in the object but at the object's new position in the scene.

There are many instances in MAX where it is practical to adjust the pivot point of an object. The most common is when you import an object from another program. Its center point may not be in the center of the object. You can correct this with Align to Center. Another common use includes moving the pivot point to affect how the object is rotated. When you get more into animation, you will see the importance of this feature.

Now that you have a little background on how the transform commands work, it is time to take a closer look at each command.

Working with the Basic Transforms

The most common transform is the Move command. This enables you to take any selected object, or group of objects, and reposition them anywhere in the scene. This works by choosing the command and then clicking the selected object and dragging it to its new location. When using the Move command in this manner, the object snap system in MAX becomes very handy for helping you quickly and accurately place objects.

The Rotate command works in the same method as the Move command, except that you end up rotating the selection set. By default, rotations are handled in a view reference coordinate system and around the Z axis. This enables you to rotate the object in the same way in any Orthographic viewport. If you rotate a box in the Top viewport, and then in the Front viewport, it will appear to be the same, but the rotate is applied along two different axes. Rotate is commonly used in conjunction with the Angle snap toggle. This enables you to restrict the rotation of objects to specific increments such as 5 degrees or 1 degree.

The Scale command, on the other hand, is a little more complicated because there are three scale commands that you can use in MAX:

♦ **Scale:** Performs uniform scaling along all three axes of the selected object(s). Axis restriction has no effect on this command.

  You can scale objects in terms of percentages. For example, 200% is twice as large and 50% is half size. This is commonly used in conjunction with the Percent snap toggle to restrict the scale to percentage increments such as 10%.

♦ **Non Uniform Scale:** This version of scale enables you to scale the object nonuniformly along an axis or plane. The application of the scale is controlled by the axis restriction.

♦ **Scale and Squash**: This is another axis-independent command that essentially squashes the object in multiple axes.

All of the scale commands rely heavily upon the location of the center or pivot point. If you have an object that has a center 5 units away from the actual pivot point and you scale that object 200%, the object will end up 10 units away from its pivot point. In other words, all parts of the object are scaled, including the distance to the pivot point. In general, when scaling, it is best to have the pivot point in the center or at the bottom of the object.

Now that you know what the transforms are capable of, let's see how to put them to work. In the following exercise, you will import some objects from the last chapter and position them in the bowling scene, which already contains some existing objects.

EDITING OBJECTS IN THE BOWLING ALLEY

1. Load the file **MF05-02.MAX** from the accompanying CD. This is the beginning of the bowling alley scene. As shown in figure 5.11, you have several basic objects. The entire scene consists of boxes and three different extruded splines. (If you want some more modeling practice, see if you can re-create this portion of the scene on your own, using the file as a guide.)

Figure 5.11

*The bowling alley
scene with some
prebuilt objects.
You will Merge
some objects that
you created in the
last chapter and
use the editing
commands from
this chapter to
correctly position
the objects.*

2. Choose File, Merge from the pull-down menus. Merge the file **MF04-01a.MAX** that you created in the last chapter. The file is available on the accompanying CD if you do not have it. Select all the objects listed in the scene and choose OK.

3. Repeat step 2 and merge the files **MF04-02a.MAX**, **MF04-03a.MAX**, **MF04-04.MAX**, **MF04-05c.MAX**, and **MF05-07.MAX** from the last chapter. Again, these are available on the CD if you did not complete the exercises. Now, you will use the transform commands to place these objects in the scene.

   When you have loaded all of the objects, you will notice that they are rotated wrong, in the incorrect positions, and even in the wrong scale in some places.

4. Activate the Top viewport and choose Zoom Extents.

5. Choose Select by Name and select the Bowling Pin 1 object.

6. Choose Select and Rotate. Set the axis restriction to X and turn on the Angle snap toggle.

7. In the Top viewport, click the Bowling Pin object (zoom in if you need to) and rotate it 90 degrees. Watch your coordinate readouts.

8. Repeat steps 5 through 7 for the Alley Text object.

9. With the Alley Text object still selected, choose Select and Move. Set the axis restriction to XY.

10. In the Front viewport, move the Text object so it is positioned about the triangles and centered on the back wall.

11. Set the axis restriction to Y. In the Top viewport, move the object to the back wall of the alley.

12. Select the bowling pin and move it to the back of lane 2 in the Top viewport as well. In the Left viewport, move the bowling pin vertically, so it sits on top of the lane.

13. Choose Select by Object and select the Alley Wall and Door1 objects.

14. Choose Select and Move. In the Top viewport, move the wall to the left side of the alley. Then position the wall correctly along the length of the alley. You will notice that the door is at the wrong end at this point.

15. Choose Select and Rotate. Set the axis restriction to Z and rotate the selected objects 180 degrees. Now, use Move to correctly place the wall again. The wall is still a few feet too high in the scene, but that will be handled in a later exercise.

16. In the Top viewport, move the chair into the eating area behind the steps. Select the NGon and Line01 objects and delete them.

17. Choose Select and Scale. Select the Banana object (which is way too big) and scale it down to 4% of its original size. Figure 5.12 shows the scene at this point.

Figure 5.12

The bowling alley scene after adding several objects that you created.

18. Save the scene as **MF05-02a.MAX**.

As you can see, using the transform commands is relatively easy. Based on the work done in the last exercise, you should also begin to see exactly how much these commands are used in day-to-day work in 3D Studio MAX.

Working with the Type-In Dialog Box

Up to this point, you have been applying transforms using the mouse in combination with axis restrictions, snaps, and reference coordinate systems. These are all handy tools for quickly placing objects. With the exception of the snaps, however, they are not very accurate. To help with this, MAX has a Type-In dialog box, where you can precisely type in the transforms that you want (see figure 5.13).

Figure 5.13

*The Move
Transform Type-In
dialog box where
you can precisely
control the
transforms of
objects.*

You can access the Move Transform Type-In dialog box through Tools, Transform type in the pull-down menu. This dialog box is used in conjunction with the Move, Scale, and Rotate commands exclusively. You select the object, activate one of the transform commands (but don't actually use it on the object), and then open the Type-In dialog box if it is not already open. At this point, you can use the mouse to move objects, or simply type in the desired transforms in the dialog box.

The Transform Type-In dialog box also changes to match the type of transform you are working with. Figure 5.13 shows the dialog box for the Move command. If you select Scale, the dialog box shown in figure 5.14 appears.

Figure 5.14

*The Scale
Transform Type-In
dialog box,
showing specific
type-in controls for
the Scale
command.*

The Scale Transform Type-In dialog box enables you to work with transforms in two different ways: Absolute or Offset. With the Absolute type-ins, all transforms are applied in the world coordinate system. If you select an object and apply a Move transform with a Z value of 3, the object will move 3 units in the Z axis. If you exit the transform and come back, the Z axis value will still be 3.

With Offset, on the other hand, you are applying the transform relative to the current position of the object. Offset makes use of the current reference coordinate system in the context of the current viewport to define the direction that the transform will be applied to. In the previous example, you can move the object 3 units in the Z axis. If the reference coordinates are set to Local, this will be applied along the local Z axis. When you return to the dialog box, the Z value will be 0 again as it is relative to the current position.

The following exercise shows how to use the Transform Type-In dialog box to modify some objects from the last exercise.

USING THE TRANSFORM TYPE-IN TO TRANSFORM OBJECTS

1. Load the file **MF05-02a.MAX** if you do not have it still loaded from the last exercise.

2. Choose Select by Name and select the Alley Wall and Door1 objects.

3. Choose Select and Move. From the pull-down menus, choose Tools, Transform Type-In to access the Transform Type-In dialog box.

4. With the Top viewport active, enter a value of –24 in the Z spinner under Offset:Screen. This moves the two objects 24 inches down in the Z axis and correctly positions the wall.

5. Select the Chair object. You will notice that because one object is selected, the Absolute:World coordinates are now available. Z is at 18.86 because of the location of the pivot point.

6. Set the Z spinner under Absolute:World to –5.5. This moves the chair approximately –24 units in the Z axis.

7. Close the Type-In dialog box.

8. Save the file as **MF05-02b.MAX**.

Many times, transforming objects with the mouse is accurate enough. But every once in a while, you will need the ability to accurately and precisely transform the object to match your needs. In the previous exercise, two objects needed to be moved precisely 24 inches. It was easier to use the Type-In dialog box than to set up a grid and snap that would accomplish the same task.

Transforming objects is a simple, yet powerful, method of editing in MAX. But, transforms have more capabilities than just moving, scaling, or rotating objects in a scene. You can use transforms to clone (copy) objects in a variety of ways. This cloning process makes use of the MAX reference system.

Working with the MAX Reference System

Even as simple as the transforms are in MAX, you can begin to see just how flexible and powerful they really are. Now, you can take this one step further by using the transforms to create new objects. You accomplish this by using the MAX reference or cloning system.

The reference system is a general method of handling how an object is copied in MAX. Making a copy of an object in MAX is easy enough. Simply hold down the Shift key when performing a move, rotate, or scale. When you select the new location for the object, you will be prompted for an object name and type. Figure 5.15 shows this dialog box. Actually, copying an object in MAX is called cloning, and there are three types of clones that you can create.

Figure 5.15

The Clone Options dialog box where you can tell MAX what type of object clone you want to create.

Copy

The first type of clone is a Copy. A Copy is an exact duplicate of the object in every manner, except for the name. The second copy of the object takes up just as much memory as the first. As your create clones, MAX will automatically rename the cloned objects by numbering them, unless you give the new object a new name every time. You may run across objects named tree01, tree02, and so on. This might indicate that they were cloned.

The second type of clone is an Instance. An Instanced object does not take up additional memory in the scene, except at render time, thus making your files much smaller. An Instance is an exact duplicate of the original object, but it is still related to the original. With an Instance, if you apply a modifier, it will be applied to all instances of the object in the same way. This makes it easy to create effects such as a set of flowers blowing in the wind. Each flower can be an Instance. Then, simply apply the Bend modifier to one instance and all the flowers will bend at the same time. By animating one instance of the Bend modifier, you animate all as well.

The last type of clone is a Reference. A Referenced object is similar to an Instance but is considered a one-way Instance. In other words, if you apply a modifier to the original object, the Reference is affected as well. But if you apply the modifier to the Reference, the original is not affected. The Reference maintains its own modifier hierarchy.

Throughout MAX, you will find places where you can use References, and more commonly, Instances. You can, for example, Instance bitmaps in the Materials Editor or animation controllers in TrackView. In all cases, the copies' objects are the same as the original, and any changes made to one affect all Instances. As you progress through the many areas where you can use Instances, you will see how and why they are a very powerful tool.

In addition to using the transform commands, there is a Clone command in the Edit pull-down list. This makes a clone of any selected object, in the exact same position. When this is done, the original object is deselected and the clone is selected, so that you can immediately transform it.

Using Move, Scale, and Rotate, with their associated functionality, is a common task that you will perform in everyday work with MAX. But there are still a few other, less used, transform commands to look at.

Using Align, Array, and Mirror

Three other types of transform commands exist in MAX that you should be aware of: Align, Array, and Mirror. These commands are transforms because they change the position of objects and, in some cases, create one or more copies of the objects as the position is changed. You can find these commands in the main toolbar, as shown in figure 5.16, as well as in the Tools pull-down menu.

Working with Align

The Align command is used to align one object to another. The alignment can occur as a position, rotation, or scale. To perform this operation, you simply select the object you want to align. Choose the Align command, and then select the object you want to align to. At this point, the dialog box shown in figure 5.17 appears.

Figure 5.16

*The Align, Array,
and Mirror
commands are
less-used
transform
commands. These
commands can
transform an
object and make
multiple copies at
the same time.*

Figure 5.17

*The Align
Selection dialog
box, where you
can align one
object to another
by scale, rotation,
and/or position.*

As shown in figure 5.17, there are several very powerful options to the Align command. Each is listed here and briefly described:

♦ **Align Position (Reference Coordinate System):** These controls define which coordinates of the selected object are aligned to the destination objects. You simply select each check box and the transformation is applied. In addition, you can define which center point of the objects are aligned by choosing Minimum, Center, Pivot, or Maximum. This alignment occurs in the selected reference coordinate system, which is read back in the parentheses. So, alignment is also coordinate system specific.

♦ **Align Orientation (Reference Coordinate System):** These check boxes control which axes are also aligned to the destination object. This occurs in the local coordinate space at all times.

♦ **Match Scale:** Lastly, you can match the scale of the aligned object at the X, Y, and Z axes, regardless of the coordinate system.

As you can see, the Align command provides you with a lot of detail. But, there are also several other Align commands available in the Align toolbar flyout, which is shown in figure 5.18.

Figure 5.18

The Align toolbar and associated flyout. Here you will find various commands to align objects with.

There is an Align to View command that aligns objects to the current viewport. There is also an Align Camera command that can align objects to a camera view. Many of these are specialty commands that are only used in certain circumstances. Coverage of these commands is beyond the scope of this book.

Working with Array

The next transform command is the Array command. The Array command enables you to create multiple copies of an object in either a circular or gridlike fashion. Arrays can occur in one dimension, two dimensions, or even three dimensions. You can even set the array to create copies, instances, or references of the original object. To array an object, select the object and then select the Array command. The Array dialog box shown in figure 5.19 appears.

Figure 5.19

Use the Array dialog box to create one-, two-, or three-dimensional arrays of an object.

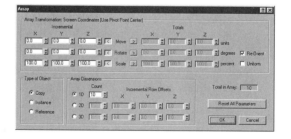

The Array dialog box includes several controls you can use to define how the array works. These controls are listed and briefly described here:

♦ **Array Transformation:** These controls define the spacing of the array components. This can be done in an incremental or a total fashion. Incremental sets a defined spacing between objects, and total defines an overall length and the objects are created within that length. You may select which is active by clicking the arrows between incremental and total. This may be applied to the move, rotate, and scale aspects of the array.

♦ **Type of Object:** These controls enable you to define whether the array is created as a Copy, Instance, or Reference.

♦ **Array Dimensions:** These control the overall dimensions of the array and whether it is one-, two-, or three-dimensional.

Figure 5.20 shows an example of an arrayed set of spheres.

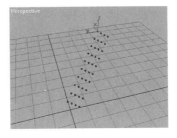

Figure 5.20

A set of spheres that have been transformed using the Array command.

Working with Mirror

Probably the most-used special transform command is the Mirror command. This command creates an exact mirror duplicate of a selected object and enables you to mirror an object about a single axis. Simply select the object and choose Mirror. When you do this, the Mirror dialog box shown in figure 5.21 appears.

Figure 5.21

The Mirror dialog box, where you can create mirrors of objects around any axis.

The Mirror command simply provides you with two sets of controls. The first control is the mirror axis. This can be defined just like the axis restriction controls are. The offset spinner shown in figure 5.21 enables you to set the mirrored object a specified distance from the mirror line. Like the other transformation commands, the Mirror command makes use of the selected reference coordinate system to perform the mirror operations.

The second control enables you to define the clone options. By default, the Mirror command does not create a clone, but you can set it to create a Copy, Instance, or Reference.

In the following exercise, you will mirror a wall and a door from one side of the bowling alley to the other side. You accomplish this with a clone and move operation, but it's sometimes easier as a simple mirror.

MIRRORING A WALL AND A DOOR

1. Load the file **MF05-02b.MAX** from the last exercise if it is not already loaded.

2. Choose Select by Name and select the Alley Wall and Door1 objects.

3. Select the Mirror command.

4. Set the clone type to Instance and set the mirror axis to X.

5. Adjust the offset value to 274 units, which is approximately how wide the bowling alley is.

6. Choose OK to finish the command.

7. In the Top viewport, choose Zoom Extents.

8. Select the Chair object with Select Objects.

9. Choose the Mirror command.

10. Set the mirror axis to Y and the offset to −60. The clone options should already be set to Instance from the last mirror operation.

11. Choose OK to create the mirror.

12. Choose Select and Rotate. Select both chair objects.

13. Set the center point type to selection set.

14. Turn on the Angle snap toggle. Hold the Shift key down and rotate the chairs 90 degrees.

15. When you let go, you are prompted with a Clone Options dialog box. Set the clone type to Instance and choose OK.

16. Choose Select and move the chairs to the center of the eating area.

17. Now create a mirror of the four chairs to create a second set. Figure 5.22 shows the scene with eight chairs, one of which is a true chair; the rest are instances of the one.

18. Save the file as **MF05-03.MAX**.

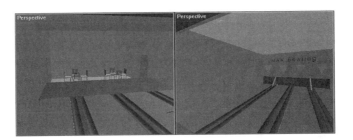

Figure 5.22

The bowling alley with eight chairs. Seven copies of the original chair were created using Mirror and Rotate.

From the last exercise, you can see how to use the Mirror command in combination with standard transformations to quickly create and position multiple copies of objects.

Conclusion

This chapter focused on basic editing skills using some of the most commonly used commands in 3D Studio MAX. Overall, basic editing skills such as transforms and cloning are vital to working with the MAX system. You will use these skills every day that you work with MAX to create your scenes, manipulate objects, assign materials, or perform hundreds of other tasks in MAX.

- ♦ **Transforms:** The Move, Scale, and Rotate commands, which are used to position objects correctly in the scene.

- ♦ **The MAX Reference System:** Provides three (Copy, Instance, and Reference) different methods for creating copies of objects in the MAX scene. By controlling the type of copy, you can control how the copied objects are related to other objects in the scene.

- ♦ **Reference Coordinate Systems:** Objects are always transformed around a specific point and a specific coordinate system. The reference coordinate system enables you to define the position and orientation of a coordinate system that MAX will use when transforming objects.

- ♦ **Align, Mirror, and Array:** These are advanced transform commands that provide automated methods of transforming objects. You can use Shift+Move to make a clone of an object, or you can simply mirror the object.

Now that you have seen how to do some basic editing, it is time to look at some additional editing methods, including the use of the stack and modifiers. These methods, which are covered in the next chapter, provide you with even more powerful ways of editing objects to create other objects.

C H A P T E R

6

Exploring More Editing Methods

In the last chapter, you explored the basic transform and editing tools that are available in MAX. Now, it is time to look at additional editing tools that you will use. These include modifiers, the stack, and space warps. These tools enable you to quickly change and modify one object into another to create a variety of effects.

In particular, this chapter covers the following topics:

- ♦ Working with Modifiers

- ♦ Understanding the Modifier Stack

- ♦ Editing Objects at Different Levels

Working with Modifiers

One of the most powerful and useful features of 3D Studio MAX is the ability to use modifiers. Modifiers are routines that change and transform objects in specific ways. You may create an object that you want to twist, such as the ice cream on an ice-cream cone. You can accomplish this by applying a Twist modifier to the ice cream object and twisting it around the world coordinate system Z axis.

Modifiers work by adjusting all or part of the geometry. A twist modifier works by adjusting the location of the vertices of an object, for example. Other modifiers work at various sub-object levels such as vertex, edge, or even face level. As such, modifiers are useful modeling tools, as well as powerful tweaking tools.

Like the modeling methods in MAX, the modifiers are parametric in nature. This means that each modifier has an associated set of controls that you can set and adjust at any time. The parameters of a modifier can even be animated providing you with many powerful animation tools. You apply modifiers to selected objects through the Modify command panel, shown in figure 6.1. You may apply modifiers to more than one object at a time, but it is recommended that you apply modifiers on an object-by-object basis.

Figure 6.1

The Modify command panel where you assign any modifiers to currently selected objects.

Modifiers that appear in the command panel are smart enough to recognize the type of geometry selected. In other words, modifiers only work on certain types of geometry (patches versus NURBS versus meshes versus splines). In such cases, if you select a spline, only modifiers that can work on the spline will be active. The others will be grayed out.

MAX has many modifiers already built into it. As you add plug-ins, you will get more and more modifiers to use. Obviously, not all of these modifiers will fit in the Modify command panel. As such, the Modify command panel is fully configurable and customizable.

To access modifiers that do not appear in the default set of buttons, select the More button, which displays the dialog box shown in figure 6.2. This dialog box enables you to select any of the modifiers that are currently available.

Figure 6.2

The Modifiers dialog box, where you can select a modifier from the list of all modifiers available in MAX.

As you work with MAX, you will find modifiers that you use more than others. In such cases, you will probably want to add them to the Modify command panel, so you do not have to use the More button every time you want to apply the modifier. You can accomplish this by choosing Configure Button Sets in the Modify command panel. This displays the Configure Button Sets dialog box, where you can change buttons in the Modify command panel (see figure 6.3).

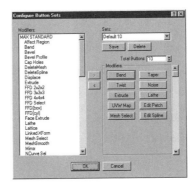

Figure 6.3

The Configure Button Sets dialog box, where you can define which modifiers appear as buttons in the default Modify command panel.

The Modify command panel supports up to as many as 32 modifier buttons at any given time. If you want to run this many modifier buttons, run MAX at 1280x1024 or higher. When you increase the number of modifiers, blank buttons will appear in the dialog box. To assign a modifier to one of these buttons, simply select the button. Then select the modifier you want that button to represent from the list on the left side of the dialog box. Then click on the right arrow button and the assignment is complete. You may assign modifiers to blank buttons or change existing buttons.

Objects and Sub-Objects

Many modifiers work on the principle of objects and sub-objects because all objects in MAX are sub-objects that form objects. Boolean compound objects use the original operands as sub-objects. Hence, all objects have sub-objects of some sort.

Through various modifiers, you can access each of the sub-object parts that exist. Each modifier can control different types of sub-objects, including their own sub-objects, called *gizmos*. If you look at the Modifiers command panel shown in figure 6.4, you will see a Sub-Object button that is grayed out under Selection Level.

When sub-objects are available, you can activate the sub-object selection and then select the type of sub-objects you want to work with in the accompanying drop-down list. When active, you can only select the type of sub-object in the drop-down list, and only on the current selected object. Figure 6.4 shows a sphere and several vertices selected as sub-objects. When a particular sub-object is active, the rollout will change to present you with controls specific to that sub-object type you are working with.

Gizmos

The gizmo sub-object is available in many modifiers such as bend, twist, or UVW Map. The gizmo is a helper object that tells MAX how to apply the selected modifier to the object. Figure 6.5 shows an object with a Bend modifier applied to it. The cage that surrounds the object is the gizmo and usually appears as yellow in the MAX viewports.

When the Sub-Object gizmo selection option is active in the Modifiers command panel, you can apply standard MAX transforms such as Move, Copy, and Rotate to the gizmo to determine how the bend effect is applied. Figure 6.6 shows three examples of this.

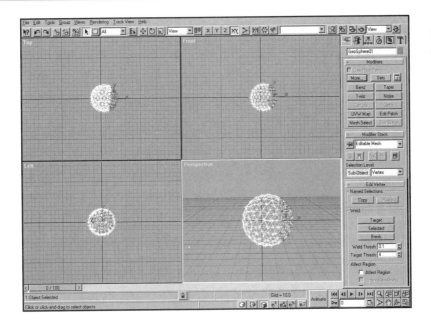

Figure 6.4

A sphere with vertices selected through sub-object selection.

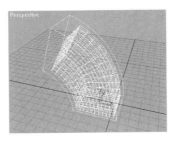

Figure 6.5

The Bend modifier sub-object gizmo as applied to a standard box with 10 segments.

In addition to the standard gizmo, the Bend modifier also has a center point sub-object gizmo, which determines the location of the center point of the bend effect. By adjusting either the gizmo or the center point, you can create a wide variety of effects with just the one modifier. Other modifiers in MAX may or may not make use of one or more gizmos.

When you are creating objects, you might need to apply only one modifier to create the effect you want. Many times, however, you will apply more than one modifier to a single object. The list of modifiers applied to the object is called the history or the stack.

The following exercise explores how to use modifiers such as the Bend modifier to create a sign that uses curved text. Without the use of modifiers, this sign would be tedious to create because you would have to create each letter individually.

Figure 6.6

The box on the right has the Bend modifier gizmo scaled up, which results in a smaller bend on the object. The box in the middle has the Bend modifier gizmo rotated 45 degrees, which bends the box in the selected direction. The box on the left has the Bend modifier gizmo moved, resulting in an exaggerated bend effect.

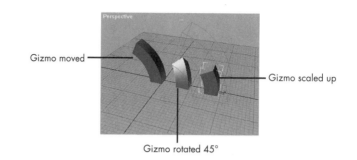

Gizmo moved

Gizmo scaled up

Gizmo rotated 45°

CREATING A CURVED TEXT SIGN USING MODIFIERS

1. Load the file **MF06-02.MAX** from the accompanying CD. This file contains a few shapes and a box that you will apply modifiers to.

2. Choose Select Object and select the Milky Way text object.

3. Go to the Modify command panel and select the More button.

4. Select PathDeform under World space modifiers.

5. Choose Pick Path and select the long curved line behind the text.

6. Set the Path Deform axis to X, the Percent spinner to 50, Rotation to 180, and choose Move to Path once.

7. While the text is still selected, choose More again.

8. Select Bevel Profile from the modifier list and choose OK.

9. Select the Pick Profile button and select the small red profile just below the text in the Top viewport. You will probably get a very weird result at this point.

10. Turn on Keep Lines from Crossing to clean up the text. This will take a few minutes, so have a little patience. Figure 6.7 shows the resulting text.

Figure 6.7

The text after applying a bevel profile. Notice how the profile was applied in all directions.

11. Select Tools, Display Floater, and choose All under Unhide.

12. Apply the Path deform modifier to the box that appears exactly as before in steps 5 and 6. You now have a curved sign with curved and beveled text.

13. Once applied, use the Move command to move the box vertically in the Top viewport so the text is correctly centered.

14. In the Left or Front viewport, move the box so it is just below the text. Figure 6.8 shows the final image.

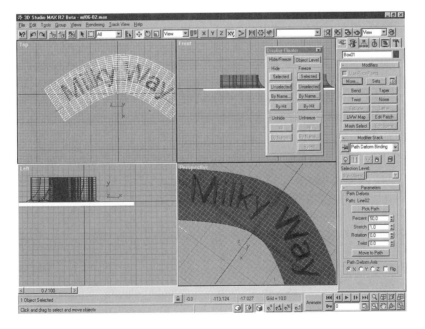

Figure 6.8

The completed sign showing the use of several different modifiers to create an interesting effect.

15. Save the file as **MF06-02A.MAX** for use in a later chapter.

As you can see, MAX has many powerful modifiers that you can use to create a wide variety of effects.

 NOTE   MAX 2 has many modifiers that are not covered in this book. Refer to your MAX documentation for information on features and how to use modifiers that are not covered here.

Understanding the Modifier Stack

In MAX, modifiers are applied linearly, creating the modifier stack. The stack is a linear history of modifiers that have been applied to the selected object. The stack is what enables you to return to any modifier that was assigned earlier in the stack and make adjustments to see the results in the final object.

You can create a box and apply bend, twist, and taper modifiers to it, for example. But, at any point, you can return to the original box and make it taller or wider but still see the effect of the applied modifiers. This results in practically unlimited opportunities to explore, modify, and change your objects.

The ability to modify any portion of an object or its history is possible through the MAX geometry pipeline, which enables you to work parametrically with modified objects.

Understanding the MAX Geometry Pipeline

The geometry pipeline in MAX is important because it helps you understand how modifiers work and how they are applied to the geometry. To demonstrate the geometry pipeline, consider an object that has five modifiers applied to it. While you work on the object, you can see the end result, as if you had built the object without modifiers.

When you come in the next morning, restart MAX, and reload the file, MAX will rebuild the object by recreating the original object and then reapplying each of the modifiers (with their saved settings) to the object. Without the rebuilding process of the geometry pipeline, the stack could not be possible. The only downfall to this is that sometimes the application of a modifier can take a few minutes to process, depending upon the complexity of the object. When this occurs, every time you load the object, it will have to be rebuilt and you will have to wait. This is part of the price of a truly parametric system. Fortunately, because of how optimized MAX is, you will rarely run across this problem.

As you apply various modifiers, they pass the geometry up to the next modifier in the stack list. So, if you have applied a twist to an object and then decided to apply a bend, the bend will operate on the geometry in the state it is in after the twist modifiers. In other words, the twist modifier passed the object geometry to the bend modifiers, after applying its effect.

Working with the Stack

The stack is an extremely powerful tool in MAX, and fortunately it is easy to use. When you select a newly created existing object, the stack is already active with just one entry in it. As you apply modifiers to the object, they will appear in the stack drop-down list, which is shown in figure 6.9.

Figure 6.9

The stack drop-down list, where you can select which modifier you want to edit.

Through the stack drop-down list, you can select a particular modifier or even go back as far as the original object and adjust its parameters. You will immediately see the result of the changes in the viewports. Below the stack drop-down list are five stack control buttons (see figure 6.10) that further enable you to work with the stack.

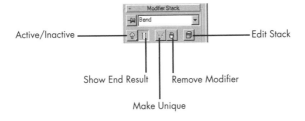

Figure 6.10

The stack control buttons, which provide you with precise control over the stack.

Each button shown in figure 6.10 is listed here and briefly described:

+ **Active/Inactive:** Activates or deactivates the current modifier.

+ **Show End Result:** Toggles the display of the end result. When active, you see the object after all the modifiers in the stack have been applied. When inactive, you see the object with all modifiers up to and including the current modifier applied.

+ **Make Unique:** Turns an instanced modifier into a unique one.

+ **Remove Modifier from Stack:** Deletes the current modifier from the object and the object's stack.

+ **Edit Stack:** Accesses the Edit Stack dialog box, where you can perform operations such as reordering the stack or collapsing the stack.

 NOTE   If you click on the Edit Stack button without any modifier applied to the object, you will get a pop-up menu that asks whether you want to convert the geometry to an editable mesh or a NURBS surface. Also on this menu is an option to access the Edit Stack dialog box. This is the easiest way to convert an object from mesh to a NURBS surface. (NURBS are covered in Chapter 7, "Exploring Other Modeling Methods.")

You can access many of the important stack functions through the Edit Modifier Stack dialog box. The most important functions are the capability to reorder the stack using Cut, Copy, and Paste and the capability to collapse the stack.

Reordering the stack enables you to move modifiers to different locations in the stack. This can result in quite different objects because the modifiers are applied to the result of the last modifier. You can reorder by selecting a modifier in the stack and choosing either Cut or Copy. Then select a new location and choose Paste. MAX places the new modifier above the selected position in the stack.

Obviously, the more modifiers you apply to an object, the more memory that particular object will take. At some point, you will decide that the object you have created is correct and no longer needs any changes. At that point, the parametric aspects of the object are also no longer needed. To conserve memory, you can collapse the stack. Collapsing the stack removes all the modifiers from the object and leaves the final result as an editable mesh object. Thus, it takes up much less memory.

If you decide to collapse the stack on an object, make sure you want to do so. The Collapse Stack command cannot be undone. Also, collapsing the stack will remove any animated parameters that might have been a part of any modifier. If you have animated modifiers, do not collapse the stack. Collapsing the stack also removes the parametric capabilities of the object. If you want to keep those, do not collapse the stack either.

WARNING

There are several new features to the Edit Stack dialog box, most notably the Cut, Copy, and Paste options. But you also have the ability to give any modifier in the stack its own name, as well as create instances of modifiers.

The following exercise will show you how to make use of the stack to create the ice cream on an ice-cream cone. During this exercise, you will see how to apply and work with modifiers as well as the stack.

CREATING AN ICE-CREAM CONE

1. Load the file **MF06-01.MAX** from the accompanying CD. This file is an ice-cream cone with a block of chocolate ice cream that you will modify. Figure 6.11 shows this file.

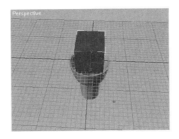

Figure 6.11

The ice-cream cone scene before you begin to apply modifiers to make ice cream.

2. Choose Select Objects and select the box on top of the cone.

3. Click on the Modify command panel.

4. Select the Taper modifier. When its controls appear in the command rollout, set the amount to –0.50.

5. Select the Twist modifier. When its controls appear, set the angle to –360.

At this point, the twisted box looks very bad. The reason for this is the lack of detail in the box itself for the Twist modifier to work on. You will now go back into the stack and adjust the detail in the box so that it will correctly deform.

6. Click on the Stack drop-down list and select Box. Set the Length, Width, and Height segment spinners each to 20. This immediately corrects the problem, but the ice cream is still not correct.

7. Click on the drop-down list again and select Taper.

8. Adjust the Taper amount to –0.75.

9. The last thing to do is adjust the size of the ice cream to more approximately match that of the cone. Select the Stack drop-down list and choose Box again.

10. Set the Width and Length spinners to 83.

11. Now that the ice cream looks good, it is time to collapse the stack because you will not be changing it anymore. Select Edit Stack.

12. Choose Collapse All.

13. Choose Yes to the warning message about the consequences of collapsing the stack.

14. Choose OK. Figure 6.12 shows the completed ice-cream cone.

15. Save this file as **MF06-01a.MAX** for use later in the bowling alley scene.

Figure 6.12

The completed ice-cream cone, illustrating how easy modifiers are to use and manipulate.

Working with Non-Uniform Scale

When dealing with modifiers in a stack situation, you must be careful about using the Non-Uniform scale and Squash transforms. When you apply this type of transform, it is applied after any modifiers that are already in the stack. If this is what you want, no problem. But, if you want to apply the Non-Uniform scale at a specific point in the stack, you must use an Xform modifier and apply the Non-Uniform scale as a sub-object.

Editing Objects at Different Levels

One of the most powerful uses of modifiers is the ability to edit objects at different sub-object levels. Each type of object in MAX, such as a Patch object or a Mesh object, is composed of different types of sub-objects. So when you edit at the sub-object level of these objects, you will run across different types of sub-objects, depending on the type of geometry you are working with. A Mesh object has vertex, face, and edge sub-objects, whereas a spline has vertex, segment, and spline sub-objects.

Editing objects at different levels of detail enables you to refine, or even model, complex objects out of simple objects. By exploring the different sub-objects with which you can work by geometry type, you can begin to see the power of sub-object editing.

Editing Spline Objects

As you saw in Chapter 4, "Basic Modeling Methods," you can create spline objects fairly easily. But, the true power of spline modeling is the ability to edit and refine the shape. Without this capability, you cannot create many of the shapes you will need for your projects.

To edit a spline or shape, simply select the shape, and then go to the Modify command panel. In most cases, you will immediately see the Edit Spline controls. If you don't, click the Edit stack button and select Editable Spline. This converts the object to an editable spline. You can edit splines at four different levels: shape (called the object level), vertex, segment, and spline. Vertex, segment, and spline are all sub-object editing modes.

Editing Splines at the Object Level

Object-level editing of splines is the default method when you enter the Modify command panel with a spline selected. Figure 6.13 shows the rollout that appears.

Editing splines at an object level enables you to perform three basic functions. First, you can attach one or more splines to the current shape. Remember, when you create splines, you have the option of deciding whether or not the splines are created as part of the current shape or created as a new shape through the Create New Shape button. Object-level spline editing enables you to combine splines into a single shape after you have created them. In addition to adding splines to a shape, you can also create lines that are added to the shape as you create them.

Figure 6.13

The Edit Object rollout for splines. Here, you can perform several object- or shape-level operations.

Second, you can control the interpolation options, otherwise known as the detail settings, of the splines in the current shape. These settings will override any settings that you applied when you created the splines and are applied to all splines in the shape.

Lastly, you can set the rendering options of the splines. This enables you to make all the splines in the shape-renderable entities.

By far, most of the object editing that you will do with splines involves attaching one or more splines to the current shape.

Editing Splines at the Vertex Level

The first, and most important, sub-object level that you can work with in splines is the vertex level. This is accomplished by activating the Sub-Object button in the Modify command panel and selecting the vertex option from the drop-down list. This displays the vertex level controls as shown in figure 6.14.

Figure 6.14

The spline vertex sub-object rollout. Here, you can make fine adjustments to splines that you have already created.

When the vertex sub-object controls are active, you can access any of the commands present in the command panel rollout, or you can use any of the standard MAX transforms to position and adjust the vertices of a spline.

When the vertex sub-object selection is active, all you can select in the scene are vertices on the currently selected spline. So if you choose Select Object, you can select one or more vertices to edit. When the vertex is selected, it will turn red and an axis tripod will appear. Depending on the type of tangents this particular vertex is using, you might also get a set of green tangent handles. Figure 6.15 shows a selected vertex with tangent handles.

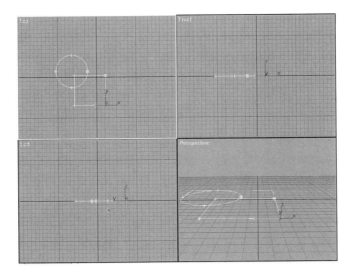

Figure 6.15

A spline with a selected vertex. This vertex is now ready to be transformed and adjusted.

If you right-click the selected vertex, you can select the type of transform to apply in the pop-up menu that appears. But more importantly, you can also select the type of tangents that are being used by the vertex.

If you remember from Chapter 3, "Understanding Modeling Concepts," a spline vertex can have four different types of tangents. You can set these corner types while creating the spline if you are using the Line command. But if you are using the other spline commands, the only way to set the tangents is to use sub-object editing.

After you have set the tangent types, you can transform the vertex or the tangent handles with the Move, Scale, and Rotate commands. The Scale command, in particular, affects only the tangent handles. When you scale a vertex, the distance of the tangent handles away from the vertex is scaled. So the Scale command does not affect the Corner or Smooth tangent types.

Beyond the transform commands, you can use the commands located in the command panel to edit splines at the vertex level. These commands include the following:

♦ Connect

♦ Break

♦ Refine

♦ Insert

♦ Make First Vertex

♦ Weld

♦ Lock Handles

By making use of the transform commands in combination with the rollout commands, you can take a spline such as a rectangle and adjust it to practically any other shape, without ever creating a new spline.

Editing Splines at the Segment Level

The next level at which you can edit a spline is the segment level. If you remember, a segment is the part of a spline that appears between vertices. You access these commands by selecting the Segment option under the Sub-Object drop-down list, which produces the Edit Segment rollout (see figure 6.16).

Figure 6.16

The Edit Segment rollout, where you can refine and adjust a spline at the segment level.

Like vertices, you can select and transform segments at will. Also like vertices, there is a pop-up menu that appears when you right-click any selected segment.

This menu is the same as the vertex menu, except for the last two entries. Here you can select whether the segment is a curve or a straight line. Choosing one or the other will have no effect on the vertices themselves, only on how the segment between the two is interpreted.

Many of the commands found here in the command panel are the same as those found under the vertex-level editing commands but work on a segment instead. The only two differences are the Detach command that enables you to detach the selected segment(s) and create a new shape or create a copy of the segment as a new shape. You can also use the Divide command to equally divide any segment into smaller segments by placing equally spaced vertices along the spline.

Editing Splines at the Spline Level

The last level of spline editing occurs at the spline level. Here you will find a set of commands that enable you to combine open and closed splines in a variety of methods. When you select the Spline option from the sub-object drop-down list, you get the rollout shown in figure 6.17.

Figure 6.17

The Edit Spline rollout, where you can edit individual splines that are part of a larger shape.

Editing at a spline level involves manipulating individual splines that exist within the larger, more complex shape. You can create a mirror of a spline, and the resulting copy is still a member of the current shape.

The most basic command at the spline level is the Close command, which connects the first vertex to the last vertex and creates a closed spline within the shape.

You can use the Outline command to create parallel copies of the spline. Creating an outline of a circle, for example, will create a donut shape. The distance between the original spline and the offset copy is defined by a spinner or drag of the mouse.

Alternatively, just as you can Boolean 3D objects together, you can Boolean splines. The only conditions that must be met for this to work correctly are that the splines must be closed, must be part of the same shape, and must overlap in some way. If these conditions are met, you can create a union, intersection, or subtraction of the splines.

The last rollout command is the Reverse command, which is very similar to the First Vertex command. The Reverse command simply reverses the order of the vertices of a spline and is extremely useful when using the spline as an animation path or as an edge for a surfacing operation.

Overall, most of the editing that you do to a spline will occur at a vertex or a spline level. Vertex editing is used to refine the shape of a spline, whereas spline editing is used to combine two or more splines or create new splines.

Through the use of sub-object editing, you can modify and control a spline or shape all you want. The following exercise shows how to use some simple spline editing to refine an object for use in the bowling alley scene. In particular, you will take a simple rectangle and modify it into the profile of the scorer's desk, which can then be lofted and added to the scene.

CREATING A SCORER'S TABLE USING SPLINE SUB-OBJECT EDITING

1. Start a new file in MAX.

2. In the Create command panel, go to shapes and select rectangle. Create a rectangle that is 30 units by 30 units starting at 0,0 and dragging up and to the right in the Top viewport.

3. Use Region zoom to zoom in on the rectangle in the Top viewport.

4. Go to the Modify command panel and click the Edit Stack button. Select Editable Spline to convert the object over.

5. Activate sub-object selection. This brings up Vertex mode. Choose Select and Move and move the upper-left corner vertex of the rectangle to –6,36. (When watching the coordinates, you might need to place the vertex and then check to see its exact location.) If you want, use the Transform Type-In dialog box to perform this transform.

6. Move the upper-right vertex to 56,53. Move the lower-right vertex to 50,0. Right-click each vertex and change the tangent type to Corner.

7. Select the Insert button. On the top segment, insert a vertex and place it at 18,38. Place another vertex at 19.5,34.5. Continue placing vertices at approximately the following coordinates: 36.5,41.5; 46,1.5; 18,1.5; 14.5,18; 2,14.5; –3,36.5. Right-click to stop placing vertices.

8. Select Insert again and click the right vertical segment. Place a vertex at 40,43 and then place another at 57,50. Right-click to stop.

9. Deactivate Sub-Object mode.

10. Apply an Extrude modifier and extrude the object 60 units.

11. Rotate the object 90 degrees in its local X axis. Figure 6.18 shows the resulting object and the spline that you created.

12. Save the file as **MF06-03.MAX** for use in a later chapter.

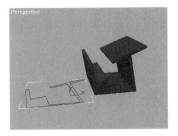

Figure 6.18

The scorer's table created from a simple rectangle using Edit Spline and Extrude.

From the last exercise, the power of sub-object editing, whether it is used on splines or other types of objects should be obvious. You took a simple rectangle and modified it into a much more complex shape with very little effort.

Using Other Modifiers to Edit Splines

In addition to the standard editable spline rollouts, there are two other spline modifiers worth covering at this point. In particular, two very useful modifiers are Fillet/Chamfer and Trim/Extend. These provide spline editing controls that were previously only available in an illustration program or drafting program.

You can use Fillet/Chamfer to create curved (filleted) or flat (chamfered) corners on a spline. To make use of this modifier, you must have a spline with a corner vertex. If the vertex has a Smooth, Bézier, or Bézier Corner tangent type applied, the modifier will not work. By default, this modifier is not located on the Modifier command panel, but you can access it through the More button. Figure 6.19 shows the rollout that appears.

Figure 6.19

The Fillet/Chamfer rollout, where you can set and apply the Fillet/Chamfer effect.

To use the Fillet/Chamfer modifier, select the spline and apply the modifier. The modifier is applied at a vertex sub-object level. Once you access the sub-object controls, select the vertex around which you want to create the fillet or chamfer. Then adjust either the Fillet or Chamfer spinner and select the Apply button. Figure 6.20 shows a spline and the result after applying Fillet to it.

Figure 6.20

Two splines, one before and one after applying the fillet. Notice the extra vertices that were created.

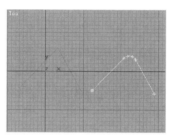

The Trim/Extend modifier works a little differently. This command is used to extend a spline to match another, or trim a spline back to match another. To make use of this, you must have at least two separate splines that are a part of the same shape. When you have this condition, apply the Trim/Extend modifier. You get the rollout shown in figure 6.21.

Figure 6.21

The Trim/Extend rollout, where you can control how the Trim/Extend modifier is applied to the selected splines.

To make use of the modifier, simply choose the Pick Locations button and click the spline you want to trim or extend. If a valid trim or extend operation is possible, MAX will create it.

By combining the editable spline controls with Fillet/Chamfer and Trim/Extend, you can create and work with splines to create any shapes you will need. Just as you can modify splines at a sub-object level, you can edit Mesh objects such as primitives and Loft objects at a sub-object level.

Editing Primitives and Other Mesh Objects

When you create an object such as a primitive, the object is considered a primitive and not an editable mesh. When in this condition, you can convert the object from a primitive to an editable mesh or NURBS object by selecting the object and clicking the Edit Stack button in the Modify command panel. A pop-up menu will appear from which you can select the type of object you want to work with. After it is converted to an editable mesh, you can edit the object at a sub-object level. Other objects, such as lathes and lofts that cannot be converted to an editable mesh, can be edited by applying an Edit Mesh modifier to them.

Many of the functions that you saw in the editable spline controls are also available but at a mesh level here. One example is the ability to attach one or more other mesh objects to the currently selected object. This makes it easier to apply materials, mapping coordinates, and so on to large meshes that will share the same information in the scene. In addition, you can also edit the mesh at a vertex, face, and edge level.

Editing Objects at a Vertex Level

If you select a vertex after enabling sub-objects, the selected object will have a bunch of tick marks, representing the vertices. Figure 6.22 shows this on a sphere. If you select one or more vertices, the vertices will turn red to indicate their new state. You can then apply standard MAX transforms to the vertices to adjust your object.

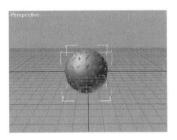

Figure 6.22

A sphere with a set of selected vertices, which you can transform or modify.

Beyond the basic transforms, you also have several vertex commands in the command rollout. Some of these commands are the same as their spline cousins, such as Weld Vertices or Create, Delete, and Detach. Others perform new functions. You can, for example, use the Affect Region command to define a larger region of the object that will be affected when you transform the selected vertex. This makes it easier to create bulges in objects and control how those bulges appear.

The only other different feature for vertex-level editing of a Mesh object is Vertex Colors. Vertex Colors enables you to assign different colors to different vertices. This makes it easy to select a group of vertices. In general, these are for game developers and programmers, but they are handy for selections.

The following exercise shows an example of how to use vertex editing to create a pear out of a sphere.

USING VERTEX EDITING TO CREATE A SPHERE

1. Create a basic sphere in MAX with 32 segments and a radius of 40.

2. While the sphere is selected, go to the Modify command panel and select Edit Mesh.

3. Select Sub-Object when it becomes available and choose Vertex.

4. Choose Select Object from the main toolbar, and select the vertex that would be the north pole of the sphere.

5. Turn on Affect Region and select Edit Curve. The Affect Region dialog box appears.

6. Set the Falloff to 40, the Pinch value to –0.85, and Bubble to 0.50, and choose OK.

7. In the Perspective viewport, choose Select and Move, and set the axis restriction to Z.

8. Move the selected vertex. A shape resembling that of a pear will be created, as shown in figure 6.23.

Figure 6.23

The pear shape created after adjusting a single vertex on a sphere.

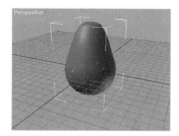

Obviously, you will not do a lot of modeling by editing vertices. But it is always good to make fine adjustments to a model through the use of vertex sub-objects.

Object Editing at a Face Level

Like vertices, when working at a face level, you can select faces and transform them with the standard MAX transform commands. In addition, you can perform many functions, including the following:

♦ Attach and detach faces

♦ Surface normals

♦ Select by surface normals

♦ Assign materials IDs

♦ Smoothing groups

♦ Tessellate

♦ Extrude

Many of these functions are available as separate modifiers in MAX, enabling you to apply them through Edit Mesh or individually. If you apply them individually, you should use Mesh Select first to select the faces you want to apply the modifiers to.

Editing Objects at an Edge Level

The last sub-object level supported under Edit Mesh is Edge. Here you can control the edges of the faces, most notably their visibility. A nice feature is Auto-edge, which enables you to hide shared edges of faces based on the angle between their surface normals.

One of the more interesting edge-level controls is only available if you collapse the object to an editable mesh. If you do this, you can create a shape based on the edges you select. In other words, you can create a spline that matches the surface edges of an object. This would make it easy to loft an object along the surface of another or perform other interesting modeling chores that require you to work on the surface of an object.

Most of the editing that you will do to a Mesh object will occur at a vertex or a face level. At the vertex level, you can reposition, add, or delete vertices to change the shape of an object. At the face level, you can add or remove surfaces from the object, as well as increase the detail, assign Material IDs, or perform many other operations. Face-level editing is powerful when you work with geometry that was imported from another modeling program. The import process will not always work perfectly, so some editing must be done to correct the errors. This is generally done at the face level.

Overall, the ability to edit objects, whether they are meshes or splines, at any level of detail is important to creating crisp, accurate models that use as little detail as possible, while still creating stunning imagery. As you grow with your modeling experience, you will see more and more where sub-object editing and modeling are important.

Conclusion

This chapter showed how to work with and edit objects at a sub-object level. You learned about the following topics:

♦ Working with Modifiers

♦ How the Stack Works

♦ Using Modifiers to Edit at Sub-Object Levels

This chapter showed how powerful the MAX modifier system and the stack are for creating parametric models. By creating objects and then applying modifiers to them, you can change the object into totally different objects. As this occurs, MAX tracks a history of changes to the objects with the Stack feature. Working with modifiers and the Stack were the two key points covered in this chapter.

As mentioned earlier, sub-object level editing is primarily used to fine-tune objects more than it is used for modeling purpose. The exceptions to this rule are Patch and NURBS surfaces that handle modeling in a different manner. Patches and NURBS, which are covered in the next chapter, use sub-object editing as their primary modeling tools.

C H A P T E R 7

Exploring Other Modeling Methods

Besides the basic primitive, spline, and compound objects that you can create in MAX, you can also create patch, NURBS, and particle system objects. You can use patches and NURBS to create much more complex surfaces quicker and easier than you can with primitives and splines. In addition, you can use particle systems to model complex systems over time, such as smoke, fire, a flock of birds, and so on.

This chapter focuses on how to use the modeling tools to begin to create more complex objects than those found in the last chapter. In particular, this chapter focuses on the following topics:

- ♦ Using Patch Modeling
- ♦ Modeling with NURBS
- ♦ Working with Particle Systems

Using Patch Modeling

Patch modeling makes use of surfaces that are controlled and deformed through the use of a lattice. This lattice has vertices (called control points) that you can adjust to control the surface of the patch. By adjusting a simple control point, you can affect an area of the surface of a patch. Figure 7.1 shows a simple patch (on the left) and the same patch after adjusting one control point (on the right).

Figure 7.1

On the left: a patch surface that is ready to be transformed into a more complex surface. On the right: the patch surface after transforming the center control point. Notice the smooth curvature of the resulting surface.

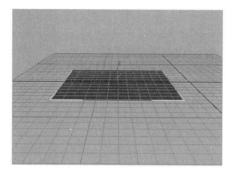
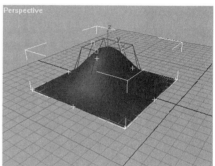

When you adjust a patch surface by moving a control point, it is deformed as a Bézier curve. In other words, the deformations are smooth, not angular like you might find when you adjust a vertex on a mesh. Like a Bézier tangent on a spline, the control points of a patch surface also have tangent controls that you can adjust to givee a different look to the curvature of the surface. Figure 7.2 shows the same surface with tangent adjustments to one corner.

The process of creating and editing patches is fairly easy. You create a patch surface in the Create command panel. In general, one surface is good enough to start modeling with because you can add additional surfaces later. Then you apply an Edit Patch modifier in the Modify command panel to actually modify the surface, add additional surfaces, and perform your modeling tasks.

MAX supports two types of patches: a quad and a tri patch (see figure 7.3). The basic difference between the two is the underlying geometry and the use of quads versus triangles. The quad patches are more commonly used because they generally deform more smoothly than tri patches.

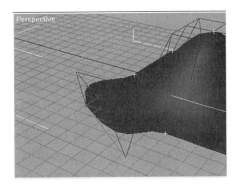

Figure 7.2

The patch surface after adjusting the tangents of the lower left control point. Again, notice how smooth the resulting mesh is.

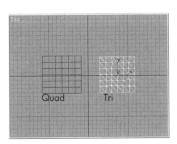

Figure 7.3

The quad patch versus the tri patch. Quads are more common because they deform better than tri patches.

Patch modeling is a push-pull type of modeling system where you push and pull on the control points of the patch surfaces to create the object you want. You accomplish all of this through the Edit Patch modifier.

Modeling Methods with Edit Patch

The Edit Patch modifier is your primary method of modeling patch surfaces in MAX and provides you with many levels of controls. By adjusting one or more of the patch parameters, you can create a wide variety of objects. The patch parameters are as follows:

- Object level patch editing

- Vertex level patch editing

- Edge level patch editing

- Patch level patch editing

Object Level Patch Editing

Object level patch editing is available through the Edit Patch modifier when Sub-Object Selection is disabled. The primary purpose of the object level editing capabilities of Edit Patch is to control the resolution of the patch surface. As a patch, the surface must be converted to polygons at render time. This is handled by the MAX rendering engine, because it can only render polygons. The controls in the Edit Object rollout enable you to set the tessellation of the surface when it is converted to polygons (see figure 7.4).

Figure 7.4

The Edit Object rollout for Edit Patch. Here, you can control the tessellation and density of the resulting patch surface.

Under the Topology section of the rollout, you can set the number of steps in the patch surface. In other words, you can set how many quads appear in the surface. Higher values result in more accurate surfaces but take longer to render.

Under the Tessellation section of the rollout, you have another set of controls that you can use to override the default patch settings. These controls are the same as the NURBS tessellation controls and come from that technology. (You will learn more about the NURBS tessellation controls in the "NURBS Modeling" section later in this chapter.) As a patch, the surface must be converted to polygons at render time so that it can be processed correctly by the rendering engine. The tessellation controls provide you with four methods of controlling the tessellation of the surface to match a wide variety of surface shapes.

The tessellation controls work at two levels: Viewport and Renderer. This enables you to select whether the tessellation settings you are about to adjust apply to the viewport or only at render time. Many times you will set more accurate tessellation values for the rendering engine than you will for the viewports. Only when Viewport is active will you see the tessellation of patch surfaces. After you select where you want to apply the tessellation, you can select the type, of which you have four choices: Fixed, Parametric, Spatial, and Curvature.

Fixed provides no tessellation of the surface. The detail in the patch surface is derived from the Steps setting under Topology. You can set the Steps value to as high as 100 per patch surface. In all other tessellation cases, the Steps setting is ignored.

Parametric, however, enables you to subdivide the surface into even numbers of U and V steps. For each U or V step, one row of faces will appear between each vertex. Figure 7.5 shows a normal patch versus a parametrically tessellated patch.

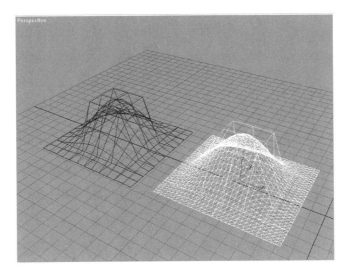

Figure 7.5

The difference between Fixed and Parametric tessellation is readily apparent, as Parametric provides many more faces and is much more accurate.

The Spatial tessellation option sets the tessellation of the object based on the spatial distances within the patch. Spatial tessellation uses an analytical routine to correctly tessellate the surface. Figure 7.6 shows a normal patch versus a spatially tessellated patch.

The Curvature option sets the tessellation of the patch surface based on the amount of curvature in the surface. In areas where the curvature is higher, the tessellation is higher. This is another analytical method and will produce the best results when the lowest number of polygons possible is important. Figure 7.7 shows an example of a Curvature tessellation.

The only other options you can control at an object level for patches is the display of the lattice and the actual patch surface.

Figure 7.6

Figure 7.6

The difference between a fixed and a spatially tessellated patch.

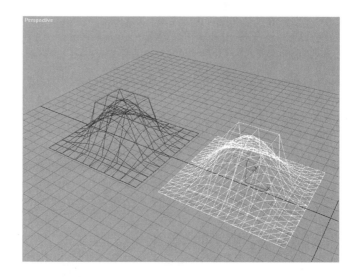

Figure 7.7

A fixed patch versus a curvature tessellated patch.

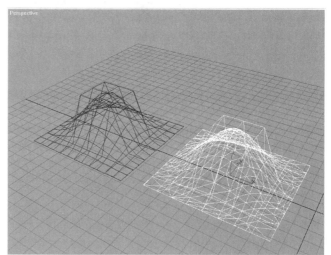

Vertex Level Patch Editing

The most basic level of patch editing is at the vertex level. In reality, even though MAX reports that you are working with vertices, you are really only working with the lattice control points to deform the surface. When you select the Sub-Object button, vertex editing immediately becomes available and the Edit Vertex rollout appears (see figure 7.8). You can perform the vertex-level editing functions from this rollout.

Figure 7.8

The Edit Vertex rollout for the edit patch modifier.

The most important aspect of vertex level editing is the ability to select a vertex and transform it with the standard MAX transform commands. This is how you push and pull on the patch surface to create the shape you want. As with Bézier splines, when you select a vertex, you also get two or more handles that you can use to control the tangents of the surfaces as they enter and leave the vertex. Just like spline Bézier tangents, these tangents also work completely in 3D. Figure 7.9 shows a selected vertex and the associated tangent handles.

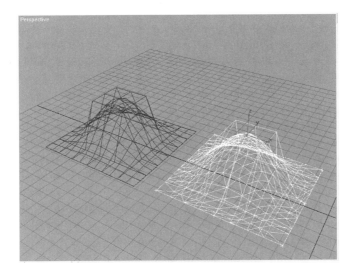

Figure 7.9

A selected vertex and its associated tangent handles. By adjusting the handles, you can affect the curvature of the patch as it enters and leaves the control point.

You can adjust the tangent handles independently, or, by selecting Lock Handles in the Command Panel rollout, you can lock the handles together so when you adjust one, the other adjusts as well.

Beyond these basic capabilities, the only other feature of the Edit Vertex rollout is the ability to weld vertices together. This becomes important when you add other quad or tri patches to the surface. Where the vertices overlap, you will need to weld them together to create a uniform surface; otherwise they will still transform independent of each other.

Edge Level Patch Editing

The next level that you can edit a patch at is edge level. Through this level, you can select the edge of a patch and add another patch to it. Figure 7.10 shows the rollout that appears.

Figure 7.10

The Edit Edge rollout, where you can add patches to the overall surface.

To add a patch, select an edge and then choose the type of patch you want to add under Add Patch. Figure 7.11 shows you a surface before and after adding a patch. Notice how the added patch automatically takes on the shape of the selected edge.

Figure 7.11

A patch surface before and after adding another patch to it.

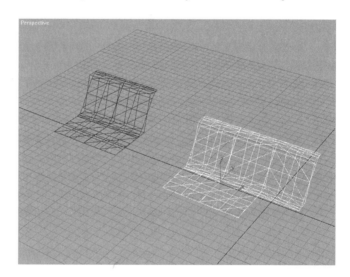

After you add a patch to the surface, you will want to go back to the vertex sub-object level and weld the coincident vertices together. You can do this by selecting the overlapping vertices of the patch with a crossing or window and then choosing weld.

Patch Level Patch Editing

The last level you can edit a patch at is the patch level. Here you can detach or delete patches you have previously added. You can also assign material IDs to individually selected patches. (Note that it is impossible to assign more than one material ID to a single patch.) Figure 7.12 shows this rollout.

Figure 7.12

The Edit Patch rollout, where you can detach or delete patches from the current selected surface, as well as apply material IDs.

Now that you have seen how to model with patches, it is time to put that knowledge to practical use. The following exercise shows how to create the basic topology of an island using patches.

CREATING ISLAND TOPOLOGY

1. Select patch grids under the Create command panel and create a quad patch that is 50 units by 50 units.

2. Go to the Modify command panel and select Edit Patch.

3. Set the sub-object type to Edge.

4. Choose Select Objects and select the right edge of the patch. Choose Add Quad.

5. Repeat adding quads until you have created a 4x4 grid of quad patches. (You can simplify the process by selecting more than one edge at a time with a region window.)

6. After you add the patches, you must weld the vertices. Select Vertex as your sub-object level. When you do, you will see the interior vertices appear as ticks.

7. Use a window to select one set of vertices; then click Weld. Repeat for all of the interior vertices. Only select vertices that are on top of each other for welding. Do not try to select two or three sets of vertices and weld them all at once.

8. After you weld the vertices, select each vertex around the edge of the patch, and move or adjust the vertex to create a random shoreline. Figure 7.13 shows one possible island shoreline created by moving the vertices and tangent handles.

Figure 7.13

The shape of the island after adjusting the outer vertices and tangent handles.

9. Select the center vertex and move it along the Z axis approximately 100 units.

10. What's left over at this point is a set of vertices between the center vertex and the outer vertices. Using Select and Move, place these vertices at random heights and positions to create the rest of the island. (Try experimenting with the tangent handles in the Z axis to further control the slopes.) Figure 7.14 shows one possible island at this point.

Figure 7.14

The completed island, showing how you can quickly use patches to create rather complex organic shapes.

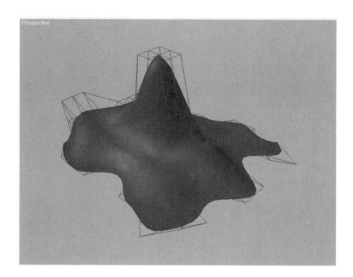

11. Save the file as **MF07-01A.MAX** for use in a later chapter.

From the previous exercise, you can begin to see the power of modeling in MAX with patches. Another powerful modeling method is NURBS.

NURBS Modeling

NURBS (Non-Uniform Rational B-Spline) is a powerful and commonly used modeling method for creating organic shapes or any objects that require accurately curved surfaces. NURBS are used to model everything from cars to dinosaurs to bicycles. If the object has a lot of complex curves in it, it is a perfect candidate to be modeled with NURBS curves and surfaces.

Unlike patch modeling, NURBS comes in two forms: curves and surfaces. NURBS curves are similar to regular splines in MAX but are much more accurate and easier to precisely control. You can use NURBS curves as a skeleton upon which you create surfaces in MAX. You cannot do this with any other modeling tool in MAX except Lofting, where you don't have the control you do here. NURBS provides the following advantages over the other modeling methods in MAX:

♦ It is easier to create organic surfaces or surfaces that require complex curves.

♦ NURBS models render smoother around the edges because of analytical tessellation. This is different from Polygonal models, which are generally faceted. Figure 7.15 shows an example of this.

Figure 7.15

A polygonal sphere versus the same sphere as a NURBS object. Notice the differences around the edges of the sphere.

MAX supports most of the standard NURBS features except surface trimming. This option will be made available by Kinetix as a separate feature set sometime after MAX 2 ships.

NOTE

There are two approaches to working with NURBS in MAX. The first method is to create NURBS curves and generate surfaces based on those curves. The second option is to go straight to creating the surfaces, much like patch modeling. The more flexible of the two methods is working with curves first.

NURBS Curves

NURBS curves are very similar to MAX splines but are based on a slightly different mathematical formula. Thanks to the different mathematics behind the scenes, you can use NURBS curves to create very smooth curved lines to create very organic shapes that can be lofted, extruded, lathed, or otherwise formed into complex curved 3D objects.

NURBS curves in MAX are located under the Shapes button in the Create command panel. To access the NURBS curves, click the Splines drop-down list and select NURBS curves. The NURBS Curves command rollout appears (see figure 7.16).

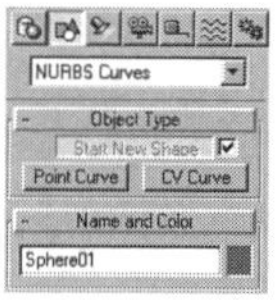

Figure 7.16

The NURBS Curve commands in MAX, where you can create one of two types of NURBS curves.

Like regular splines, NURBS curves are treated as shapes and as such can form multiple curves together to create a single shape. You control this through the Start New Shape button, which works exactly like the spline version.

Two types of curves are available in NURBS modeling in MAX 2: Point and CV. A point curve draws the NURBS curve through each point that you choose in the scene. CV (standing for control vertices), however, works much like a lattice by providing control points upon which the curve is based. Figure 7.17 shows both types of NURBS curves.

Point curves are more accurate than CV curves. However, controlling the curvature of a NURBS curve is sometimes easier with CV curves because when you adjust the position of a CV curve, it affects the curvature of the line but not to the degree that the same change in a point curve would.

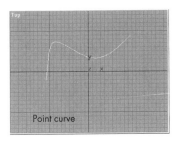 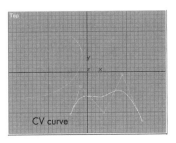

Figure 7.17

A point curve, where the line is draw directly through each vertex you select to create the NURBS curve, and a CV curve, where control vertices are used to create the NURBS curve.

In either case, when you compare NURBS curves to standard MAX splines, you will find creating curved splines much easier than using the Line command and adjusting in and out tangents. But because of their capability to create smooth curved lines, it can be difficult to create a straight line with a NURBS curve. If you need a straight line segment, regular MAX splines can be imported into NURBS curves through the use of Attach or Import in the Modify command panel.

The following exercise illustrates how easy it is to create curved shapes with NURBS curves. In the following exercise, you will recreate the wine glass profile you created in Chapter 4, "Basic Modeling Methods."

RECREATING THE WINE GLASS

1. Go to the Shapes section of the Create command panel and access the NURBS curve controls.

2. Select CV curve. (This type of curve is used because it is easy to approximate the wine glass shape with it.)

3. In the Top viewport, click once each at approximately the following coordinates:
   0,0
   60,0
   60,10
   10,10
   10,100
   10,120
   80,150
   80,250
   70,250

4. At this point, select coordinates on your own to approximate the interior curve of the shape. When finished, click the start point to close the shape. When prompted if you want to close the curve, choose Yes. You should get a curve similar to the one shown in figure 7.18.

Figure 7.18

The approximate NURBS curve of the wine glass profile. Now, you must refine the shape to match the profile you are looking for.

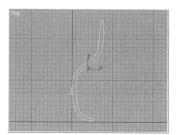

5. Now that the basic curve is complete, go to the Modify command panel and turn on Sub-Object selection. Here, you can edit the CVs of the curve.

6. Manually edit each CV using Select and Move until you have a shape you like. Figure 7.19 shows an example of one possible glass shape.

Figure 7.19

The completed wine glass shape, showing the power and accuracy of the NURBS curve system.

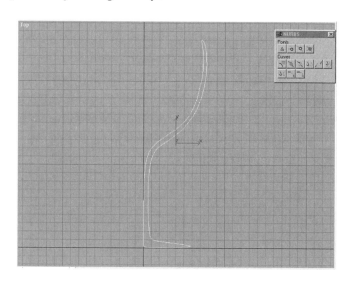

7. Save the file as **MF07-02a.MAX**.

Editing NURBS Curves

As you saw briefly in the last exercise, you can edit NURBS curves after creation, just like you can splines. But, unlike other MAX objects, you do not need to apply a modifier to the object or convert it into an editable form. All you have to do is access the Modify command panel, and the NURBS controls are immediately made available to you.

There are two levels you can work on with NURBS curves in MAX. You can edit the curve as a whole, or edit the sub-objects of the curve. The easiest way to edit the curve as a whole is to use the NURBS floater, which is accessible by choosing the NURBS creation toolbox button. Figure 7.20 shows the resulting dialog box.

Figure 7.20

The NURBS toolbox dialog box for NURBS curves. Through this dialog box, you can access most of the curve controls found in the command panel.

The NURBS toolbox is interactive with the command panel rollout. In other words, because the commands are duplicated in both places, when you select a command in the toolbox, the command panel version becomes active and the rollouts appear for that command. Many times, you will not need the command panel rollouts, but occasionally they are nice to have when you want to type in specific values for a command such as a Transform.

The commands in the NURBS toolbox for curves are broken down into two sections: Points and Curves. The Points controls provide different methods of adding points to the currently selected curve for various reasons. The most common of these buttons is the Create point command, which enables you to add independent points to the curve, points that can later be connected with other curves.

NOTE Many of the NURBS commands are based on the concept of independence and dependence. An independent NURBS object does not rely upon other NURBS objects for its shape. A dependent NURBS object relies upon other NURBS objects to define it. A blended surface, for example, is a surface that is formed between two separate surfaces. In this case, the two separate surfaces are independent objects, but the blend surface is dependent. It is possible to convert a dependent surface to an independent surface but not the other way around.

In addition to the regular NURBS curve commands, you also have a complete set of curve tools you can use to create additional NURBS curves based on existing curves. These tools enable you to create and modify the NURBS curves in many different ways. Many of these tools create copies of selected curves. When this occurs, all curves are considered part of the same larger NURBS curve that you can later convert into a surface.

In addition to the toolbox commands for object level curve editing, you can also attach or import MAX splines for use in NURBS curves. This is accomplished by selecting a NURBS curve and accessing the Modify command panel. You will immediately see the Import and Attach commands. That Attach command works like the Mesh attach commands and converts the selected spline to a NURBS curve. Import, however, imports the object while maintaining its edit history and base parameters. Use the Import command when you want to go back and edit the original object at any time. You also have Import Multiple and Attach Multiple commands that use a Select by Name dialog box to select the objects you want to use in your NURBS curve.

NOTE Like spline shapes, NURBS curves are formed from one or more smaller curve objects. You can form curves out of point, CV, or both types of curves. When you use both types, the individual NURBS lines within the curve must be separate to be different.

Editing NURBS at the Sub-Object Level

Beyond editing the NURBS curves at an object level, you can also edit them at a sub-object level, much like you can a spline. The NURBS curves contain up to three levels of sub-object controls: CV Curve (available when you have CV curves in your NURBS object), Point (available when you have point curves), and Curve. By editing at a sub-object level, you gain precise control over the curves.

Editing Point Curves

If you are editing a NURBS curve with a point line in it, you can edit the points of that line by selecting the point sub-object in the Modify command panel while the line is selected. This produces the rollout shown in figure 7.21.

Figure 7.21

The Point rollout for editing point curves. The controls shown here provide all the controls you will need to adjust the NURBS curve at will.

When point sub-objects are active, the points on a NURBS curve appear as green boxes. You can select one or more of these boxes and edit them using the standard MAX transform commands. In general, the Scale and Rotate commands will have no effect on a point in a point curve. Only the Move command is useful here.

In the Point rollout you will see two buttons (Single Point and All Points) at the top of the rollout under the word Selection. These buttons determine how many points are selected. The left button enables individual point selection. The right button enables curve selection so that when you select one point in a curve, all the points in that curve are selected.

Aside from the standard transform controls, there are several controls in the Modify command panel that you can use to edit point curves. Many of these commands are similar to the commands used for editing splines in MAX. These include the following:

♦ Hide

♦ Unhide All

♦ Fuse

♦ Unfuse

♦ Refine

- Delete

- Extend

- Make Independent

- Affect Region

By working at a sub-object level, you have all the controls for point curves that you have for splines, plus some additional controls that are specific to NURBS curves.

Editing CV Curves

CV curves are very similar to point curves, except for how the vertices are interpreted. Because of this, the rollouts for CV editing are very similar to those for point editing.

The only different CV command is the Weight spinner. Because CV works with a lattice, you can assign a weight value to each vertex. This value is relative to the other vertices in the curve. The higher the weight value, the closer the curve is drawn toward the point. The lower the value, the less influence the point has on the curve. This is part of the reason why CV curves are a little easier to control. But CV curves are relative to each other. This means that if you adjust one CV to a weight of 2 and leave the others at 1, the adjusted CV will be stronger. But if you adjust all the CVs in a curve to 2, the curve will still be the same.

Editing Curves

As you can edit NURBS curves at a point or vertex level, you can also edit them at a curve level. This is important because a NURBS curve can be formed from smaller NURBS lines. This is very similar to the shape-spline relationship that you find when modeling with splines. When you select the Curve sub-object type, you get the rollout shown in figure 7.22.

Like point or CV editing, you can select any individual curve and transform it with the standard MAX transform commands. But in this case, you can use Scale and Rotate in addition to the Move command. MAX also provides you with two different selection methods, just like points. The first selects individual curves; the second selects the curve and any attached curves.

Figure 7.22

The Curve Common rollout, where you can edit NURBS curves.

In addition to the transform commands, there are several specific curve-related commands that you can use to modify the selected curve. Many of these are the same as those found in the Point and CV rollouts but work at a curve level. The others are listed here:

♦ **Reverse:** Reverses the order of the points in the curve. When you select a curve, a green circle will appear at one end. This indicates the first point. Reversing is sometimes necessary when you create a surface based on the curve. Both curves that form the edges of the surface must have the first point on the same side or the surface will twist.

♦ **Make Fit:** Creates a fit curve from the selected point curve. A fit curve has many more points in it and is much higher in detail. This commands spawns a dialog box where you can set the number of points in the fit curve. Figure 7.23 shows the Make Point Curve dialog box and a curve that has been transformed from a four-point curve to a fit curve.

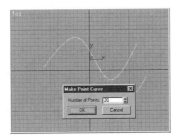

Figure 7.23

The Make Point Curve dialog box and associated curve. Notice how the points on the curve are evenly spaced, creating a very smooth curve.

♦ **Detach:** Enables you to detach the currently selected curve as a separate curve element. You may opt to copy the curve instead of a straight detach with the Copy check box.

+ **Break:** Breaks the selected curve into two separate curves at the point you select.

+ **Join:** Enables you to join the endpoint of one curve to another. This is done with a click-and-drag operation from one endpoint to another. A blended curve is then created between the two.

In addition, there are some controls related to the specific type of curve (for example, point or CV) that you can select. These include:

+ **Close:** Connects the first and last vertices of a curve with a blended curve, resulting in a closed curve. This is available for both CV and point curves.

+ **Degree:** On a CV curve, you have a lattice. The Degree spinner effects the overall strength of the lattice. The higher the degree, the less influence the lattice has over the shape of the curve. You may set the Degree spinner to 2, 3, or 4.

By editing the NURBS curves, you can create curves that you can use to create 3D objects. Because these are NURBS objects, you must use NURBS surface commands to create the 3D objects. Later in this chapter, you will get the chance to create and edit some NURBS curves and surfaces when you create a return carriage for the bowling alley.

NURBS Surfaces

MAX can also create NURBS surfaces. These surfaces can be based on either standard surfaces, much like patches are, or NURBS curves. You create standard NURBS surfaces in the Create command panel under the Geometry button with NURBS surface selected in the drop-down list. Like NURBS curves, there are two types of surface: Point and CV. Figure 7.24 shows an example of each.

Figure 7.24

A point surface and a CV surface. Notice how the CV surface uses a lattice to handle deformations.

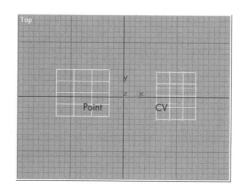

Like NURBS curves, you can create many types of surfaces based on other surfaces or curves. In addition, you can create NURBS surfaces based on NURBS curves by converting these to NURBS surfaces for skinning and editing. You accomplish this by selecting the NURBS curve or shape (it must be one curve with one or more smaller curves) and clicking the Edit Stack button in the Modify command panel. In the resulting pop-up menu, you can convert the object to a NURBS surface. When you do, the rollouts and the NURBS toolbox will change to show you the Surfaces commands. Figure 7.25 shows the NURBS toolbox.

Figure 7.25

The NURBS toolbox with the NURBS Surfaces commands active, in addition to the NURBS curves.

There are 11 different methods you can use to create new NURBS surfaces. These include CV, Point, Transform and more. Some of the surfaces you can create will be dependent; that is, they are dependent upon other surfaces in the model to derive their shape and form from. Others will be independent and will not require other curves or surfaces to define their form.

After you create the surfaces, you can edit them as you would any other NURBS object in MAX. A full NURBS object in MAX can contain point curves, CV curves, point surfaces, and CV surfaces, all in the same object. By editing at a sub-object level, you can individually control any of these parts. If you select the Surface sub-object, you can work with individual surfaces in the object. At this point, you can use either MAX transforms, as usual, or change the parameters in the command panel shown in figure 7.26.

Many of the commands here are the same as those found in editing NURBS curves. The different commands include the following:

♦ **Make Loft:** Converts the selected surface to a loft surface. In this case, a NURBS surface is generated by U and V lines, which define how the surface appears. A loft surface enables you to control the number of U or V lines in the surface, enabling you to create highly detailed surfaces.

♦ **Renderable:** Defines whether the selected surface will appear when rendered.

Figure 7.26

*The Surface
Common rollout,
where you can
adjust and modify
individual NURBS
surfaces within a
NURBS object.*

♦ **Display Normals:** Displays the surface normals for the surface.

♦ **Flip Normals:** Enables you to flip the normals for the entire surface. Many commands such as Lathe will require this operation to correct flipped face normals. This occurs in commands such as the Lathe command because the normals rely upon curves. The order of the points in the curves determines the direction of the face normals.

♦ **Materials:** Includes various controls for working with materials on NURBS surfaces. These controls will be covered in Chapter 11, "Exploring Other Material Methods."

♦ **Break Row:** Enables you to break the surface along a U row. This physically splits the surface into two separate surfaces.

♦ **Break Col:** Enables you to break the surface along a V column. Again, this breaks the surface into two separate surfaces.

♦ **Break Both:** Enables you to break the surface along both the U and V contour lines. This breaks the surface into four separate surfaces.

All other commands that you might find in the surface sub-object rollouts will function similarly to those found in the NURBS curve rollouts, the only difference being that they work on surfaces instead of curves.

By making use of the curve and surface object and sub-object controls for NURBS objects, you can create a wide variety of complex objects in MAX. The following exercise shows how to create a return carriage for the bowling alley.

CREATING A RETURN CARRIAGE FOR THE BOWLING ALLEYS

1. Load the file **MF07-03.MAX** from the accompanying CD. This file contains two sets of NURBS curves that you will use to create a bowling ball return machine for use in the bowling alley scene. Figure 7.27 shows the initial scene.

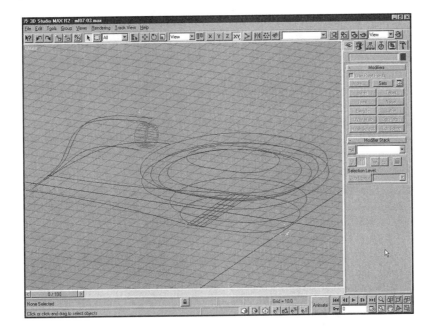

Figure 7.27

The NURBS curves that you will use to create a bowling alley ball return.

2. Select the Return Carriage curve (in dark red). In the Modify command panel, click the Edit stack button and convert the object to a NURBS Surface.

3. Open the NURBS toolbox. Select Create Uloft Surface.

4. Select the bottom curve. Then, select the next three curves, working your way up the outside of the object. As you do, a NURBS surface will be generated. Figure 7.28 shows the object at this point.

5. Select the Ruled surface command from the NURBS toolbox. Starting at the upper outer ring, click and drag from ring to ring, working your way inward until you reach the center ring. This creates the surface where the ball will roll around.

Loft was not used here because it adjusts the curvature across the selected curves. This would cause unusual results if you continued to surface the interior of the object with Uloft.

NOTE

Figure 7.28

The carriage assembly after applying Uloft.

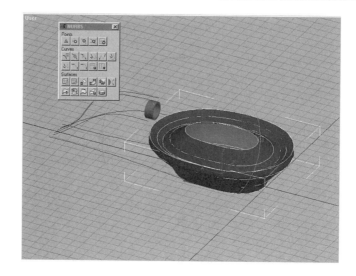

6. Select the Create Cap Surface command from the NURBS toolbox and select the center ring. You may need to adjust the view to correctly select the area. Figure 7.29 shows the completed return carriage.

Figure 7.29

The carriage assembly after adding rule surfaces and capping.

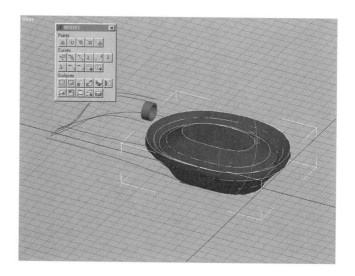

7. Hide the Return Carriage object.

8. Select the remaining NURBS curves. Again, convert these to a NURBS surface.

9. In the NURBS toolbox, select Uloft.

10. In the Top viewport, select the lines in order from left to right to create the surface. In the

Modify command panel, go to Surface sub-object editing, select the curve, and then turn on Flip Normals to correctly orient the normals. (If you render the object without doing this, it will appear incorrect.) Figure 7.30 shows you the surface at this point.

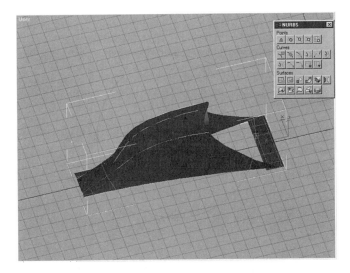

Figure 7.30

The surfaced ball return with corrected face normals. Note, two-sided display is turned on in the viewport to show the exact result.

11. Select the Blended Surface tool from the toolbox.

12. Select the Open edge of the surface you just created. Then drag down to the ground and select the inner edge of the square surface at the bottom. Figure 7.31 shows the correct edges. A basic surface is created.

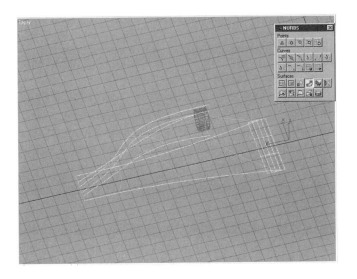

Figure 7.31

The correct surface edges to select in order to create the blended surface.

13. Activate the Sub-Object selection and choose Surface as your sub-object.

14. Select the surface you just created. In the Modify command panel, scroll down until you see the Blend Surf parameters. Turn on Flip End 1 and set Tension 1 to 0 and Tension 2 to 3.0.

15. Unhide the Return Carriage object. Save the file as **MF07-03a.MAX**. Figure 7.32 shows the final object.

Figure 7.32

The completed Return Carriage object.

As you can see, the NURBS objects are very powerful but somewhat complex. This has been just an introduction to a robust set of tools that enables you to model many complex models. Take the time to explore these tools more fully than they were presented here. You will find many places where you will want to use them.

Working with Particle Systems

Particle systems are the last type of objects that you can model in MAX. Particle systems vary from all the other modeling tools because they occur over time. A particle system creates a series of small particles controlled by a variety of parameters. Examples of where particle systems are handy include rain, snow, smoke, fire, flowing liquids, starfield simulations, and many others.

Particle systems can also be affected by various space warps (modifiers that affect objects in world space coordinates) such as wind, gravity, and deflectors to control the motion of the particles through the scene. (You will learn more about space warps in Chapter 14, "Exploring Basic Animation Methods.") MAX supports six different types of particle systems:

- **Spray:** Creates basic sprays such as water fountains or rain. Use this system when you want simple particle effects.

- **Snow:** Creates a simple snow effect and has a few more parameters related to the particle shape, size, and tumble. Again, this system is great for simple snow effects.

- **Pcloud:** Creates a static cloud of particles and can be used to create effects such as 3D starfields or a flock of birds. Particles can be restricted to a variety of object shapes.

- **Parray:** Great for creating particles that emit from any type of object or for advanced explosion effects.

- **SuperSpray:** A much-enhanced version of the standard spray system and will probably be the most-used particle system. You can create most, if not all, of the particle effects you will need with this system.

- **Blizzard:** A much-enhanced version of snow.

The last four particle system types have literally hundreds of configurable parameters. Fortunately, outside of the basic parameters, all four systems share the same parameters. Even so, there are many more particle parameters covered in this book, so you will get an overview of the more important particle functions from SuperSpray.

Particle systems are created by selecting the object type (they are available in the Create command panel under Particle Systems) and clicking and dragging in any viewport to create the particle dummy object. The particle system emitter (or dummy object) is not a renderable object and is only used to control the location and orientation of the emitter system. Figure 7.33 shows the Particle System icon and emitter for a SuperSpray particle system.

Adjusting the Parameters

After you create the particle system, you must go to the Modify command panel to adjust the parameters. You cannot immediately edit the parameters in the Create command panel. They will not have any affect until you edit them in the Modify command panel. This is because of the complex nature of the particle systems and how they have to be implemented.

Figure 7.33

*The SuperSpray
Particle System
icon that
represents the
location and
orientation of the
particle emitter.*

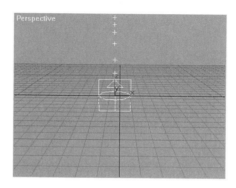

After you create the particle system, there are eight parameter rollouts that appear in the command panel. Each of these rollouts provides a specific set of controls for the particle system. The eight parameter rollouts include the following:

♦ Basic parameters

♦ Particle generation

♦ Particle type

♦ Particle rotation

♦ Object motion inheritance

♦ Bubble motion

♦ Particle spawn

♦ Load/Save Presets

Basic Parameters

These types of parameters vary from particle system to particle system and define how the system appears. In the SuperSpray particle system, for example, you can control the formation of particles such as their axes and spread, as well as what type of geometry appears in the viewports while you work on the system.

Particle Generation

These parameters define the number of particles in the system, as well as their life and size. Because particles occur over time, each particle has a life that is defined by a certain number of frames. If a particle has a life of 60 frames, for example, the particle will appear in the scene for 60 frames. So if a particle appears at frame 30, it will show in the scene until frame 90. In addition to controlling the life parameters, you have precise control over the size of the particles, including variations.

Particle Type

Particle type parameters enable you to define the type of particle that appears when you render the scene. The viewports will generally use ticks to represent the particle system, but in the final rendering, you will probably have more particles of specific shapes or types. There are three types of particles that you can use:

- **Standard Particles:** Includes standard particle types such as triangles, cubes, facing, spheres, tetrahedrons, sixpoint, constant, and special. These options provide various shapes of renderable surfaces that are substituted for each particle in the system.

- **MetaParticles:** Replace each particle with metaballs. Metaball modeling works by creating surface tension between spheres to create an organic surface. You can use Metaparticles to create flowing liquids and other types of effects. Be careful when using this particle type because they can take large amounts of time to prepare and render.

- **Instanced Geometry:** Replaces each particle in the system in an instance of a selected piece of geometry. This can be great for creating effects such as flying flocks of birds. You can create a single bird with animation and then substitute it into the particle system to create the flock.

After the particle type is selected, various parameters associated with that type will become available.

Particle Rotation

Particle rotation parameters enable you to control the rotation of an object over its life. You can control the speed and axis around which the particles rotate. This is regardless of the type of particles you use.

Object Motion Inheritance

The particle emitter, like many objects in MAX, can be fully animated. When it is, object motion inheritance parameters control how the motion of the emitter (regardless of whether the emitter is an object or a helper) effects the motion of the particles as they are emitted.

Bubble Motion

Bubble motion parameters enable you to add a little wobble to the particles such as you might see in a bubble stream under water. Generally, you will use these parameters on thin directed particle streams. The bubble motion parameters are not affected by space warps.

Particle Spawn

Particle spawn parameters control the spawning of secondary particle systems from events such as particle collisions. This makes it easy to create effects such as drops landing in water or collisions in space.

Load/Save Presets

The Load/Save Presets parameters enable you to load and save preset particle system settings. As you can see, there are so many parameters to deal with, the ability to load and save the settings is very important.

By combining the parameters found in these eight rollouts, you can create almost any kind of particle system effect that you will possibly want. Only a few highly specialized effects (such as breaking an object down into particles and reassembling it into another) cannot be created with these systems.

Now that you have an idea of how the particle systems work and some of the parameters associated with them, it is time to see how to create one. The following exercise shows how to create a simple water fountain.

CREATING A WATER FOUNTAIN

1. Load the file **MF07-04.MAX** from the accompanying CD.

2. Open the Particle Systems rollout under the Create command panel and select SuperSpray.

3. In the Top viewport, click and drag to create the system at the center of the fountain.

4. In the Front or Left viewport, use the Move command to position the system at the top of the fountain, as shown in figure 7.34.

To actually create the correct fountain effect, you need to make use of a gravity space warp, which applies a gravity effect to the particles. Space warps are fully covered in Chapter 14. You will use only the one space warp at this time.

Figure 7.34

The correct position of the SuperSpray emitter to create the water fountain effect.

5. Select the Space Warps button under the Create command panel. In the drop-down list, select Particles and Dynamics, and then select the Gravity space warp from the accompanying rollout.

6. Click and drag in the Top viewport to create the space warp. Then, use Move to position the space warp in the center of the fountain about 40 or 50 units above the fountain.

7. Choose Select and Bind to space warp from the main toolbar. Click the space warp and drag over to the SuperSpray emitter; let go when you see the cursor change. This binds the particles to the gravity effect and makes them active.

8. Go to the Modify command panel while the space warp is still selected.

9. Set the strength to 0.25.

10. Select the SuperSpray emitter.

11. Set the animation time slider to 50. This sets the current time to frame 50, where you can better see the particle effect.

12. In the Modify command panel, under the Modifier Stack drop-down list, select SuperSpray. Set the following parameters:

Under Basic Parameters
1st Spread 20
2nd Spread 75

Under Particle Generation
Under Use Rate, set the spinner to 20
Speed 5
Emit Stop 100
Life 50

Under Particle Type
Select Sphere

13. Choose the Play Animation button in the lower right corner of the scene to see the particle effect. Click again on the same button to stop the playback. Figure 7.35 shows the completed water effect.

Figure 7.35

*The completed
SuperSpray
particle system,
showing the
versatility of the
particle systems in
MAX.*

14. Save the file as **MF07-04a.MAX** for use in a later chapter.

As you can see, the particle systems require a decent understanding of the animation system in MAX. Don't worry if some of the information in the last exercise was a little confusing. You will see how to work more with particle systems in later chapters.

Overall, particle systems provide you with the only true dynamic modeling system in MAX. With particles, you can create endless special effects such as smoke, fire, and more.

Conclusion

This chapter introduced you to some of the more powerful modeling tools in MAX. In particular, you learned about the following:

♦ Patch Modeling

♦ Working with Sub-Objects to Model

♦ NURBS Curve Modeling

♦ NURBS Surface Modeling

♦ Working with Particle Systems

MAX provides many modeling tools that you can use to create just about any type of object. The most popular tools for modeling objects that have many curves or complex curves are patch and NURBS modeling tools. In addition, you have dynamic modeling through the use of particle systems. When combined with the standard modeling tools such as splines, primitives, and compound objects, you can create all the geometry you need quickly and efficiently.

After you have created that geometry, you will want to put it into a scene and render it with materials and lighting. This is called composition. Before looking at how to compose your scene, you need to become familiar with the theory behind scene composition, which is the focus of the next chapter.

PART

SCENE COMPOSITION

FUNDAMENTALS

C H A P T E R 8

Understanding Composition Concepts

Now that you have a basic sense of how to model in 3D Studio MAX, it is time to look at the aspects of MAX that enable you to create photo-realistic or near photo-realistic renderings. To create these types of renderings, you need a good understanding of scene composition. Scene composition is the application of cameras, lighting, and materials to a scene to make it render well.

Before looking at specific techniques, you need to become more familiar with the terminology that you will encounter. This chapter focuses on the concepts and terminology behind scene composition and includes the following topics:

◆ Understanding Cameras

◆ Understanding Lights

◆ Understanding Materials

◆ Working with Colors in MAX

Understanding Cameras

The first concept in MAX that you need to understand is cameras. A camera is an object in MAX that lets you view the scene as you would see it in a real-world sense: in perspective. Most of the views in MAX viewports are orthographic, providing you with parallel projections of the scene. Many times, these are handy, but they do not provide a realistic look. MAX also provides a Perspective view that provides a much more realistic perspective of the scene. It does not, however, provide you with the precise controls necessary to accurately view a scene. Cameras enable you to have this control.

In 3D Studio MAX, the camera is a virtual camera that duplicates many of the controls and settings found on a real camera, adding some special features that real-world cameras do not have. If you are familiar with 35mm photography, many of the terms discussed here will be familiar.

The camera concepts covered in the following sections include:

♦ Lens length and FOV

♦ Focus and aperature

♦ Camera movement

Lens Length and FOV

In a real camera, the lens length (also called focal length) is the distance from the center of the lens to the image it forms of the subject on the camera's film (assumed to be an infinite distance in front of the lens). The normal lens length of a camera is considered to be 50mm, which is similar to that of the human eye. This is why the 50mm lens is also referred to as the normal lens.

There is a direct relationship between the lens length and the field of vision (FOV), which is the angle that encompasses everything that can be seen through a lens with a given focal length. The typical FOV for a 50mm lens is 40 degrees. Figure 8.1 shows you an example of several lens lengths and their associated FOVs.

When the lens length of a lens is changed, the field of view changes in an inversely proportional manner. If you reduce the lens length of a lens to 28mm, the FOV widens to 65 degrees. This is why lenses from 20mm to 35mm are considered wide angle lenses. By the same token, if the focal length is increased to 200mm, the field of view drops to 10 degrees. Lenses with 85mm and longer lens lengths are known as long lenses or telephoto lenses.

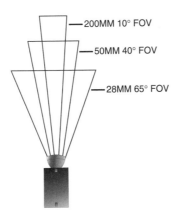

—200MM 10° FOV

—50MM 40° FOV

—28MM 65° FOV

Figure 8.1

Lens length has a direct effect on the field of view. As the focal length is reduced, the FOV is widened.

NOTE

As you learn about cameras and millimeters, keep in mind that film sizes such as 35mm are a related, but separate, subject that has to do with image output. This will be discussed later in this chapter.

At one time, photographers had to have many different lenses available for their cameras to shoot a wide variety of subjects, from broad vistas to distant objects. As optics became more sophisticated, however, the zoom lens was developed. This lens enabled photographers to adjust their lens lengths over a broad range of settings. These days, a photographer can generally use just two lenses: a 35–80mm zoom and a 80–200 zoom. These modern lenses often have a macro lens setting that enables the user to take extreme close-ups as though they were using a low-powered microscope.

In MAX, the lens length of a camera is calculated by mathematical formulas, so you can define almost any lens length you need for a given camera. However, real-world cameras are still used as a reference, so MAX provides you with a set of standard lens lengths. You may also type in any specific lens length you like. Figure 8.2 shows you examples of several different lens lengths. Note that there is not a need to include the equivalent of a macro setting because virtual cameras can be placed very close to the subject to achieve that effect.

As you can see, in addition to adjusting the size of the subject, the wide lens settings have a tendency to exaggerate the perspective in a scene, whereas the longer lenses reduce it. As a result, wide lens angles often impart a feeling of massiveness to a subject, whereas telephoto lenses are used to flatten scenes, compressing them so that distant objects seem like they're closer together.

Figure 8.2

Sample Lens Lengths: (a) 15mm, (b) 20mm, (c) 24mm, (d) 28mm, (e) 35mm, (f) 50mm, (g) 85mm, (h) 135mm, (i) 200mm.

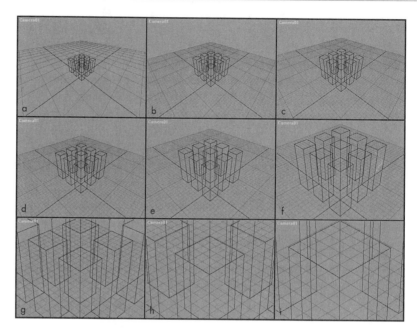

Focus and Aperture

Lens length isn't the only part of a real camera lens. One of the most commonly used controls on a manual camera is the focus adjustment. Focus adjusts the optics in the camera so that the subject is sharp and clear. However, focus is not object-specific; it is a range, a set of near and far distance settings called depth of field. Figure 8.3 shows you an example of depth of field. Depending upon the lens settings, the depth of field may be narrow, with only a few objects within a few inches of the focus point being clear, or wide (like many fixed focus cameras), where everything from a few feet away to infinity is in focus.

Real-world camera effects, such as depth of field, are not supported by cameras in MAX. But with the addition of a lens effects package to MAX, you can create many optical effects in the digital world that you would normally see from using a real camera. Chapter 17, "Exploring Video Post Fundamentals," discusses these effects and how they are created.

Figure 8.3

Depth of Field effects: (a) MAX does not create a depth of field, so everything is in focus. (b) Variable depth of field enables you to select a portion of the image to be in focus, although the rest is out of focus.

Camera Movement

When it comes to movement, cameras in MAX hold a massive advantage over their real-world counterparts. In 3D Space, cameras are free to move anywhere in the scene, even inside of objects. In addition, multiple cameras can be defined, enabling the action to be viewed from several angles at the same time.

In addition to mimicking 35mm cameras, MAX can imitate their motion picture and video counterparts. Although most of the following moves require a real camera to be mounted on a tripod or dolly (wheeled platform), there are no such restrictions for virtual cameras, even though they can behave in the same manner. Many of the camera moves discussed here are implemented as viewport controls when you work in a camera viewport.

Pan and Tilt

Two of the most common moves in filmmaking are pan and tilt. A *pan* is a horizontal rotation of the camera from right to left or vice versa (as shown in figure 8.4). A pan is often used to move the camera from one subject to another or to see more of a landscape than will fit in the frame.

Figure 8.4

Pan and tilt camera movements: A pan is a horizontal rotation of the camera. A tilt is a vertical rotation of the camera.

TOP VIEW

SIDE VIEW

Pan

Tilt

A *tilt* is the vertical equivalent of a pan, rotating the camera up or down. Tilts are often used to showcase tall objects, such as buildings, but also may be used on a character to give the impression that the viewer is sizing them up.

Tracking and Dollying

A *dolly* is a wheeled platform that a camera is mounted on. The term dolly, or truck, also refers to moving the camera around on the floor during the shot to get closer to or further away from the action, or to view it from a different side, as shown in figure 8.5. In MAX, the Dolly command moves the camera closer to or farther away from the subject, without changing the lens length.

Figure 8.5

Dolly and Truck camera movements. Dolly moves the camera around, usually on the same "floor plane" as the subject. Truck moves the camera horizontally or vertically.

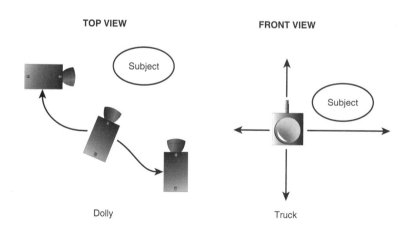

TOP VIEW

FRONT VIEW

Subject

Subject

Dolly

Truck

In film making, a dolly is sometimes mounted onto a steel track, enabling the camera to move smoothly along a predefined path. Therefore, *truck* usually refers to the movement of the camera along a single axis, either horizontal or vertical.

Bank and Roll

In the real world, banks and rolls are difficult to do unless the camera is hand-held or mounted in a motion control rig, but MAX cameras handle them with ease. *Roll* means to rotate the camera around its viewing axis, making the scene appear to spin (see figure 8.6). *Bank* is simply an automatic roll that occurs when a camera moves through a curve in a path. Creating the illusion you are flying in a plane or tumbling out of control are two of the most popular uses for roll.

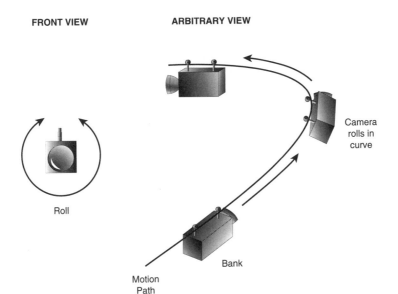

FRONT VIEW   **ARBITRARY VIEW**

Roll

Camera rolls in curve

Bank

Motion Path

Figure 8.6

Roll and bank camera movements: Roll is the rotation of the camera around the viewing axis. Bank is an automatic roll applied to cameras moving along a curved path.

Clipping Planes and Targets

Another unique feature of MAX cameras is clipping planes. A **clipping plane** is a plane that is perpendicular to the camera view at a specific distance away from the camera. MAX supports two types of clipping: near and far. With a near clipping plane, all objects between the camera and the clipping plane are not rendered. Near clipping planes are excellent for making section perspectives through buildings. Far clipping planes remove all objects beyond the clipping plane, thus reducing the geometry in the rendering pipeline, speeding up rendering in most cases.

MAX supports two types of cameras: Target and Free. A Target camera has a camera location and a defined target that it always points at. This is represented in MAX by a camera icon with a line drawn to a box that represents the target. The camera and target may be moved independently of each other, making it easier to control. The target enables you to see exactly where the camera is pointed from any other viewpoint, making it faster and easier to position. A Free camera does not have a target and is used in special circumstances such as path-based animation where you want the camera to follow a path and always look in the direction of the path. Both types of cameras are shown in figure 8.7.

Figure 8.7

The MAX camera icons: Target camera, Free camera.

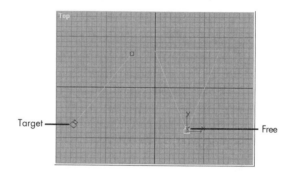

Cameras enable you to set up any true view of your scene that you want. While you are doing this, MAX will light the scene with two default lights so that you can see what is going on. But to create a realistic-looking scene, you must create and add your own lights.

Understanding Light

Visible light is composed of a spectrum of colors running from red to violet. When light rays strike an object, some of these colors are absorbed by the material, whereas others are reflected. The amount and color of the light reflected from objects enables us to see them as red, lime green, or any other color in the spectrum.

Computer displays, because they are generally viewed by producing light rather than reflecting it, use the additive color model in which white light consists of equal amounts of red, green, and blue light. If the level of one of these three colors drops slightly below the others, the result is something other than white.

Color temperature is a scale used to differentiate between these near-white spectrums of light. Color temperature is measured in Kelvins, which refers to what temperature a black object must be heated in order to have it radiate that particular spectrum of colors. This has nothing to do with the operating temperature of light sources, however—it's just a scientific scale.

What color temperature does from a practical standpoint is indicate the warmth or coolness of the light in terms of color. Note that the scale is counter-intuitive. Cool (meaning bluish) fluorescent lights are rated at 4000K, whereas typical warm (yellowish) incandescent lamps are 290K. Quantifying color temperatures can be helpful at times when you want maximum color accuracy because our eyes tend to consider the main source of light illumination to be white regardless of whether it is noon sunlight (5000K) or a halogen desk lamp (3300K). However, when the image is output, the color differences may become more noticeable. MAX does not let you specify a particular color temperature, but you can adjust the colors of a light to match. However, some plug-in renderers, such as RadioRay, let you specify every aspect of a real-world light that it will simulate when rendering.

Another important element of light is intensity: the brightness of the source or reflection. The angle at which a light ray strikes a surface and is reflected into our eyes (called the angle of incidence) has an effect on how brightly the object appears to be illuminated from our perspective. If you hold a flashlight in front of your face and point it along your line of sight at a very smooth, flat surface, most of the light is reflected back into your eyes and the surface seems brightly lit. If, however, you stand at a 45-degree angle to the surface, it will appear darker because much of the light is being reflected away from you. Figure 8.8 shows you an example of this.

a   b

Figure 8.8

The effect of angle of incidence on apparent brightness: (a) A surface lit and viewed at a 90-degree angle. (b) The same surface lit and viewed at a 45-degree angle.

Light reflecting off an object goes on to illuminate other objects as well, an effect called *radiosity*. The cumulative effect of all the light bouncing off all the objects in an area is called *ambient light*. This ambient light has no discernible source or direction but acts to illuminate everything in the scene. In MAX, ambient lighting is a very subtle control that affects the overall brightness of objects in a scene, regardless of the lighting. Radiosity can be simulated through the use of other programs such as Lightscape or plug-in renders such as RadioRay.

Another property of light is that it becomes weaker with distance, which is called *attenuation*. This occurs because the atmosphere is full of tiny particles that block and reflect the light rays. Larger particles such as those in smoke and fog dramatically increase the effect, whereas attenuation occurs to a much lesser extent in space because there are far fewer particles to block the light rays.

Types of Lights

MAX supports five different kinds of light sources that you can use to illuminate your scenes: omni (or point) lights, directional (or distant) lights, spotlights (both target and free), and the global ambient light. Figure 8.9 diagrams these types of lights.

Figure 8.9

3D light sources: An omni, or point, light casts light in all directions, a directional light casts parallel light along a single axis, and a spotlight casts a cone or pyramid of light.

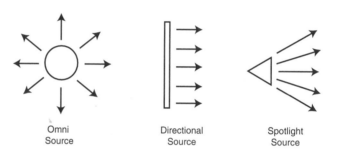

Omni
Source

Directional
Source

Spotlight
Source

An omni (omni-directional) light source casts light in all directions and is also known as a point light. This type of light is usually ideal for simulating any kind of nondirectional light source, from bare bulb fixtures hanging in an attic to the sun in an outer space scene. Figure 8.10 shows you an example of an omni light.

Figure 8.10

Omni-directional light source (white diamond) positioned in the center of the scene casts light in all directions.

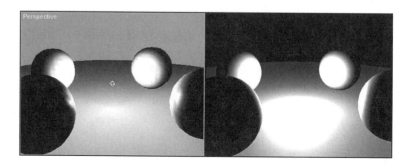

Omni lights in MAX now support full shadow casting capabilities. Be warned, however, that using a shadow casting omni light can significantly increase rendering times due to the number of shadow maps that must be generated.

UPGRADERS
NOTE

Directional lights, also called distant lights, project light along one axis only, and all the beams are parallel, not unlike a laser beam. Directional lights are good for simulating sources that are far away, such as the sun in a terrestrial scene. Because the source is so distant, it causes the light rays to appear parallel, so all the shadows cast by the light are parallel as well (see figure 8.11).

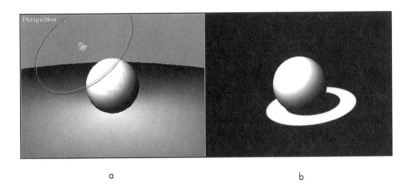

a   b

Figure 8.11

Directional light characteristics: (a) A directional light source, which casts parallel light rays, aimed down a sphere. (b) The resulting shadows are also parallel.

Spotlights are very similar to directional lights but cast light from a single point in a cone fashion, much like the light from a flashlight. Where directional lights have parallel beams, spotlights do not. Spotlights are heavily used in MAX to create general lighting, special highlighting, and light coloring.

Lighting Controls and Effects

MAX offers a standard set of controls for lights sources, including intensity, color, and shadow settings. In addition, MAX also provides include and exclude lists, as well as projection mapping and attenuation controls.

Brightness and Color

Intensity sets the brightness level of the source. In general terms, this is considered to be a color of 255, pure white. But, in MAX, you also have a multiplier setting that you can use to increase or decrease brightness. By adjusting the multiplier of a light, you can easily "blow out" the highlights of an object, giving it an overexposed appearance. MAX actually tracks colors that are brighter than 255,255,255. These colors are called unclamped colors and can be accessed by other routines such as the lens effects package.

Color is controlled by RGB and HSV color sliders and simulates the use of colored plastic gels over photography lights. The use of colored lights can give a scene a theatrical flair, complementing the material colors and adding extra interest to lit surfaces. You can also use colored lights to create some interesting effects by blending different colored light sources together.

Colored lighting doesn't have to be showy to be effective. By making subtle adjustments to the color balance of a light source, you can simulate the color temperature of an incandescent bulb, a fluorescent tube, or the sun on a hazy day.

Shadows

Lights in MAX are capable of casting shadows when they shine on objects. This is an option that must be enabled in the MAX lights and is not on by default. When you enable shadows on a light, there are two types of shadows you can use: Shadow maps and ray-traced shadows. Figure 8.12 shows you examples of both.

Figure 8.12

Shadows types: (a) Shadow mapping produces natural-looking, soft-edged shadows. (b) Ray-traced shadows are sharper and more precise.

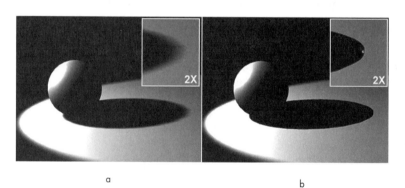

a   b

Shadow mapping is a scanline rendering technique for creating shadows. It works by creating a grayscale texture map based on the lighting and mesh objects in the scene and then applies it to the objects at render time. Mapped shadows are soft edged and more natural looking than raytraced but may become blocky and inaccurate in some situations.

You can reduce the blockiness by increasing the shadow map size, which adjusts the amount of memory that the system can use to create the map. Increasing the size to 512 KB or 1 MB (the default is 256 KB) can go a long way toward smoother shadows but obviously has an impact on render times as well, especially if there are more than a few shadow maps that need this kind of resolution. Figure 8.13 shows you an example of using different shadow maps.

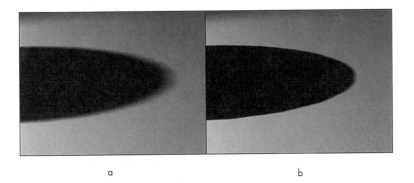

a   b

Figure 8.13

Effects of shadow map size: (a) Blockiness and smearing with a 256 KB map size. (b) Increasing the map size to 1024 KB reduces the problem but increases render time.

The other problem with shadow maps is that they may not be properly positioned in the scene. This most often occurs at the intersection of two objects, and the shadow of one is cast on the other. In some cases, the shadow may be offset from the mesh intersection. Adjusting the map bias setting moves the shadow closer to or further away from the casting object, enabling you to correct this situation.

Ray-traced shadows are defined using ray-tracing renderer techniques. Unlike the results of the soft-edged shadow mapping technique, ray-traced shadows have a hard edge but are very accurate and precise. This is good for sharp, dramatic shadows, such as those you would find in space or on airless worlds, such as the moon. Because ray-traced shadows make use of ray-tracing techniques, they can dramatically increase rendering times based on the geometry that is casting shadows.

Hotspot and Falloff

Spotlights and directional lights have controls that enable you to define the concentration of light in the beam they project. The adjustments are given in degrees and are represented onscreen by two cones that show how wide the beams are set (see figure 8.14).

Spotlight source   Hotspot cone   Spotlight target

Figure 8.14

Hotspot and Falloff settings are visually represented by cones. This aids in the positioning of the lights without doing excessive test renders.

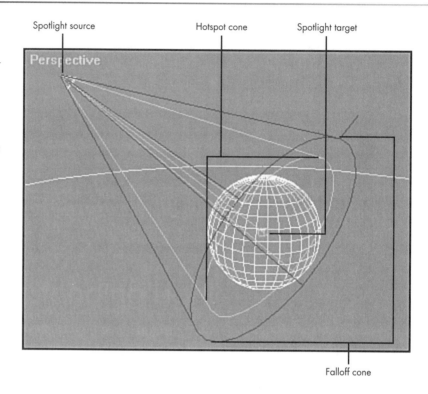

Falloff cone

The Hotspot adjustment defines the angle of the inner portion of the beam of light projected at the current intensity setting for that source. The Falloff setting sets the perimeter of the outer portion of the beam, indicating where the intensity has dropped all the way down to zero. In other words, the light is constant across the hotspot area and then falls off linearly between the Hotspot and Falloff cones.

When the Hotspot and Falloff settings are within a few degrees of each other, the light appears to be sharply focused, with very little transition between full intensity and none at all. When the differences in angles are much larger, the beam looks softer and tapers off gradually from the bright hotspot to the edges of the beam, as shown in figure 8.15.

Include and Exclude

MAX also enables you to set up your lights so that they will affect only certain objects that you identify. There are two ways to do this: Include enables you to pick a list of objects that the specified light affects, whereas Exclude is used when you want most of the objects in the scene to be affected, but you want to select a few objects that should be left out. MAX also enables you to set the type of include or exclude that the light will use. You can include or exclude an object from illumination, shadow casting, or both.

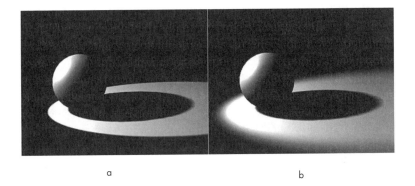

a   b

Figure 8.15

Effects of hotspot and falloff sizes: (a) When Hotspot and Falloff settings are close together, the beam appears focused. (b) Widening the difference between settings makes the beam look softer and more diffused.

Include and Exclude are something of cheats because you can't control light that way in the real world. However, because lighting is such a time-consuming process, these features are great for fine-tuning and achieving difficult effects more easily. Say that you've set up a spotlight that creates a perfect highlight on one of the objects in your scene. Unfortunately, the spill from that spot is shining on many other objects that you don't want illuminated that way. The solution is to add the desired object to the include list for that light so that only it is affected.

MAX lights and cameras are used to compose and illuminate your scene. There are literally hundreds of techniques and effects that you can create and use to set the mood of your scene. This is an art called digital cinematography that will be explored in more detail in the next chapter.

After you have set up lights and cameras, you will want to start adding materials to your objects to give them a lifelike appearance.

Understanding Materials

A material is a set of attributes assigned to the surface of an object. When rendered, MAX interprets these settings to generate the appropriate colors based on the lighting and the camera position. MAX comes with a variety of materials that have many settings you control to create different types of surfaces for your scene. Before looking closely at materials, this is a good time to take a look at how colors are interpreted by MAX.

Working with Colors

MAX interprets colors in the same way that a computer does, using the RGB color model. The RGB color model works by combining different saturation values of red, green, and blue to create an array of colors. These are sometimes called color channels. The number of shades you have in each color channel defines how many possible colors you might have. If you have 8-bit (2^8) color channels, you have 256 shades of red, green, or blue, resulting in a total of 16.7 million possible colors, often referred to as 24-bit (3 x 8 bit channels) color space. (This is calculated by multiplying 2^8 x 2^8 x 2^8)

MAX actually renders images in 48-bit color space and reduces the number of colors down to 24 bit for output in most cases. Sometimes, you can use higher colors depending upon your hardware and software configurations. Most video work is done in 24-bit color, whereas most film work is done in 24- and sometimes 48-bit color.

When working with MAX, you will find various places to make use of color; these include materials and lights. When you need to adjust a color, many times you will see a color swatch. Clicking that color swatch will launch the MAX color selector, shown in figure 8.16.

Figure 8.16

The MAX color selector, where you can select the color that you want to use.

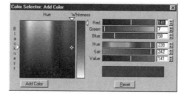

In the MAX color selector, all colors are treated as RGB, but you have three methods of selecting the color: RGB, HSV, and Blackness and whiteness. In the RGB method, you simply adjust the RGB spinners or sliders for each color channel. In HSV, a slightly different approach is taken. HSV stands for Hue, Saturation, and Value. Adjusting the Hue gives you the general color. You can then fine-tune the color using the saturation and value spinners.

The last and most intuitive method is to use the blackness, hue, and whiteness sliders found on the left side of the color selector. Here you will see a color gradient. Clicking and dragging around in the color gradient quickly selects a rough color that you can then further refine with the blackness or whiteness spinners. You may also further refine the color with the RGB or HSV spinners. In any case, adjusting colors using one method adjusts the settings of the other methods to provide the same color.

Now that you have an idea of how colors are interpreted by MAX, it is time to take a look at how colors are used in materials.

Material Colors

A basic material in MAX provides a plastic or flat look, much like paint on a flat surface. The colors on this surface are defined in three different ways: Ambient, Diffuse, and Specular, as shown in figure 8.17.

Color Sources

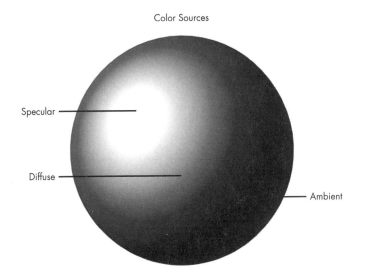

Specular

Diffuse

Ambient

Figure 8.17

An object's rendered appearance is influenced by three different sources of color and value. Ambient is the color of the object in shadow, Diffuse is the color of the objects material, and Specular is the color of the highlight.

♦ ***Ambient color*** is the hue an object reflects if it's not directly illuminated by a light source (its color in shadow). This is rarely black because the ambient light in the scene usually guarantees at least some illumination on every surface. Generally, the ambient color is a very dark shade of the diffuse color, but it can be set to whatever you want.

♦ **Diffuse color** is the hue assigned to the object. This is the color that's reflected when the object is illuminated by a direct lighting source.

♦ **Specular color** is the hue of any highlights that appear on the object.

Shading Models

MAX enables you to render objects at different levels using different shading models. A shading model is how the MAX rendering engine interprets the colors and highlight assigned to the material. In MAX, you determine the shading mode in the material. The four rendering limits in MAX are Flat, Phong, Blinn, and Metal. Additionally, you can set the material to render as a wireframe object. Figure 8.18 shows you examples of each type of shading level.

Figure 8.19

The various shading levels supported by MAX. Correctly choosing a shading level will help define how accurate your scene is.

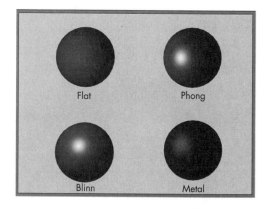

UPGRADERS NOTE

In MAX 2, Gouraud shading has been removed and Blinn shading has been added. Blinn provides slightly smaller specular highlights than Phong and results in less plastic-looking materials.

Each shading mode is listed here and briefly described:

♦ **Flat:** Renders objects without any smoothing. Colors on objects will be consistent across each individual face. This is a fast method of rendering and is good for test renders, but the quality is not very high.

♦ **Phong:** Renders objects after smoothing the surfaces, so they appear smooth even though they are faceted. Phong also provides highlights that give the material a shiny or glossy look. Colors are distributed across the rendered surface as necessary. This is good for any type of plastic or shiny surface.

◆ **Blinn**: Same as Phong but with smaller highlights resulting in a less plastic look. This is very good for many types of materials such as stucco or wood.

◆ **Metal**: Similar to Phong shading where the objects are smoothed and highlighted but renders the surface with a very metallic look. Only use this mode when you want a metallic look to your objects. The highlights and shininess of materials rendered in this mode are exaggerated.

By correctly choosing the rendering level for each material, you can mix and combine different rendering methods within the same scene. This provides you with the ultimate in flexibility for controlling the materials and producing realistic-looking scenes.

Material Properties

After you have set the rendering mode for the material, you set the material properties to define how the material looks. Material properties (sometimes called surface attributes) include color (which was covered earlier) but often include additional settings such as shininess or reflection.

Shininess and Shininess Strength

Shininess is the overall reflective nature of the objects—in other words, the glossiness. Shininess has an effect on the size of the specular highlight (the bright reflection of light seen on glossy objects), with matte objects having larger highlights and shiny objects having smaller ones as shown in figure 8.19.

Shininess

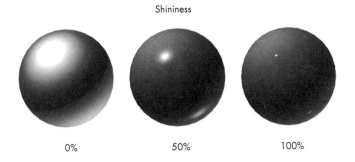

0%   50%   100%

Figure 8.19

Shininess is a measure of an object's surface gloss. At 0%, the material is matte, whereas 100% is maximum glossiness. Note how the specular highlight shrinks as the object is made glossier.

Shininess works together with Shininess Strength (sometimes called Specularity) to give the viewer information about the reflectivity and characteristics of the material, so pay attention to how the two affect a material's appearance.

Shininess Strength adjusts the intensity of the object's highlight, if it has one (see figure 8.20). By adjusting Shininess, in combination with Shininess Strength, you can create a wide range of glossy to matte materials.

Figure 8.20

Shininess Strength sets the intensity of a material's highlight. Shininess and Shininess Strength work together to define an object's glossiness. They also play a major role in simulating metallic materials.

Specularity

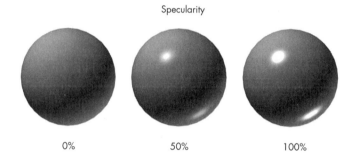

0%   50%   100%

Opacity

Opacity is a material attribute that controls the amount of light that can pass through an object. If opacity is set to 0%, the object is virtually invisible, whereas if opacity is set to 100%, the object is opaque. Any other settings make the object more or less translucent, as shown in figure 8.21.

In addition to setting a general opacity to the material, you can also control exactly how the opacity is interpreted through extended material parameters. These options will be covered in the Chapter 10, "Working with Materials," and Chapter 11, "Exploring Other Material Methods," where necessary.

Self Illumination

Self illumination adjusts how much an object appears to be lit from within. As the percentage of self illumination increases, it flattens out the effects of the ambient and diffuse lighting sources until the object appears to be one solid value (see figure 8.22). Self illumination has no effect on specular highlights, however. Self illumination is used in several instances, most commonly when you have a bright light source such as the lights on a car. By making the lights self illuminated, they appear brighter and more realistic.

Transparency

90%   50%   10%

Figure 8.21

Opacity controls the amount of background imagery that can be seen through an object.

Using Mapped Materials

Beyond the basic material properties, MAX can also make use of Mapped material properties. Mapped materials (sometimes called Texture Maps) use either scanned in bitmaps or procedural (mathematically defined) maps in place of various aspects of a material such as the diffuse color. To create a wood material, for example, you would replace the diffuse color with an image of a real piece of wood. You can then adjust Shininess and other parameters to make the wood appear more or less polished.

Max provides you with many different opportunities to make use of mapping in materials. Each is listed here and briefly described:

♦ **Ambient:** Replaces the ambient color of a material with a map. This is rarely used.

♦ **Diffuse:** Replaces the general color of a material with a map. This is the most commonly used map. Materials generated this way rely upon mapping coordinates on the objects themselves to correctly place the map on the surface of the object.

Luminosity

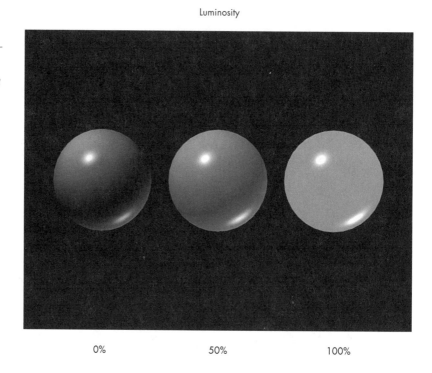

Figure 8.22

Self illumination adjusts how much an object appears to be lit from within. 0% is completely unlit, and 100% is totally self illuminated.

0%   50%   100%

♦ **Specular:** The specular highlight of an object can be perturbed (distorted) with a map to give the appearance of a less smooth, but still shiny, surface. In this case, the intensity of the colors of the map determines where the highlight appears and where it doesn't.

♦ **Shininess:** Similar to a specular highlight, but affects the shape of the highlight instead of just the colors.

♦ **Shininess Strength:** Enables you to use a map to vary the shininess strength.

♦ **Self Illumination:** Enables you to use a map to control where an object is self-illuminated and where it is not.

♦ **Opacity:** Enables you to use a map to control where an object is opaque and where it is not.

♦ **Filter Color:** Enables you to adjust the colors of an object using a map. This is generally only used with transparent objects where you can see the background behind the object. The filter color is used to tint the transparent colors.

♦ **Bump:** Enables you to apply a 3D look to an object through the use of a map. This is the second most commonly used map and is used to make a surface have the appearance of 3D geometry without ever having to create the geometry.

♦ **Reflection:** Reflection is a property of a material that reflects its surroundings. Usually, you see reflection in highly polished or waxed surfaces such as new cars, silver goblets, or even water. MAX implements reflection as a procedural map that can either be ray-traced or environmentally generated.

♦ **Refraction:** Refraction is the bending of light as it passes through an object such as water or glass. Refraction may be handled as a map or as a procedural map and can be raytraced.

Figure 8.23 shows you an example of each of these types of maps and their effects on a material.

Map Channels

Figure 8.23

A wide array of material characteristics can be altered by using bitmaps in the different types of mapping available.

Because mapped materials make use of a bitmap image such as a GIF, Targa, TIF, or JPEG, they require mapping coordinates. Mapping coordinates are simply a method of telling MAX how and where to apply the bitmap to the surface of an object. You will see how to create and use mapping coordinates in Chapter 11.

Mapped materials also make use of procedural materials, which are materials that are defined by mathematical formulas instead of scanned images or colors. MAX provides you with several procedural materials. Many more are available as plug-ins from various developers. With this kind of capability, you can create or have access to almost any kind of material property you may ever need.

After you have created and applied lights, cameras, and materials to your scene, you render the scene. *Rendering* is simply the process where MAX takes into account all of the geometry, lights, materials, and cameras and produces an image. Rendering can take anywhere from a couple of seconds to minutes or even hours depending upon a wide variety of factors. Rendering is covered in Chapter 12, "Exploring Rendering Techniques."

Conclusion

Lights, cameras, and materials all work together to take the geometry that you have created and produce a photorealistic rendering of the scene based on those settings. Actually creating lights and materials is not a cut-and-dry process; you should try one setting and see if it produces the result you are looking for. If not, try again.

In this chapter, you learned about the basic theories behind composition. In particular, you learned about the following:

♦ Cameras and How They Are Handled by MAX.

♦ Lights and the Variety of Lights that MAX Can Make Use Of.

♦ Materials and How They Are Applied to Objects in a MAX Scene.

Now that you have a basic idea of what lights, cameras, and materials are, it is time to see how to put them together to create a photo-realistic scene. The next chapter covers how to create and use lights and cameras in a scene.

C H A P T E R 9

Working with Lights and Cameras

Lights and cameras are key elements in producing a good rendering or animation. First, there is the camera. This provides a method for viewing your scene in a realistic method. By carefully placing your camera, you compose the scene for the viewer. After it is composed, you light the scene by strategically placing one or more lights in the scene to achieve a variety of effects.

This chapter focuses on the techniques necessary to quickly—yet accurately— compose a scene. In particular, this chapter covers the following topics:

♦ Creating a Camera

♦ Manipulating Cameras

♦ Camera Perspective Matching

♦ Working with Lights

♦ Controlling Shadows

♦ Creating Basic Lighting Special Effects

NOTE In this chapter, cameras are created before the lighting. You do not necessarily have to work in this order. You may create lights at any time. Because MAX creates default lighting for the scene using two omni lights, cameras and a lot of other work can be done before lights are even created. You may even want to create materials before you add lighting. The actual order of creating the scene is up to you.

Creating a Camera

There are two types of cameras in 3D Studio MAX: target and free. A target camera has an eye position (the location of the camera) and a target point (a 3D point in space) where the camera is looking. A free camera does not have a target but is otherwise the same.

NOTE A free camera is the same as a target camera but with one difference: A free camera does not have a target. Free cameras are intended for use in animation in which the camera is attached to a motion path or a trajectory. You can control the direction of the free camera by using any standard transform on the Free Camera icon. When you create and place a free camera, it appears perpendicular to the current construction plane and must be transformed to the correct position.

The camera controls are located in the Create command panel under the Cameras button. Selecting this button will reveal the two camera commands. If you select the Target button, you will get the Target Camera rollout, where you can create a target camera. Figure 9.1 shows the rollout.

Creating a target camera is most easily done in the Top viewport because you can easily select the camera and target locations and then simply move the camera and target vertically along the Z axis into the position you want. Of course, you can create cameras in any view, including the Perspective view.

To create the camera, click in the Top viewport at approximately the location where you want the camera to be. Drag toward the area of the scene where you want the camera to look, then let go. A camera icon will appear, as shown in figure 9.2. This icon is representative of the camera and is not considered geometry. As such, it will not render in the scene.

Figure 9.1

The Target Camera rollout, where you can set camera parameters either before or after you create the camera.

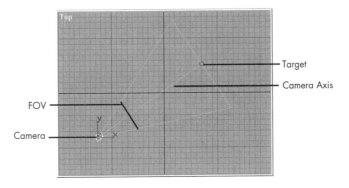

Figure 9.2

A camera icon and its various parts.

Creating a Camera View

After you create the camera, you can transform the camera or the target independently or together to correctly position the camera. Of course, to make transforming the camera a little easier, it is a good idea to view what the camera is seeing, hence you need to convert one of the viewports to a Camera view. You accomplish this by selecting the viewport and pressing the C key. The view will be switched to the currently selected camera. If no camera is selected and more than one exists in the scene, you will get a dialog box that enables you to select the camera you want to use.

Alternatively, you can also switch the view through the Viewport Configuration dialog box, or by right-clicking the name of the viewport and selecting the Camera view that you want from the resulting pop-up menu. Cameras will appear under the Views section of the menu under their own names. As you create cameras, it is a good idea to name your cameras so that they are easily recognizable in circumstances such as this.

After you create a Camera view, you can either use the MAX transform commands (except Scale) on the camera icons in the other viewports or use the camera viewport controls to manipulate the Camera view, as described in the following section. Either way, you end up adjusting the Camera view.

TIP   When you are transforming a camera with MAX transforms, you need to select the camera, the target, or both. You can easily select both by selecting the camera axis line that runs from the camera to the target.

When you are happy with the Camera view from the Camera viewport, you can select the camera, go to the Modify command panel, and adjust the camera parameters.

Working with Camera Parameters

After you create the camera, you can fine-tune it to match the view that you are looking for. There are three sets of controls that you can use to fine-tune a camera: Lens Length, Environment Ranges, and Clipping Planes.

Lens Length

The lens length is the most important camera parameter. If you remember from the last chapter, this setting works in conjunction with the FOV (field of vision) to determine how much you can see in you Camera view. MAX 2 comes with nine presets that match 35mm camera lenses, such as 35mm, 50mm, and 200mm. Selecting one of these presets sets the Lens spinner and FOV spinner. Alternatively, you can type in any value that you might need for either spinner.

The FOV spinner in MAX is exceptionally flexible, enabling you to specify the FOV in one of three ways: horizontally, vertically, or diagonally. You accomplish this through the flyout toolbar that is to the left of the FOV spinner. These adjustments enable you to match almost any real camera that you might run across. Adjusting the FOV in a different axis does not alter the aspect ratio of the camera, only the relative size in that particular direction. The other directions and lens length will adjust to match. As an option, you can also set your camera to an orthographic projection, but this is generally not used because it is the same as a User view, which nullifies the use of the camera.

Below the lens length presets are two noteworthy check boxes. First is Show Cone. The cone is a visible representation of the viewing area of a camera. The cone is visible when the camera is selected. When this check box is active, the cone is visible even when the camera is not selected. This can be very useful when you are positioning objects in your scene and you do not have a Camera view visible. The other check box is the Show Horizon check box, which causes a black line (which does not show in the final rendering) to be drawn across the Camera viewport that represents the horizon of the scene. This line moves as you move the camera. Horizon lines are used in camera matching, which is covered later in this chapter.

Environment Ranges

The next set of parameters is the Environmental Ranges. You use these controls in conjunction with environmental effects such as fog. There are two types of ranges you can set: near and far. By default, these are set to 0 and 1000 units, respectively, and the near range can never be set larger than the far range. Use these range settings to define where, in the depth of the scene, effects such as fog appear. If you check the Show check box, you can visibly see the ranges on the camera icon, as shown in figure 9.3.

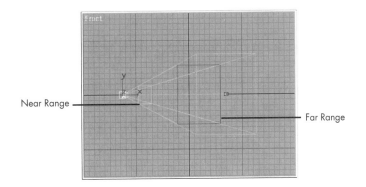

Near Range

Far Range

Figure 9.3

The near and far environmental range markers on a camera icon. These markers determine where camera-dependent environmental effects, such as fog, start and stop.

By adjusting the near and far settings, you can control where camera-dependent effects, such as fog, appear. Fog is an environmental effect that you can apply by selecting Render/ Environment from the pull-down menus. Fog and other environmental effects are covered in Chapter 12.

Clipping Planes

Clipping planes are the last settings you can use to clip off either the front or rear of a Camera view. Clipping off the front removes all the objects between the camera and the front clipping plane. You can use this to create effects such as cutting a hole in the side of a building to view into it. The far clipping plane removes any objects beyond that plane, which removes objects that would otherwise be too small to render. You can also use this feature to make objects disappear or appear in the distance.

Like environmental ranges, clipping planes have both near and far settings and show in the camera icon when you activate Clip Manually. Figure 9.4 shows the resulting camera icon.

Figure 9.4

The clipping planes in a camera icon. You can use these markers to control where objects are clipped in the scene.

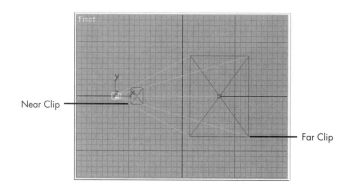

After you have fine-tuned your camera, you will probably not need to make any further adjustments unless you animate the camera, which is covered in Chapter 14.

The following exercise shows you how to create a few Camera views for the bowling alley scene.

CREATING A CAMERA VIEW

1. Load the file **MF09-01.MAX** from the accompanying CD. This is the bowling alley after the last exercise from Chapter 7, "Exploring Other Modeling Methods." You can load the file you worked on from Chapter 7 if you want.

2. In the Create command panel, select the Cameras button. Then, select Target in the rollout that appears.

3. In the Top viewport, click around the right side of the eating area and drag toward the other end of the bowling alley.

4. In either the Front view or the Side view, move the camera vertically 72 units.

5. Select the camera target and move it up 48 units, so that you are looking at a slightly down angle along the length of the alley.

6. Activate the User view and hit the C key on your keyboard to set it to the current Camera view. Figure 9.5 shows this view.

Figure 9.5

The bowling alley viewed through a camera. The default camera settings created a slightly narrower view than would be good, so further adjustment is needed.

7. The view is a little too narrow in the Camera viewport. Select the camera and go to the Modify command panel.

8. Set the lens length to 35mm. This widens the view and makes it look a little better.

9. Save the file as **MF09-01a.MAX**.

10. Repeat steps 1–7 and create a camera that looks from the other end of the alley toward the eating area. Figure 9.6 shows you this Camera view.

Figure 9.6

The bowling alley second Camera view showing the eating area and scorer's tables.

11. Save the file again.

Working with Camera Matching

The last feature of a camera to look at is camera matching. Camera matching enables you to match the perspective of a background image for composition purposes. An example might be an architectural rendering. You could take a photograph of the existing site and place the digital building directly over the top of the image. Normally, this is not a problem, but the perspective of the building needs to match the perspective of the site photo. This is where camera matching comes in.

There are two ways to perform camera matching. Both rely upon the display of the image in the viewport. The first method makes use of the camera horizon line, which is perspectively matched to the background image. The second method uses the Camera Match utility, where you place helper objects on top of the photo and create a camera based on the location of each point. In general, if you know the camera settings used to create the background image, you can use horizon lines; otherwise, you will need to use the Camera Match utility to accurately match the view.

To assign a bitmap as the background in a viewport, choose Views/Background image. In the dialog box that appears, select the Files button to select the actual bitmap that you want to use. After you have selected the file, at the bottom of the dialog box, make sure Display background is checked. In general, you will also want to select Match Bitmap under Aspect Ratio so that you do not end up compressing the image in the X or Y direction. Finally, when you render the image, you should set your output size to match the background image size.

The following exercise shows you how to create a camera match using horizon lines.

CREATING A CAMERA MATCH WITH HORIZON LINES

1. Load the file **MF09-02.MAX** from the accompanying CD. This is a simple file with a camera and three boxes that you will match perspectively.

2. Activate the Camera viewport.

3. Select Views, Background Image. Select the Files button in the Viewport Background dialog box.

4. Select the file **Lake2.tga**. This file ships with MAX and is available on the MAX CD if you do not have it installed.

5. Set the Aspect Ratio to Match Bitmap. Choose OK. Figure 9.8 shows you the viewport at this point.

6. In another viewport, select the Camera object.

7. Go to the Modify command panel and turn on Show Horizon.

8. Activate the Camera viewport. Turn off the grid in the Camera viewport.

9. Use the Camera viewport controls to manipulate the view so that the horizon line matches the horizon of the background image. (In this case, the horizon line is between the mountain base and the lake waterline.) The boxes in the scene should approximate the perspective lines of the image at this point, as shown in figure 9.8.

Figure 9.7

The MAX viewport after loading the bitmap background. Now, you must adjust the camera position and settings to match the background perspective.

Figure 9.8

The MAX viewport after approximating the perspective of the background image by using the horizon line.

10. To complete the rendering, you need to set the background as the environmental background. This is covered in Chapter 12, "Exploring Rendering Techniques." Save the file as **MF09-02a.MAX** so that you can apply the background information after exploring Chapter 12.

The Camera Match utility works in a slightly different manner. To make use of this utility, you create helper objects in the scene (which are just points) that contain true X, Y, and Z locations for the point in the background image but are positioned correctly in the viewport. After you create the helpers, go to the Utility command panel and activate the Camera Match utility to create the camera. The following exercise shows the steps you must take to make this work.

CREATING A CAMERA MATCH WITH THE CAMERA MATCH UTILITY

1. Find a photo of the image you want to match and scan it in. (You can also use any background image that you might already have.) In this photo, you must know the exact location of five points in 3D space, such as the corner of a building or the top of a pole.

2. Assign the bitmap as an Environment background, using screen coordinates.

3. Set the rendering output to the same resolution as the bitmap.

4. Assign the same bitmap as a viewport background; check Use Environment Background instead of selecting the Files button. Then set MAX to display the background in a viewport, such as the Perspective viewport.

5. In the Create command panel, go to the Helpers button. In the drop-down list that appears, select CameraMatch. Use the CamPoint function to create at least five CamPoint helpers. As usual, when you create these points, assign them recognizable names such as Pole Top.

 NOTE   You must use at least five CamPoint objects to successfully use the Camera Match utility. The more points you use, the more accurate the match is likely to be.

6. As you create each camera point helper object, you can use the keyboard entry rollout to position the helpers. Each helper is positioned in 3D space where it would be if it were a part of the background image. If the top of a pole in the photo were at 350,200,20 in real life, for example, that is where the camera helper object would appear. You can also use Transform type in to adjust the position after creating the helper. For best results, space the helpers relatively far apart.

7. Access the Camera Match utility and click the Assign Position button. Select each of the CamPoints in the Camera Match list, and then click the corresponding visual location on the 2D bitmap for that coordinate.

8. Click the Create Camera button in the Camera Match utility to create a camera that matches the Bitmap view. (If a camera already exists, select the camera and click the Modify Camera button instead.)

9. Assign the camera to the current viewport.

10. Save the file at this point.

Objects created in the scene should now appear to match the perspective of the background. Any objects that you create in the viewport will match the perspective as well.

Working with Lights

One of the most important, if not the most important, aspects of a high-quality rendering or animation is lighting. Lighting provides the illumination for the scene, as well as a sense of depth and realism through the use of shadow. A well-lit scene will always look better than a scene with the greatest camera angles and materials, but poor lighting.

As such, lighting lends itself to experimentation and trial and error. Even minor adjustments to the lighting of a scene can be the difference between a good scene and a great scene.

MAX provides you with four types of light to work with, including ambient, spotlights, ambient lights, and directional lights. Ambient light is present in every scene, regardless, whereas you must create the others. So take a look at ambient first because it is always there.

Controlling Ambient Lighting

The most basic type of lighting in a scene is the ambient lighting, which gives the scene an overall brightness. Ambient lighting is present in all scenes in MAX by default. In most cases, you may not ever need to adjust the ambient lighting. But occasionally you will. A daytime scene will work just fine with the default ambient lighting, for example, but a nighttime scene may require reducing the ambient light so that objects do not appear to almost glow in the reduced lighting.

You control the ambient light of a scene through the Environment dialog box, shown in figure 9.9, which you access through the Render pull-down menu.

Figure 9.9

The Environment dialog box, where you can set the ambient lighting levels for a scene.

Ambient light is controlled through the color swatch under Global Lighting. By clicking on this swatch, you can access the color selector. Ambient light is interpreted as a shade of gray, with darker colors resulting in less ambient light. So in general, all you will have to do is adjust the Whiteness Slider to adjust the ambient lighting. The default is 11, 11, 11 when interpreted as RGB.

Creating a Light

Creating a light in MAX is very similar to creating a camera. Some lights are created with sources and targets, like a camera, whereas others are simple points, like a free camera. Beyond this similarity, lights are a totally different animal to work with. The basic lights beyond ambient include: target spot, free spot, target direct, free direct, and omni. The most commonly used of these light types are target spot and omni.

To create a target spot, you select the Target Spot command in the Create command panel for Lights. Then you click at the location you want the light to be and drag out until you reach the target; then let go. Like a camera, the spotlight and target are individual objects that may be transformed individually using the standard MAX transform commands. You can even set one of the viewports to be a Spotlight viewport, showing you the view from the selected spotlight. Figure 9.10 shows a Target Spotlight icon and its parts, as well as an Omni Light icon.

Figure 9.10

The MAX Target Spotlight and Omni Light icons, showing you the various parts of a target spotlight.

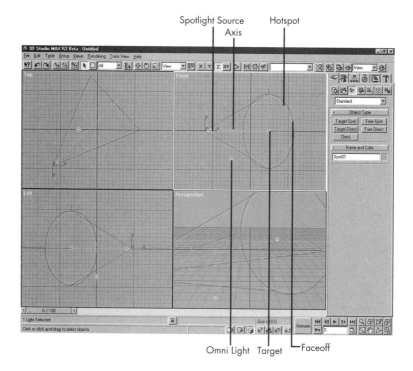

An omni light is even easier to create. Simply selecting the Omni command and selecting a point in 3D space creates the omni light at that point.

Also, like cameras, after you create the light, you need to go back and fine-tune the light settings to create the type of effects you want. This is generally accomplished by selecting the light and going to the Modify command panel. Figure 9.11 shows you the rollout for a spotlight. Omni and direct lights have similar rollouts.

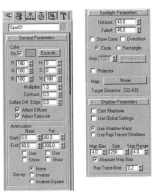

Figure 9.11

The Spotlight rollout, where you can customize and modify the light to match the needs of your scene.

At the top of the Light rollout, you will notice an On check box. This lets you enable or disable a light without having to delete it from a scene. This can be very handy for testing the influence of a light on a scene.

NOTE

The only effective way to test the effect of a light is to render the scene. Because these are test renders, only the necessary geometry should be used, to minimize the amount of time necessary. Rendering is covered in Chapter 12, but you will be introduced to the basics of rendering during the exercises in the next three chapters.

After you have created the light, you can go back to adjust and fine-tune the parameters of the light to match the various aspects of your scene. One of the more important properties of a light is its color.

Light Color

To the right of the On check box is the color swatch for the light, indicating the color of the light that is cast from this source. Below you will find the RGB and HSV spinners for the light color. You can adjust these to set the color of the light, or you can double-click the color swatch to use the MAX color selector. The default color is 180, 180, 180, or a light gray.

All lights in MAX also have a Multiplier spinner, which defines just how intense the light is. By adjusting the Multiplier, you can create low intensity lights that have subtle effects on the scene, or completely blow out portions of the scene with highly intense lights.

The following four features—Contrast, Soften Diff. Edge, Affect Diffuse, and Affect Specular—are new to MAX 2 and provide you with precise control over the lights and how they affect the ambient and diffuse color of a material. The first is the Contrast spinner. This spinner sets the amount of contrast between the ambient and diffuse colors on a lit surface. The default is a contrast of 0. By setting a higher contrast value, you can create harsh lights such as those that might be found in outer space.

The Soften Diff. Edge spinner enables you to soften the edge between diffuse and ambient lighting. This is most effective when you have two lights shining on the same surface and a crossing pattern appears in the lit area. Setting a value of 100 here will eliminate that crossing but will also result in slightly less light on the surface.

Lastly, you can control which portion of the material color the light is affecting. There are two check boxes, Affect Diffuse and Affect Specular, that you can use to control this effect. By default, both are on, but you may want to turn one or the other off. When this occurs, you can use one light to affect the diffuse color and another to affect the specular color differently.

Light Includes and Excludes

You can find the Exclude button to the right of the light color swatch in the light rollout. This button is actually the Include/Exclude button, depending on the type of operation you decide to use. Selecting this button displays a dialog box where you can select objects to be either included or excluded from the influence of the currently selected light.

You can select one or more objects from the left side of the dialog box and copy them to the list on the right. Then, depending upon your settings at the top of the dialog box, the selected objects will either be excluded or included in the illumination, shadow casting, or both properties of the selected light.

Includes and excludes are very important for controlling light in a scene, especially when you want to illuminate a single surface only with a little extra light. Unfortunately, a single light can only exclude or include objects, not both. In cases where you need to do this, clone the light and use one light for excludes and the other for includes.

Light Attenuation

Lights can also be attenuated. In other words, you can control where they are in effect. In real life, the intensity of light will die off the farther away from the source you get. This is similar to attenuation. Attenuation also works just like the ranges on a camera. You can set near and far ranges and where they start and end. Figure 9.12 shows a Light icon with near and far ranges.

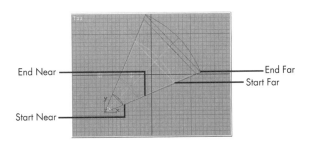

End Near — **End Far**
— **Start Far**

Start Near —

Figure 9.12

The Near and Far range markers for a spotlight. These determine where a light is in effect in MAX.

Another method of attenuation that you can use is decay. Decay does not make use of the attenuation settings and forces a more realistic decay of light over distance. There are three choices: None, Inverse, and Inverse Square. When set to None, the light has full intensity from start to end. With Inverse, the light is not reduced quickly, as shown in figure 9.13. Figure 9.14 shows the Inverse Square option, which is considered to be fairly close to the way light decays in real life.

Figure 9.13

A volumetric light using the Inverse method of light decay.

After the attenuation of lights, you can control specific parameters related to each type of light. A spotlight has the most parameters, such as shadow control, cone size, shape control, and others. These parameters will be explored here. Other lights, such as omni lights, have a subset of spotlight parameters. An omni light has all of the shadow controls, for example, but does not have cone control because omni lights do not have light cones.

Figure 9.14

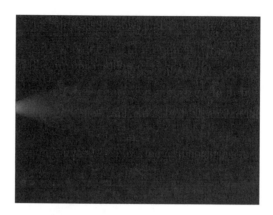

The same volumetric light using the Inverse Square method of light decay. Notice how quickly and more realistically the light decays.

Hotspot and Falloff Controls

First, you can set the hotspot and falloff settings for the spotlight. These are given in degrees and represent the angle of the cone of light. In the hotspot (shown as a light blue in the Light icon), the light is constant at full intensity. Between the hotspot and falloff (shown in a darker blue line), the light reduces from full intensity to none. By adjusting these two parameters, you can create spotlights with crisp, sharp-edged shadows to very soft, very diffuse shadows, when shadows are enabled for the light.

No light will show outside of the hotspot and falloff ranges unless you turn on overshoot, which forces the spotlight to become a point light that casts shadows only in the hotspot and falloff ranges but does cast light in all directions.

Of course, the basic spotlight uses a circular projection, but you can set the light to be rectangular by selecting the Rectangular radio button. When you do this, you can control the aspect ratio of the light, which is its ratio of width to height. Thus, you can create and control circular and rectangular shapes of light in MAX.

In addition, you can assign a bitmap to the rectangular light to turn it into a projector. This enables you to project the bitmap, as you would out of a film projector. This is great for creating effects such as a drive-in movie theater.

Working with Shadow Control

All of the basic light types in MAX are capable of casting shadows, including omni lights. Shadows are very important to the realism of a scene. Without shadows, the scene will not have the 3D depth that is necessary to make it look real. It can also be hard to tell where objects exist in the scene without shadows.

Look at figure 9.15, which shows a box with a sphere on the surface. Without shadows, it is difficult to tell where the object is above the box it is sitting on. But, if you add shadows, as shown in figure 9.16, the box is clearly sitting on the surface of the box below. Hence, shadow control is very important.

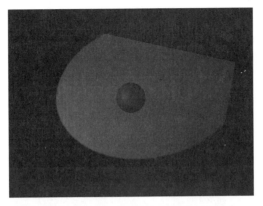

Figure 9.15

A scene with a sphere and a box, but no shadows. The position of the sphere in the scene is not obvious.

Figure 9.16

The same scene but with shadows determining the correct location of the sphere on top of the box.

In MAX 2, omni lights can now cast shadows and act as projector lights, providing a whole new level of capability. Just be careful, because shadow-casting omni lights create six shadow maps per light. This means that when you render the scene, the omni light will take up as much RAM as six spotlights, if the settings are the same.

UPGRADERS NOTE

MAX provides two methods of creating shadows with lights: shadow maps and raytracing. But, by default, all lights created in MAX have shadow casting turned off. Under the Shadow parameters of the Light rollout, you must turn on Cast shadows for the light to have shadows. Once it is on, you select the type of shadows and the associated settings.

You can select to use either shadow maps or raytraced shadows. Shadow maps make use of generated grayscale bitmaps to create the shadows, whereas raytracing physically traces each shadow with rays. In general, shadow maps are used for speed and for soft shadows, whereas raytracing is used for accurate, hard shadows.

Shadow maps are generally used when you do not need crisp, clear, hard shadows, or highly detailed shadows. If you created a 3D tree and set a spotlight to cause the tree to cast shadows, for example, it would depend on the type of lighting you are looking for as to the type of shadow you would use. On a crisp clear fall or spring day, you might use raytracing to get crisp shadows. But, on a slightly overcast or hazy day, a shadow map will do. Figure 9.17 shows a Douglas fir with shadow maps; the same fir is shown in figure 9.18 with raytraced shadows.

Figure 9.17

A Douglas fir lit with a shadow map casting light. Notice how the shadow is somewhat accurate but still fuzzy.

Figure 9.18

The same fir tree lit with a ray-tracing shadow casting light. Notice how the shadows are much crisper and more accurate now.

For shadow maps, there are three sets of controls: Bias, Map Size, and Sample Range. The Bias controls how far away from the shadow-casting object the shadow will appear. The default is 4 units. For tight, accurate shadows, you might set this to 1. But setting a low Bias setting might result in streaking in the shadows. If so, choose a slightly higher Bias setting.

The Map Size determines the overall size of the shadow map. A default size of 256 creates a map 256x256 pixels in size. Larger maps are more accurate but use more memory exponentially. A map that is 2048x2048 will take a considerable amount of RAM itself. You should use the smallest Map Size possible. Never use a map larger than 2048. If you need more accuracy than that, use a raytraced light.

The Sample Range spinner determines how many times the shadow is sampled. Larger values are used here to prevent aliasing in the shadow, but at the cost of increased render time. Raytracing only has a single Bias setting.

Once you create your lights and set the settings, you are ready to test render the scene and make any adjustments that are necessary. The following exercise shows how to create several different types of lights, including omni and spotlights, for the bowling alley scene.

LIGHTING THE BOWLING ALLEY

1. Load the file **MF09-03.MAX** from the accompanying CD. This is the bowling alley with most of the modeling completed.

2. Go to the Create command panel, select the Lights button to access the Light commands, and choose Omni.

3. Click at approximately 60,100 in the Top viewport to create an omni light. Name the light **General Light1**.

4. Move the light vertically in the Front or Right viewports until it is about 70 units above the floor.

5. Using Shift+Move, make a copy of the omni light and place it over the eating area at around 60, –300. Make the copy as an instance. The omni lights you just created provide general lighting for the scene.

6. Select Target Spot from the Create command panel.

7. In the Right viewport, click near the ceiling but just below it to place the light. Drag to the floor and let go to place the target. Try to position the target so the axis line of the light is vertical. Name the light **Main Lighting1**.

TIP

Even though this bowling alley model does not make use of it, you can create extra geometry to represent the actual light sources such as overhead fluorescent lights. This will add a further touch of realism to the scene. If you want to do so, go ahead and create some boxes or other types of geometry to represent the lights. Then, place the spotlights just below the geometry so the geometry does not interfere with the light source.

8. In the Top viewport, right-click the selected light and choose Select Target. This selects the target and light so you can move them together.

9. Move the light to approximately 50,100 in the Top viewport.

10. Make two instances of the light and place them at 50,-70 and 50, -300. Right-click the last instance and choose Deselect Target.

11. Select the light, without its target, and go to the Modify command panel. Set the Hotspot to 70 and the Falloff to 160. Turn on Cast Shadows and set the Map Size to 512. Because the light is an instance, the other two main lights will automatically update to match.

12. Activate the Camera01 viewport and choose Render Scene. Set the size to 640x480 and choose Render. A Virtual Frame Buffer dialog box will appear and the scene will be rendered. Figure 9.19 shows approximately what the scene should look like at this point.

Figure 9.19

The bowling alley scene after adding the general lighting and main lights.

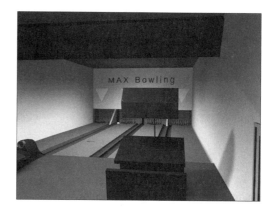

At this point, you have created the main lights for the scene. Now, it is time to add some lights for special highlights in the scene.

13. Close the Virtual Frame Buffer dialog box after the rendering is complete. Go back to the Create command panel.

14. Select Target Spot again. In the Right viewport, zoom in on the scorer's desk. An overhead projector box is present.

15. Click and drag from just below the bottom of the overhead to the top of the center of the writing surface and let go. Name the light **Desk Light1**.

16. Set the Multiplier to 1.5 to make a brighter light source. Set the Hotspot to 50 and the Falloff to 90. Turn on Cast Shadows and set the Map Size to 256.

17. In the Top viewport, select the target again and position the light over the top of the desk. Clone the light as an instance and place the other copy over the other desk.

18. Select Free Spot from the Create command panel.

19. In the Top viewport, zoom in on the bowling pins. Click to place the light in the center of one set of pins.

20. Set the Hot Spot to 40 and the Falloff to 90. Turn on Cast Shadows and set the Map Size to 512. Set the Map Bias to 2.0 to produce more accurate shadows.

21. In the Right viewport, zoom in on the new light you just created.

22. Move the light so it is about 50 units above the bowling alley floor.

23. Make three cloned instances of the light, and place them over the top of the other bowling pin sets.

24. Render the Camera01 viewport again. Figure 9.20 shows the scene at this point.

Figure 9.20

The bowling alley after adding special lighting to the desks and the bowling pins.

25. Save the file as **MF09-03a.MAX**.

Up to this point, you have explored creating omni, spot, and free spot lights. Through these light types, you created some basic lighting effects. In the next exercise, you will add a light that will highlight the MAX Bowling sign in the back of the alley. This is an accent light that you might see on a typical sign.

ADDING LIGHTING HIGHLIGHTS TO THE BOWLING ALLEY

1. You can continue from the last exercise, or load **MF09-03a.MAX** from the accompanying CD.

2. Activate the Right viewport and zoom in on the right half of the alley.

3. Access the Light commands in the Create command panel. Choose Target Spot.

4. Click at approximately 115,140 in the Right viewport. Drag the target and place it in the center of the MAX Bowling sign.

5. In the Top viewport, select the light and target, and position the light in the center of the alley.

6. Select only the light and go to the Modify command panel.

7. Double-click the color swatch and set the color of the light to 252,255,171 in RGB. Close the color selector, and then set the Multiplier to 0.25 to reduce the strength and make the highlight more subtle.

8. Under Spotlight Parameters, set the Hotspot to 40 and the Falloff to 60. Change the cone type from Circle to Rectangular and set the Aspect Ratio to 12.

9. Under Shadow Parameters, turn on Cast Shadows and set the Shadow Type to Use Ray Traced Shadows.

10. Click the Exclude button at the top of the rollout.

11. Set the Exclude type to Include.

12. In the list on the left side, select End Alley Wall and Alley Text, and add them to the right side. Choose OK.

13. Render the Camera01 viewport. Figure 9.21 shows the resulting image.

Figure 9.21

The bowling alley scene after adding highlight lighting to the text.

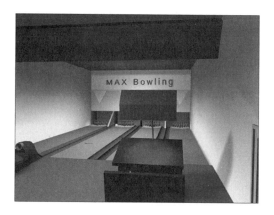

14. Save the file as **MF09-03b.MAX.**

As you can see, adding lighting to a scene can be a time-consuming task. It is also a trial-and-error type of task where you will create lights, adjust their settings, and then possibly decide that you want to take a different approach. Don't be afraid to experiment with the lighting. As you gain experience, you will become more proficient because you will have a better idea of what settings you want to use before you even create the light.

Basic lighting provides you with a lot of flexibility. But simple adjustments such as setting a light to be rendered as a volumetric light (which looks like a light shining in fog) can also create some very basic special effects.

Creating Basic Lighting Special Effects

You can use lights to create certain basic special effects that evoke a mood or are necessary for accurate lighting. With MAX 2, for example, you can use volumetric lights to create effects such as fog-filled lights or lights shining through misting water. As a matter of fact, most bright light sources that shine at night, such as a searchlight, have some sort of volumetric quality about them.

Another type of special effect is the creation of a projector light that projects an image or sequence of images from a spotlight source. You can use this to create effects such as movie projectors or drive-in theaters.

Working with Volumetric Lights

A volumetric light is a light that appears to have a foggy aspect to it wherever the light actually appears. Figure 9.22 shows you an example of a volumetric light.

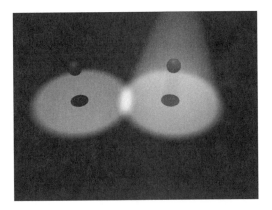

Figure 9.22

A volumetric light in MAX. Use this type of light to invoke a mood or illustrate a characteristic of the atmosphere that is otherwise not readily discernible.

Volumetric lights are actually modifications of existing shadow-casting lights in your scene. To turn a light into a volumetric light, it must cast shadows and must use shadow maps. A raytraced shadow light will not work. The only other requirement is that the scene must be rendered in a Camera viewport to see the volumetric light.

Volumetric lights are added and set up through the Environment dialog box, which you can access by selecting Render, Environment from the pull-down menus.

To add a volumetric light, choose the Add button and select Volumetric light from the list of Environmental Effects. After you select the volumetric light type, the rollouts for a volumetric light will appear. Figure 9.23 shows you these rollouts.

Figure 9.23

The volumetric controls. Here, you can fine-tune the volumetric light effect.

To add one or more lights to the volumetric effect, choose the Pick Light button and select various lights in the scene. When this is active, you can select only light objects, making selection a lot easier. As you select lights, their names are added to the drop-down list on the right.

After you have selected the lights you want to apply the same volumetric effect to, set all of the volumetric parameters, and then close the Environment dialog box. When you render the scene, MAX will automatically process the volumetric information. Volumetric light controls are broken down into three categories: Volume, Attenuation, and Noise.

The Volume controls enable you to set the color of the fog, as well as the density, minimum and maximum light percentages, and the filtering of shadows. Most of the time, you will vary the density, color, and min and max spinners to control the effect.

You can use attenuation to cause the volumetric effect to decay, along with the light source, if the light is making use of attenuation.

Lastly, you can apply various types of noise to the volumetric light to make it appear less constant. Through the use of the Noise parameter, you can make the volumetric fog look like smoke or very subtle fog.

The following exercise shows you how to create a couple of subtle volumetric lights for use in the bowling alley scene.

ADDING VOLUMETRIC LIGHTS TO THE BOWLING ALLEY

1. You can continue from the last exercise, or you can load the file **MF09-04.MAX** from the accompanying CD. This is the bowling alley at the end of the last exercise.

2. Choose Rendering, Environment.

3. Choose Add to add an environmental effect. Choose Volume Light and choose OK.

4. Choose the Pick Light button in the rollout that appears. Select the two lights that are above the scorer's desk.

5. Set the Density to 10.0.

6. Click the Noise On check box to turn noise on.

7. Set the Amount spinner to .75 and the Type to Fractal.

8. Set the Size spinner to 2 and the Levels to 6.

9. Close the Environment dialog box.

10. Render the Camera01 viewport and you should get the scene shown in figure 9.24.

Figure 9.24

The bowling alley after adding a couple of volumetric lights. Notice the subtle smoky haze effect around the scorer's desk.

11. Save the file as **MF09-04a.MAX**.

As you can see, volumetric lights are powerful in the effects they can create. But they do come with the cost of much longer rendering times. The more volumetric lights you have in a scene, the longer it will take to render. Use them only when necessary.

Creating Projector Lights

Projector lights are used to project the image of a bitmap onto the surface of an object, much like a movie projector. You can enable these simply by turning on the

Projector check box in the light rollout and selecting a bitmap image to work with. Figure 9.25 shows an example of a projector spotlight.

Figure 9.25

A spotlight that has been set to project an image instead of light.

The following exercise will create two projector lights to simulate the overhead bowling scores that are seen in many modern bowling alleys.

CREATING OVERHEAD PROJECTORS IN THE BOWLING ALLEY

1. Load the file **MF09-04a.MAX** from the accompanying CD or continue with the last exercise.

2. Activate the Right viewport and zoom in on the scorer's desk and the overhead projector.

3. Create a target spotlight that has a source just above the desk and shines on the overhead screen. Figure 9.26 shows you this light.

Figure 9.26

The correct placement of the spotlight, from the Right viewport.

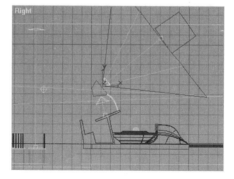

4. In the Top view, position the light and its target so that it is over the projector. Make an instance copy to the other projector as well.

5. Deselect the target and go to the Modify command panel.

6. Under Spotlight Parameters, turn on Projector.

7. Set the Hotspot to 25 and Falloff to 27. Set the Type to Rectangle.

8. Open the Materials Editor by choosing the Material Editor button.

9. With the first material selected, expand the Maps rollout.

10. Click the None button next to Diffuse. Select the Bitmap Map Type and choose OK.

11. Select the None button next to Bitmap in the rollout that appears. Select the file **Bscore.tga** that is available on the CD.

12. Turn off the Tile check boxes.

13. Choose the Go to Parent button. Click and drag the Map#1 button and drop it on the None button next to Map in the Spotlight Parameters rollout. Set the Copy Type as an instance. This copies the map from the Materials Editor to the projector.

14. Close the Materials Editor.

15. Choose Bitmap Fit. Select the **Bscore.tga** file again.

16. Set the light to include only the Overhead Score Screen object.

17. Render the Camera viewport. Figure 9.27 shows you the result.

Figure 9.27

The scene with overhead projector lights displaying blank scorecards.

18. Save the file as **MF09-04b.MAX**.

Lights and cameras provide the most basic methods of composing your scene so it has a realistic look. Through careful use of both lights and camera angles, you can create realist images.

Conclusion

This chapter showed you how to create lights and cameras for use in your scenes. In particular, you learned the following:

♦ How to Create Cameras

♦ How to Adjust Cameras

♦ How to Create Lights

♦ How to Adjust Lights

♦ How to Create some Basic Lighting Effects

You need cameras to view the scene in a way that looks correct. Cameras in MAX match the cameras used in the real world, so there is a nice correlation. After you have a view of the scene, you need to illuminate it with various light types that are available in MAX in order to provide your scene with a greater sense of realism.

After you have illuminated the scene, you are ready to apply materials. The next chapter focuses on how to create and apply basic materials to your scenes.

CHAPTER 10

Working with Materials

Up to this point, you have seen how to model, illuminate, and view your scenes. But for the most part, no thought has been given to the objects in the scene, other than their shape. All objects in real life are made up of some sort of material, whether that material is plastic, wood, or plasma.

Materials are part of what brings a scene to life. The correct creation and application of material to objects will make your scenes jump to life. But, just as there are many types of materials in the world, there are many types of materials that you can work with in MAX.

This chapter focuses on working with basic materials such as plastics and metals. The following chapter focuses on texture mapped materials. In particular, this chapter covers the following topics:

- ♦ Working with the Material Editor
- ♦ Working with Standard Materials
- ♦ Assigning Materials to Objects
- ♦ Working with Materials other than Standard

Working with the Material Editor

The key to working with materials in MAX is the Material Editor. The Material Editor is a single dialog box, through which you create, manipulate, and assign materials. You access the Material Editor by choosing the Material Editor button on the main toolbar or selecting Tools, Material Editor. Figure 10.1 shows the Material Editor.

Figure 10.1

The Material Editor dialog box in MAX, where you create and assign all of the materials you will use in a scene.

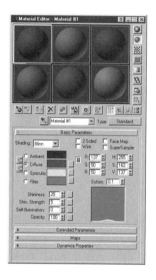

The Material Editor is broken down into two basic sections: the preview windows and the material controls. The preview windows provide you with a sample of what the material would look like on a sample object. The material controls enable you to actually manipulate and change the currently selected material. Now take a look at the preview windows first.

The Material Editor Preview Windows

When you first open the Material Editor in a new scene in MAX, there are 6 material preview windows. These represent materials 1 through 6 initially. (Later in this chapter, you will see how to open 15 or even 24 preview windows.) Like objects, MAX materials can also have (and should have) individual material names. Until you change the names, MAX names the basic materials Material #1 and so forth.

The preview windows make use of the MAX scanline renderer. This means that the preview of the material is just as accurate as the final rendering will be. You can configure the preview windows to use any rendering engine that you have installed in MAX, and you should configure the Material Editor to use the engine you are going to render the scene with. This will help to give you a more accurate preview of what the material will look like when loaded into the scene. In these cases, it helps a lot to run Windows 95 or NT at 24-bit color for best viewing of the material previews.

A white box surrounding the material preview indicates the currently selected material. Like the MAX viewports, you can make any material preview window and the material associated with that window active simply by clicking it.

On the right side of the preview windows is a set of buttons, called the Material Editor Preview Window controls, that enables you to control some of the basic features of the material previews. Figure 10.2 shows the names of each of these buttons.

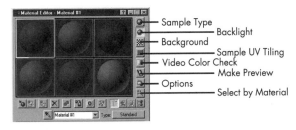

Figure 10.2

The MAX Material Editor Preview Window controls. These enable you to change the material preview to more closely match your scene conditions.

Each of the Material Editor Preview Window controls provides you with control over a specific aspect of the Material Editor preview window. For example, the Sample Type button enables you to select the type of geometry that appears in the preview window. You can select box, cylinder, or sphere. In addition, you can also configure MAX to use any custom object as a sample type.

The Material Editor previews are lit by two omni lights, one in front and one in the rear to provide backlighting. The Backlight button enables or disables the backlighting. Because most objects have some sort of backlighting to bring out the details in the shadows, this is usually left on.

Some materials that are somewhat transparent such as glass or water are difficult to see in the default material preview window. You can use the Background button to set the background of the preview window to either gray or a colored checkerboard. Other materials, such as materials that make use of maps, can make use of the Sample UV Tiling button to set the number of times the sample bitmap is repeated over the surface of the object, so you can preview the material as a tiled material.

For output to video tape, you can use the Video Color Check button to check the colors of the material versus a video output color palette, such as NTSC or PAL video formats. This enables you to check your material for colors that are illegal or unreadable under those video formats. This relies upon the Rendering Preferences to determine which format is used. Along the same lines, you can use the Make Preview button to make quick previews of any materials that have animated material properties.

The last two buttons don't affect the material previews but are still very useful. Options enables you to set the various options for the Material Editor previews such as lighting, custom objects, and anti-aliasing. The Select by Material button enables you to select one or more objects in the scene that have the current material assigned to them. This command makes use of the Select by Name dialog box, but only objects with the current material will show in the list.

Beyond these basic material preview controls, you can also set different preview settings by right-clicking any preview window. This brings up the pop-up menu shown in figure 10.3.

Figure 10.3

The Material Editor Preview Window pop-up menu, where you can quickly configure the preview windows, such as the number of visible material preview slots, loading a custom object into the preview through the Options entry on the menu.

Through this pop-up menu, you can set and control several features. First, you can set the mouse state for the preview window. The default is Drag/Copy, which enables you to drag the current material preview and drop it on another preview window to make a copy of the material. You can also use this feature to assign materials to objects in the scene by dragging the material preview and dropping it on the object.

You can also set the mouse type to Drag/Rotate. This essentially gives you the viewport command Arc Rotate in the material preview. When active, the mouse cursor changes to the same cursor as Arc Rotate. All clicks and drags end up rotating the sample object. You can also reset the rotation once you are done.

At the bottom of the preview window pop-up list, you can select from three viewport configurations. The default six windows are actually a 2x3 grid of preview windows. You can also select 5x3 and 6x4 to work with more materials at once. Figure 10.4 shows the Material Editor with 6x4 loaded.

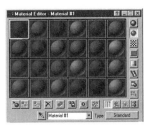

Figure 10.4

The Material Editor with 24 material previews loaded (6x4 Sample Windows option). This is the maximum number of active previews you can have in MAX 2.

With the 5x3 or 6x4 Material Editor preview options, the preview windows have a tendency to get fairly small, even on large displays. Fortunately, the pop-up menu has a Magnify option that creates a resizable dialog box that provides you with a larger preview. This dialog box uses the scanline renderer, so when using maps or procedural materials, updates to the Magnify preview window might take a few seconds, especially if you made the window fairly large. Figure 10.5 shows the Magnify window.

The last option of the pop-up menu is the Options button, which enables you to configure the rest of the Material Editor options. The resulting dialog box is shown in figure 10.6.

Figure 10.5

The Magnify preview window, which gives you a larger rendering of the current material, enabling you to precisely adjust the material before applying it to an object and rendering the scene.

Figure 10.6

The Material Editor Options dialog box, where you can configure most of the important options, such as lighting, related to the Material Editor.

As mentioned earlier, the material previews make use of two omni lights to illuminate the sample object. In the Material Editor Options dialog box, you can set the light color and multiplier values for each light, so you can more closely approximate what is in your scene. You can also set the Material Editor to use a custom sample object by selecting the blank button to the right of File Name. If you elect to use this option, you should try to use relatively simple custom objects because using more complex objects will result in longer preview times. Use custom objects to see what the material will look like on an object that is more complex than a cube, cylinder, or sphere. This way, you can make use of the preview windows, instead of having to render the entire scene or portion of a scene to see the material on the object.

If you use plug-in renderers, such as RadioRay or RayMAX, you can set the Material Editor to use that rendering engine instead of the default MAX scanline rendering engine to create the material previews. This requires that the plug-in rendering engine is set as the current rendering engine in the MAX Preferences. You can do this by choosing File, Preferences and going to the Rendering tab in the Preferences dialog box. There you will find the buttons that enable you to select both the production and draft rendering engines.

The material preview controls are very powerful in helping you see what the material will look like under just about any condition, before you ever apply it to an object. But they are only part of the Material Editor; the rest is the actual material controls themselves.

Material Controls

The material controls enable you to load, save, assign, and manipulate materials in the Material Editor. The material controls include everything below the material previews, including the buttons and the material rollouts. Figure 10.7 shows these controls.

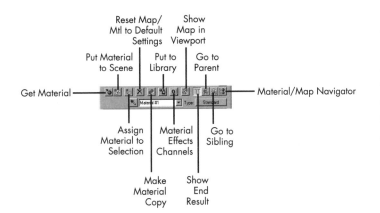

Figure 10.7

The Material Editor material controls where you can load, save, assign, and manipulate materials.

Like the MAX commands and modifiers in the command panels, the Material Editor makes use of rollouts. There are four basic rollouts with a material: Basic Parameters, Extended Parameters, Maps, and Dynamic Properties.

The Basic Parameters include features such as shading level, color, shininess, opacity, and so on. Many simple materials such as plastic only make use of basic parameters. With the Extended Parameters, you have greater control over material properties such as opacity, wireframe rendering, and reflection dimming.

The Maps rollout provides you with the ability to assign bitmaps to various material properties, which are covered in full detail in the following chapter. The Dynamic

Properties rollout provides you with a set of commands to set the properties when you use the MAX dynamics system. These properties are covered in Chapter 15, "Exploring Other Animation Methods."

Above the rollouts and below the preview windows is a set of buttons in the Material Editor that enable you to load and assign materials in MAX. These buttons are shown in figure 10.7.

You can use the Get Material button to start the material/map browser, where you can load new materials or maps or previously created materials from a library into the current material slot. If you make a copy of a material with the same name as a material already in the scene, you can use Put Material to Scene to replace the material properties of the existing material in the scene with the new material.

Use the Assign Material to Selection button to assign the material in the current active slot to the current active object selection. This works very well for both single object selections and multiple object selections. If you want to reset a material to its default settings, you can use the Reset Map/Mtl to Default Settings button. Then, you can start the material from scratch if you want. Another method that you can use to create a new material is to use the Make Material Copy button, which makes a copy of the current material, with all the parameters the same, including the name. Then, you can simply change the name and the parameters as you want to create a new material.

Of course, after you create a new material or set of materials, you should save it to a library so that you don't have to create it again. The Put to Library button saves the material in the active slot to the current materials library that is loaded.

The Material Effects Channel button assigns the material a channel effect number, which is used in Video Post to apply special effects such as a glow to objects or parts of objects, based on their materials. There is a total of 16 material effects channels that you can assign to various materials. These are covered in Chapter 17, "Exploring Video Post Fundamentals."

When working with materials that have a bitmap or procedural map applied to them, you can use the Show Map in Viewport button to make the current bitmap visible in the interactive renderer, when the viewport shading level is set to Smooth+Highlights.

Like an object with a long modifier stack, materials can also have multiple levels of effects. You can use the Show End Result button to isolate a specific section of the material that you are working on or enable you to see the material with all sections active. Along a similar line, you can use the Go to Parent button in complex materials with many levels of effects to navigate from one level to another. For example, multi-sub object materials have several levels of material controls. In a multi-sub object, you have more than one material assigned, each assigned to different material IDs. The overall material is the parent. The Go to Sibling button enables you to move sideways in the material hierarchy instead of vertically.

The last button is the Material/Map Navigator, which spawns the Material/Map Navigator dialog box, which you can use to navigate through the materials and maps of the currently selected material. This is convenient way to drag part of a material back into the same material, such as copying a bitmap into the bump channel. This dialog box is different from the browser and is used only for information purposes. Figure 10.8 shows the Material/Map Navigator dialog box.

Figure 10.8

The Material/Map Navigator, where you can look through the current materials assigned to the scene.

As you can see, the Material Editor is a powerful interface you can use to create just about any type of material that you want. Now that you are familiar with the interface, it is time to look at how to create some simple materials such as paints, plastics, and metals.

Working with Standard Materials

MAX materials can be broken down into two categories: material types and maps. A *material type* is a specific configuration of material properties and maps to achieve a specific purpose. For example, MAX comes with several material types, including a standard material and a Double Sided material. The standard material contains all of the basic material properties that you would use to create most of your materials. For example, a teak wood material and a flat white paint material are both created as standard materials. Other material types are used in special circumstances; for example, when you render a scene with two-sided rendering turned on, the standard material renders the same material on both sides of the face, whereas the Double Sided material renders two different materials, one on each side of the face.

Maps are a collection of bitmap controls and procedural materials used in the context of MAX material types or in other commands such as Projector spotlights, covered in the last chapter.

For the most part, you will use standard materials to create most of your materials. The default settings for the Material Editor create standard materials. The process for creating a material is relatively simple, as demonstrated in the following exercise.

CREATING MATERIALS

1. Select a material preview window to be active. If all material windows are used by current materials, you can select the Get Material button to start a new material. This spawns the Material/Map Browser (see figure 10.9) where you can select the material type or map type to work with. For a standard material, double-click Standard.

Figure 10.9

The Material/Map Browser dialog box. Use this box to select new material types or maps for use in the Material Editor. Entries with a blue sphere are material types and entries with a Green Parallel-ogram are maps.

2. Just below the Material Preview slots is a drop-down list showing the name of the material (refer to figure 10.1). Because you just created the material, it should be named Material #*n*, where *n* is the next available material number. You should rename the material to something more appropriate, such as Yellow Plastic or Blue Glass, or whatever material you are about to create.

3. After you name the material, use the Basic Parameters rollout to set the shading level, colors, shininess, opacity, and other basic parameters.

4. If necessary, set any extended parameters.

5. When you are happy with the material preview, assign the material to one or more objects in the scene. You can accomplish this in two ways. First, you can click and drag the material preview and drop it on the object. Second, you can select the object, and with the material active, choose the Assign Material to Selection button in the Material Editor. You will know that the material has been assigned in a shaded viewport because the color of the object should change immediately to that of the new material.

6. Once assigned, the active material preview window shows white triangles in the corners. This indicates that the material is now "hot." In other words, if you make any changes to the material at this point, they are immediately reflected in the scene. Figure 10.10 shows a hot material preview.

Hot Material —

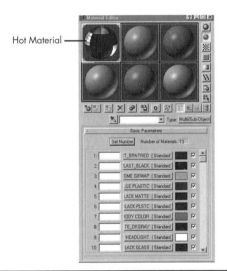

Figure 10.10

The Material Editor preview window with a "hot" material. This is a material that is currently assigned to one or more objects in the scene and is active.

After you have assigned the material or materials, you test render the scene and then make any adjustments you see fit in the context of the lighting and cameras from the scene.

Now, take a closer look at some of the material properties you can control.

Working with Basic Material Parameters

When you create a new standard material, the Basic Parameters rollout appears by default. This rollout, shown in figure 10.11, enables you to change the basic properties of the material. As such, it is the most commonly used rollout.

Figure 10.11

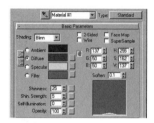

*The Basic
Parameters rollout
of the Material
Editor. Here, you
can set the basic
properties of a
material in MAX.*

First, you can select the shading level for the material. In this case, you have a choice of four different levels: Flat, Phong, Blinn, and Metal. Each of these levels was described in Chapter 8, "Understanding Composition Concepts." Selecting the correct shading level has a large impact on the overall quality and believability of the materials. A glossy metal surface is difficult to create without using the Metal shading level, for example. By contrast, a flat paint is easier to create with a Blinn shading level, whereas plastics are easier with Phong. As you work with the various shading levels, you will gain experience and get a better feel for when to use each shading level.

To the right of the shading level, there are four check boxes. These check boxes are rendering parameters for the material such as 2-Sided, which forces the material to render on both sides of a face. Wire forces the material to become a wireframe version, as shown in figure 10.12. Use Face Map when you have a texture mapped material to force one copy of the texture maps onto one face. Last is SuperSample, which you can use with bump maps, described in the next chapter.

Figure 10.12

*A material when
Wire mode is
active. In this
mode, the object
is rendered with
the material only
along its visible
edges.*

The most important part of a material is, of course, the colors. There are four color swatches that you can work with: Ambient (the color of the material in shadow),

Diffuse (the general color of the material), Specular (the color of any highlights on the material), and Filter (the color of transparent materials when filtered over a background image).

To the left of each color swatch is a radio button indicating the currently active color channel. This affects the values shown in the RGB and HSV spinners to the right. You can adjust colors by changing any of the RGB or HSV spinners or by double-clicking the color swatch and using the MAX color selector.

NOTE

When working with colors, you should always think about the lighting conditions. You might choose different material colors if you have a red light in the scene than if the light is white or a light yellow, for example. Also, subtle variations in color can make large differences in the final rendering. The use of a very light yellow instead of a white will make outdoor scenes look more realistic because the sun is a light yellow color and provides correct color tinting. You will need to make test renderings to see the final results.

Some colors can also be "locked" together; if you change one color, the other locked color changes to match. Ambient and Diffuse can be locked, as can Diffuse and Specular, through the two buttons at the far left of the color swatches. You might want to lock two colors together to ensure consistent colors across the surface of the object.

To the right of the color swatches are three smaller blank buttons. These buttons launch the Material/Map Browser and enable you to replace that color of the material with a bitmap or procedural map. This same bitmap will appear in the Map rollout as well. Again, bitmapped materials are covered in the next chapter.

Below the color swatches, you can set the shininess and shininess strength spinners. To the right is a graph of the shininess of the material, enabling you to see a visual representation of how strong the specular highlights are. Above this graph is a Soften spinner that enables you to soften specular highlights if you need to.

Lastly, you can set the Self-Illumination and Opacity spinners. When using the Opacity spinner, it is a good idea to set the material preview background to a checkerboard or bitmap so you can better see the transparency of the material.

Having said all that, it is time to see how to create some basic materials. The following exercise shows you how to create four materials for use in the bowling alley scene: White Plastic, Tan Flat Paint, Glass, and Red Metal.

Creating a White Plastic Material

1. Open the Material Editor in a new MAX session.

2. Click the first material slot to make it active. In the material name drop-down list, set the name to **White Plastic** instead of Material #1.

3. For a plastic material, Phong shading is good because it gives good highlights. Set the Shading level to Phong.

4. Click the Diffuse color swatch to access the Color selector. Set the Blackness slider completely to black. Then, adjust the Whiteness slider until RGB reads 250,250,250. This is not pure white but rather a very light gray.

5. With the Color selector still open, click the Ambient swatch and set the colors to RGB 230,230,230. Close the Color selector.

6. Set the Shininess to 50 and the Shininess Strength to 75, which results in a fairly shiny and glossy surface, such as a polished plastic.

    Now that you have a plastic material that makes use of shininess properties, you can create a flat paint in a similar manner.

7. Click the next material preview slot and name the material **Tan Flat Paint**.

8. Set the Diffuse color to 206,179,122, using the Color selector or RGB colors. Set the Ambient color to 161,110,0 for a darker version of the same color.

9. Set the Shininess Strength to 0 and Shininess to 0 to create a flat material.

10. Click the next open material preview slot. Name the material **Glass**.

11. Set the Diffuse color to 64,49,179 for a dark blue.

12. Set the Ambient color to 16,182,243 for a lighter blue.

13. Turn on the Background button so a checkerboard background appears.

14. Set the Shininess to 60 and the Shininess Strength to 75 to make the material more like glass.

15. Set the Opacity to 50 to make the material appear like a fairly transparent blue glass.

16. Click the next active material slot and name the material **Red Metal**.

17. Set the Shading level to Metal.

18. Set the Diffuse color to 167,57,49 for a dark red.

19. Set the Ambient color to 71,18,16 for a very dark red.

20. Set the Shininess to 60 and the Shininess Strength to 70. This creates a dark cherry red metal.

21. Leave the Material Editor open to continue with this exercise later in the chapter.

Obviously, after taking the time to create these materials, you do not want to have to create them again. Instead, it would be better to save these materials into a library of materials that you can use in any scene. Fortunately, MAX provides you with that exact ability.

On the toolbar under the preview windows in the Material Editor is a Put to Library button. This button creates a copy of the current material and places it in the current material library under the name that you gave the material. After the material is added to the library, you can save the library to keep the material handy.

To view the contents of a material library, you use the Material/Map Browser. You can access this in the Material Editor by choosing the Get Material button. Once in the Material/Map Browser, select Mtl Library under Browse From. At this point, the contents of the current material library will appear in the browser, as shown in figure 10.13.

Figure 10.13

The Material/Map Browser, showing you a currently loaded material library. You may select any material and load it into the Material Editor to assign to objects in the scene.

Obviously, the Material/Map Browser is a powerful dialog box, so the following section takes a closer look at it.

Working with the Material/Map Browser

The Material/Map Browser, shown in figure 10.13, is your only method for browsing and managing materials that you are currently working with. Because you are working with a browser, you can browse materials and maps from a variety of sources. As a matter of fact, there are six sources that you can select from under the Browse From section of the dialog box: Mtl Library, Mtl Editor, Active Slot, Selected, Scene, and New.

The MTL Library button enables the display of materials that are contained in the current material library. At the bottom left of the Material/Map Browser are the library file functions where you can open, merge, and save library files. They have a *.MAT extension on them and are generally saved in a Matlibs directory under your 3D Studio MAX installation, but can be saved and loaded from anywhere on the system.

The merge function enables you to merge the material library from a specific MAX file so that you may use materials that were used in that file.

The Mtl Editor button displays materials that are currently in the Materials Editor. Since there are 24 slots in the Materials Editor, a list of 24 materials will appear when active, regardless of the number of materials you have created.

You can also display materials that are in the active slot, assigned to the currently selected object, assigned in the current scene, or new materials, by selecting the appropriate option.

At the top of the Material/Map Browser dialog box are seven buttons that enable you to further control the display of the materials in the browser. The four buttons on the left define whether or not a material preview is active, and if so, how large the preview is. Figure 10.14 shows the library material list with material previews active.

Figure 10.14

The Material/Map Browser using material previews to show the material lists.

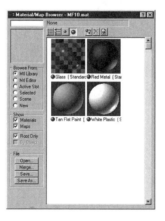

The three buttons on the right provide additional library functions. The first button is Update Scene Materials from Library. This updates all the materials in the scene with the materials of the same name from the current library. Next is Delete from Library, which deletes the selected material from the current library. Last is the Clear Library button, which deletes all the materials in the current library. This is essentially how you create a new material library. Delete all the materials in the current one, add new materials to the library, and then use Save As to save the library under a different name.

The following exercise takes the materials that you created in the last exercise and adds them to a material library.

CREATING A MATERIALS LIBRARY

1. If it's not already open, open the Material/Map Browser.

2. Set Browse From to Mtl Library.

3. Choose Clear Library.

4. Select each new material in the Material Editor and choose the Put to Library button. When you do so, you will be asked to give the material a name. Because you already did this, choose OK. As you add them, they will appear in the Material/Map Browser.

5. In the Material/Map Browser, choose Save As.

6. Name the file **MF10.MAT** and save it to your Matlibs directory.

Now that you have seen how to create materials and save them to a library, explore loading that material library and adding those materials to the bowling alley scene.

Assigning Materials to Objects

One of the more important aspects of working with a material is the ability to assign the material to objects in the scene. MAX provides two primary methods for accomplishing this. First, you can click and drag the material preview and drop it on the object you want to assign the material to. When you do, as you place the cursor over the object, a tooltip will appear telling you the name of the object so that you know exactly which object you are assigning the material to. This works great for individual material assignments.

The other method involves selecting one or more objects in the scene. Then, with the objects selected, choose the Assign to Selected button in the Material Editor to assign the materials. This is the best method to use when you need to assign the same material to more than one object at a time.

Eventually, you will assign a material to an object and then want to edit the material. But due to the large number of materials in your scene, the material is no longer loaded in a preview window and you may not remember the name of the material you assigned. This presents a problem that is easily solved in several ways. First, in the Material Editor, next to the Material Name drop-down list is an Eyedropper button. Selecting this and then clicking an object in the scene will load the material on that object into the current material slot. This is the easiest method.

You can also opt to choose Get Material and then set the Browse From options to Scene, which displays all the materials in the scene. MAX 2 then lists the objects that have the material assigned to them to the right of each material. Furthermore, you can use object properties to find out the name of a material assigned to an object. Or you can use MAX's Summary Info to see what materials are assigned to objects.

Assigning materials to objects is relatively easy, as is retrieving materials from the scene into the Materials Editor, even when you have forgotten the name of the material.

The following exercise shows you how to assign basic, nontextured materials that you created earlier in this chapter to the bowling alley scene. (In the next chapter, you will retrieve these same materials and change a few of them to texture-mapped materials.)

LOADING AND ASSIGNING MATERIALS

1. Load the file **MF10-01.MAX** from the accompanying CD. This is the bowling alley at the end of the last exercise.

2. Open the Material Editor in MAX.

3. Choose Get Material. In the Material/Map Browser, select Mtl Library under Browse From. Choose Open under File.

4. Select the file **MF10.MAT** from the accompanying CD (or the file you created earlier in this chapter). This loads four materials.

5. Double-click the Red Metal material. This assigns it to material slot #1.

6. Close the Material/MAP Browser.

7. In the MAX scene, select both the scorer's desks and the overhead projector and supports that are attached to the desk. (Each desk is located behind the ball returns.)

8. Choose Assign Material to Selection to assign the materials.

9. Click in slot #2 to activate that slot. Choose Get Material, and double-click White Plastic to assign the material to the slot.

10. Select the scorer's desks, all of the bowling pins, and the tables and chairs and assign the White Plastic material to them.

11. Activate another material slot and assign the Tan Flat Paint material from the library to it.

12. Select all of the wall objects, the bowling alley lanes, the floors, and steps and assign the material to them.

13. Render the scene to see the results, shown in figure 10.15.

14. Save the file as **MF10-01b.MAX**.

Figure 10.15

The scene after applying three basic materials to the objects. Notice how the scene is beginning to look more realistic with the materials applied.

At this point, the scene has roughly half the materials it needs. Take a few minutes and generate your own materials for the remaining objects. For example, you can generate a material for the ceiling, gutters, doors, return carriages, signage, and so on. Also, you can experiment with variations or changes in the material assignments chosen for this exercise.

Working with Material Types Other than Standard

Until now, you have seen only the standard material in MAX. Unfortunately, the standard material is not applicable to all situations. In these cases, you might need special materials. For example, in the bowling alley, you can use a raytrace material type on the alley lanes to make them appear very shiny and glossy with high reflections. Fortunately, MAX provides several other material types that you can make use of that are extremely powerful. In addition, you can purchase plug-in material types to add even more material types to MAX.

NOTE   You can find plug-ins for MAX in many places on the Internet, such as http://
www.mcp.com/newriders/MAX, where New Riders maintains a list of plug-ins
for MAX. Or you can purchase plug-ins from various vendors such as Digimation
(www.digimation.com), CadCrafts (www.cadcrafts.com), and Kinetix
(www.ktx.com).

There are seven material types in MAX, including the standard material. Blend,
Double Sided, Multi/Sub-Object and Top/Bottom are discussed in the following
sections; Matte/Shadow and Raytrace are covered in the next chapter.

Blend

The Blend material simply blends two separate materials (whether they are a
standard material or other material) by adjusting the strength as a relative percentage. Figure 10.16 shows the rollouts for the Blend material.

Figure 10.16

*The Blend
material controls,
where you can set
up and define the
materials to be
blended and how
they are blended.*

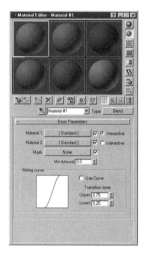

Selecting either the Material 1 or Material 2 button takes you directly to another
standard material. As such, you will get the standard rollouts and properties. You
can even change this material to a different material or even another blended
material to create multilayered blending effects.

TIP   When working with materials such as blended materials, it may become
difficult to remember which level you are working at. You can use the Go to
Parent control to move back up the material hierarchy, or you can use the Go
to Sibling control to move to other materials at the same level.

To the right of each material in the blended material is a check box that makes that material active. To the right of that check box is an Interactive radio button. This determines which material appears in the Interactive viewport. The interactive renderer cannot handle blended materials, so you can see only one at a time. To see the actual blended material, you must use the MAX rendering engine.

You can also apply a bitmap that acts as a mask between the two blended materials so that only portions of one material show. But the most important aspect of the blended material is the mix amount, which determines which material is viewable. At a mix amount of 0, Material 1 is visible. With a mix amount of 100, Material 2 is visible. Any other value is some sort of blend between the two.

As an alternative, you can also use the mixing curve to create different types of blends between the materials. By animating the mix amount or the mix curve, you can create effects such as materials blending into other materials over time.

Double Sided

Double Sided materials are used in conditions where you are rendering a model with Two Sided turned on. In this case, both sides of a face are rendered, regardless of the direction of the face normal. This material enables you to apply a material to both sides of the face. Normally, in two-sided rendering, the material on the normal side of the face is repeated on the back side. Figure 10.17 shows the controls for the Double Sided material.

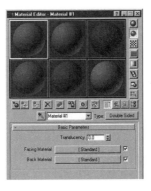

Figure 10.17

The Double Sided material controls, where you can set up which material is on the face and which material is on the back.

Like a blended material, the Double Sided material makes use of two separate materials, which are standard materials by default but can be any material type. You can also activate or deactivate these materials at will. Double Sided materials also have a Translucency spinner, which enables the material on the back side to affect the material on the front side, or vice versa, by changing the transparency of the face.

Double Sided materials are helpful whenever you want to render the inside of an object without having to model the inside. You can create a vase with paint on the outside and clay on the inside, for example. But Double Sided materials only work if you are rendering the scene with the Two Sided option turned on. Figure 10.18 shows an example of this type of material.

Figure 10.18

A vase rendered with a Double Sided material. The facing material is the outside pattern material and the backing material is the clay-colored interior.

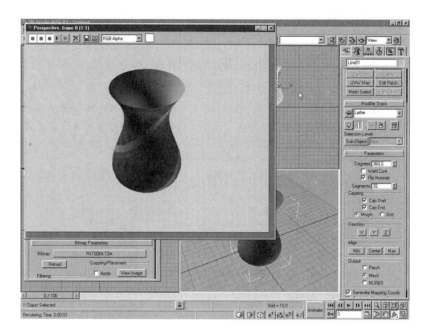

Multi/Sub-Object

One of the more popular alternative materials is the Multi/Sub-Object material, which enables you to assign multiple materials to a single object. Multi-Sub/Object materials are used when you want to keep complex objects as a single object but apply different materials to different portions of the same object.

In this material, there are sub-materials that can be any type of material. The default Multi/Sub-Object material has 10 sub-materials. These are assigned a number from 1 to 10 and can each be given a name. If you remember back to Chapter 6, "Exploring More Editing Methods," and the face level editing commands, you can select a set of faces and assign them a unique material ID number. This number corresponds to the material number from the Multi/Sub-Object material.

If you assign a material ID of 3 to a set of faces and then assign a Multi/Sub-Object material to that object, the material in channel #3 of the Multi/Sub-Object material will be assigned to those faces. Figure 10.19 shows the Multi/Sub-Object rollout.

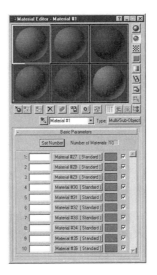

Figure 10.19

The Multi/Sub-Object material, where you can set up the different materials that are applied to the same object.

There are many reasons why you might want to keep a large complex object as a single object, such as staying a single object might be a requirement for a certain animation technique. In situations such as these, the only way you have to assign multiple materials to the same object is through a Multi/Sub-Object material. Figure 10.20 shows an example of the usage of a Multi/Sub-Object material.

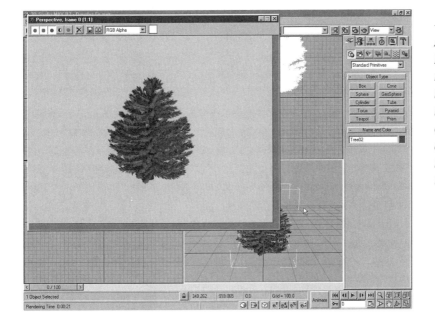

Figure 10.20

A tree with a Multi/Sub-Object material applied to it. The tree is treated as a single object but has different materials for the leaves and branches.

The actual controls are very simple for a Multi/Sub-Object material. You can set the total number of sub-materials and define which materials are on or off.

Top/Bottom

The last material to look at in this chapter is the Top/Bottom material, which enables you to apply two materials to the same object and place them based on a percentage distance from top to bottom. For example, you can set a position value of 50. In this case, the material division is halfway up the object. Figure 10.21 shows you the controls for the Top/Bottom material.

Figure 10.21

The Top/Bottom material, where you can set up and define materials whose location is based on a vertical position of the object.

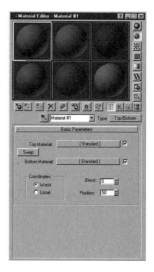

A Top/Bottom material is made up of two materials, the top and bottom materials, which can be swapped. As with other materials that make use of sub-materials, you can turn each individual material on and off at will.

The Position spinner defines the location of the break between the top and bottom materials. A setting of 50 is the midpoint of the object. The Blend spinner enables you to blend the materials at the transition point, instead of making a hard break between the materials. Lastly, you can use either world coordinates to determine the orientation of the break line or you can use local coordinates. When using world coordinates, the break line will always be horizontal, along the X,Y plane. With local coordinates, the break line between materials will keep its orientation with the object when it is animated.

As you can see, the various material types that MAX provides give you enough power and flexibility to spend literally years developing different materials for different purposes. With the addition of plug-in materials, this power is extended even further.

The following exercise shows how to add a Top/Bottom material to a bowling ball from the bowling alley scene.

ADDING A TOP/BOTTOM MATERIAL TO THE BOWLING BALL

1. Load the file **MF10-02.MAX** from the accompanying CD. This file contains a bowling ball.

2. Open the Material Editor. Click the first material slot.

3. Choose Get Material.

4. In the Material/Map Browser, make sure New is selected under Browse From and double-click Top/Bottom. Close the Material/Map Browser.

5. Click the Standard button next to Top Material. This displays a standard material. Name the material Bowling Ball Top, so that it is easily distinguished. (This actually creates a separate material that can be assigned independently of the Top/Bottom Material.)

6. Set the Diffuse color to a dark red, the Shading level to Metal, the Shininess to 60, and the Shininess Strength to 60.

7. Choose Go to Sibling to go to the Bottom Material.

8. Name this material Bowling Ball Bottom.

9. Set the Color to a dark blue, the Shading level to Blinn, the Shininess to 70, the Shininess Strength to 70, and the Opacity to 75.

10. Choose Go to Parent to return to the Top/Bottom Material.

11. Set the Blend Amount to 30 and the Coordinates to Local.

12. Assign the material to the bowling ball.

13. When you render the Perspective view, you get a bowling ball that is metal on the top and glass or plastic on the bottom, as shown in figure 10.22.

14. Save the file as **MF10-02a.MAX**.

Figure 10.20

The bowling ball after applying the Top/Bottom material. This creates a unique effect of a bowling ball that is metal and plastic.

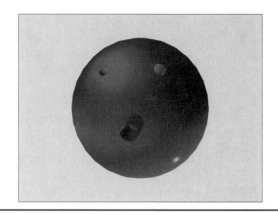

As you can see from the last exercise, experimenting with various material types and settings can produce unusual, but interesting, results. The rule of thumb with materials is: Don't be afraid to experiment.

Conclusion

In this chapter, you learned how to create simple materials. In particular, you explored:

♦ The Material Editor

♦ Standard Materials

♦ Creating Material Libraries

♦ Assigning Materials to Objects

♦ Working with Materials other than Standard Materials

Basic materials, while lacking texturing, are still very powerful and provide you with a high degree of control over surface properties such as Opacity, Shininess, and Color. By carefully, and sometimes ingeniously, working with the parameters, you can create thousands of real-world materials.

However, basic materials only get you so far. The second half of materials is texturing, or the use of bitmaps in the materials themselves. That is the focus of the next chapter.

C H A P T E R 11

Exploring Other Material Methods

In the last chapter, you were introduced to basic materials that made use of several surface properties to create a variety of material effects. Now, you will learn how to make use of texture-mapped materials that make use of bitmaps, or scanned photos of materials. You can use these bitmaps to create a large number of effects, such as animated materials or 3D effects on a surface, without having to model the details of the surface.

This chapter focuses on the following topics:

♦ Working with Bitmaps

♦ Using Bitmaps in a Material

♦ Working with Mapping Coordinates

♦ Working with Procedural Materials

Working with Bitmaps

A *bitmap* is a scanned-in or computer-generated image that is encoded as a series of pixels. When these pixels are small enough and close enough together, they form an image. Bitmaps are stored in a variety of different file formats such as TIFF, Targa, GIF, JPEG, PNG, RLA, and AVI (which is an animated bitmap format).

Each pixel in a bitmap has a color value assigned to it. Depending upon the size of the color value supported, the number of colors in an image will vary. A 24-bit image, for example, can have any of a possible 16.7 million colors assigned to each individual pixel. An 8-bit image only has a possible palette of 256 colors. Obviously, a 24-bit image looks a lot better than an 8-bit image but results in a much larger file. Some file formats supported by MAX (such as PNG and RLA) support up to 48-bit color images, which provide the greatest color fidelity.

When it comes to materials, you can use bitmaps to simulate real-world materials. You might take a photograph of a piece of wood, scan the photograph into a bitmap format, use the format in a material, and apply the material to an object. Then, when you render the object, it will look like it was made of the same wood material. Obviously, it is not quite as easy as that, but using bitmaps in a material greatly increases the realism of the material.

When you do use a bitmap in a material, it does have a profound impact on the memory requirements that MAX will need to render the image. Each bitmap that is used in a material must be loaded into memory (whether real or virtual memory) to render. As such, a 2 MB bitmap will require 2 MB of memory. So, it is always a good idea to use smaller bitmaps and as few as possible.

 TIP   When working with materials, you may sometimes do a lot of test renderings to see how the materials look. In such cases, you may use 8-bit materials for test renders and then substitute 24-bit color images for the final renderings. This will save some memory and increase the rendering speed for test renders somewhat.

Using Bitmaps in a Material

You can use bitmaps in materials to replace one of the various parts, such as the diffuse color. In other instances, you can use the bitmaps to add effects to the material that cannot otherwise be created. An example of such an effect might be a bump map, which adds small shadows to the material to make it look like the material is a true 3D surface. Figure 11.1 shows a diffuse mapped material and figure 11.2 shows the same material using a bump map.

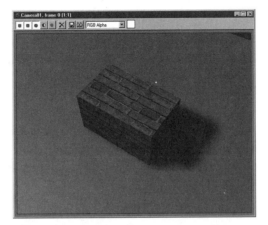

Figure 11.1

The box shows a material that uses a diffuse bitmap. This map replaces the diffuse color and makes the material look more realistic.

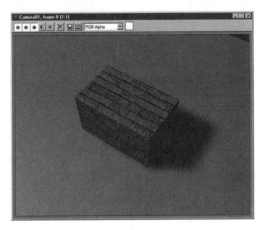

Figure 11.2

The same box with a material that makes use of a bump map. Notice how the surface appears to have more detail than it really does.

As you can see from figures 11.1 and 11.2, using a bitmap in a material can create subtle and large-scale changes in a material. In figure 11.1, a large-scale change in the material is achieved by applying the map to the diffuse channel, directly affecting the look of the material. Figure 11.2 shows a subtle change where a bump map is applied to the material to give it a 3D look.

Use the Asset Manager to keep track of all of the bitmaps you might use in MAX. It is a powerful and quick tool for viewing and selecting bitmaps from hundreds of choices. The Asset Manager is covered in Chapter 2, "Touring the MAX 2 Interface."

TIP

You can apply bitmaps to a wide range of material properties. In some cases, all of the colors of the bitmap will be used; in other cases, only the black and white or saturation values will be used. Each material property you can apply a map to is listed here and briefly described:

 NOTE   If you want to create an effect such as seeing a movie on a TV screen in your scene, use an animated file format, such as an AVI file, or an IFL (Image File List) in the diffuse channel. All you have to do is find some digitized video and make use of it.

- ♦ **Ambient:** Even though it is rarely used, you can apply a bitmap to the ambient color of a material. The bitmap will appear when the object is in shadow. In general, this color channel is locked with the diffuse color channel, so a bitmap applied to the Diffuse is automatically applied here.

- ♦ **Diffuse:** As mentioned earlier, the diffuse color is the general color of the material. Using a bitmap in place of the diffuse color results in a material that looks like the bitmap.

- ♦ **Specular:** The specular highlight can also be replaced by a bitmap, which can give the impression of a slightly reflective surface or other such effects.

- ♦ **Shininess:** The shininess of a material can be controlled through the use of a bitmap. Here, the grayscale colors of the bitmap are used to control where the shininess or specular highlights appear.

- ♦ **Shin. Strength:** Just as shininess and shininess strength are related, so are the bitmap versions. Here the strength of the shininess is controlled by the grayscale colors of the bitmap.

- ♦ **Self-Illumination:** Using a bitmap in place of Self-Illumination provides you with control over where the object is self-illuminated. Black colors of the bitmap are not self-illuminated whereas white are. Colors in between are interpolated appropriately.

- ♦ **Opacity:** A bitmap can also be used to control which parts of an object are solid and which are transparent. Black areas are transparent, white areas are solid, and grayscales are different levels of translucency.

- ♦ **Filter Color:** In this channel, which is used in conjunction with Opacity, you can control the filtering of background colors with a map on transparent materials.

♦ **Bump:** The second most heavily used map channel is the bump map. Here, the bitmap colors are interpreted to give shade and shadow to the surface of an object. This provides the illusion of a 3D surface, without having to create one.

The Bump Map strength controls are slightly different from the other map types. The others range from 0 to 100 in strength. Bump maps range from 0 to 1000 in strength, providing you with a higher degree of control.

NOTE

♦ **Reflection:** Here, a bitmap can be used to simulate the reflection of the surrounding environment.

♦ **Refraction:** You can apply a bitmap to the refraction channel; the bitmap is refracted according to the shape of the geometry.

The areas where you can apply a bitmap are shown in figure 11.3.

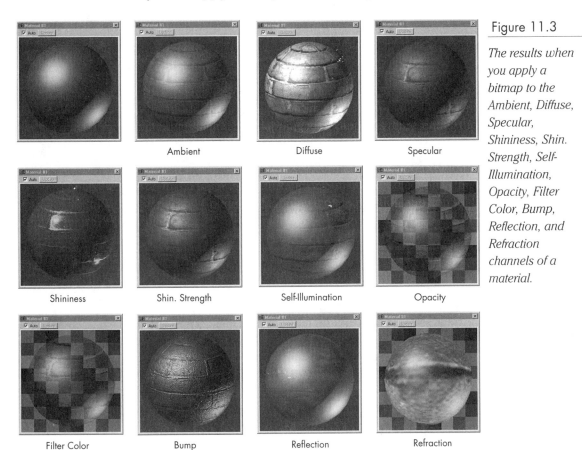

Ambient   Diffuse   Specular

Shininess   Shin. Strength   Self-Illumination   Opacity

Filter Color   Bump   Reflection   Refraction

Figure 11.3

The results when you apply a bitmap to the Ambient, Diffuse, Specular, Shininess, Shin. Strength, Self-Illumination, Opacity, Filter Color, Bump, Reflection, and Refraction channels of a material.

In all cases, when you apply a bitmap to use in a specific portion of a material, you can control the strength of the bitmap and whether or not the bitmap is on or off. You accomplish this in the Maps rollout shown in figure 11.4.

Figure 11.4

The Maps rollout of the Material Editor where you can define which Map channels are active and how strong they are.

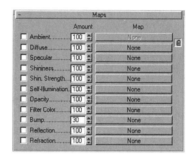

Creating a Mapped Material

To create a mapped material, you can either access the Maps rollout in the Material Editor or simply click the blank button to the right of many of the material properties such as diffuse color or transparency. Either action brings up the Material/Map Browser where you can select the type of map you want to apply to that particular portion of the material. Map types that you can apply to a material are shown with a green symbol to the left of the map name. Most of the time, you will select Bitmap. The other types of maps are called *procedural maps* and are discussed later in this chapter.

NOTE Many times you will want to create your own maps for use in MAX. Two of the best tools for doing this are Adobe Photoshop and Fractal Design Painter. Both provide a lot of features that you can use to create your own maps. MAX will accept Targa, GIF, JPG, PNG, TIF, and other formats from these programs.

When you select the Bitmap entry and choose OK, the rollouts of the Material Editor change so you can control the Bitmap. Figure 11.5 shows you these rollouts.

NOTE When you access the bitmap rollouts of a material, you are working at a child level of the material. In other words, the bitmap is dependent upon the rest of the material. To return to the standard material controls, choose the Go to Parent button in the Material Editor. To return back to the bitmap level, click the appropriate bitmap button in the Maps rollout.

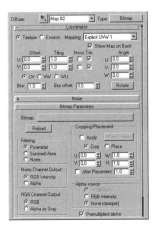

Figure 11.5

*The Bitmap
rollouts for a
material. Through
these rollouts, you
can precisely
control the usage
of the bitmap in
the material.*

There are two main rollouts to the Bitmap Controls: the Coordinates rollout and the Bitmap Parameters rollout. The Coordinates rollout is covered in the "Working with Mapping Coordinates" section later in this chapter.

The first thing you do is work with the Bitmap Parameters to select which bitmap you want to use in the material. Clicking the blank button next to Bitmap will provide you with a file selector where you can select any supported file type. After the bitmap is loaded, it will appear in the material preview according to the map channel it is assigned to.

TIP

For you to use a Bitmap in MAX, the bitmap file must reside in a directory that MAX is aware of, known as a Map Directory. You can select one or more Map Directories by choosing File, Configure Paths from the pull-down menu.

After you have assigned the appropriate bitmap, you can set the bitmap controls, if necessary. There are five sets of controls for each bitmap that you load into a material. These are: Filtering, Mono Channel Output, RGB Channel Output, Alpha Source, and Cropping/Placement.

The filtering controls determine how the map is antialiased when rendered. Aliasing is the appearance of artifacts in a scene, such as jagged lines instead of smooth lines. Antialiasing is the process of smoothing out these artifacts. MAX provides two methods of antialiasing bitmaps used in a material. You can select either Pyramidal or Summed Area filtering. Both achieve good results but Summed Area is slightly better, although it requires a lot more memory. In most cases, you should use Pyramidal, unless you are getting aliasing artifacts in your maps, or have maps that appear to travel across the surface of the object. If this is the case, Summed Area is better. But only use Summed Area when absolutely necessary.

There are two sets of channel outputs. Depending upon the material property you applied the bitmap to, one of these channels will be used. The RGB channel is used for properties such as diffuse color or reflection. The mono channel is used for properties such as bump maps or opacity. Under the mono channel, you can select whether the mono colors are chosen from the intensity values of the RGB colors or from the alpha channel of the image, if it has one. The RGB output enables you to select the RGB colors or use the alpha channel as a grayscale map, if the bitmap has an alpha channel.

NOTE
The alpha channel of a bitmap image is an extra 8 bits of color (making the image 32 bit instead of 24 bit) that represents the transparency of the image. The alpha channel is encoded as a 256-level grayscale image, providing 256 levels of transparency. In general, only images that are rendered out of MAX or some other 3D program have alpha channels. For the most part, alpha channels are most heavily used in the Video Post for compositing purposes. Video Post is covered in Chapter 17, "Exploring Video Post Fundamentals."

When you select the Alpha option for either the RGB or mono output channels, you can select the source of the alpha channel under Alpha Source. The three options are Image Alpha, RGB Intensity (which calculated the transparency from the intensity of the colors) or None, where no alpha channel is present.

The last set of controls are very powerful for working with bitmaps. These are the Cropping/Placement controls that enable you to precisely place a copy of the bitmap, such as a decal, on the surface of an object, or crop the image inside of MAX instead of cropping the bitmap in an image editor such as Photoshop.

The easiest way to make use of the Cropping/Placement controls is to use the View Image button. Depending upon whether Cropping or Placement is active, you will get an interactive editor (shown in figure 11.6) where you can interactively scale, position, or crop the bitmap.

In the interactive cropping/placement editor, a dashed outline appears, representing either the cropping or placement boundaries. By adjusting the handles of this box, you can interactively adjust the bitmap. Alternatively, you can use the Number spinners at the top of the dialog box.

After you apply the bitmap to the material, you can select Go to Parent to return to the main material controls and further adjust the strength of the map in the Maps rollout.

Figure 11.6

The Specify Cropping/ Placement editor where you can interactively set the cropping and placement of bitmap images. In this figure, the Placement option is active.

The following exercise shows you how to create three different mapped materials for the bowling alley scene. These materials will be applied in an exercise later in this chapter.

CREATING A MATERIALS FOR THE BOWLING ALLEY SCENE

1. Load the file **MF11-01.MAX** from the accompanying CD. This is the bowling alley scene at the end of the last chapter. You may also load the file that you created at the end of the last chapter.

2. Open the Material Editor. Click Material Slot #4 because it is unused.

3. Name the material **Alley Floor**.

4. Expand the Maps rollout and click the None button next to Diffuse.

5. In the Material/Map Browser, double-click Bitmap. This opens the Bitmap rollouts in the Material Editor.

6. Select the blank button next to Bitmap.

7. Select the file **CEDFENCE.TGA**. (This file should be either in your MAX Maps directory or on the accompanying CD. If on the CD, copy into the Maps directory first.)

8. Set the U Tiling spinner to 2.

9. Choose Go to Parent.

10. Set the Shininess and Shin. Strength spinners to 0.

11. Put the material into the Material Library.

The wood floor material is complete. Now you will create the bowling pin material.

12. Select an open Material Slot. If you need to, switch your Material Previews to 5x3 for more slots.

13. Name the material **Bowling Pin**.

14. Expand the Maps rollout and select the None button next to Diffuse.

15. Select Bitmap again from the Material/Map browser and choose OK.

16. Select the Blank bitmap button again and select the file **Bowling.tga** that is on the accompanying CD.

17. Choose Go to Parent.

18. Set the Shininess Strength to 75 to make the pin appear polished.

19. Put the material into the Material Library.

    After the floor and bowling pin have been surfaced, it is time to create the bowling ball material.

20. Select another open material slot.

21. Name the material **Bowling Ball.**

22. Apply the file **Marbteal.tga** to the Diffuse channel as in the other materials. This file should have been installed with MAX. If not, it should be available on the MAX 2 CD.

23. Put the material into the Material Library.

24. Save the scene as **MF11-01a.MAX**.

As you can see from the last exercise, creating a mapped material is not difficult. You simply apply bitmaps to selected areas of the material to generate specific effects. Only the Diffuse channel was used in the previous exercises. In later exercises in this chapter, you will make use of other mapping channels.

After you create the material, you assign the material to objects in the scene, just like any other material. Then, you have to apply mapping coordinates to the objects (if they do not already have them) so MAX will know where and how to place the maps on the objects.

Working with Mapping Coordinates

All mapped materials make use of mapping coordinates to correctly place the bitmap on the object. These mapping coordinates make use of a different coordinate system called UVW. This is the same as XYZ, but corresponds to the bitmap dimensions. UVW is used to help reduce the confusion surrounding which coordinates you are using.

If you were to look at a flat bitmap, for example, the X axis is the U direction and the Y axis is the V direction. The W direction is only used with procedural materials.

There are essentially two different ways to create mapping coordinates for an object. The first method is to turn on Generate Mapping Coordinates when you are creating the object. These coordinates are then generated based on the type of geometry you are creating. The second, and more flexible, method is to apply the UVW Map modifier to the object. With the UVW Map modifier, you can apply the mapping coordinates, scale them, rotate them, and even select various types of mapping coordinates. This is not possible with the Generate Mapping Coordinates options.

If you use the UVW Map modifier, it should be the last modifier, or one of the last modifiers, that you apply in the Stack for the object. If you apply a UVW Map modifier, for example, then use Edit Mesh to attach more geometry. The attached geometry will not have mapping coordinates because it was attached after the UVW Map modifier in the Stack.

When you apply the UVW Map modifier to an object, you get the rollout shown in figure 11.7.

Figure 11.7

The UVW Map Modifier rollout, where you can select the type of mapping coordinates and how they are applied to the selected object.

When you apply the modifier, mapping coordinates are automatically generated for the object, and a gizmo (sometimes called the Mapping icon) appears representing the mapping coordinates. Figure 11.8 shows a box with this gizmo present.

The Mapping icon is representative of the scale, orientation, and position of one copy of the bitmap that is used in the material. By turning on Sub-Object selection in the UVW Map rollout, you can Move, Scale, and Rotate the Mapping icon to position and control the location of the bitmap on the object.

Figure 11.8

A box with a Mapping icon showing. Adjusting this icon at a sub-object level enables you to position the mapping coordinates.

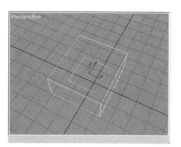

 TIP When transforming the Mapping icon, it is helpful to see the material on the object. If you turn on Smooth+Highlight Shading in the viewport and turn on the Show Map in Viewport button in the Materials Editor, you will see a representation of the bitmap in the viewport that you can interactively adjust. The Show Map in Viewport button is only available when you are adjusting the Bitmap parameters in the Bitmaps rollout. The Show Map in Viewport button is only available if the map you are using can be shown in the viewport. Many procedural maps cannot be displayed in the interactive viewports.

If the icon is smaller than the object, the bitmap will be tiled or copied across the surface. This presents one of the problems with using a mapped material. If the bitmap is a picture of an organic substance such as wood or grass, placing copies of the bitmap next to each other will show a seam. Figure 11.9 shows an example of a box that uses a grass material and shows a tiling error.

Figure 11.9

A box with a grass material showing a tiling error. This error results in a repetitive pattern that detracts from the quality of the rendering.

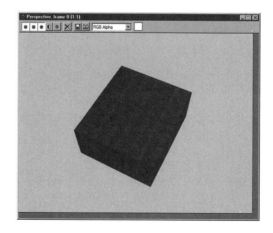

You can solve the problem presented in figure 11.9 using several different material techniques, such as blended materials and secondary mapping coordinates. But, the easiest method is to simply use a tileable bitmap. A tileable bitmap is one that when tiled across the surface of an object will not show seams. You can either purchase these as material sets from various vendors or use a program such as Photoshop to edit your material until it is tileable.

The best method for solving tiling problems is not to tile the bitmap at all. Instead, create a high resolution version that has enough detail for your scene, and place it on the object so that it only tiles once. The disadvantage to this method is that the higher resolution bitmap will require more memory and slightly more time to render.

Mapping Coordinate Types

MAX provides six different types of mapping coordinates to match the various types of geometry that you may encounter. These mapping types include: Planar, Cylindrical, Spherical, Shrink Wrap, Box, and Face. Figure 11.10 shows an example of each type of mapping coordinate.

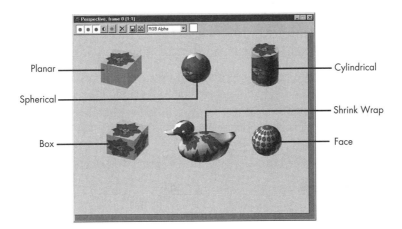

Figure 11.10

The different mapping coordinate types as applied to different types of geometry. Correctly selecting and placing mapping coordinates will add to the realism of the material on the object.

The Planar mapping type places the bitmap on the surface of an object in a planar fashion. This works well if the object is flat or relatively flat. The downside is that Planar mapping does not work in all conditions. If you apply Planar mapping to a box, for example, the mapping will look good on one side of the box but will appear stretched along the sides of the box that are perpendicular to the Mapping icon. You can get around this by rotating the Mapping icon, but then you will have a material that stretches a little across the surface of the object. In general, Planar is great if one surface of the object is showing.

Spherical mapping creates a sphere around the object and places the mapping coordinates along that sphere. Use Spherical mapping coordinates with objects that are round, or spherical, in nature such as bowling balls, golf balls, or rocks.

Use Cylindrical mapping on objects that have a cylindrical shape, such as a can or a bowling pin. The bitmap is wrapped around the vertical axis of mapping coordinates and then projected inward to the center on the ends. As an option, you may have the ends capped where a copy of the bitmap will appear on each end of the cylinder as well.

The Box mapping coordinates are just like Planar mapping but provide mapping on six sides so that you do not have the problem of stretched mapping coordinates. Box mapping is great for boxes, walls, or other objects that have the same material on all sides.

Shrink Wrap is a special mapping coordinate designed to work with highly organic shapes where cylindrical or spherical mapping isn't good enough. Imagine a sphere made of cellophane surrounding a sculpture. If you sucked all the air out of the interior of the cellophane sphere, the sphere will shrink wrap itself to the sculpture. This is how Shrink Wrap mapping works. This type of mapping is most commonly used on human or animal figures or other such complex mapping tasks.

The last type of mapping is Face mapping, which applies one copy of the bitmap to the center of each face in the object. This can be great for creating complex tiled patterns if the faces on the object are evenly spaced.

Applying the UVW Map Modifier

When you apply the UVW Map modifier to an object, Planar mapping coordinates are applied by default. If you select one of the other mapping coordinate types, the Mapping icon will change to match.

After you have applied and selected a mapping coordinate type, there are several controls that you can use. First, and most notable, is the Channel number. MAX 2 supports two sets of mapping coordinates per object. When you apply a second set, you must apply a second UVW Map modifier and set it to the other mapping channel. Then, in the Material Editor, you can set individual bitmaps to use either the first or second channel in the Coordinate rollouts. In such cases, you can have a material with a diffuse map on one set of mapping coordinates and bump mapping on the other.

Next, you can choose the type of alignment for the Mapping icon. A Cylindrical Mapping icon is generally created along the Z axis, for example, but can be set to X or Y as well. Along with the axis, there are several commands—Fit, Center, Bitmap Fit, Normal Align, View Align, and Region Fit—in the UVW Map modifier rollout that you can use to quickly position and manipulate the mapping icons.

First is Fit, which makes the Mapping icon fit the size of the selected geometry. The Center button centers the Mapping icon around the geometric center of the selected geometry. Bitmap Fit is one of the more commonly used mapping icon controls. Each bitmap has its own aspect ratio (ratio of width to height). Bitmap Fit sets the Mapping icon to match the aspect ratio of the bitmap. This prevents unnecessary scaling of the bitmap when rendered. Along the same lines is the Region Fit command, which enables you to fit the Mapping icon to a region you select with the mouse.

There are two alignment commands: View Align and Normal Align, which align the Mapping icon to either the current viewport or to the Normals of the selected object. Lastly, you can reset the Mapping icon to its original state or acquire a Mapping icon from another object that already has mapping coordinates. The Acquire command is particularly useful because it enables you to match material scaling between objects.

All of these Mapping icon controls can be adjusted interactively and represent mapping at an object level. You can also control, to an extent, mapping at a material level.

Working with Mapping Coordinates at a Material Level

When you select a bitmap for use in a material, several rollouts appear, including the Bitmap Parameters and the Coordinates rollouts. The Coordinates rollout enables you to control the mapping at a material level and apply the mapping changes to all objects with the material assigned to them.

In the Coordinates rollout, you can control the type of coordinates that the map will use. You can choose either Texture or Environmental. Texture coordinates rely upon coordinates applied to the geometry the material is assigned to. The Environmental coordinates are used when the bitmap is applied as a background or environment for your scene.

To the right of the coordinate type radio buttons is a drop-down list that enables you to select the type of texture or environmental coordinates that you will use. If you select Texture coordinates, for example, you can select to use UVW channel 1 or 2 or Planar XYZ coordinates.

The next set of parameters in the Coordinates rollout controls the position of the bitmap within the Mapping icon. Use the Mapping icon to apply, scale, and rotate the mapping coordinates onto an object. In general, by default, one copy of the bitmap appears within the Mapping icon.

You can set the offset, tiling, mirror the bitmap, set the bitmap to tile if necessary, rotate the bitmap, and blur the bitmap. All of these controls, except for map blurring, can be controlled either at the material level or at the object level through the UVW mapping modifier.

In the following exercise, you will take some of the materials you created in the last exercise and apply them to objects in the scene. Then, you will apply mapping coordinates to make the materials appear correctly on the objects.

APPLYING MAPPING TO A BOWLING PIN

1. Load the file **MF11-01a.MAX** that you created in the last exercise. This file may also be loaded from the accompanying CD.

2. Select all the Bowling Pin objects and hide all the other objects in the scene.

3. Open the Material Editor. The Bowling Pin material that you created in the last exercise should be present. Select and highlight it.

4. Expand the Maps rollout and click the Bowling Pin.tga button next to Diffuse.

5. When the bitmap rollouts appear, choose Show Map in Viewport.

6. Choose Apply Material to Selection to apply the bowling pin material.

7. Minimize the Material Editor.

8. Set the upper right viewport to a Right view. Choose Zoom Extents, and then set the shading level to Smooth and Highlights. The pins will appear with the maps showing, but the mapping coordinates generated during the lathing of the pins are incorrect.

9. With all the pins still selected, go to the Modify command panel and select UVW Map.

10. Set the Mapping type to Cylindrical and the Axis to Z. The bowling pin material should almost immediately appear on the pins as shown in figure 11.11.

    Now that the bowling pins have the material and mapping coordinates applied, you will do the same to the bowling alley.

11. Hide all of the bowling pins and unhide the Lane1 through Lane 4 objects and the Bowler Setup object.

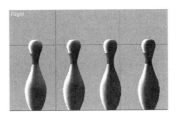

Figure 11.11

The bowling pins after applying the material and mapping coordinates.

12. Open the Material Editor and apply the Alley Wood material with Show Map in Viewport option turned on to the Lane and Bowler Setup objects. Again, these objects have mapping coordinates resulting from the modeling process.

13. Select all of the objects and apply a UVW Map Modifier. Set the mapping type to Planar.

14. Select the Sub-Object button, and then uniformly scale the Mapping icon down to 20% of its original size. You should see the results in the shaded Camera01 viewport. This is shown in figure 11.12.

Figure 11.12

The bowling alley with material and mapping coordinates applied.

15. Save the file as **MF11-01B.MAX**.

16. On your own, apply the bowling ball material and mapping coordinates to the bowling balls that are in the scene.

> If you are running MAX with the Software Z Buffer, you may notice that the material in the interactive viewport appears to be bent. This is due to a speed optimization in the SZB driver. If you right-click the viewport name and select Texture Correction, the material will appear correct but will take a little longer to redraw. If you are using a Hardware accelerator such as a Glint card, Texture Correction is not available as it is handled in the hardware of the accelerator.
>
> **NOTE**

As you can see, thanks to the interactive renderer, working with mapping coordinates is much easier than it used to be. Don't be afraid to explore and test different mapping coordinates if you feel you need to.

Working with Procedural Materials

Bitmaps are a powerful method of creating materials, but they are not the only types of maps that you can use in a material. The other types of maps are procedural maps and are mathematically generated. As such, procedural maps have several distinct advantages over bitmaps.

First, a procedural map is mathematically generated, so it uses a lot less memory. Sometimes, this is at the cost of speed. Second, procedural materials do not require mapping coordinates. You can use mapping coordinates if you want, but most of the time, procedural materials will use the world space XYZ coordinates. Take, for example, a case where you subtract a sphere out of a box with a Boolean operation. The resulting void is difficult to correctly map with UVW coordinates. But procedural maps make the object look like it was cut out of a solid.

You may use procedural maps anywhere you can apply a map to a material. You may also mix and match procedural maps with bitmaps in your scene. The application of a procedural material is the same as a bitmap, except instead of selecting the Bitmap option in the Material/Map browser, you can select any of the procedural materials with a green trapezoid next to them.

Each procedural material will have its own unique set of controls to define how the material works. A procedural wood has two color controls where a procedural gradient has three.

 NOTE   Max 2 has many procedural maps, some of which will not be covered in this book. Refer to the MAX documentation for information on procedural maps not covered in this book.

The following exercise will show how to create a procedural stucco for the bowling alley scene. You will apply this stucco as a bump map to the wall material.

CREATING A PROCEDURAL STUCCO

1. Load the file **MF11-01B.MAX** that you created in the last exercise. You can also load this file from the accompanying CD.

2. Open the Material Editor.

3. Select the Tan Flat Paint material.

4. Expand the Maps rollout and select the None button next to Bump.

5. Double-click Stucco in the Material/Map browser to select the procedural map. The Stucco rollouts will appear as shown in figure 11.13.

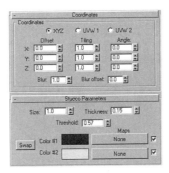

Figure 11.13

The Stucco controls where you can define how this procedural map is generated.

6. Set the Size spinner to 1.0 and leave the rest set to default parameters.

7. Choose Go to Parent.

8. Set the Bump map strength to 150.

9. Unhide all the objects in the scene and render the Camera view. You will now see stucco indentations in the walls.

10. Save the file.

As you can see from the last exercise, using procedural maps is not difficult. But, procedural maps do not provide interactive previews, so the only way to see what they look like is to render the scene, which can be a time-consuming process.

Ray-Traced Materials

The last material issue to look at is another procedural material, which is a very special material. This is the Raytraced Material. Ray tracing is a technique for tracing reflections and refractions in scenes. Normally, ray tracing is a type of rendering engine, but due to some unique programming, MAX 2 now provides ray tracing as a material. As such, it is faster than a regular ray tracer and can be selectively applied to objects in the scene.

The Raytracer comes in two forms in MAX: a ray tracing material and a ray tracing map. The map version is covered here, and you can explore the ray tracing material on you own. The map provides a simple, quick method of getting accurate reflections and refractions and is applied like any other procedural material.

The material version of the Raytracer provides numerous controls over ray tracing parameters, reflection, refraction, material properties, antialiasing, and other advanced topics. Use the material version when you need full control of reflection and refraction parameters in all parts of the material. As such, it is a fairly complex material and is considered beyond the scope of this book. Consult your MAX documentation for more information on this material.

The following exercise shows you how to apply a ray trace map to the reflection of the bowling alley to make the floors look shiny and well-oiled.

Using Raytracing to Create Reflections and Refractions

1. Load the File **MF11-01b.MAX** that you created in the last exercise. You can also load this file from the accompanying CD.

2. Open the Material Editor.

3. Select the Alley Wood Material.

4. Expand the Maps rollout and click the None button next to Reflection.

5. Select Raytrace as the map type from the Material/Map browser.

6. The default settings of the Raytracer automatically select the type of raytracing to be done. So no adjustment is necessary.

7. Choose Go to Parent.

8. Set the Reflection strength to 20. (Reflections are usually subtle additions to materials, so their strengths are relatively low.)

9. Render the Camera01 viewport to see the results shown in figure 11.14.

10. Save the file as **MF11-01c.MAX**.

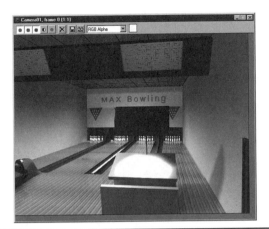

Figure 11.14

The bowling alley scene after applying several materials. Notice the reflections in the alley lanes.

This would be a good point to stop and explore applying materials to the bowling alley scene. Many objects still do not have materials and can be used to explore many of the different material features of MAX. The MAX Material Editor is an extremely powerful tool. Don't feel intimidated by it. Even experienced users are always learning new ways of creating and using materials in scenes.

Including on the accompanying CD is a file called **MF11-03.MAX** that is the bowling alley with a set of materials already applied. Several maps were created for this scene. Explore the scene to see how certain elements were created, or make changes to explore how certain material parameters work.

Conclusion

This chapter explored the power of the MAX materials system, including the use of bitmaps in materials, mapping coordinates, procedural methods, and ray tracing. Even though only a small portion of that power was uncovered here, you created several materials and added a lot of realism to the bowling alley scene. This chapter covered the following topics:

♦ What a Bitmap Is and How to Work with One

♦ Applying a Bitmap to a Material

♦ Creating and Adjusting Mapping Coordinates

♦ Using Procedural Maps in Materials

♦ Using Raytracing to Create Easy Reflective Effects

Now it is time to look at how to render the scene and generate still images. That is the focus of the next chapter.

CHAPTER 12

Exploring Rendering Techniques

Now that you have seen how to model, compose, and set up a scene for rendering, it is time to learn the ins and outs of rendering. This chapter concentrates on the techniques associated with rendering a still image. In particular, this chapter focuses on the following topics:

♦ Exploring Rendering Options

♦ Rendering Parameters

♦ The Rendering Process

♦ Virtual Frame Buffer Tools

♦ Environmental Effects

Exploring Rendering Options

In MAX, you can render any active viewport, except for a Track View viewport. You can also render any section of a viewport. You can control what you are rendering by using the three Render buttons and a drop-down list on the main toolbar (see figure 12.1).

Figure 12.1

The Render buttons on the main toolbar, where you can control what view or section of a view you are going to render.

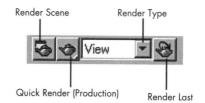

These buttons enable you to choose how and which view to render. Render Scene brings up the Render Scene dialog, where you specify which frames to render, the render parameters, and the output filename. Quick Render renders the active viewport at the current frame. Render Type enables you to specify which part of the viewport to render, and Render Last re-renders the last view you rendered with the same settings.

MAX enables you to define two sets of rendering parameters: the production settings and the draft settings. These settings are defined in the Render Scene dialog box. When you are creating or animating your scene, you may frequently want to quickly render low-quality images just to check object placement and motion. For these renders you'll want to turn off as many of the time consuming render options as possible. You may want to turn off, for example, shadows, reflections, map filtering, and motion blur in the draft settings. In the production settings, you want to specify your final production render settings. By having two sets of rendering parameters, you are less likely to forget to turn on render options when moving from draft renderings to production renderings. By clicking and holding on the Quick Render button, a flyout enables you to choose whether to perform a quick render using the draft or production settings.

In the Render Type drop-down list are four options (View, Selected, Region, and Blowup) that enable you to choose which part of the viewport to render. When starting a render using Region or Blowup, a window is displayed in the active viewport as a black dashed line. After resizing or moving this window, you execute the rendering by choosing OK in the lower-right corner of the viewport.)

To render a scene, first activate the viewport you want to render and choose the Render View button from the main toolbar to display the Render Scene dialog box, shown in figure 12.2.

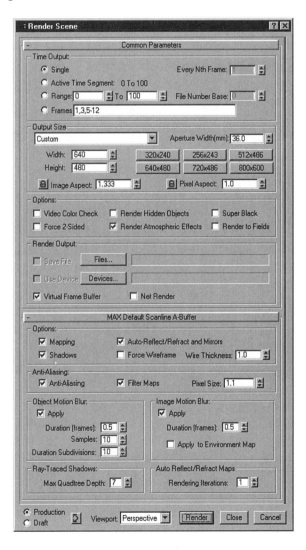

Figure 12.2

The Render Scene dialog box where you can set up rendering parameters and actually execute the rendering process.

Rendering Parameters

The Render Scene dialog box parameters shown in figure 12.2 are described here, section by section. The Render scene dialog box is divided into two rollouts: Common Parameters, which contains the rendering parameters that are independent of the rendering engine; and the rendering engine rollout, which contains the rendering parameters specific to the rendering engine. The engine shipped with MAX is the Scanline A-Buffer, and the rollout's name is MAX Default Scanline A-Buffer.

At the bottom of the Render Scene dialog box are buttons or options to switch between the Production and Draft render settings, transfer settings between the Production and Draft render settings, select the viewport to render, and start the render process.

Two complete sets of common and rendering engine-specific settings are stored by MAX. One set is called the Production settings, the other the Draft settings. Changing the settings in one set has no impact on the other. To switch between the sets, simply select the appropriate option. If you click the Transfer Settings button, you will be warned that a copy of all the settings will be transferred to the current set. If you click OK, all the current settings will be replaced.

Common Parameters

The Common Parameters rollout is divided into four areas: Time Output, Output Size, Options, and Render Output. This rollout contains the render parameters that are common to all render engines, specifying which frames to render, the size of the output images, and where to store the output images.

Time Output

The Time Output area parameters specify which frames are to be rendered. To render just the current frame of the animation, the Single option is used. To render the currently active time segment, choose Active Time Segment. To specify a contiguous range of frames, use the Range option and specify the first and last frames of the range. To render a set of individual frames or a set of ranges, use the Frames option.

When you render ranges using the Active Time Segment or Range options, you can use the Every Nth Frame spinner to determine whether to render every frame, every other frame, and so on. Often you can do this simply to test an animation.

When you render to a file using any Time Output option other than Single, the frame number is appended to the filename. For example, if you specified an output file name of **file.tga** and rendered a range of frames from 0 to 10, the output file names would be **file0000.tga** to **file0010.tga**. The File Number Base lets you specify the base file number from which the filename will increment. For example, if the Range of frames is set to 0-30, Every Nth Frame is 10, and the File Number Base is 100, the output filenames would be **file0100.tga**, **file0110.tga**, **file0120.tga**, and **file0130.tga**.

In File, Preferences, Rendering, there is an option called Nth Serial Numbering. If this option is on, file names are incremented by 1 when rendering sequences, no matter what the value of Every Nth Frame is set to. In the previous example, the output file names would be **file0100.tga** to **file0103.tga**.

Output Size

Options in the Output Size section of the dialog box enable you to set the height and width of the final image in pixels, which are single dots in the image. The higher the resolution is, the crisper the image, the longer the rendering time and the larger the output file.

The Output Type pop-up list lets you choose either Custom or one of a number of standard film or video formats.

With all output types, you can change the width or height of the image by adjusting those fields, or by clicking one of the preset rendering resolutions. You can also define your own preset by right-clicking one of the buttons, which displays the Configure Preset dialog box shown in figure 12.3. After you set the width and height, the button displays the new values.

Figure 12.3

The Configure Preset dialog box, where you can set Preset Buttons to rendering resolutions and aspect ratios you commonly use in your work.

In Custom mode, you can also set the Aperture Width of the camera, the Image Aspect ratio, and the Pixel Aspect ratio. When you choose any of the standard formats, all of these values are locked to the values associated with the standard.

Aperture Width specifies the aperture width of the camera, which alters the relationship between the Lens spinner and the FOV spinner. It has no effect on the view of the scene through the camera. Unless you are trying to match a specific type of camera, this value should not be changed.

The Pixel Aspect ratio refers to the "squareness" of a pixel on the output device. The ratio is formed by dividing the height of the pixel by its width. For computer screens and film, the Pixel Aspect is 1—the pixels are square. For other output devices, such as video, the pixels are not square and the Pixel Aspect should be set appropriately.

The Image Aspect ratio refers to the squareness of the entire image on the output device. For a Pixel Aspect ratio of 1.0, the Image Aspect ratio is the image width divided by the image height.

Both the Image Aspect and Pixel Aspect ratios can be locked to their current values by clicking their respective lock icons. If one or both of these are locked, changing the height, width, or aspect ratio fields will cause the other fields to adjust to maintain the locked values.

Options

In the Options section of the Common Parameters dialog box is a set of rendering options that are either enabled or disabled. Depending upon your preferences, these options will either be enabled or disabled by default.

If the Video Color Check option is on, MAX checks the colors of the output image versus accepted color standards for NTSC and PAL video outputs. Depending upon the preferences set in File, Preferences, Rendering (Video Color Check area), MAX will either correct any colors that are unacceptable or change them to black to warn you.

If the Render Hidden Objects option is on, hidden objects will be rendered. As you are working, you often will hide objects to make a scene easier to work on. By enabling this option, you can render these objects without having to unhide them.

The Super Black option limits how dark an object can be and is primarily used for compositing purposes. If Super Black is on, no object will be rendered darker than the Super Black Threshold value set in File, Preferences, Rendering. Areas of the image not covered by an object are unaffected by the Super Black option.

The Force 2-Sided option forces the renderer to always render both sides of a face. This is used a lot when you import geometry from other programs because most other modeling programs, such as AutoCAD, do not track face normals. Objects imported from these programs usually have their face normals pointing in different directions. Using the Force 2-Sided option is effective but increases the rendering time for each frame of an animation.

Turning the Render Atmospheric Effects option off disables the atmospheric effects to speed up test renders. Fog and other such atmospheric effects are intensive and not normally needed if you are just checking your animation.

The Render to Fields option applies only to animation and video output. See Chapter 16, "Exploring Animation Rendering Methods," for information about using this option.

Render Output

The Render Output area of the dialog box enables you to determine where the final rendered image goes. Output files can be sent to either a file or to a device. If the Virtual Frame Buffer option is selected, MAX also displays the image in a window called the Virtual Frame Buffer (VFB). Figure 12.4 shows the VFB with a rendering. The Net Render option enables you to use a network of machines to render your animation. See Chapter 16 for more information on this feature.

MAX can save to a variety of file types. You can set the file type by choosing the Files button in the Render Scene dialog box and then choose a file type from the List files of the type drop-down list. The file types most commonly used are AVI, which is used for playing back animations on a computer; JPEG, which uses a lossy algorithm to greatly compress images; and Targa, which is used for high-quality images and for images that will be used for video.

You can set up parameters for most file types. Simply choose the file type from the drop-down list and select the Setup button in the Render Output File dialog box. Figure 12.5 shows the setup dialog box for a Targa image file. The image file setup varies from file type to file type.

Before you save an image to a specific file type you can also correct the file's gamma. Gamma measures the contrast that affects the midtones of an image, and gamma correction affects the overall brightness of the image. For some output devices (such as video), gamma correction may be necessary for the image to look right. To correct the gamma, you choose the Gamma button and then change the settings in the Output Gamma Settings dialog box.

Figure 12.4

The Virtual Frame Buffer, where you can see rendered images as they are generated.

Figure 12.5

The Targa Image Control dialog box, where you can set the Targa image output options.

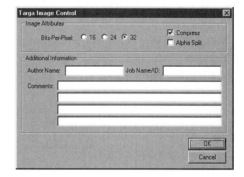

NOTE   Enable Gamma Correction must be turned on in File, Preferences, Gamma before the Gamma button can be selected in the Render Output File dialog box. The system default gamma values are also set up in File, Preferences, Gamma.

Gamma corrections are generally somewhere between 1.0 and 2.5. The higher the value is, the brighter the image. You will have to experiment with your output equipment to see whether you need gamma correction at all.

The following exercise steps you through the most common render options available in the Render Output dialog box.

EXPLORING THE COMMON RENDER OPTIONS

1. Load file **rendopt1.max** from the accompanying CD. The scene consists of a teapot sitting on a table in a room.

2. Click Render Scene and then click Render to render the scene. The Rendering dialog box is displayed, showing the phase and progress.

3. The steam from the teapot and the fog in the room are created using atmospheric effects. Click Render Scene, turn off Render Atmospheric Effects, and click Render. The scene is then rendered without the steam or fog.

4. Click Render Scene, turn on Render Hidden Objects, and click Render to render the scene. A hidden object, a banana sitting on the table, is rendered.

5. Turn Render Atmospheric Effects back on and, in the Output Size area, click the 640x480 button. Click Files, and specify an output filename of **TEST.JPG**. After specifying the filename, click Setup. In the JPEG Image Control dialog box, set Quality to 65 and click OK. Then click OK to exit the Render Output File dialog box. Click Render to render the scene. The scene is rendered at the higher resolution and the image is saved to file **TEST.JPG**.

The parameters in the Common Parameters rollout are used by MAX to determine what is to be rendered. These parameters are used no matter what rendering engine is used. The rendering engine specific parameters have their own rollout. The next section will describe the parameters associated with MAX's default render engine.

MAX Default Scanline A-Buffer

The options in this rollout are specific to the default rendering engine in MAX. If you have a plug-in rendering engine, you may see different settings here. For MAX's default renderer, this rollout is broken up into six areas: general options, anti-aliasing options, motion blur options, ray-traced shadow options, and reflection/refraction map options.

Options

The options in the Options area turn on or off different aspects of the renderer. These options are frequently turned off for draft renderings where you want to quickly render the scene to check object placement and motion. In this area, you can turn on and off texture mapping, shadow generation, and computation of automatic reflection and refraction maps. If the Force Wireframe option is on, all geometry will be rendered as wireframes, regardless of the material settings. The Wire Thickness value defines the thickness of the wires in pixels.

The following exercise takes you through the Options area.

EXPLORING THE RENDER ENGINE OPTIONS

1. Reload file **rendopt1.max** from the accompanying CD.

2. Click Render Scene and then click Render to render the scene. As you can see while performing the render, the generation of the auto reflection maps is time-consuming. Click Render Scene, turn off Auto-Reflect/Refract and Mirrors, and then render the scene. The scene is rendered without the reflections on the teapot.

3. Click Render Scene, turn off Mapping and Shadows, and render the scene. The scene is rendered without texture mapping or shadows.

4. Click Render Scene, turn on Force Wireframe, and render the scene with all objects rendered as wireframes.

Anti-Aliasing

The options in the Anti-Aliasing area control how texture maps and edges of objects are rendered. *Anti-aliasing* is the process of smoothing out edges in an image to prevent jagged or broken-up edges. When this option is disabled, the image renders faster, but the image quality suffers. Figure 12.6 shows the same scene with and without anti-aliasing, respectively. Note the breaking up of the thin helix the jagged edges on the cylinder on the left in figure 12.6, and how much smoother these areas look on the right.

Figure 12.6

A scene without Anti-Aliasing turned on (left). The same scene with Anti-Aliasing turned on (right).

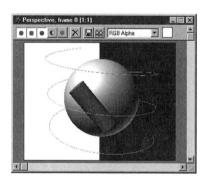 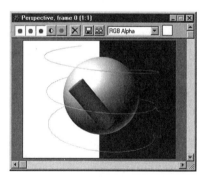

Filter Maps is the second option in the Anti-Aliasing section of the Render Scene rollout. Turning off Filter Maps disables the filtering of all bitmaps. Bitmap filtering is a memory-intensive task that slows down rendering times. Generally, unless you are doing test renders, this should always be left on because it will produce the best looking materials that use bitmaps. Figure 12.7 shows the same scene with and without bitmap filtering. Note the pixelation of the map on the cylinder, and the sharpness of the world maps when filtering is turned off.

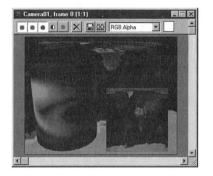 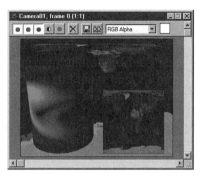

Figure 12.7

A scene with Filter Maps turned off (left). The same scene, with Filter Maps turned on (right).

The third option in the Anti-Aliasing section of the rollout is Pixel Size. Higher Pixel Size values provide extra smoothing during anti-aliasing. The effect is seen mainly along nearly vertical or horizontal edges. Valid values are from 1 to 1.5, with a default value of 1.1. The default value provides satisfactory results for most cases. If the resulting image is being blown up (for prints or film), you should try setting this to 1.5 and inspect the results. Although this setting will increase render times, the quality may be much better. Figure 12.8 shows renderings with a pixel size of 1.0 and 1.5.

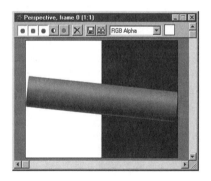 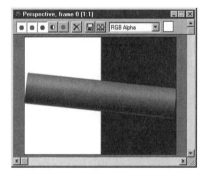

Figure 12.8

In the left scene, Pixel Size is set at 1.1. In the right scene, Pixel Size is set at 1.5.

The maximum Pixel Size value available in the Render Scene dialog box can be increased to 2 in File, Preferences, Rendering. Pixel Size values greater than 1.5, however, can cause render artifacts along edges.

The following exercise explores the Anti-Aliasing options for the render engine.

EXPLORING THE RENDER ENGINE ANTI-ALIASING OPTIONS

1. Reload file **rendopt1.max** from the accompanying CD.

2. Click Render Scene and then click Render to render the scene. Click the Clone Virtual Frame Buffer button to create a copy of the VFB.

3. Click Render Scene, turn off Anti-Aliasing, and render the scene. Compare the rendering in the VFB to the previous render. Notice the jagged edges on the objects.

4. Click Render Scene, turn on Anti-Aliasing, turn off Filter Maps, and render the scene. Compare the rendering in the VFB to the original render. Notice the graininess of the texture mapping.

5. Click Render Scene, turn on Filter Maps, increase Pixel Size to its maximum value, and render the scene. Compare the rendering in the VFB to the original render. Notice that the edges of the objects are not as sharp and, to a lesser degree, that the features on the textures are not quite as sharp.

Object and Image Motion Blur

The Motion Blur parameters control the blurring of objects that results from their motion. These parameters are used for rendering animations and are described in Chapter 16.

Auto Reflect/Refract Maps

In the Auto Reflect/Refract Maps area, you can set the number of rendering iterations to use while calculating the Auto Reflect/Refract maps. When rendering reflective surfaces, you may be able to see other reflective surfaces in the first reflective surface, and so on. The Rendering Iterations parameter controls the number of levels of reflections you can see in a single surface. The On/Off state of Auto-Reflect/Refract and Mirrors does not affect the generation of ray-traced reflections and refractions.

NOTE Flat mirrors are always rendered with only a single iteration. If, in your scene, a flat mirror will be seen in another reflection, use the Raytrace map type for the flat mirror.

The following exercise steps you through several options in the Reflection/ Refraction area of default renderer rollout.

EXPLORING THE RENDER ENGINE REFLECTION/REFRACTION OPTION

1. Load file **rendopt2.max** from the accompanying CD. The scene consists of a teapot, a sphere, and two boxes sitting on a table in a room. Automatic reflection maps have been applied to the teapot, sphere, and front faces of the boxes.

2. Click Render Scene and then click Render to render the scene. Click the Clone Virtual Frame Buffer button to create a copy of the VFB.

3. Click Render Scene, set Rendering Iterations to 2, and render the scene. Compare the rendering in the VFB to the original render, particularly at the reflection of the sphere on the teapot. In the second rendering, you can see a reflection of the teapot in the sphere's reflection, although no secondary reflection is seen in the original render. Notice that in neither render do you see a secondary reflection in the reflection of boxes' front mirrors.

Ray-Traced Shadows

The Max Quadtree Depth parameter controls the time versus memory requirements for ray-traced shadows. Higher values make the process of creating ray-traced shadows faster but take more RAM than lower values. The lower the value, the slower the ray-traced shadows are to create, but the less RAM you use. Recommended values are between 4 and 8. Below 4, the quadtree gets too small and performance suffers. Above 8, too much RAM will be used and the render speed does not increase proportionally.

The following table shows the render time and memory requirements for different Max Quadtree Depth settings in a simple scene. The default setting is 7.

Max Quadtree Depth	Render Time	MAX Memory Requirements
4	16:01 minutes	42.0 megs
5	6:06 minutes	43.0 megs
6	2:36 minutes	43.2 megs
7	1:31 minutes	43.3 megs
8	1:09 minutes	44.4 megs
9	1:04 minutes	46.2 megs
10	1:04 minutes	50.5 megs

The Rendering Process

As MAX performs a render, the Rendering dialog box is shown. This dialog box shows which phase of the rendering process is being performed, a progress bar showing how far into that phase MAX is, and a summary of the common and render-engine specific parameters.

Figure 12.9 shows a rendering in progress. At the top of the Rendering dialog box is a Pause and a Cancel button. The Cancel button is used to cancel the render operation. If a range of frames is being rendered, no further frames are rendered. The Pause button is used to temporarily pause the render operation. Because the render operation is highly CPU intensive, little CPU time is free for other applications you may be running. By pausing the render, you can work in other applications at their normal speed. When you click the Pause button, its title changes to Resume. Click this to resume the render operation.

Figure 12.9

A rendering in progress, showing the Rendering dialog box.

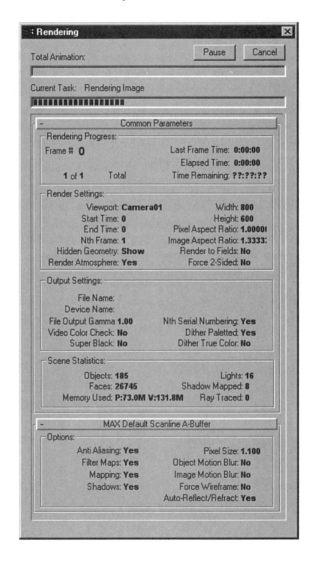

One of the most important parts of the Rendering dialog box is the Scene Statistics. These statistics tell you not only how many faces, objects, and lights are active in the scene, but also, and more important, how much memory you are using. This number is approximate and can be used to guess the amount of memory you need.

For rendering speed, it is very important that you have enough RAM to run the rendering completely from RAM. The second you start swapping to disk, speed drops dramatically. For MAX, 32 MB of RAM is an absolute minimum. For small to medium scenes, you should have 64 MB of RAM. For large scenes, greater than 300,000 faces, you should have more than 64 MB of RAM.

To see exactly how much memory MAX is using, you can use the NT Performance Monitor, which is located in the Administrative Tools program group. (Consult your NT documentation on how to use the Performance Monitor.) Add a line to the chart that shows the Memory/Committed Bytes. This line shows the amount of memory NT is using for itself and all running applications. Figure 12.10 shows an example of the Performance Monitor, showing committed bytes usage for a typical MAX session. If this number is greater than the amount of RAM in your system, you need more RAM to get the most effective use of your hardware with MAX. Figure 12.10 shows that the system is currently using 83 MB of RAM. (For more information about the Performance Monitor, consult your NT documentation.) An alternative method for displaying committed bytes is to right-click the task bar, select Task Manager from the pop-up menu, and select the Performance tab.

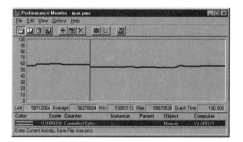

Figure 12.10

The Performance Monitor, showing committed bytes memory usage for a typical MAX session.

Multithreaded Rendering

One reason Kinetix decided to develop MAX for the Windows NT operating system was to take advantage of its multithreaded and multiprocessing capabilities. Multithreading breaks down program tasks into threads, each of which can then be executed on the next available processor. With the advent of the Pentium and Pentium Pro processors, dual and quad-processor computers are increasingly common.

Without multithreading, running MAX on a dual-processor machine is no more effective than running it on a machine with a single processor (in fact, it might even be a little slower). With multithreading, however, you will see rendering speeds that are between 1.6 and 1.9 times faster on still images, depending upon the complexity of the scene.

You can enable and disable multithreaded rendering in MAX in File, Preferences, Rendering. The check box for multithreaded rendering is in the lower-right corner and is on by default. Other than making you feel good that you bought a dual-processor machine, there is no reason to ever turn this option off.

Working with the Virtual Frame Buffer

When you render an image, you will typically output to the Virtual Frame Buffer (VFB), as well as to the output file or device. The VFB remains open after the render operation is complete, showing the results of the last frame rendered. The VFB is also used when viewing bitmap files in Materials Editor or via File, View File.

Virtual Frame Buffer Tools

Located across the top of the VFB are a set of command buttons, a drop-down list, and a color swatch, as shown in figure 12.11.

Figure 12.11

The Virtual Frame Buffer command buttons.

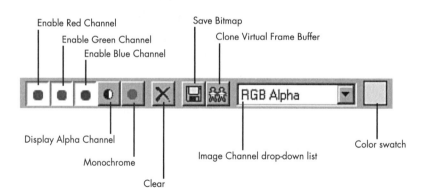

The first three buttons, Enable Red Channel, Enable Green Channel, and Enable Blue Channel, turn on and off the display of the red, green, and blue components of the image, respectively. If the button is pushed in, that color component is included in the image display. The Display Alpha Channel button causes the alpha (transparency) channel of the image to be displayed rather than the RGB channel data.

The Monochrome button displays the image in monochrome. The monochrome (or grayscale) value shown for each pixel is the average of the enabled color channel values. If all three color channels are enabled, this provides the same values used by monochrome material map channels, such as for bump or opacity maps.

The Clear button clears all values in the image. The Save Bitmap button enables you to save the image shown in the VFB to a file. The Clone Virtual Frame Buffer button creates a new VFB containing the image shown in the original VFB. Cloning a VFB is useful when you are adjusting materials or lighting by enabling you to see before and after images. To do this, render the scene, clone the VFB, modify the materials or lighting, and re-render.

The Image Channel drop-down list enables you to display additional image channels if present in the image. Typically, only the RGBA (Red, Green, Blue, Alpha) channels are present in an image. If you are outputting to an .rla file, or if the image was rendered in Video Post, additional channels may be present.

You can read the color/alpha value and coordinate location of any pixel in the Virtual Frame Buffer image. To do this, right-click and hold over the image. While the right mouse button is held down, a dialog box displays the following information about the pixel under the mouse pointer (see figure 12.12).

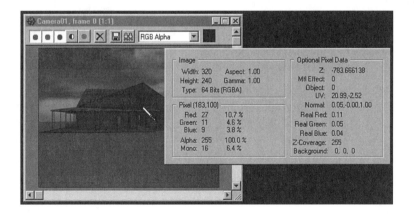

Figure 12.12

Right-clicking in the Virtual Frame Buffer shows detailed information for each pixel.

- ◆ **Image:** Displays general information about the image (Width, Height, Aspect, Gamma, and Image Type).

- ◆ **Pixel (X, Y):** For the pixel under the mouse pointer, Pixel displays the RGBA color values and the percentage of each color. Also shown is the monochrome value of the pixel.

♦ **Optional Pixel Data:** If the image contains additional information, (such as that saved in an .rla file), this area displays that information.

In addition, a color swatch in the title bar stores the color value of the last pixel you clicked. You can drag and drop this color swatch to any other color swatch in MAX, or you can click the color swatch to display the Color Selector dialog box for further detail.

Zooming and Panning the Virtual Frame Buffer

You can zoom in and out and pan the image in the VFB. You can even do this *while* a scene is rendering. To zoom in by 2, press Ctrl and left-click. To zoom out by 2, right-click. To pan the image, press Shift and left-click and drag, or use the VFB scroll bars.

If you have a three-button mouse or a Microsoft Intellimouse, you can use its third-button/wheel to zoom and pan. Roll the wheel to zoom in or out. To pan, press the wheel and drag, or drag using the middle button on a three-button mouse.

NOTE You must have the Pan/Zoom option chosen in File, Preferences, Viewports dialog box in order to use the third button for panning and zooming.

You should now have a good understanding of the rendering process and the effects of the rendering options on the rendered image. Because a full production rendering can take a significant amount of time, it is important to understand the effect of the various options on the rendering speed and image quality. Understanding these trade-offs is actually more important for rendering still images than for rendering animations. Any rendering defects are usually quite noticeable in a high-resolution still image. Animations are typically rendered at a lower resolution and object motion tends to draw the viewers' attention, making rendering defects less noticeable.

In the next section, special effects that can be rendered in the scene are described. These special effects, called environmental effects, are not based on scene geometry. Rather, they form the background against which the scene geometry is rendered, or are effects which are applied to part of or the entire scene volume.

Working with Environmental Effects

For many scenes you create, you will need to be able to simulate real-world environments so that you can create the realism and sense of space that are critical to a rendering. For example, a nighttime scene in the early spring or late fall, such as around Halloween, would greatly benefit from the use of fog to create a sense of ambiance and mood. These environments may be earthly or alien, day or night, but in all cases, careful use of environmental effects greatly enhances the realism and the overall impact of the image or animation.

This section focuses on how to create environmental effects. In particular, you will learn how to work with the following:

♦ Volumetric fog

♦ Fog

♦ Combustion

♦ Environment background

Environmental effects in MAX are accessed by choosing Environment from the Render pull-down menu. This displays the Environment dialog box, shown in figure 12.13. The dialog box is divided into three areas: Background, Global Lighting, and Atmosphere. The environment background controls in the Background section of the dialog box are covered later in this chapter.

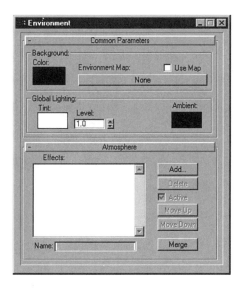

Figure 12.13

In the Environment dialog box, you can create many environmental effects.

The Global Lighting section contains the Ambient color swatch, along with two controls that globally affect all lights in the scene, except the ambient light. The Tint color swatch tints all lights in the scene by that color. Click the color swatch to display the color selector. The Level value acts as a multiplier to all lights in the scene, except ambient light. Thus, a level of 1 (default) preserves the normal light settings, whereas higher numbers raise the lighting, and lower numbers reduce the lighting.

The Atmosphere section enables you to create and add four types of atmospheric events to your rendering: Combustion, Fog, Volumetric Fog, and Volumetric Lights. Choosing the Add button in the Atmosphere section displays the Add Atmospheric Effect dialog box, in which you can add one of these four atmospheric effects. Volumetric Lights were previously described in Chapter 9, "Working with Lights and Cameras."

Volumetric Fog

Volumetric fog is similar to a volumetric light, except that the fog can permeate the entire scene or can be confined within an atmosphere gizmo. Many of the parameters for volumetric fog are the same as for volumetric lights. Volumetric fog is used instead of regular fog to give it some irregularity and make it look more realistic. When you choose this option from the list in the Add Atmospheric Effect dialog box, MAX displays the Volume Fog Parameters rollout shown in figure 12.14.

Figure 12.14

The Volume Fog Parameters rollout.

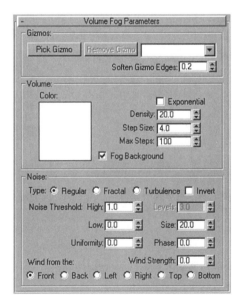

An atmospheric gizmo specifies the volume in the scene that an atmospheric effect is limited to. Atmosphere gizmos are created using the Helpers category of the Create panel, choosing Atmospheric Apparatus from the pop-up menu list. You can create gizmos in three shapes: box, cylinder, and sphere. Spherical gizmos can be created as a sphere or a hemisphere. Gizmos are created in the same way as their matching geometry types—by dragging the mouse to create the initial dimensions.

Once created, an atmospheric gizmo can be moved, rotated, or scaled. By performing non-uniform scaling on the gizmo, you can directionally stretch or compress the fog. If you scale an atmospheric gizmo up in its vertical direction, for example, you can create effects such as steam rising off of water.

The atmospheric gizmos to apply a Volume Fog to are specified in the Gizmos area of the Volume Fog Parameters rollout. If no atmospheric gizmo is specified, the Volume Fog is applied to the entire scene. When applying Volume Fog to gizmos, the fog fills the entirety of the gizmo. You can soften the fog at the edges of the gizmo so that the shape of the gizmo is not noticeable by increasing the Soften Gizmo Edges value. Normally you want the fog to apply to both the objects in the scene and the background. If you are compositing the rendered image with other images, you might want only the objects to be fogged. In this case, you should turn Fog Background off, which will prevent fogging of areas where no objects are located.

MAX renders a Volume Fog by stepping through the fog and calculating the fog intensity at each step. The number of steps evaluated is specified by the Max Steps value. In most cases, a much lower Max Steps setting can be used for Volume Fogs that are applied to atmospheric gizmos. Because the higher the Max Steps value is, the longer the render time, it is best to perform test renders starting with a low value and increasing it until the aliasing that occurs at low values disappears.

For Volume Fogs applied to a gizmo, the step size is based on the size of the atmospheric gizmo. Because Volume Fogs that are not applied to an atmospheric gizmo extend to infinity, you need to specify the Step Size for MAX to use. Again some experimentation is needed to determine the proper Step Size value to use, but an initial value can be estimated by taking the distance from the camera to the furthest object, and then dividing that distance by the Max Steps value.

The following exercise shows how to create and use volumetric fog.

Creating and Using Volumetric Fog

1. Load the file **TEMPLE.MAX** from the accompanying CD. Render the Camera viewport to see what it looks like at the moment (see figure 12.15).

Figure 12.15

The scene before adding volumetric fog.

2. Choose Rendering, Environment and select the Add button.

3. Choose Volume Fog from the Add Atmospheric Effects dialog box. Set Density to 5, Size to 10, Uniformity to 0.1, and turn on Exponential and Turbulence.

4. Render the Camera viewport. Figure 12.16 shows the rendered scene.

Figure 12.16

The scene with volumetric fog applied to the entire scene.

5. In the Helpers branch of the Create command panel, choose Atmospheric Apparatus from the drop-down list.

6. In the Top viewport, create a CylGizmo centered on the camera, and give it a radius of about 1000 and a height of 15.

7. In the Environment dialog box, click Pick Gizmo and click the CylGizmo.

8. Render the Camera viewport to see what it looks like at the moment (see figure 12.17).

    Notice that the horizon isn't fogged and it looks like a fog bank behind the temple. This is typical of fogs, which look better against a close-in background.

9. Unhide object Sky. This is half of a geosphere with its normals reversed. The sky texture is then applied to the geosphere.

Figure 12.17

The scene with volumetric fog applied to an atmospheric gizmo.

10. Decrease the CylGizmo radius to 500. In the Environment dialog box, set Density to 10, Soften Gizmo Edges to 0.5, and Max Steps to 50.

11. Render the Camera viewport. Figure 12.18 shows the final rendered scene.

Figure 12.18

The scene with the same volumetric fog, except against a backdrop object.

Volume Fog creates a three-dimensional fog in the scene. You can use Volume Fog to create fog that moves through the scene over time, and fog or clouds that you can walk or fly through. By assigning Volume Fog to atmospheric gizmos, you limit the volume of the scene to which the Volume Fog is applied.

Fog

The Fog atmospheric effect is a standard generic fog. When compared to a volumetric fog, a standard fog does not have very much in the way of noise controls to add non-uniformity and realism to the fog. Standard fog is based on the Near and Far range settings for the current camera view. In other words, Fog is view dependent. When you choose Fog from the Add Atmospheric Effect dialog box, you see the rollout shown in figure 12.19.

Figure 12.19

The Fog Parameters rollout.

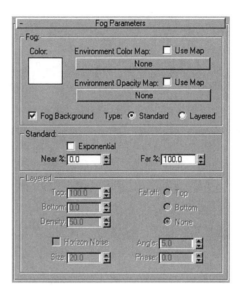

The Fog Parameters rollout is divided into three areas: Fog, Standard, and Layered. The Fog area controls the way the fog appears in the scene, regardless of fog type.

Choosing the Standard fog type activates the Standard area of the dialog box, which has only three controls. Near % sets the percentage of fog at the near camera range, Far % sets the percentage of fog at the far camera range, and the Exponential control works the same as with Volumetric Lights.

Choosing the Layered fog type activates the Layered area of the dialog box. With a layered fog, you can vary the density of the fog from top to bottom.

The following exercise shows how to create a Fog atmospheric effect.

CREATING AND USING FOG

1. Load the file **TEMPLE.MAX** from the accompanying CD. (Reload this file from scratch if you worked on the last exercise.)

2. Select the camera and, in the Modify command panel, choose Show in the Environment Ranges area.

3. Set the Near range to 70 and the Far range to 500. The fog will start at the Near range and grow progressively more dense as it approaches the Far range.

4. Choose Rendering, Environment and select the Add button.

5. Choose Fog from the Add Atmospheric Effects dialog box. In the Standard section, set Near % to 20, and Far % to 75.

6. Render the Camera viewport. Figure 12.20 shows the rendered scene.

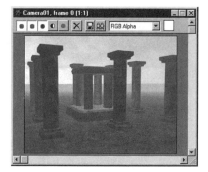

Figure 12.20

The scene, rendered with standard fog.

7. Change the fog type to Layered, set Top to 20, Density to 15, and Falloff to Top.

8. Render the Camera viewport. Figure 12.21 shows the rendered scene.

Figure 12.21

The scene, rendered with Layered fog.

In this rendering, the fog at the horizon is an abrupt, straight-edged line. Let's clean this up.

9. Turn on Horizon Noise and set Angle to 3.2. Unhide object Sky.

10. Render the Camera viewport. Figure 12.22 shows the final rendered scene.

Figure 12.22

*The scene with
the same Layered
fog, except
against a
Backdrop object.*

For further practice on your own, experiment with the Horizon Noise angle to see how increasing the angle "pushes down" the solid fog in the rendered image. Also try using either an environment or opacity map to see how it affects the fog.

In most cases, it is better to use Volume Fog applied to a Box atmospheric gizmo rather than Fog. Volume Fog provides better control over the fog generation, and you can adjust its parameters to achieve a more realistic fog effect.

Combustion

Combustion is used to produce animated fire, smoke, and explosion effects. Because there's no geometry required to produce these effects, they're virtually RAM-free and render much more quickly than would a particle system. When you choose Combustion from the Add Atmospheric Effect dialog box, you see the rollout shown in figure 12.23.

Combustion is similar to Volume Fog in that it is applied to an atmospheric gizmo. The combustion effect is constrained to the atmospheric gizmo, which can be moved, rotated, or scaled. By performing non-uniform scaling on the gizmo, you can directionally stretch or compress the combustion effect. For example, if you scale an atmospheric gizmo up in one direction, you can create a jet's exhaust.

Combustion can be used to create either fires or explosions. How the various Combustion parameters affect the Combustion effect depends on which of these you are creating. To create fires, the Explosion option in the Explosion area is turned off. To create explosions, this option is turned on.

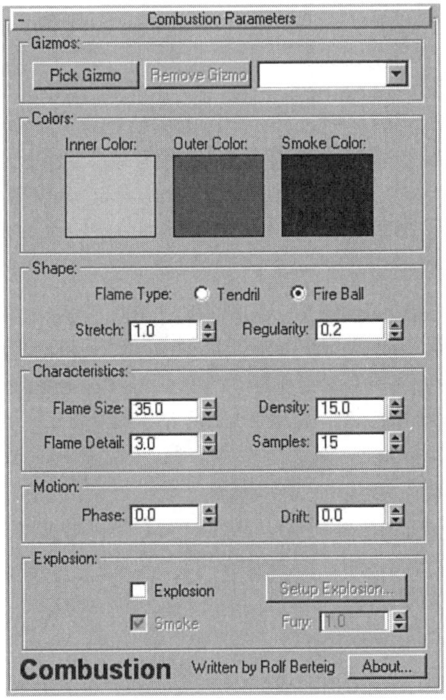

Figure 12.23

The Combustion Parameters rollout.

When Explosion is off, the color of the flame varies between the Inner and Outer colors defined in the Colors area. The flames rise based on the rate of change of the Drift value and churn based on the rate of change of the Phase value. Typical fires, such as camp fires and candles, have fairly high rates of change for the Drift value, and low rates of change for the Phase value. For pool fires (such as an oil spill), the rate of change on the Phase value would be high to give a turbulent fire.

If Explosion is turned on, the Phase value controls the timing of the explosion. An explosion has three phases that it goes through: Expansion (Phase=0 to 100), Burnoff (Phase=100 to 200), and Dissipation (Phase=200 to 300). The maximum intensity of the explosion occurs as a Phase value of 100. When Smoke is turned on, the flame colors will turn to the smoke color as the phase parameter goes from 100 to 200. The flames rise based on the rate of change of the Drift value and churn based on the Fury value.

There are two Flame Types from which you can choose in the Shape area: Tendril, in which the flames are pointy at the ends and have veins along their centers; and Fire Ball, in which the flames are more puffy and round, as if they were balls of fire. Tendrils are most often used for fire effects, whereas Fire Ball is typically used for explosions.

The length of individual flames in the gizmo is controlled by the Stretch parameter, whereas Regularity controls how parameter affects the overall shape of the fire. You can pull the flames in from the edges of the gizmo so that the shape of the gizmo is not noticeable by decreasing the Regularity value. The Stretch value is usually based on the intensity of the fire—weak fires have a low Stretch value, whereas a blazing bonfire has a high stretch value. Open fires would typically have low Regularity values whereas constrained fires, such as a fireplace, would have higher Regularity values.

The Characteristics area lets you adjust the characteristics of the flames. Flame Size specifies the size of the individual flames or tendrils. This does not affect the overall size of the effect but instead affects the characteristic appearance of the fire. Flame Detail specifies the amount of detail within the individual flames. If this parameter is low, then the flames will be smooth with little detail; larger values provide more detail. Density specifies the density or overall strength of the effect and samples specifies the rate at which the volume is sampled. Higher values give more precision and generally produce better results but at the expense of slower rendering times.

The Setup Explosion button is an aid for quickly setting up explosions. Clicking this button displays the Setup Explosion Phase Curve dialog box in which two spinner controls specify a start and end time for the explosion. After clicking OK, the existing phase curve is discarded and a new phase curve is created that represents an explosion over the specified interval. Only the Phase values are set using Setup Explosion, and the remaining parameters need to be adjusted to give the desired effect.

The following exercise uses Combustion to add jet exhausts to an airplane.

USING COMBUSTION

1. Load the file **COMBUST.MAX** from the accompanying CD. The scene consists of an airplane flying over a lake. We want to use Combustion to add the jet exhausts. Two SphereGizmos have already been created in the scene and are non-uniformly scaled to achieve the proper shape.

2. Choose Rendering, Environment and select the Add button.

3. Choose Combustion from the Add Atmospheric Effects dialog box.

4. In the Gizmos area, click Pick Gizmo and select one of the SphereGizmos in the Top viewport. Repeat and select the other SphereGizmo.

5. In the Shape area, set Stretch to 0.01 and Regularity to 0.5. In the Characteristics area, set Flame Size to 4, Flame Details to 3, and Density to 200.

6. Render the Camera viewport. Figure 12.24 shows the rendered scene.

Figure 12.24

The scene rendered with Combustion applied to the jet's exhaust.

The parameter values to be used in Combustion vary greatly, depending on the type of fire or explosion you are modeling. Typically you use an atmospheric gizmo approximating the overall shape of the fire or explosion, specify the shape of the flames as Tendrils or a Fire Ball, and specify whether a fire or explosion is being modeled. If an explosion is being modeled, the Phase values are then set to establish the timing of the explosion. Next, the colors and density are adjusted to set the overall color and brightness. Finally, the remaining parameters would be adjusted to give the flames the desired look. A lot of experimentation may be required to get the exact effect you desire.

Environment Maps

There are two places environment maps are used in MAX: the Background environment map and the Fog color and opacity maps. Environment mapping enables you to map a bitmap to the environment, rather than to a particular object. If you wanted to render your scene on top of a city background, you could use a Background environment map with screen environment mapping. Also, if you wanted to create an animation of a scene with a sky background, you could use a Background environment map with Spherical or Cylindrical environment mapping.

The mechanics of applying and using environment maps for Fog are the same as for the background. In this section, only the background environment map will be discussed, but the discussions are also applicable to the Fog environment maps.

You can use four types of mapping for environmental mapping: screen, spherical, cylindrical, and shrink wrap. Spherical mapping, for example, creates an infinitely large sphere around your scene and maps the background to the inside of the sphere. The background controls are located in the Background area of the Environment dialog box (see figure 12.25).

Figure 12.25

The image background is specified in the Common Parameters rollout of the Environment dialog box.

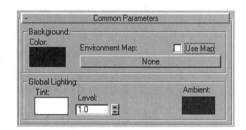

The Background controls are rather simple to use. By clicking the Color swatch, you can use the standard color picker to define a color for the background. For all areas of the rendered image where no object appears, the background color will be displayed. To the right of the Color swatch is the Environment Map button. To assign a map to the background, click the Environment Map button to display the standard material/map browser dialog box.

Because the environment map is a map, you can use any of the standard map types, such as Gradient, Bitmap, Mask, and so on. When you choose a map type, its name is displayed in the Environment Map button. To adjust the parameters associated with the map, or to assign a bitmap if the Bitmap map type is chosen, you must assign the map to a slot in the Materials Editor. You can do this by opening Materials Editor and dragging from the Environment Map button to a Material Editor slot. This will display the Instance (Copy) Map dialog box, in which you should specify to instance the map. That way any changes made to the map in Material Editor are automatically reflected in the environment map. Alternatively, you can define a map in Material Editor and drag that map to the Environment Map button. At this point, you adjust the map parameters in Material Editor in the same fashion you would adjust any other map.

If the assigned map is a 2D map (such as Bitmap, Checker, or Gradient), at the top of the Coordinates section of the rollout you will see options on whether to use Texture or Environment coordinates and which type or subset of mapping coordinates to use (see figure 12.26). For environment maps, Environment coordinates must be chosen. In the Mapping drop-down list you can choose the type of environment coordinates you are going to use. Descriptions of the four choices follow:

♦ **Spherical:** Enables you to map the environment to the inside of an infinitely large sphere. The map is applied around the sphere, and then its upper and lower edges are pulled in to the poles of the sphere. Two things to watch out for: First, be sure to use a high-resolution bitmap; otherwise, the background will look stretched and fuzzy. Second, there will always be a seam where the map starts and ends on the sphere. You should always try to keep that seam behind the camera and out of view when rendering. Both of these warnings apply also to cylindrical mapping.

♦ **Cylindrical:** Enables you to map the environment to the inside of an infinitely large cylinder instead of a sphere.

♦ **Shrink Wrap:** Enables you to map the environment to the inside of an infinitely large sphere. The map is draped around the sphere, with all four edges pulled in to one pole of the sphere.

♦ **Screen:** Enables you to map the environment directly to the view. As the view changes, the screen mapping travels along with the view. This is great for still images and can be used when you want to match your scene to a real background.

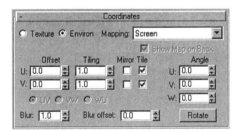

Figure 12.26

The Materials Editor Coordinates rollout with an environment map loaded.

After you have chosen the environment mapping type, the environment is set; this is the way it will render until you disable the environment mapping in the Environment dialog box. You can disable the environment map by turning off Use Map in the Background area of the Environment dialog box.

The following exercise shows you how to create an environment map.

CREATING AND USING AN ENVIRONMENT MAP

1. Load the file **TEMPLE-N.MAX** from the accompanying CD.

2. Choose Rendering, Environment from the pull-down menus.

3. Click the Environment Map button in the Background area. Double-click Bitmap in the Material/Map browser to assign it as the map type.

4. Open Materials Editor and drag from the Environment Map button to Materials Editor slot #6. In the Instance (Copy) Map dialog box, specify to Instance the map.

5. In Materials Editor, click the blank button next to Bitmap in the Bitmap Parameters rollout and load bitmap **Cloud2v.jpg**.

6. In the Coordinates rollout, make sure that Environ is selected and set Mapping to Screen. Set the W Angle to 90.

7. Render the Camera view. Figure 12.27 shows the rendered scene.

Figure 12.27

The scene with a background bitmap applied with Screen mapping.

8. In Materials Editor, change the map type from Bitmap to Cellular, discarding the old map.

9. In the Cell Characteristics area, change Size to 2 and Spread to 0.02.

10. Render the Camera view. Figure 12.28 shows the rendered scene.

Figure 12.28

The scene with a Cellular map applied as a background.

Environment maps are useful for assigning fixed or animated backgrounds to your scene. This can reduce the amount of modeling required to duplicate the background or allow the use of "real-world" images in the background. If the background objects in a scene aren't affected by the foreground objects, the background objects can be rendered to an image, which can be used as the background. This can also significantly reduce rendering time.

Perspective Matching

Perspective matching makes use of a screen-environment mapped background and the camera's horizon line to match the perspective of your scene to the background. This is done when you want to render your scene into a photograph or other such background. Architects often use this feature to render buildings into the site context. For best results, and to decrease rendering time, always try to use background bitmaps that are the same size and resolution as your final output.

After you have set up the environment map, use a shaded view of your Camera viewport to perform the perspective match. In this shaded view, you can turn on the background and use the camera controls to change the Camera view to match the perspective of the background. To turn on a background image, choose Views, Background Image, which displays the dialog box shown in figure 12.29.

In the Background Source section, choose Use Environment Background to use the same bitmap that you are using as the screen environment map. Alternatively, if you want to be able to zoom in and pan on a bitmap background in orthographic viewports, click Files and select the bitmap file being used as a background. In the Aspect Ratio area, turn on Match Bitmap and turn on Lock Zoom/Pan.

Figure 12.29

The Viewport Background dialog box where you can select a bitmap or a map to appear in the background of a viewport for perspective matching.

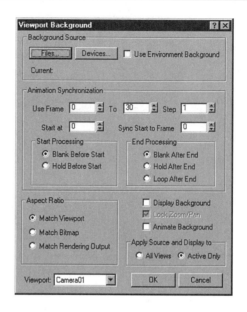

 NOTE   You can zoom in and pan on a bitmap in Perspective and Camera viewports, but you need to use virtual viewports to do so. See the MAX documentation for information on virtual viewports.

To turn on the background display in the viewport, turn on Display Background at the bottom right of the Viewport Background dialog box. When you choose OK, the image is displayed as the background of the current viewport.

The following exercise shows how to create and use perspective matching.

CREATING AND USING PERSPECTIVE MATCHING

1. Load the file **BACKGROU.MAX** from the accompanying CD.

2. Choose Rendering, Environment. Assign bitmap **LAKE_MT.JPG** as the background environment map and set the environmental mapping type to Screen.

3. Close the Environment and Material Editor dialog boxes.

4. Click the Camera viewport name to activate it, if it is not already active.

5. Choose Views, Background Image, and turn on Use Environment Background and Display Background.

6. Select the camera and, in the Modify command panel, turn on Show Horizon option for the camera. A line will appear in the Camera viewport, as shown in figure 12.30.

Figure 12.30

The horizon line is visible in the viewport.

7. Activate the Camera viewport if it is not active.

8. Choose Orbit Camera from the viewport control buttons.

9. Click and drag around in the viewport until the horizon line matches the shoreline in the background image, then release the mouse button.

10. Render the Camera viewport. Figure 12.31 shows the final rendering.

Figure 12.31

The final perspective-matched rendering.

Perspective matching enables you to set up the camera so that the ground plane associated with the objects in your scene matches that of the background image. Special effects that show objects in the scene interacting with the background image can be accomplished with "shadow catchers," created by assigning Matte/Shadow materials to objects in the scene, and using the Camera Mapping modifier to apply mapping to objects that matches the background image mapping.

Conclusion

Rendering and output are important issues in MAX, and they will grow familiar as you work with MAX. Environmental effects are important to creating ambiance and mood in certain scenes. Backgrounds are necessary to provide an extra hint of realism to most renderings or animations. Making use of these tools will greatly enhance not only your skills, but your overall output quality. This chapter taught you the following:

♦ Common Rendering Parameters

♦ Multithreaded Rendering

♦ Working with the Virtual Frame Buffer

♦ Creating and Rendering a Scene

♦ Working with Environmental Effects

This concludes the fundamentals on composition and rendering. While you have learned the basics here, there is much more to learn. This learning will come with experience. Practice these tools, as they are the most important tools in producing a rich, powerful rendering.

Now that you have seen all the basic elements involved in creating still-image renderings, it is time to move on to animations.

PART

IV

ANIMATION
FUNDAMENTALS

13

Understanding Animation Concepts

Up to this point, you have explored numerous features of MAX: the user interface, modeling, editing, composition, materials, rendering, and environments. But these are only part of what MAX brings to you. One of the most powerful features of MAX is its capability to animate almost any geometry, light, camera, or modifier.

This chapter examines the basics of computer animation in MAX. In this chapter, you will learn about the following topics and how they apply to animating with MAX:

- ◆ What Can Be Animated in MAX

- ◆ Animation Basics

- ◆ Advanced Animation Topics

The rest of the chapter discusses the basic and advanced concepts of animation in relation to 3D Studio MAX. You will read about practical application of these concepts in the next several chapters.

What Can Be Animated in MAX

You can animate all object, sub-object, and gizmo transforms in MAX, as well as most object, modifier, material, and atmospheric effect parameters. In Video Post, you can animate the Blend parameter in the Negative filter, as well as most parameters in the Lens Effects filters. Parameters that you cannot typically animate are time-related parameters (such as the detonation time in the Bomb space warp and the start and life parameters in the particle systems) and space warp and particle system icon sizes. On/off or multiple choice options in the command panels are sometimes animatable, sometimes not.

The easiest way to discover which parameters you can animate is to create the object, apply the modifier, or create the material, and then display all the tracks for the object, modifier, or material in Track View. Track View, which will be described in Chapter 14, "Exploring Basic Animation Methods," will show all the animatable parameters available by name.

Another way to discover whether a parameter that has a spinner is animatable is to turn on the Animate button and adjust the spinner. If a red bracket appears around the spinner, the parameter is animatable.

Animation Basics

In this section, you will be introduced to concepts associated with basic animation. As you become familiar with the more basic animation concepts and methods, you will find it easier to perform your job as an animator. The concepts covered include understanding controllers and understanding time in computer animation.

Understanding Controllers

Whenever you create animation in MAX, an animation controller is assigned to each animated parameter for the objects. These controllers store the data associated with the animation. There are four basic types of controllers:

♦ Key-based controllers

♦ Procedural controllers

♦ Compound controllers

♦ System controllers

The following sections describe the basic differences between these four controller types. The various controllers themselves will be described in Chapter 14 and Chapter 15, "Exploring Other Animation Methods."

Key-Based Controllers

The most common method used for creating animation is keyframing. *Keyframing* is a process whereby objects are positioned at critical frames and someone—or in the case of MAX, something—fills in between the critical frames. A *keyframe* is any frame of an animation in which a specific event is supposed to occur. The frames between keyframes are called *in-betweens*, or *tweens*.

Keyframing in MAX works by setting the current frame of the animation to the desired time, turning on the Animate button (which tells MAX that the following changes are to be animated over time), and creating the Keyframe event. In MAX, the Keyframe event can be not only a change in the transform (Position, Rotation, or Scale) of an object, but also a change in any of its animatable parameters. The new value for the transform or parameter is stored by an animation controller assigned to the object's transform or parameter in a *key*.

Let's say, for example, that you want to create an animation of a cylinder bending 90 degrees over 30 frames. You would first create a cylinder and apply a Bend modifier. You would then move to frame 30, turn on the Animate button, and change the Bend modifier's Angle parameter to 90. At this point, MAX will assign a controller to the Angle parameter, create a key at frame 0 to store the initial Angle value, and then create another key at frame 30 to store the new Angle value. If you play back or render the animation, the cylinder will smoothly bend 90 degrees over the 30 frames.

You can tell if an object has a position, rotation, or scale key at a specific frame because a white bounding box will appear around the object. For other parameters, a red bracket will appear around the parameter's spinner if a key for it exists at that frame.

MAX ships with a variety of key-based controllers. Examples of these are the Bézier, Linear, and Smooth controllers. Each of these controllers stores the animation data in keys. The difference between the controllers is how the output values between keys (the tween values) are calculated.

Procedural Controllers

Procedural (or parametric) controllers do not store keys; rather, their output is based on initial data values supplied by the user and the equation the controller implements. Procedural controllers enable you to create motions or effects that would be difficult or tedious to create using key-based controllers, such as attaching an object to the animated surface of another object, having an object travel along an existing spline, or having a light blink on and off in a complex periodic fashion. Examples of procedural controllers are the Surface, Path, and Waveform controllers.

Compound Controllers

Compound controllers simply combine the output of a set of controllers and output the results in a format that MAX expects. An example of a compound controller is the Position/Rotation/Scale (PRS) controller. The PRS controller takes as inputs the output of individual Position, Rotation, and Scale controllers and outputs to MAX the transform matrix for the object. Other compound controllers include the Look At, List, and Euler XYZ controllers.

System Controllers

Although the previous controllers all control a parameter or transformation of a single object, system controllers control multiple aspects of multiple objects. Typically, although the parameters associated with the system can be animated, the parameters or transforms of the individual objects cannot be animated. In those cases where the individual object transforms can be animated, the system controller still maintains control over these transforms and can limit the transforms to meet the requirements of the system. Examples of system controllers are the new Bone IK controller, the Sunlight controller, and the Biped portion of Character Studio.

As previously described, keys store the data values for a parameter at a particular point in time. In MAX, as with most animation packages, time is not continuous but rather is defined in small discrete chunks.

Understanding Time in Computer Animation

Time is one of the most important elements to understand when learning about computer animation. Computer animation is achieved by displaying a series of individual frames at a speed fast enough to create the illusion of motion. This is the same principle used in simple hand-drawn animation, film, and television.

In general terms, animation playback is not considered smooth unless you can achieve a speed of at least 20 frames per second (FPS), but the actual speed for which you will design your animation depends on what medium you use to record the animation. The film industry, for example, has standardized on 24 FPS, whereas 30 FPS is the standard for video in the United States.

MAX supports three standard frame rates—two for video and one for film—and a user-defined custom frame rate. The three standard frame rates are:

♦ **NTSC:** Stands for the National Television Standards Committee and is the standard for television broadcast in the United States and Japan. The frame rate for NTSC is 29.97 frames per second.

Although the true NTSC frame rate is 29.97 frames per second, MAX uses a frame rate of 30 FPS when the NTSC frame rate option is selected. The difference between MAX's and the actual NTSC frame rate is one frame in 33.33 seconds, or about one second in 1,000 seconds. Although this should not normally affect you, you need to be aware of this if you are lip synching or need the animation to have a specific duration.

♦ **PAL:** Stands for Phase Alternate Line and is the standard for television broadcast in most European countries. The frame rate for PAL is 25 frames per second.

♦ **Film:** The frame rate for film is 24 frames per second.

MAX enables you to set the overall playback speed of the animation to any of these standards or to any frame rate you want. After you have set this information, you can display and work with time in MAX as frames, minutes and seconds, or fractions of seconds.

Advanced Animation Topics

In this section, you will be introduced to concepts associated with more advanced animation methods and techniques. As you become familiar with the more basic animation methods, you will start to run into situations where these techniques will make it easier to perform your job as an animator. The techniques covered are the following:

- ♦ Trajectories

- ♦ Ghosting

- ♦ Pivot points

- ♦ Links and chains

- ♦ Skeletal deformation

- ♦ Morphing

- ♦ Space warps

- ♦ Character animation

- ♦ Motion blur

- ♦ Dynamics

Trajectories

When you create animations in MAX where the position of the objects are changing, the object motions can be thought of as *trajectories* or motion paths. Trajectories are usually a line such as a Bézier spline, which passes through each keyframed position. As described earlier, the trajectory between the keyframes is a function of the controller being used. The controller affects the curvature of the trajectory and how fast the object moves between the keyframes. By viewing an object's trajectory, you can see how the object will be moving and detect any unexpected motion resulting from how the controllers interpolate the motion between keyframes. MAX provides the ability to display object trajectories from the Motion and Display command panels (see the "Trajectories" section in Chapter 14). Figure 13.1 shows the trajectory for a sphere whose position is animated over time.

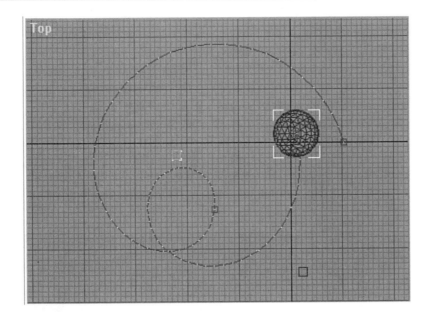

Figure 13.1

Trajectories show the motion path of an object as a line in the viewports.

Ghosting

Ghosting is a method of displaying wireframe or shaded "ghost" copies of an animated object at a number of frames before and after the current frame. Although showing an object's trajectory shows how the object is moving over time, ghosting will give you "snapshots" of what the object looks like over time. These snapshots show the effect of any object's rotation and scaling, as well as the effect on the object of any modifiers or space warps. Ghosting is particularly useful in character animation, where it gives you a sense of the timing of the character's motion. MAX provides the ability to display object ghosts from the Views menu option, with ghosting options being set in File, Preferences, Viewports. Figure 13.2 shows three frames of ghosting before and after the current frame for a character.

Figure 13.2

Ghosting shows snapshots of an object at frames before and after the current frame.

Pivot Points

Every object you create in MAX has an associated *pivot point*. Think of the pivot point as the anchor point of the object. As you move, rotate, or scale an object, these transforms are applied to the pivot point, and then the transform is passed on to the object geometry. The practical effect of this is that if you are rotating or scaling an object, the object geometry is rotated or scaled relative to the pivot point. Figure 13.3 shows two boxes, and ghosts of the boxes, which have identical rotation and scaling but different locations for their pivot point. The location of the pivot point for the top box is located at the center of the box (as indicated by the axes tripod), and the pivot point for the bottom box is located at its left-hand edge.

As can be seen from the ghosts, the rotation and scaling on the two objects are applied relative to pivot points. The effect is useful when animating both mechanical objects and characters. In both cases, you should locate the pivot points at the joint location. You can even move the pivot point away from the object, making it appear that the object is rotating about another object. You can adjust the pivot point location and orientation in the Hierarchy command panel (see the "Working with Hierarchies" section in Chapter 15).

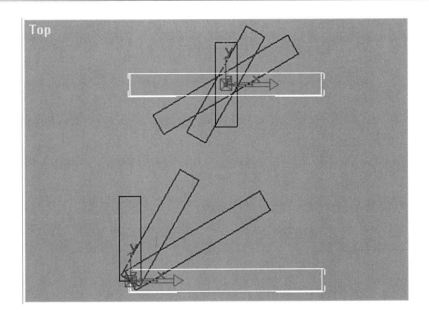

Figure 13.3

The location of an object's pivot point affects how the rotation and scale transforms are applied to the object geometry.

Links and Chains

Clearly, adjusting the pivot point of an object is of great benefit when you are animating a single object. But there are other times, especially in character or mechanical modeling, when you want to animate an object by transforming it, and have other objects repeat the same transform. If, for example, you rotate the upper arm of a character, you want the lower arm, hand, and fingers to move along with the upper arm, as they would in real life. Although you can manually keyframe their motion, this would quickly become tedious and frustrating.

The solution here is to link one object to another and form a hierarchical chain. The linked object becomes the child and the object linked to becomes the parent. You can build entire chains of linkages this way, with the restriction that a child can have only a single parent. You perform object linking using the Link tool, described in the "Working with Hierarchies" section in Chapter 15.

When you transform a portion of a linked chain, the transform can be propagated in two directions: up the chain or down the chain. If the transform is being propagated down the chain, forward kinematics is being applied. If the transform is being propagated up the chain, inverse kinematics is being applied. Figure 13.4 shows two arms and their ghosts. The top arm was animated by rotating the upper arm and uses forward kinematics. The bottom arm was animated by repositioning the hand and uses inverse kinematics.

Figure 13.4

Forward kinematics propagates motion down a linked chain, whereas inverse kinematics propagates motion up a linked chain.

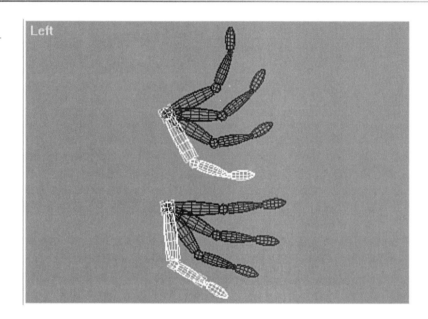

Forward Kinematics

With forward kinematics, when you transform a parent object, any children objects are transformed along with the parent. The effect is as if a rigid bar had attached the child's pivot point to the parent's pivot point. If you move the parent, the child will also move so that its position relative to the parent remains constant. If you rotate the parent, the child will both move and rotate such that the position and orientation of the child relative to the parent remains constant. This can be seen in the top arm in figure 13.4, where, as the upper arm was rotated, the lower arm and its children were moved and rotated to remain fixed relative to the upper arm.

Although the children are being rotated and moved as the parent is transformed, transform keys are not being generated for the children. By linking the objects, you have told MAX to perform these transforms automatically.

Forward kinematics affects only the children of an object. If you select and move an object in the middle or at the end of a chain, that object will move away from its parent object.

Inverse Kinematics

With inverse kinematics (IK), you transform a child object, and MAX calculates the position of the parent objects. Other than the fact that the motion is being propagated up the chain rather than down the chain, the other main difference between forward and inverse kinematics is that there is only one possible result from forward kinematics, whereas multiple results are possible from inverse kinematics. The final position of the parents is called the IK solution. This solution is based on the motion of the object transformed and the joint constraints applied to the object and its parents.

In the bottom arm shown in figure 13.4, joint constraints were applied to each object to ensure that the objects would not move away from one another, and to ensure that the joints only rotated about the appropriate axes. After activating IK, the hand was then moved. While the hand was being moved, MAX calculated the IK solution in real time, showing the position of each of the objects in the arm.

If you selected and moved the lower arm, both forward and inverse kinematics would be applied; forward kinematics would be applied to the hand and inverse kinematics to the upper arm.

Further details on inverse kinematics is provided in the "Basics of IK" section in Chapter 15.

Skeletal Deformation

For the arms shown in figure 13.4, the upper arm, lower arm, and hand are all separate objects. If the arm were a single object, then there obviously wouldn't be any way to set up a linkage to achieve the desired motion of the arm.

If you wanted to deform an object such as an arm that is modeled as a single mesh, a method called skeletal deformation is commonly used. A skeleton is constructed beneath the object and is animated. The mesh is then attached to the skeleton using a skeleton deformation modifier or space warp. This modifier or space warp takes the movement of the skeleton and deforms the mesh of the object to match.

MAX does not ship with a Skeletal Deformation tool, although you can simulate simple skeletal deformation using some MAX tools such as Linked XForms. The two available plug-ins that provide more skeletal deformation are the Physique portion of Character Studio and Bones Pro for MAX.

Morphing

Morphing is a method you can use to create an animated mesh by transforming one object into another over time. To morph, you establish two or more target objects and set keyframes that specify the percentage influence of each target object at that time. The resulting morph object is based on the relative position of the targets' vertices from the targets' pivot points and the percentage influence of the target objects. One restriction when using morphing is that each object must contain the same number of vertices, and the vertices in each target must be created in the same order. In practical applications, one initial morph target is usually created, and then the remaining targets are created by cloning the initial target and editing the clones at the sub-object level.

Morphing is a handy tool for detailed and fluid animation of objects. A common application is for facial animation, where targets are made representing different facial expressions using sub-object editing for skeletal deformation. The animator then can combine the different targets with varying influence levels to achieve fluid movement and unique facial expressions. An example frame from a facial animation using morph targets is shown in figure 13.5.

Morphing is described in more detail in the "Animating Using Morphing" section in Chapter 15.

Figure 13.5

Morphing enables you to combine several target objects to form a new, unique object.

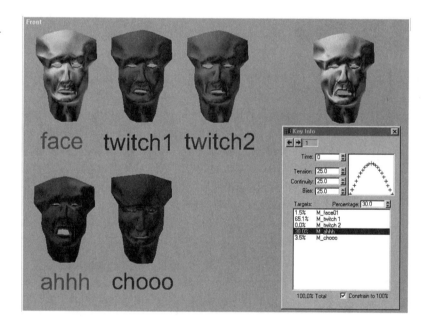

Space Warps

Space warps are a means of defining an area in 3D space that has an automatic effect on selected objects passing through its influence. Only objects bound to the space warp are affected by the space warp. The difference between a modifier and a space warp is that a modifier always has the same effect on an object no matter where the object is located, whereas the effect a space warp has on an object is dependent on the location and orientation of the object relative to the space warp. Depending on the type of deformation selected, the object may respond to gravity effects, become wavelike, disintegrate, or change its path. Figure 13.6 shows an example where the text is deformed along a spline and a wave is applied to a box.

Space warps make it easier to cause certain effects to occur on cue, such as having an object shatter as it strikes a floor, or to apply external forces to particle systems. Further details on using space warps is provided in the "Using Space Warps" section in Chapter 15.

Figure 13.6

Space warps deform objects based on the location and orientation of an object relative to the space warp.

Character Animation

The goal of *character animation* is to provide a sense of life and personality to a character. The character can be not only a human or animal model, but any object. As Buzz Lightyear would say, "Character animation is moving with style." In television commercials and in films, we have seen dancing cars, gas pumps, and cereal boxes. What makes the objects appear alive is not how they look, but how they move.

In fact, performing character animation for an "inanimate" object is easier than for a human or animal. Because the viewer does not have any preconceived notions of how the inanimate object would move if it were indeed alive, you have the freedom to have the object move as you want. After a lifetime of observing the movement of humans and animals, the viewer will quickly detect nonlifelike movement associated with these types of models.

Generally, you will base how a character would move on how you would perform the same motion. The use of full-length and hand-held mirrors allow you to see how you would perform the motion both overall and in detail. Using a camcorder and a stopwatch to record yourself performing the motion, you can identify "keyframes" and the timing between those keyframes.

Motion Blur

If you take a picture of a fast moving object, you will notice that the edges of the object are not sharp and that the position of the object appears to be spread out. This is a result of the object being in one position when the shutter opens and in another when the shutter closes. The image captured on film is actually of the object in all of its positions between the opening and closing of the shutter.

The use of *motion blur* in MAX approximates this effect. In still images rendered with motion blur, fast moving objects are blurred more than slower-moving objects, giving an impression of the relative speeds. In playback of animated sequences, motion blur provides a smoothness of motion that is not present if motion blur were not applied. Figure 13.7 shows a rendering of two bowling pins that each have the same motion. One pin was rendered with motion blur, the other without.

Figure 13.7

A rendering of two bowling pins that each have the same motion. The right pin was rendered with motion blur, the left pin without.

Three different types of motion blur are available in MAX and are described in the "Motion Blur" section in Chapter 16, "Exploring Animation Rendering Methods."

Dynamics

The term *dynamics*, as used in MAX, refers to a system of controls used to produce animation that simulates real-world physics. Using dynamics allows the animator to create virtual environments where realistic object movements can be achieved based on the object's physical properties and the forces acting on the object. You can, for example, create a scene representing a bowling alley and set up the scene for dynamics by selecting the objects to be included in the dynamics simulation, defining the object properties, defining which object collisions to detect, and applying an initial motion on the bowling ball. The dynamics system then uses this information to calculate and generate keys for the position and rotation of each object in the dynamic simulation over a range of frames.

There are two types of dynamics: rigid-body and soft-body. In rigid-body dynamics, when objects change their velocity or collide with another object, the objects are not deformed. With rigid-body dynamics, if a sphere hits another object, the sphere will remain spherical. The dynamics utility shipped with MAX is a rigid-body dynamics package, described in the "Working with Dynamics" section in Chapter 15. In soft-body dynamics, when objects change their velocity or collide with another object, the objects can deform based on their physical properties. With soft-body dynamics, if a sphere hits another object, the sphere will be squashed. HyperMatter, a plug-in for MAX, implements soft-body dynamics.

Conclusion

This chapter described the fundamentals of computer animation upon which the following chapters will build. From this chapter, you should have a basic understanding of the following terminology and techniques:

◆ Basic Animation Controllers Types

◆ Animation Frame Rates

◆ Using Ghosting and Trajectories as Animation Aids

◆ Forward and Inverse Kinematics

◆ Object Deformation Using Skeletal Deformation, Morphing, and Space Warps

♦ Character Animation

♦ Motion Blur

♦ Hard- and Soft-Body Dynamics

Although this was only an overview, you should now have an understanding of the basic animation concepts and how they are applied in MAX. In the following chapters, you will delve into the methods and techniques of animation in MAX.

C H A P T E R 14

Exploring Basic Animation Methods

In Chapter 13, you were introduced to the basic types of animation controllers and learned how to set and control time in MAX. This chapter builds upon those concepts to create and adjust animations. The following topics are covered:

♦ Configuring Time in MAX

♦ Creating Basic Keyframed Animations

♦ Viewing and Moving Keys in Track View

♦ Viewing and Working with Function Curves in Track View

♦ Working with Different Controller Types

♦ Procedural and Compound Controllers and Their Uses

♦ Advanced Track View Controls

Configuring and Moving Through Time in MAX

In this section, you will learn how to configure and move through time in MAX, and how to use the interactive renderer to help you create your animations. The following MAX tools are covered:

♦ Using the Time Configuration dialog box

♦ Using the Time Controls

♦ Working with the Interactive Renderer

♦ Previewing Animations

Using the Time Configuration Dialog Box

All animation time in MAX is configured through the Time Configuration dialog box (see figure 14.1). This dialog box is accessed either by clicking on the Time Configuration button or right-clicking on any animation playback button. The frame rate, time display, playback options, key step options, and the start and end of the active time segment are configured and controlled through this dialog, where you also can rescale the amount of time in the active time segment.

Setting the Frame Rate

MAX provides three predefined frame rates and enables you to define your own custom frame rate. The three cover the standard frame rates used for video and for film. If the Custom frame rate is selected, you can adjust the FPS spinner to set the frame rate.

Internally to MAX, all time-related data is stored in a unit of measure called *ticks*. Each second is divided into 4,800 ticks. The number of ticks per frame varies, based on the frame rate. This feature ensures that even as you change the frame rate, the length of the animation in seconds remains constant. You can create an animation of a given duration for television, and then output for film with the same duration by simply changing the Frame Rate to Film. If you had a 30-second animation developed for video at 30 FPS, for example, the total number of frames would be 900. If you then changed the frame rate to Film (at 24 FPS), the length of the animation would still be 30 seconds, but the new frame count would be 720.

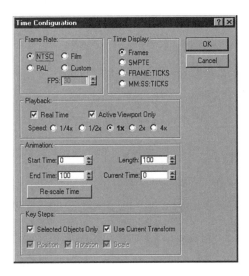

Figure 14.1

The Time Configuration dialog box is where you can define the length, playback rate, and time display format for the active time segment.

Setting the Time Display

The Time Display options control how time is displayed on the Time Slider and in any dialog box where you change the current time of the animation. Each of these options is described in the following list:

♦ **Frames:** Displays time as frames.

♦ **SMPTE:** Stands for the Society of Motion Picture and Television Engineers. This option displays time as Minutes:Seconds.Frame.

♦ **Frame:Ticks:** Displays time as frames, followed by the tick offset from the frame. For a frame rate of 30, each frame contains 160 ticks. Thus you would display the time and control the animation at a resolution of 1/160 of a frame.

♦ **MM:SS:Ticks:** Displays time as minutes and seconds, followed by the tick offset from the second.

Changing the Playback Options

Two Playback options are available in the Time Configuration dialog box: Real Time and Active Viewport Only. If the Real Time option is chosen, MAX tries to play back the animation in the viewport at a user-specified multiple of the given frame rate. MAX will skip frames of the animation if it is unable to maintain this frame rate. To see all frames in the viewport playback, turn off this option.

If the Active Viewport Only option is chosen, viewport playback will occur only in the active viewport. If this option is off, playback will occur in all viewports.

Changing and Re-scaling Animation Time

The Start Time and End Time fields enable you to change the length of the active time segment. The active time segment is the time range you can move within by using the Time Slider and the animation playback buttons. When you change the Start Time, End Time, or Length in the Time Configuration dialog box, only the definitions of the begin and end points of the active time segment are changed. The time associated with any keys in the animation does not change.

The Re-scale Time button brings up the Re-scale Time dialog box, where you can re-scale the current time segment. MAX re-scales the time segment by stretching or shrinking the time between animation keys within that segment. Any animation keys that occur either before or after the current time segment are moved earlier or later in time, depending on whether you adjust the Start Time or the End Time. Any time-related parameters are also affected. For example, parameters in the particle systems include the start time and life of the particles. The time value for these parameters will be scaled appropriately.

NOTE Depending on the current frame rate and the percentage reduction or increase in the time segment, the re-scaled animation keys might not be placed on a frame boundary, but rather might have a tick offset within the frame. In such a case, if you are in Frames or SMPTE time display mode and use the Key Mode Toggle button to step through the animation keys on an object, MAX will automatically switch the Time Display either to Frame:Ticks or MM:SS:Ticks to display the exact timing of the key.

Changing the Key Steps Options

The Key Steps options are used in conjunction with the Key Mode Toggle button and the Previous Key and Next Key buttons discussed in the next section. When the Selected Objects Only option is chosen, MAX will jump to the previous or next frame containing a transform (position, rotation, scale) key for the selected object only. If this option is off, MAX will jump to the previous or next frame containing a transform key for any object in the scene. Which transform keys are searched for depends on the setting of the Use Current Transform option.

If the Use Current Transform option is chosen, MAX will only jump to frames containing a transform key of the same type as the current transform that is selected in the toolbar. If the Use Current Transform option is off, the Position, Rotation, and Scale options at the bottom of the dialog box are enabled, and you can specify which types of transform keys MAX will jump to.

In the following example, you will use the time configuration tools to change the length of an animation.

CHANGING THE LENGTH OF AN ANIMATION

1. Load the file **anim-k-d.max** from the accompanying CD.

2. Access the Time Configuration dialog box either by clicking on the Time Configuration button or right-clicking on any animation playback button.

3. The current time display is SMPTE, the Frame Rate is NTSC, and the length of the animation is 4 seconds. Switch between the different frame rates and notice that the length of the animation remains at 4 seconds.

4. Change the Time Display to Frames and again switch between the different frame rates. Notice that the length of the animation in frames changes as you switch between frame rates.

5. Change the Time Display back to SMPTE and click on Re-scale Time. In the Re-scale Time dialog, change Length to 2 seconds and click on OK. The total length of the animation is now 2 seconds. If you play back the animation now, the animated changes in the scene will happen twice as fast.

6. Change the End Time to 4 seconds. If you play back the animation now, the animated changes in the scene will still occur over the first 2 seconds and then stay constant over the remaining 2 seconds.

Using the Time Controls

The Time controls are used for creating animation and moving between frames in an animation. The Time Slider, Animate button, and animation playback buttons are located in the lower portion of the main MAX window, as shown in figure 14.2.

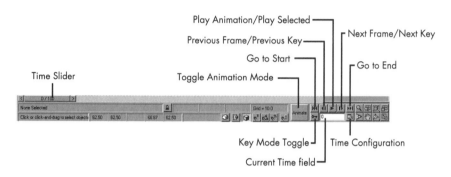

Figure 14.2

The Time Slider and animation playback buttons, where you control the interactive playback of animations in the viewports.

The Time Slider displays the current frame or time of the animation, as well as the overall number of frames or amount of time in the active time segment. By positioning this slider with the mouse, you define the current frame or time. The small arrow keys on either side of the Time Slider duplicate the function of the Previous Frame/Previous Key and Next Frame/Next Key buttons, which are described soon.

The Animate button toggles MAX in and out of Animation mode. When MAX is in Animation mode, changes to any animatable parameter or object transform cause an animation key to be generated. You know MAX is in Animation mode when the current viewport is outlined in red, and the Animate button turns red.

TIP For an even more blatant indication that the system is in Animation mode, add the following two lines to your **3dsmax.ini** file:

```
[RedSliderWhenAnimating]
Enabled=1
```

When Enabled is set to 1, the Time Slider background turns red whenever Animation mode is on. When Enabled is missing or is set to 0, the background color of the Time Slider does not change.

To the right of the Animate button is a series of buttons that enable you to move through time and control the interactive playback of animations in MAX. By using these buttons, you can move the start or end of the active time segment, play back the animation, or manually set the current frame. As described previously, the Key Mode Toggle enables you to move between frames containing transform keys for the selected objects.

As you move through time, the MAX viewports update to reflect the animated changes to the scene objects. Typically, you will view your objects by using the Wireframe rendering level of the interactive renderer. By using the Smooth or Facets rendering level, you can more easily visualize the completed animation. Unfortunately, most scenes will not play back smoothly in the interactive renderer, but you can use the speed of the renderer to generate preview animations.

Previewing Animations

A preview animation uses the interactive renderer to create a simple version of the animation. Animators use these mostly to check the motion of objects in the scene. Because a preview animation is generated with the interactive renderer, lighting, opacity, and materials can be applied. None of these are as accurate as the scan line renderer, however, and should only be used to help test the motion. For the final testing of the lighting, opacity, and materials, render individual frames of the animation by using the scan line renderer.

Generating a preview animation is a simple task. Under the Rendering menu, you can choose to make, view, and rename previews. The Make Preview command displays its dialog box, shown in figure 14.3, in which you set the preview settings.

The Make Preview dialog box is broken into six sections:

♦ **Preview Range:** Enables you to define the time segment to render. You can choose the active time segment or a custom range.

♦ **Frame Rate:** Enables you to set the target frame rate for the animation file. Every Nth Frame enables you to create a preview of a regular sampling of the animation.

♦ **Image Size:** Enables you to set the resolution of the preview images as a percentage of the image resolution set in the Render Scene dialog box.

♦ **Display in Preview:** Enables you to pick the type of objects to be shown in the preview animation.

♦ **Rendering Level:** Enables you to select the rendering level used by the interactive renderer while generating the preview animation.

♦ **Output:** Enables you to choose the output file type or device. The default file type is AVI.

Figure 14.3

*Use the Make
Preview dialog
box to select the
options necessary
to create a preview
animation.*

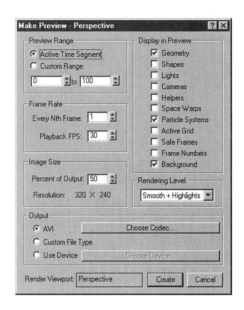

After setting the desired options, generate the preview animation by choosing Create.

The View Preview command loads the media player and the last preview animation that was generated. The Rename Preview command enables you to change the name of the file so you do not overwrite it the next time you generate a preview animation.

Creating a Keyframed Animation

The mechanics of creating a keyframed animation are simple: You move to a frame other than 0, turn on the Animate button, and adjust an object's position, rotation, or scale, or adjust a parameter in a command panel or dialog box.

The following exercise shows you how to create a simple keyframed animation in which you will animate a variety of objects.

CREATING A KEYFRAMED ANIMATION

1. Load file **anim-k.max** from the accompanying CD. Figure 14.4 shows what this file looks like before any animation is applied.

Figure 14.4

The scene before any animation has been applied to the objects.

2. Click on the Time Configuration button and set the time display to SMPTE. The time will be displayed as MIN:SEC:Frames, a readout that is much easier to understand than raw frame numbers. Set the End Time to 0:4.0 (4 seconds) and click OK.

3. At time 0:0.0, turn on the Animate button and select the tubular object in the middle of the viewports.

4. Open the Modify command panel and expand the Deformations rollout. Click on Scale to apply a scale deformation to the Loft object. Click on the right endpoint of the scale deformation spline and drag it down to a value of 5, as shown in figure 14.5.

Figure 14.5

The scale deformation grid, where you can control the scale deformation of the Loft object.

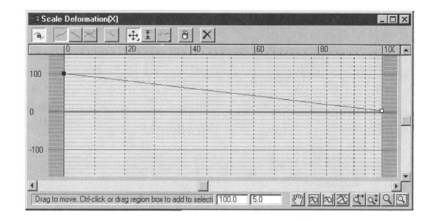

5. Set the current frame to 0:4.0 and drag the right endpoint of the scale deformation spline back to its original value of 100. Close the Scale Deformation window.

6. Play back the animation. If MAX skips too many frames during playback, go back to the Time Configuration dialog box and turn off Real Time Playback.

7. Set the current frame to 0:2.0 and select the sphere on the right side of the scene.

8. Apply an XForm modifier to the sphere. Click on Select and Non-uniform Scale in the MAX toolbar. In the Front viewport, scale the sphere down in the X and Y axes to approximately 50 percent. The scene should appear similar to that seen in figure 14.6. Turn off the Sub-Object mode button for the XForm modifier.

Figure 14.6

The sphere non-uniformly scaled to provide a slightly different animation effect.

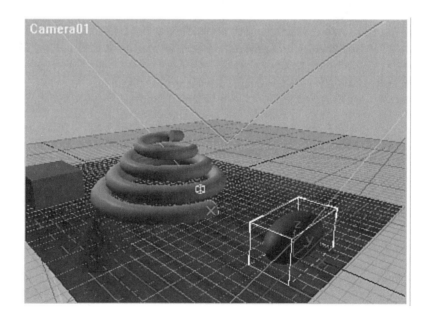

9. Set the current frame to 0:4.0, click on Select and Rotate in the MAX toolbar, and rotate the sphere 720 degrees in the Top viewport.

10. Set the current frame to 0:2.0. Open the Material Editor by clicking on the Material Editor button in the MAX toolbar. Select the second material slot (material Cone). In the Basic Parameters rollout, set the Opacity value to 100.

11. Set the current frame to 0:4.0 and set the opacity to 0. Turn off Animate and close the Material Editor dialog box.

12. In the MAX menu bar, click on Rendering, Environment. Add a Volume Light to spotlight Spot01. Set the following parameter values:

    Density: 1.0
    Noise On: Checked
    Amount: 0.5
    Uniformity: 0.5
    Size: 5.0
    Wind Strength: 0.5

13. Close the Environment dialog box.

14. Set the current frame to 0:4.0 and turn on the Animate button.

15. Select spotlight Spot01. Click on Select and Move, and move Spot01 to the right side of the scene in the Top viewport, as shown in figure 14.7.

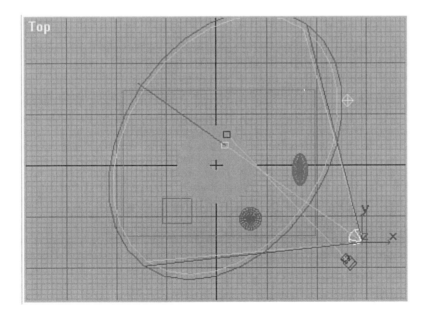

Figure 14.7

The light in its new position provides a simple animation of the light.

16. Set the current frame to 0:1.0 and select the camera. Move the camera to the upper-right corner of the Top viewport.

17. Set the current frame to 0:2.0 and move the camera to the upper-left corner of the Top viewport.

18. Set the current frame to 0:3.0 and move the camera to the lower-left corner of the Top viewport.

19. Set the current frame to 0:4.0 and move the camera back to its original position at the lower right corner of the Top viewport.

20. Save the file as **anim-k-d.max**. This file is provided on the CD for reference purposes and will be used in later exercises to illustrate other points, so keep it handy.

20. Turn off Animate, activate the Camera viewport, and play back the animation. Although the animation should play back relatively quickly, it won't play back in real time.

21. In the menu bar, select Rendering, Make Preview. Click on Create in the Make Preview dialog box to create an animation preview. After MAX finishes creating the preview, Media Player is automatically started to show the preview. Click on the Play button to play the animation.

At this point you should see the camera view rotate around the model, the lighting constantly changing, the sphere spinning and shrinking, and the wound-up tube getting larger at the top.

This exercise illustrates some points about keyframe animation and how easy it is to use. For now, you will not render the file; that will come later. However, if you want to see the final rendering, load **anim-k-d.avi** from the accompanying CD by choosing File, View File.

Trajectories

Clearly, being able to control motion in a scene is terrific but so is being able to see the motion path in the scene. To see the motion path, select the object that is in motion and then choose the Trajectories button in the Motion command panel. MAX displays the motion path for the selected object, as shown in figure 14.8.

The motion path is displayed as a blue line; the white boxes on the line represent the position keys for the object. Depending on which position controller you use, this path can be a straight line, a Bézier line, or a TCB line. In this figure, it is a Bézier line.

To interactively change the position of keys, choose the Sub-Object button at the top of the Trajectories rollout and then use a transform (such as Select and Move) to reposition any key. As you do this, you can watch the changes that occur in the motion path.

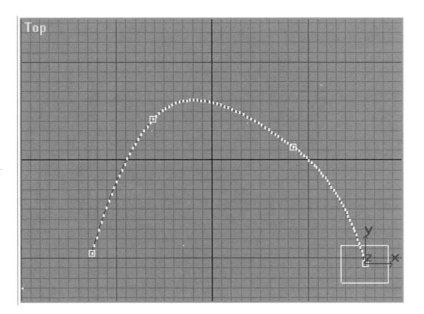

Figure 14.8

The motion path for an object.

> You can display an object's trajectory in other command panels. When the object is not selected, however, you can show its trajectory in two ways:
>
> ♦ By turning on Trajectory in the Display Properties rollout of the Display command panel
>
> ♦ By right-clicking on the object, selecting Properties from the pop-up menu, and turning on Trajectory in the Display Properties area of the Object Parameters dialog box

NOTE

In the following exercise, you will use the Trajectory display to show and adjust the motion of an object.

EDITING AN ANIMATION BY USING TRAJECTORY

1. Continue using the scene that resulted from the previous exercise or load **anim-k-d.max** from the accompanying CD.

2. Select the camera in the Top viewport.

3. Click on the Motion command panel tab and click on Trajectories. The trajectory of the camera is shown in the viewports. Click on Zoom Extents to zoom the Top viewport back to show the entire trajectory.

4. Move to frame 0:2.15 and turn on Animate. Move the camera in the Top viewport. As you move the camera, the trajectory display is updated to show the new trajectory.

5. In the command panel, click on the Sub-Object button to enter Sub-Object Keys mode.

6. In the Top viewport, select any of the keys along the trajectory and move it. As you move the key, the trajectory display is updated to show the new trajectory. Moving a key is the same as setting the current frame to the frame associated with the key and moving the object.

You have learned in this section how to set keys and display the trajectory for an object in the viewports. Although the values for keyframed parameters can be adjusted in the viewports or in the command panels, you first need to move to the frames associated with those keys. There is no way to move between frames containing keys for a parameter other than transform keys. Track View provides a direct way of viewing, adding, and modifying keys for all parameters.

Introduction to Track View

Adding keyframes to an animation in MAX is a relatively simple task. But editing, modifying, and deleting one or more keys can be difficult unless you use Track View, which is a powerful dialog box that enables you to edit all keys in your scene along a time line. Through this dialog box you can control the speed, motion, and spacing of keys, as well as create, delete, move, and copy keys.

Opening Track View

You can access the Track View dialog box at any time by choosing the Open Track View button on the main toolbar (see figure 14.9).

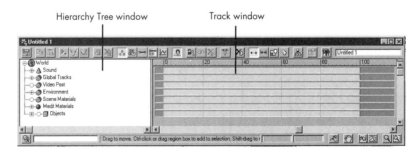

Hierarchy Tree window   Track window

Figure 14.9

The Track View dialog box.

The Track View dialog box is divided into two windows and two rows of buttons: the Hierarchy Tree and Edit windows, and the Control and View buttons. These elements of the Track View dialog box are explored in the following sections.

The Hierarchy Tree and Edit Windows

The Hierarchy Tree window, on the left of the Track View dialog box, is an expandable tree list of all elements in the scene, including materials, sounds, objects, and environmental effects. You can expand any of the tree's branches by clicking on the plus (+) button next to the branch name. Figure 14.10 shows an expanded tree.

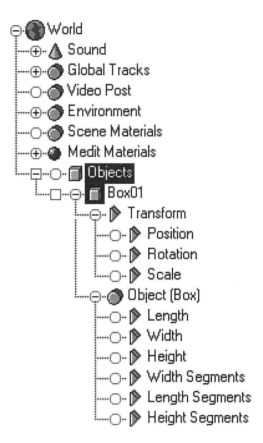

Figure 14.10

An expanded Track View Hierarchy Tree, showing the animatable parameters for a simple object.

As you can see from figure 14.10, even something as simple as a box can have 10 or more animatable parameters associated with it. When you create a key, you create it for a specific parameter of an object, such as its position or rotation, and at a specific time. If an object parameter has a key, that key will appear in the Edit window in the parameter's track at the frame where the key is located. Frames are numbered across the top of the Edit window, in a time line. If a parameter is not animated, the static data value for that parameter is shown in the track. Figure 14.11 shows a Track View with some keys assigned.

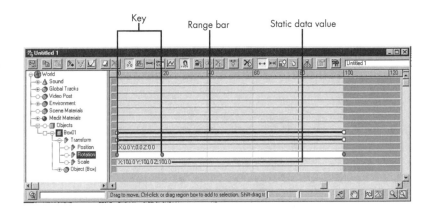

Figure 14.11

The Track View with animation keys on an object's Rotation track.

Take the Box01 object shown in the Hierarchy Tree window, for example. If you expand its tree as shown in the previous figure, you can access the transforms or the object parameters themselves. In this example, the box was rotated 200 degrees at frame 20 and an additional 520 degrees at frame 100. The keys for the rotation of the box show up under the Rotation transform track. Because the position and scale of the box were not animated, the static data values for these parameters are shown in their respective tracks.

In the Edit window, the start and end times of the animated transforms are represented by the white boxes at each end of the range (the heavy black line) in the Transform track. The range represents the total length of time that this object is being animated by some sort of transform. The specific transforms are located below the Transform entry in the tree.

In the Rotation track in figure 14.11, the gray spheres at frames 0, 20, and 100 represent the keys created in the animation. From Track View, you can delete the individual keys, move them, copy them, and so on. If you click on one of the gray spheres, it turns white to indicate that it has been selected. After it has been selected, you can easily transform the key at will.

Track View works with different modes to achieve different levels of functionality. When Track View is set to a specific mode, you can only edit the tracks in certain ways, depending upon the mode. In Edit Key mode, for example, you can edit individual keys, but in Edit Ranges mode, you can edit only a range of keys, not an individual key. Each mode is activated by selecting the appropriate mode button from the Track View toolbar (see figure 14.12). Each mode is listed below:

♦ **Edit Keys:** Edit the time or value of individual keys or selected sets of keys.

♦ **Edit Time:** Add, delete, copy, stretch, or shrink time. Underlying keys are affected based on the changes made to time.

♦ **Edit Ranges:** Slide or move time ranges and their underlying keys quickly. Individual keys are not displayed.

♦ **Position Ranges:** Edit ranges independently of their underlying keys. Used primarily with Out-of-Range Types.

♦ **Function Curves:** Displays curves showing how animation values change over time.

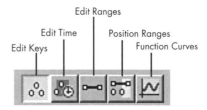

Edit Ranges

Edit Time   Position Ranges
                    Function Curves
Edit Keys

Figure 14.12

The Track View mode control buttons.

Making Basic Adjustments to Keys

In Edit Keys mode of Track View, you can adjust both the time and values associated with keys in many different ways. Figure 14.13 shows Edit Keys mode Track View toolbar buttons. To add a key to a track, click on Add Keys and click in the track to add a key at that location in time. The data value assigned to the key is the interpolated value at that time if the track was animated or the track's static data value if the track was not animated. To delete one or more keys, select the key(s) either by clicking on them (hold down Ctrl while clicking to add keys to the selection set) or dragging a selection box around them, and click on Delete Keys. If an object name label (signified by the yellow cube in the Hierarchy Tree window) is selected when you click on Delete Keys, MAX will ask you whether you want to delete all keys for that object. If you respond yes, all of the object's keys will be deleted. If you answer no, no keys (including any selected keys) will be deleted.

Figure 14.13

The Edit Keys mode Track View toolbar buttons.

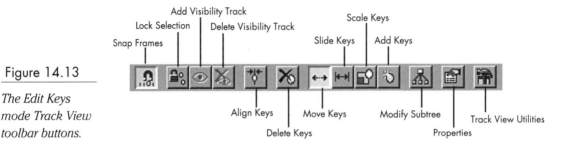

To move one or more keys, simply select the key(s), click on Move Keys, and drag the keys left or right. Moving keys does not affect the data values associated with the keys, only the time at which the keys are located. To clone one or more keys, select the key(s), click on Move Keys, and drag them left or right while holding down the Shift key. For each of the selected keys, a new key containing the same data value as the original key will be created when you release the mouse button. The position of the new keys in time will offset from the original keys by the amount that you dragged the mouse. Figure 14.14 shows the same object as in figure 14.11; however, the key at frame 20 was moved to frame 30 and then cloned to frame 50. Note that the key at frame 100 was unchanged.

Figure 14.14

The Track View, showing the effect of moving and cloning keys.

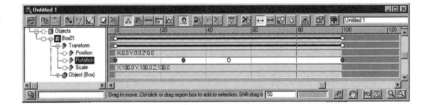

Moving a set of keys does not affect non-selected keys. At times you will want to slide the preceding or subsequent keys by the same amount that you move the selected keys. To slide a set of keys, perform the same actions as moving the keys, except click on Slide Keys rather than Move Keys. As you move the selected keys to the left, any preceding keys are also moved to the left. As you move the selected keys to the right, any subsequent keys are moved to the right. Again, the data values associated with the keys are not changed, only the time at which the keys are located. Figure 14.15 shows the same object as figure 14.14, but the keys at frames 30 and 50 were shifted right 10 frames. Note that the key at frame 100 is now at frame 110.

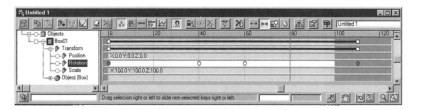

Figure 14.15

The Track View, showing the effect of sliding keys.

In some cases, you will want to modify not only the keys on selected objects or tracks but also keys on their descendants. You might have a completed animation where keys are present on multiple objects at frame 100, for example, but you need to move all of these keys to frame 120. The easiest way to do this is to click Modify Subtree to turn it on, select the key at frame 100 in the Objects track, and move that key. This will move all the keys under Objects that occur at frame 100. If you also have animated material, Video Post, or environmental effects, you would select the corresponding key in the World track and move it. Figure 14.16 shows two Track Views of the same scene. In the top Track View, Modify Subtree is off, and range bars are shown in each parent track. In the bottom Track View, Modify Subtree is on, and keys are present in each parent track. These keys signify that at least one key is present in a descendent at that frame, and by performing an action on the parent key, all descendent keys will be affected similarly.

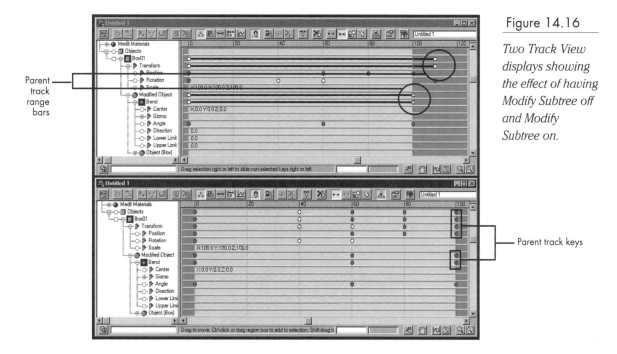

Figure 14.16

Two Track View displays showing the effect of having Modify Subtree off and Modify Subtree on.

Most key-based controllers enable you to change the data values and interpolation parameters for each key. To change these values for a key, right-click on the key. If the controller allows these values to be modified in Track View, the Key Info dialog box is displayed. Figure 14.17 shows the Key Info dialog box for a Bézier key. The fields in this dialog vary for each controller type and are described in the section "Key-based Controllers."

Figure 14.17

The Key Info dialog box for a Bézier position key.

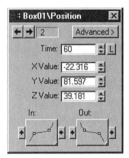

In the following exercise, you will use the various Edit Key tools to modify the keys for an animation.

EDITING KEYS IN TRACK VIEW

1. Reload **anim-k-d.max** from the accompanying CD.

2. Open Track View by clicking on Open Track View. The state of active track views is saved with the .MAX file. This file was saved with one active track view called Animated Only, which was configured to show only the animated tracks and their parent tracks. Right-click on the track name "Objects" in the Hierarchy Tree window and select Expand All from the pop-up menu to display the animated tracks.

3. Select the keys at time 0:4.0 for the Def.Scale(X) and Def.Scale(Y) points on object Loft01. With the Move Keys button active, drag these keys to 0:2.0.

4. Select the Def.Scale keys at time 0:0.0 and drag these keys to time 0:4.0 while holding down the Shift key. This clones the keys at time 0:0.0 and places the clones at 0:4.0. If you play back the animation, the wound-up tube gets larger at the top up to 0:2.0 and shrinks back down.

5. The Def.Scale keys at frame 0:4.00 are still selected. Click on Delete Keys or press the Delete key to delete these keys.

6. Click on Modify Subtree to turn on Subtree mode. Click and drag down the time ruler to show the keys in the World track. Click on the World track key at time 0:2.0 to select all the keys in the scene at time 0:2.0. Right-click on the key on the Camera01 track to deselect the camera keys. Drag the remaining selected keys to time 0:3.0.

7. Select the Position key for Camera01 at time 0:1.0. Click on Slide Keys and move the selected key to time 0:2.0. As you move the key, the keys to the right also move to the right. The time between keys remains constant.

8. Select the Position keys for Camera01 from time 0:2.0 to 0:4.0. Click on Scale Keys and move the keys so that the leftmost key moves to time 0:12.0. As you move the keys, the time between selected keys is reduced. The keys at frame 0:0.0 and 0:5.0 are not affected.

9. Select the key at time 0:0.0 for the Scale track of Sphere01's XForm gizmo and then right-click on the key. The Key Info dialog box is displayed showing the values associated with the key. Set Z Value to 100 and close the dialog box. Looking at the sphere in the viewports, the sphere is scaled up to 200 percent along the vertical.

10. Click on Add Keys and then click on the Scale track of Sphere01's XForm gizmo at time 0:2.0. A key is created at this time. Right-click on the key to display its values. The values stored in the key are the interpolated scale values at that time point. Change the X, Y, and Z values to 0 and close the dialog box. If you play back the animation in the viewports, the sphere scales down to nothing over the first two seconds and then expands back up over the next second.

In this section, you have learned how to use the Edit Keys mode of Track View to adjust the position of keys in time, create and delete keys, and change the values associated with keys by using the Key Info dialog box. Although the Edit Keys mode makes it easy to edit keys, it doesn't help you understand how the animation values change over time. For this, you will want to use the Function Curves mode of Track View.

Working with Function Curves

The Function Curves mode of Track View displays curves showing how animation values change over time for selected tracks. These curves make it easier for you to see how the object is acting in the animation. For example, a position function curve may have sloped lines. The steeper the lines, the faster the object is moving. Figure 14.18 shows you a position function curve.

Figure 14.18

The function curve for an object's position track shows the X, Y, and Z position values of the object over time.

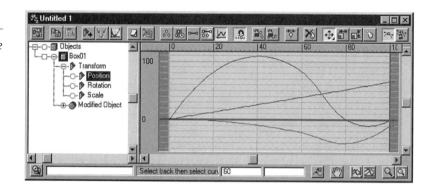

To display the function curve for a track, select the track's name in the Hierarchy Display window and click on Function Curves. The Edit window is replaced with the function curve display. The horizontal axis of this display is time, and the vertical axis is the output value(s) of the selected controller. Figure 14.19 shows Function Curves mode Track View toolbar buttons.

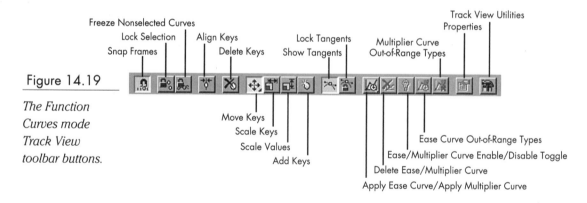

Figure 14.19

The Function Curves mode Track View toolbar buttons.

One or three curves will be displayed, depending on the type of track being displayed. For those tracks whose controllers output one value (length, width, radius), a single curve is displayed. For those tracks whose controllers output three values (scale, position, color), three curves are displayed. The red curve represents the X or red value, green the Y or green value, and blue the Z or blue value.

The only tracks that do not display a function curve are the object and modifier gizmo rotation tracks. These tracks do not display a function curve because all rotation controllers are based on what are called *quaternion controllers*, which have four data values associated with each key. A function curve display from one of these controllers would appear to be gibberish. One rotation controller, the Euler

XYZ, enables you to bypass this restriction. The Euler XYZ controller takes as input three separate controllers and outputs the quaternion representation of these three values. Although you cannot display the function curve for the Euler XYZ controller itself, you can display the function curves for its three input controllers.

Track View enables you to display the function curves for more than one track by right-clicking on the track names. By clicking on a curve, that curve becomes an active curve. You can tell which track an active curve is associated with because the green triangle next to the track name becomes highlighted. You can also set the track's curve as active by clicking on this green triangle.

When a curve is active, its vertices are displayed as solid black boxes. These vertices correspond to the keys' data values for that track. By clicking on the vertices or dragging a selection region around the vertices, the vertices become selected and the inside of the box turns white. The data values or time for these vertices can then be edited. By clicking on Show Selected Key Stats, the time and data value for each selected key is displayed. Any change to the time or value of a vertex automatically updates the values for its associated key.

Vertices can be added, deleted, moved, and scaled in a manner similar to performing the same functions in Edit Keys. The only difference with moving vertices is that you can move vertices vertically, which changes the selected vertices' data values. An additional function is the Scale Values, which lets you scale the selected vertices' data values. As you perform these functions, the function curve is updated in real time to reflect the changes made.

In the following exercise, you will use the various Function Curves tools to modify the keys for an animation.

WORKING WITH FUNCTION CURVES IN TRACK VIEW

1. Reload file **anim-k-d.max** from the accompanying CD.

2. Open Track View by clicking on Open Track View. Right-click on the track name Objects in the Hierarchy Tree window and select Expand All from the pop-up menu to display the animated tracks. Click on Function Curves to enter Function Curves mode.

3. Click on Position under Spot01's transform to display the position function curves and click on one of the curves to select the curves.

4. Click on Add Keys and click on one of the curves at time 0:2.0. A new position key is created at this timepoint.

5. Click on Move Keys and then click on one of the curves to deselect the vertex points on the key you just created.

6. The red curve shows the X coordinates of the spotlight. Click on the vertex at time 0:2.0 on this curve and drag it down to about –110 (watch the key value field at the bottom of Track View). The shape of the curve changes to show the object moving slowly in the X direction at the beginning of the animation and then moving faster in the X direction as the animation progresses.

7. Move the vertex selected in step 6 to the left and right. As this vertex is moved, the other vertices at this time point also move because all three values are stored in the same key, and changing the time value of one value changes the time value of all values.

When you are editing parameter values or changing controller interpolation parameters, you will usually want to do the editing in Function Curves mode. Because the actual parameter values used on all frames is shown by the curve, you can see the effect of changes in the controller's interpolation parameters between keyframes.

Working with Controllers

Whenever you create animation in MAX, some sort of controller is always assigned to the animated parameters of the objects. There are two classes of animation controllers: key-based and procedural. *Key-based* controllers store the animation data in keys and output values to the parameters based on the key's values and the controller's interpolation method. The different types of key-based controllers interpolate between keys in different ways. *Procedural* controllers do not store keys; rather, their output is based on initial data values supplied by the user and the equation the controller implements.

Assigning Controllers

You can assign or replace controllers for all parameters through the Track View dialog box. You can also replace controllers assigned to object transforms (Position/Rotation/Scale) through the Motion command panel.

The controller assigned to a track can be changed in Track View by selecting the track's name in the Hierarchy Display window and then clicking on Assign Controller. An Assign Controller dialog box is displayed, showing which controllers can be assigned to that track. Figure 14.20 shows the Assign Controller dialog for an object's Position track.

Figure 14.20

The Assign Controller dialog box for an object's Position track.

As you can see from the list of controllers shown in figure 14.20, thirteen different animation controllers can be assigned to the Position track of an object. If you switch between a procedural and a key-based controller or between procedural controllers, any previously defined animation for that track will be lost. If you switch between key-based controllers, any previously defined animation for that track will be transferred to the new controller.

When you select a controller from the Assign Controller dialog box, you have the option to make it the default controller. If you do, the new default controller will be used for all new controller assignments to parameters using that data type. You should be very careful about changing the default because the effects might be more widespread than you realize. For example, position controllers are used not only for the object's position, but also for the gizmo and center point of object modifiers. Making the Path controller the default position controller is a sure path to confusion because all objects will be created at the world center and are unmovable.

The controllers assigned to an object's transform tracks can also be changed in the Motion command panel. When you click on the Motion command panel tab with an object selected, a series of rollouts similar to those shown in figure 14.21 is displayed. At the top of the Motion command panel, you will see an Assign Controller rollout, which shows which controllers are assigned to the object transforms. You can change a controller by highlighting the transform track and clicking on the Assign Controller button. A Replace Controller dialog box is displayed.

The rollouts displayed below the Assign Controller rollout vary according to which transform controller is being used, which track is selected at the bottom of the transform controller's rollout, and which controller is being used for the selected track. In figure 14.21, the transform controller is the PRS (Position/Rotation/Scale) controller, so the second rollout is the PRS Parameters rollout. The Position track is selected at the bottom of this rollout. The position controller is the Bézier controller, which uses the third and fourth rollouts—Key Info (Basic) and Key Info (Advanced). While different controllers will cause different rollouts to be displayed, the general rollout structure is the same.

Figure 14.21

The Motion command panel rollouts for a PRS controller and the expanded Assign Controller rollout.

The rollouts associated with key-based controllers enable you to change the data values and interpolation parameters for each key in a manner similar to the Key Info dialog boxes in Track View. If a key is present for the selected controller on the current frame, the controller's rollouts will display these values. The various fields in these rollouts are described in the following sections for each controller type.

Key-based Controllers

All the key-based controllers store their animation data in keys. The difference between the controllers is how the output values between keys are calculated. When plotted over time, the output values of a controller forms what is known as the *controller's function curve*.

Bézier Controllers

The most used controller is the Bézier controller, which interpolates between keys based on a Bézier spline which passes through the keys' values. When you select a transform track in the Motion command panel that has a Bézier controller assigned to it, you see the Basic and Advanced Key Info rollouts shown in figure 14.22.

Figure 14.22

A Bézier controller's Basic and Advanced Key Info rollouts in the Motion command panel.

At the top of the rollout is the time, or frame number, of the current key. You can change the time of the key by adjusting this number. Use the two black arrow buttons in the rollout's top left corner to move to the next or previous key. Alternatively, you can click on the L button next to the spinner to lock the key to the specified time so that you cannot move it by accident. Below the frame number are X, Y, and Z spinner fields that show the key's data values.

Below the value spinner fields are two large buttons that control the shape of the function curve as it enters (In) and leaves (Out) the key. These buttons enable you to define how the tangent of the Bézier line is defined on the in or out side of the key. When you click and hold on the large buttons, you will see the different tangent types, as shown in figure 14.23.

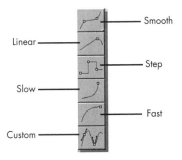

Figure 14.23

The Bézier controller's tangent type flyout.

Each of the six Bézier tangent controls causes the tangent curve of frames before or after the key to react differently. The default is the first tangent curve type, which produces a nice smooth line through the key. The reaction of the others is similar to the graphic representation on the button. For example, the third button from the top of the list (the Step tangent type) causes the output of the controller to remain at a constant value until the next key is reached. At that time, a step change to the new key's value occurs.

The last Bézier tangent type is the Custom tangent type. When you choose this button, the Key Info Advanced rollout becomes available. The In and Out controls enable you to control the rotation of the tangent handles of the function curve so that you have precise control over the tangent points. Adjusting the tangent points is better done in the Function Curves mode of Track View because it can be used to manipulate the tangent points directly, and the results of those changes on the curve can be seen immediately (see figure 14.24).

Figure 14.24

The tangent points for a Bézier controller with a Custom tangent type can be directly manipulated in the Function Curves mode in Track View.

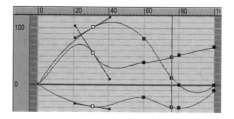

The Normalize Time control repositions the selected keys in time so that the average rate of change is equal between the preceding and following key for all selected keys. The Constant Velocity option adjusts the calculation of the interpolated values between keys to keep the absolute velocity of an object the same between the selected keys and their following key.

In the following exercise, you will use the Bézier tangent controls to adjust the movement of an object.

USING THE BÉZIER CONTROLLER

1. Load **whack1.max** from the accompanying CD. In this scene, a rotating paddle hits a ball.

2. Advance to frame 18, where the paddle is just about to hit the ball. You want the ball to remain stationary until the paddle hits the ball, so create a position key for the ball at this frame.

3. Select the ball and right-click on the Time Slider. In the Create Key dialog box, turn off Rotation and Scale and click on OK. This creates a position key for the ball, using its current position.

4. Advance to frame 100 and turn on Animate. Click on Select and Move and Restrict to X. In the Front viewport, move the ball right to the edge of the base. Play back the animation. In between frames 0 and 18, the ball is moving slightly to the left and then back to the right. This motion is due to the interpolation parameters for the controller.

5. Click on Open Track View and expand the hierarchy tree to display the position track for the ball. Select the position track name and click on Function Curves. Click on one of the curves to show the keys for the track (see figure 14.25). As can be seen from the function curves for the X axis (the red curve), the X value is not remaining constant between frames 0 and 18.

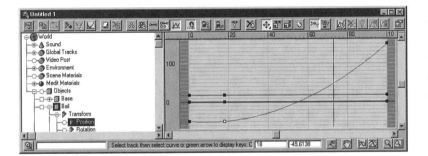

Figure 14.25

The ball's Position function curve before changing tangent types.

6. Right-click on the X axis vertex at frame 0. In the Key Info dialog box, set the Out tangent type to Step. Play back the animation. The ball now remains in position between frames 0 and 18, but the ball starts off moving slowly at frame 18 and speeds up as it approaches frame 100. We need to have the ball moving fast at frame 18 and slow to a stop at frame 100.

7. In the Key Info dialog box, click on the right arrow to move to key 2, which is the key at frame 18. Set the Out tangent type to Fast (third from the bottom of the flyout). Click on the right arrow to move to key 3 (frame 100). Set the In tangent type to Slow (second from the bottom of the flyout). Figure 14.26 shows the position function curve at this point.

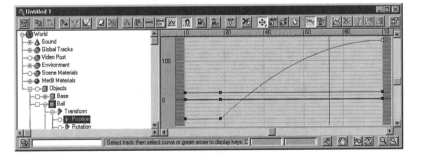

Figure 14.26

The ball's position function curve after changing tangent types.

8. Close the Key Info dialog box and Track View. Play back the animation. The ball's motion now looks okay, but you still need to do some work on the inital rotation of the paddle. Save this file as **whack2.max**. You will use this file in the next example to adjust the paddle rotation.

In the previous example, you adjusted the tangent types to control the interpolation of the ball's position between keyframes. You can fine-tune the interpolation by using the Custom tangent type and adjusting the tangent vectors at the keys to achieve the exact motion you want.

TCB Controllers

TCB controllers interpolate between keys based on five interpolation parameters assigned to each key: Tension, Continuity, Bias, Ease To, and Ease From. The shape of the controller's function curve is based on each key's data and interpolation parameter values. When you select a track with a TCB controller in the Motion command panel, MAX displays a Key Info rollout similar to the one shown in figure 14.27. To access the same controls in Track View, right-click on one of the controller's keys.

Figure 14.27

A TCB Position controller's Key Info rollout in the Motion command panel.

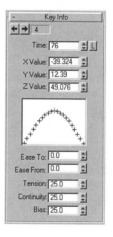

The basic Key Info rollout has the same keyframe number and lock controls and the same X, Y, and Z spinners as the TCB controller rollout. Below the frame number are X, Y, and Z spinner fields that show the key's data values. The TCB controller is assigned to an object's Position track, so these data values show the X, Y, and Z position values at the current frame. Adjusting any of these data values adjusts the position of the object.

Below the key's value fields is the TCB graph, which shows the effect of the key's interpolation parameters. The red tick at the top of the curve represents the current key, and the ticks on either side represent an even division of time on either side of the key. While handy, the TCB graph doesn't really provide a good representation of the effect of changing the interpolation parameters on the function curve. It is much better to adjust the interpolation parameters in the Function Curves mode of Track View.

The Tension value controls the amount of curvature of the function curve through the key. High Tension values result in no curvature (a straight line). Low Tension values result in increased curvature.

The Continuity value controls the angle between the In and Out tangents of the function curve. Only a setting of 25 will give you a smooth function curve through the key. High Continuity values cause the function curve to overshoot the key's value on each side of the key. Low Continuity values cause the function curve to approach a straight line between the current key and each adjacent key.

The Bias value controls the rotation of the In and Out tangents of the function curve. High Bias values cause the function curve to overshoot the key's value as it leaves the key, and low Bias values cause an overshoot as it enters the key.

High Ease To and Ease From values slow the rate of change of the function curve as it enters and leaves the key, respectively.

In the following exercise, you will use the TCB interpolation parameters to adjust the rotation of the paddle from the last example.

USING THE TCB CONTROLLER

1. If you did not complete the last example, load **whack2.max** from the accompanying CD.

2. Play the animation and watch the rotation of the paddle over the first 20 frames. The paddle rotates at a constant speed, whereas you would expect it to start off rotating slowly and speed up as it approaches the bottom of the swing.

3. To see the rotation of the paddle, choose File, Preferences, Viewports, set Ghosting Frames to 10, Display Nth Frame to 2, and turn on Ghost Before and After. Click on OK to close the Preference Setting dialog box. Click on the Views menu item and turn on Show Ghosting. Select the paddle in the Front viewport to show its ghosts (see figure 14.28). Click on Min/Max Toggle to maximize the Front viewport.

4. Click on the Motion command panel tab. In the PRS Parameters rollout, click on Rotation to display the rotation controller parameters.

5. Go to frame 0, where the first rotation key for the paddle occurs. In the Key Info rollout, set Ease From to 50.

6. Go to frame 20, where the third rotation key for the paddle occurs. In the Key Info rollout, decrease Angle so that the paddle is just hitting the ball.

Figure 14.28

The paddle's ghosts show the position of the paddle on surrounding frames.

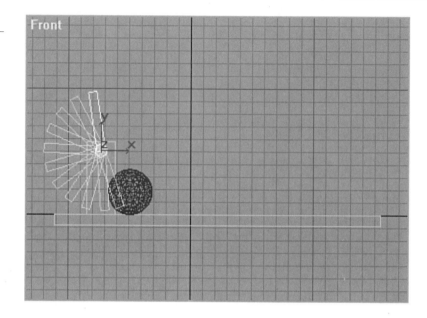

7. Look at the animation at frames 18 to 20. The paddle is hitting the ball at frame 18 and rebounding from the ball at frame 20. At frame 19, the paddle is passing slightly into the ball. In File, Preferences, Viewports, set Ghosting Frames to 1 and Display Nth Frame to 1.

8. At frame 19, note the position of the left side of the ball in the Front viewport. Go to frame 18, where the paddle is hitting the ball and the second rotation key for the paddle occurs. Use the paddle's ghost as a guide to adjust Ease From so that the paddle barely touches the ball at frame 19. The Ease From value should be approximately 20. Turn off ghosting and play back the animation.

In the previous example, you adjusted the TCB interpolation parameters to achieve the proper rotation of the paddle. Displaying ghosts while adjusting interpolation parameters enables you to see the effects of these changes quickly.

On/Off Controller

The On/Off controller is used for object and modifier parameters, which can be either on or off. In Track View, the On/Off controller displays a solid blue color in frames that are on and no blue in frames that are off. Each key that you add to an On/Off controller causes the on/off state to change at that key. An effect of this is that when you add a key, the On/Off state of all sections following that key is flipped.

The following exercise steps you through the use of the On/Off controller.

USING THE ON/OFF CONTROLLER

1. Create a box and click on Open Track View.

2. Expand the hierarchy tree to show the track immediately under object Box01. Click on the Box01 track name to select it.

3. Click on Add Visibility Track in the Track View toolbar. A Visibility track is added to Box01. The default controller is assigned to Visibility tracks in the On/Off controller. The controller state defaults to being on. Whenever the controller is in the on state, the object is visible. Whenever the controller is in the off state, the object is invisible.

4. Click on Add Keys and then click in the Visibility track at frame 20. A key is added at frame 20 that sets the controller in the off state for frame 20 on.

5. Click in the Visibility track at frame 80. A key is added at frame 80 that sets the controller in the on state for frame 80 on.

6. Click in the Visibility track at frame 40. A key is added at frame 40 that sets the controller in the on state. Because the controller state entering frame 80 changed from off to on, the key at frame 80 now changes the controller state from on to off for frame 80 on. Figure 14.29 shows the Visibility track for the box. The box would be visible up to frame 20, invisible from frames 21 to 39, and visible from frame 40 on.

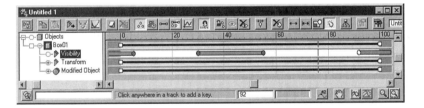

Figure 14.29

A Track View display of an On/ Off controller assigned to an object's Visibility track.

Although the On/Off controller is used as the default controller only for Visibility tracks, it can also be used for other parameters that are on or off. An example of these is the smoothing tracks for most primitives.

In this section most of the key-based controllers were described. Several additional key-based controllers were not described; however, those controllers are derived from the described controllers. For example, the Linear Position controller is the same as the Bézier Position controller, with all the tangents set to Linear.

The procedural controllers are described in the next section. Procedural controllers do not store keys; rather, their output is based on initial data values supplied by the user and the equation the controller implements.

Procedural Controllers

Most procedural controllers have an associated Properties dialog box, which is displayed by selecting the track name the controller is assigned to in the Motion command panel or in Track View, and then right-clicking on the track name and selecting Properties from the pop-up menu. Alternatively in Track View, you can select the track name and click on the Properties button, or simply right-click on the track in the Edit window.

Path Controller

The Path controller enables you to restrict the motion of an object to a spline. The position of the object is based on the spline and a percentage value. At a percentage value of 0, the object is positioned at the first vertex of the spline. At a percentage value of 100, the object is positioned at the end of the spline. As the percentage value increases from 0 to 100, the object moves along the spline. The Path controller can only be assigned to the Position track of an object.

When you assign the Path controller to an object, the rollout displayed in the Motion command panel resembles the one shown in figure 14.30. The Pick Path button enables you to choose the shape that the object is to travel along. If you select a shape that contains multiple splines, only the first spline is used as the path. In the Path Options section, the % Along Path field specifies where along the spline the object is to be located. When the Path controller is first assigned to an object, two keys are automatically created for this field. The percentage value is set to 0 at the first frame of the current time segment and at 100 for the last frame.

Figure 14.30

A Path controller's Path Parameters rollout in the Motion command panel.

When the Follow option is off, the object moves along the path without changing its orientation. Turning the Follow option on forces the object to reorient itself as it travels along the path so that the object is always pointing in the same direction as the path. The Axis options at the bottom of the Path Parameters rollout specify which of the object's local axes is to point along the path, and whether that axis points forward or backward.

The Bank option forces the object to bank as it travels along the curves of the spline. The degree of banking at a given point is a function of the curvature of the spline at that point. When Bank is active, you can set both the amount and the smoothness of the bank.

The Allow Upside Down option is used to avoid the situation where an object flips when it follows a path that is pointing straight up or down. The Path controller normally tries to keep one of the object's local axes (usually the Z axis) pointing in the same direction as the world's Z axis. However, if you have a plane doing a loop, the plane would normally be upside down at the top of the loop. Turning on the Allow Upside Down option would allow the plane to turn upside down in this case.

If the Allow Upside Down option is used, the spline used as a path should be planar, or nearly planar. If the spline is not planar, undesired rolling of the object may occur.

 WARNING

If the Constant Velocity option is off, MAX positions the object on the spline over time based on the number of spline vertices, not on the length of the spline. So if you were using a spline with three vertices (start, middle, and end), at a % Along Path value of 50, the object would always be located at the middle vertex regardless of the distance between vertices. If Constant Velocity is on, MAX positions the object on the spline over time based on the actual length of the path. If you have a path that's 100 units long, the object would be located 50 units along the path when the % Along Path value is 50.

In the following example, you will see how the various Path controller options affect the position and orientation of an object, and what type of spline paths can cause unexpected rotations of the object.

USING THE PATH CONTROLLER

1. Load file **path-con.max** from the accompanying CD.

2. Select the airplane and, in the Motion command panel, select the Position track. Click on Assign Controller and choose Path in the Assign Position Controller dialog box.

3. Click on Pick Path and select object Path01 as the path. The airplane will move to the beginning of the path, but its orientation will not change.

4. Click on Play Animation to view the animation. The airplane moves along the path, but its orientation remains fixed and the plane points in the wrong direction.

5. Turn on the Follow option and set Axis to Y. The front of the airplane now points in the direction that it is moving.

6. In the MAX toolbar, set Reference Coordinate System to Local, so you can see the object orientations more clearly. Click on Play Animation to view the animation. The front of the airplane continues to point in the direction it is moving, but the airplane rolls between frames 51 and 55, is right side up at the top of the loop, and rolls again between frames 67 and 70.

7. Click on the Allow Upside Down option to turn it on and play back the animation. The airplane no longer rolls and is upside down at the top of the loop.

8. You will notice that the airplane moves slowly over the first 20 frames and then speeds up because there is an extra vertex located near the beginning of the spline. Turn on Constant Velocity and play back the animation. The airplane now follows the path at a constant speed.

9. Click on Pick Path and select Path02 as the path. Drag the Time Slider. You will see that the plane rolls upside down at about frame 80 and returns to an upright orientation at about frame 89. This behavior occurs because Path02 is non-planar (see the previous warning). The only way to correct this behavior is to manually add rotations to the airplane to counteract the roll.

10. Select the cone, assign a Path controller to the cone, and select object Path03 as the path.

11. Turn on the Follow and Bank options and play back the animation. The cone banks excessively over frames 14 to 37 and frames 63 to 88.

12. Turn down the Bank Amount to approximately 0.05 and play back the animation. The cone now banks more reasonably at the ends of the ellipse.

The Path controller is frequently used for controlling the motion of a camera through a scene. To set up a walkthrough of an architectural model, a spline can be created representing the path of the camera, and then the camera assigned to that spline using the Path controller. By animating the % Along Path, you can have the camera pause as it moves along the path in order to look around at the scene at that point.

Noise Controllers

Noise controllers are used to generate random values. An example Noise Controller properties dialog box is shown in figure 14.31. To access this dialog box, right-click on the Noise controller and choose Properties from the pop-up menu. At the top of this dialog box, you can set the three controller parameters:

- **Seed**, which sets the initial value for the random number generator

- **Frequency**, which controls how rapidly the noise values change

- **Strength**, which specifies the range of output values

If the >0 option is unchecked, the output values are centered around 0. If this option is checked, the output values will range from 0 to the Strength value.

In the lower portion of the dialog box, Fractal Noise and Roughness specify whether to generate the noise values by using a fractal Brownian motion, and, if so, how much high frequency noise to use. The Ramp in and Ramp out parameters set the amount of time noise takes to build to or fall from full strength.

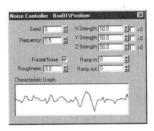

Figure 14.31

A Noise Controller's properties dialog box.

In the following example, you will add a touch of noise to the rotation of an air speed-measuring device by assigning a List controller to the Rotation track and adding a Noise controller with low strength settings.

USING THE NOISE CONTROLLER

1. Load **noise.max** from the accompanying CD.

2. Select the cylinder that forms the base of the unit.

3. Click on the Motion command panel tab and open the Assign Controller rollout.

4. Select the Rotation track and click on Assign Controller. Select the Rotation List controller from the Assign Rotation Controller dialog box and click on OK.

5. Click on the plus sign next to the Rotation controller. This displays the list of Rotation controllers that are being combined.

6. Select the track labeled Available and assign a Noise Rotation controller to the track by using Assign Controller.

7. Select the Noise Rotation track and right-click on the track. Select Properties from the pop-up menu. In the Noise Controller dialog box, set the X and Y strengths to 0, and set Z Strength to 20. Set Frequency to 0.2 and turn off Fractal Noise. Close the Noise Controller dialog box.

8. Turn on Animate and advance to frame 75. In the Top viewport, rotate the cylinder approximately –90 degrees about the Z axis.

9. Activate the Perspective viewport and play back the animation.

As can be seen in this example, adding a small amount of noise to an object's position or rotation can make the object's motion appear more realistic.

Waveform Controllers

Waveform controllers are used to generate regular, periodic waveforms. An example Waveform Controller properties dialog box is shown in figure 14.32. At the upper left of the dialog box is the Waveform List Window, which shows the currently defined waveform generators. The buttons to the right of the Waveform List Window enable you to add, delete, and re-order the waveform generators. The waveform generators are evaluated in a downward order, with each waveform generator acting on the output of the previous waveform generator.

Figure 14.32

A Waveform Controller's properties dialog box.

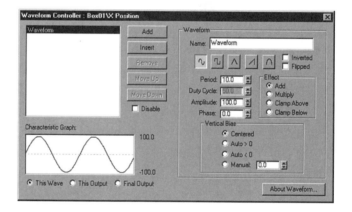

The Characteristic Graph shows one of three displays. If the This Wave option is selected, only the shape of the waveform being generated by the selected waveform generator is displayed, independent of all other waveform generators. If the This Output option is selected, the output from the selected waveform generator, including its effect on the input waveform, is displayed. If the Final Output option is selected, the output from the final waveform generator is shown.

In the Waveform area, you can rename the waveform generator and set the characteristics of the waveform (shape, period, amplitude). In the Effect area, you select how the selected waveform generator acts on the previous waveform generator's output. In the Vertical Bias area, you specify the value the waveform is centered around.

In the following exercise, you will use the Waveform controller to have a set of lights along a runway flash on and off.

USING THE WAVEFORM CONTROLLER

1. Load file **wave-con.max**, select the Camera viewport, and play back the animation.

   The scene is based on the Path controller example scene, where the airplane is coming in for a landing. Notice the runway lights that run alongside the runway. You want these lights to be flashing on and off.

2. Open Track View and expand the hierarchy to show Cylinder01. Expand Cylinder01 and then expand the Lights material track under Cylinder01. Expand the Parameters track under Lights (see figure 14.33).

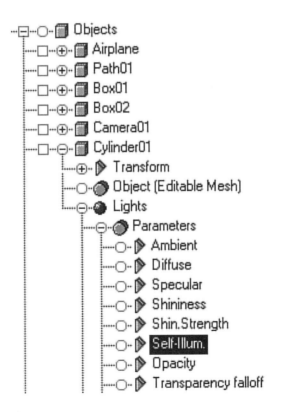

Figure 14.33

The Track View Hierarchy Tree, expanded to the parameters of the material assigned to the runway lights.

3. Select the Self-Illum. track and click on Assign Controller. Choose the Waveform Float controller and click on OK.

4. Right-click on the Self-Illum. range bar to display the Waveform Controller properties dialog box.

5. Select the Square waveform type, set the Period to 20, the Duty Cycle to 20, and the Amplitude to 50. Set the Vertical Bias to Auto > 0. Figure 14.34 shows the Waveform Controller dialog box with these settings.

Figure 14.34

The Waveform Controller dialog box.

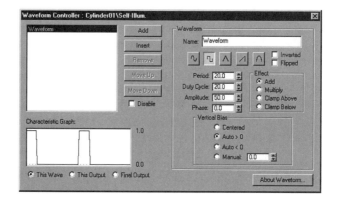

6. Close the Waveform Controller dialog box and Track View and play back the animation.

The lights now flash on and off, and the airplane approaches the runway.

As can be seen in the previous example, it is very easy to generate a periodic waveform. By combining multiple waveforms in a Waveform controller, you can generate complex periodic motions to duplicate the motion of mechanical systems. By using several waveforms whose periods can all be evenly divided into a longer period, you can generate what appears to be noise, but which can be looped over this longer period.

Attachment Controller

The Attachment controller is used to position an object on the surface of another object. The purpose of this controller is to "link" an object to the surface of another object that is being deformed. For example, if you use the Attachment controller to attach a sphere to the top of a cylinder and then bend the cylinder, the sphere will remain attached to the top of the bent cylinder.

When you apply an Attachment controller in the Motion command panel, you get the rollout shown in figure 14.35. Use this rollout to select the object to attach to by clicking on the Pick Object button. To specify the position on the object attached to, click on the Set Position button and then click and drag the mouse over the surface of the object being attached to. When you release the mouse button, the controlled object will be positioned at that point on the surface, and the face number and barycentric coordinates within that face will be displayed in the Position area of the rollout. In the Attach To area of the rollout, if Align To Surface is checked, the local Z axis of the controlled object will be aligned to the surface normal of the surface object.

Figure 14.35

An Attachment Controller's Attachment Parameters rollout in the Motion command panel.

The position of the controlled object relative to the surface can be animated by moving to another frame, clicking on Set Position, and setting a position on the surface. The parameters in the TCB area of the rollout control the interpolation of the controlled object's position between position keys (see the section "TCB Controllers" for information on these parameters). However, the results of animating the position of the controlled object may not be what you expected. The controlled object does not follow the surface between the position keys; rather, it moves in a straight line between these points. An example of this is shown in figure 14.36, where two position keys have been set and the controlled object's motion path is displayed.

Figure 14.36

The effect of animating the attachment point on a deforming object.

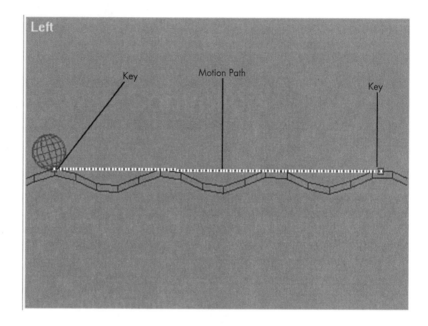

In the following exercise, you will use the Attachment controller to attach a set of weights to a bending bar.

USING THE ATTACHMENT CONTROLLER

1. Load file **attach.max** from the accompanying CD.

   This scene shows a set of weights and a weight bar. The weight bar is animated to move up and down. In this animation, you want the bar to bend as it is being lifted, and the weights to respond appropriately.

2. Select object Weights-L and, in the Motion command panel, assign an Attachment controller to its Position Track.

3. Click on Pick Object and click on the Bar object.

4. Click on Set Position and position Weights-L near the end of Bar. The orientation of the weights flips based on which face of the bar they are attached to. Make sure when you place the weights that the small weights are facing outward along the bar. Click on Set Position to turn it off.

5. Repeat steps 2 through 4 for object Weights-R.

In the Front viewport, you can see that the center of the weights isn't aligned with the center of the bar. This occurs because the pivot points of the weights are located at their center, and the pivot points are being attached to the surface of the bar.

6. To center the Weights-R on the bar, activate the Front viewport, open the Hierarchy command panel, and click on Affect Object Only. Click on Align in the MAX toolbar and select the rod to align to. In the Align Selection dialog, choose X Position, Y Position, and Center for both Current Object and Target Object. Click on OK.

7. Select Weights-L and repeat step 6.

If you play back the animation, you will see that the weights now follow the bar's motion. Now it is time to bend the bar.

8. Apply a Bend modifier to object Bar. Set the Bend Direction to 90 and drag the Bend Angle spinner up and down. The weights follow the bending of the bar. Set the Bend Angle to 0.

9. Advance to frame 8, turn on the Animate button, and set the Bend Angle to 57. Advance to frame 92 and Shift+right-click on the Bend Angle up spinner arrow to set a key at frame 92. Advance to frame 100 and set Bend Angle to 0.

If you play back the animation, you will see that the bar keeps bending between frames 8 and 92, causing the bar to form almost a full half circle. You need to stop the bending between these two frames.

10. Open Track View, right-click on Filters, and select Animated Tracks Only from the drop-down menu. Right-click on Objects and select Expand All from the drop-down menu.

11. Right-click on the second key in Bend's Angle track to display the Key Info dialog box. Click and hold on the Out tangent type button, and select the Step tangent type (third from the top).

12. Close Track View and play back the animation.

MAX provides some additional, more advanced procedural controllers. These advanced controllers are used for special purposes, such as controlling parameters based on audio files, motion control device data, and user-defined equations. These controllers are beyond the scope of a *Fundamentals* book. For more information on these controllers, please refer to your MAX documentation and to New Riders' *Inside 3D Studio MAX 2.0 Volume III, Animation*.

The compound controllers are described in the next section. Compound controllers take as their inputs the outputs of other controllers. They then combine this data with any parameter data associated with the compound controller, manipulate the data, and output the results.

Compound Controllers

Compound controllers combine the output of a set of controllers and output the results in a format that MAX expects. When displayed in the Motion command panel or in Track View, the compound controller display can be expanded to show the controller's input to it by clicking on the plus sign to the left of the controller.

PRS Controller

The Position/Rotation/Scale (PRS) controller is the default controller assigned to the Transform track of objects and modifier gizmos. There are three input controllers to the PRS controller: the position, rotation, and scale controllers. The PRS controller combines the output of these three controllers and outputs the transform matrix required by MAX.

There are no parameters or options associated with the PRS controller.

Look At Controller

The Look At controller is used to force one object to always face another. The Look At controller is used as the default controller for targeted cameras and lights. When a Look At controller is applied to the Transform track of an object, the Position/ Rotation/Scale transforms are replaced with Position/Roll Angle/Scale transforms. When you apply a Look At controller in the Motion command panel, you get the Look At Parameters rollout shown in figure 14.37.

Figure 14.37

A Look At controller's Look At Parameters rollout in the Motion command panel.

After assigning a Look At controller, click on the Pick Target button and select the object to be looked at. The Axis options specify which of the object's local axes is to point toward the target object, and whether the positive or negative direction of that axis points toward the target object.

Link Control Controller

When you link one object to another using the Select and Link tool, that object is always a child of the object it is linked to. Creating and animating hierarchical linkages is described in Chapter 15, "Exploring Other Animation Methods." By using the Link Control controller, you can animate the transfer of hierarchical linkages between objects. By using this controller, you can have one object as the parent of an object over a certain time range, and then switch parent objects. When a Link Control controller is applied, the original PRS or Look At controller becomes an input to the Link Control controller, which enables you to animate the object relative to the objects it is linked to. When you apply a Link Control controller in the Motion command panel, you get the Link Parameters rollout shown in figure 14.38.

Figure 14.38

A Link Control controller's Link Parameters rollout in the Motion command panel.

The two commands in the Link Parameters rollout are Add Link and Delete Link. Add Link enables you to specify which object is to be linked to. By selecting an object linked to in the linkage list and clicking on Delete Link, the linkage to that object is deleted. A Start Time field lies just below the linkage list. When an object is selected in the linkage list, Start Time is the time at which that object will start to act as the parent of the current object. The only exception to this is for the first object in the list. The first object in the list is the parent of the current object until the time when the second object becomes the parent. Thus, there is always a parent to the current object.

In the following exercise, you will use the Link Control controller to pass a ball between a set of rotating rods.

USING THE LINK CONTROL CONTROLLER

1. Load **link-con.max** from the accompanying CD.

   This scene consists of a ball, three rotating boxes, and a stationary dummy object.

2. Select the ball and, in the Motion command panel, select the Transform track, click on Assign Controller, and choose Link Control.

3. At frame 0, click on Add Link and then select the dummy object. The object name "Dummy-world" will appear in the linkage list with a Start Time of 0.

4. Advance to frame 5 and, with Add Link still selected, click on Box1.

5. At the following frames, add the following objects as links: frame 20 - Box2, frame 30 - Box3, frame 50 - Box2, frame 60 - Box1, frame 85 - Dummy-world.

6. Click on Add Link to turn off link selection and play back the animation. As the boxes rotate past each other, the ball is passed from the end of one box to the end of the next.

Link Control is very useful in character animation. You will often need the character to interact with objects in a scene— to pick up and carry off an object, for example. By using Link Control on the object, you can link the object to a stationary object until it is picked up and then transfer the linkage over to the character.

List Controllers

A List controller is used to combine a list of controllers whose outputs are added together. When you assign this controller type in the Motion command panel, you get the Position List rollout shown in figure 14.39.

Figure 14.39

A List controller's Position List rollout in the Motion command panel.

Each controller you add to the List controller gets added to the bottom of the list. To add a controller to the list, select the Available track in the Assign Controller rollout and click on Assign Controller. The new controller is added to the list right above the Available track.

You can cut, delete, and paste controllers into and out of this list. Any one controller in the list is set as the active controller. If the active controller is a key-based controller, you can interactively set keys for the track the List controller is assigned to, and the keys will be stored in the active controller. If a procedural controller is active, you will not be able to interactively set keys for the track. As an example, suppose you have an object with a List controller assigned to the Position track, and a Noise and a Bézier position controllers are assigned in the List controller. If the Noise controller is the active controller, you will not be able to move the object interactively in the scene. If the Bézier controller is active, you will be able to move the object, and keys will be stored in this controller.

If you want to assign a List controller to a track other than a transform track, you must perform the assignment in Track View. Although you can assign controllers to the List controller in Track View, you cannot delete controllers in the list, nor can you set which controller is active.

 TIP

List controllers are useful for offsetting the output of procedural controllers. For example, suppose you have a sphere whose radius you want to vary between 50 and 60 by using the Noise controller. In this case you would apply a Bézier controller to the Radius track and set its value to 55. You would then apply a List controller to the Radius track. The prior Bézier controller would automatically become an input to the List controller. Finally, you would add a Noise controller to the List controller and set its strength to 10.

XYZ Controllers

Many parameters in MAX don't consist of a single value, but rather a set of three values. Examples of these are the various color (red, green, blue), position (x, y, z), scale (x, y, z), and rotation (x, y, z) parameters. The XYZ controllers are used to combine the outputs of three separate controllers (each outputting a single value) into a format understood by MAX. This enables you to animate each of these values independently of the others.

Advanced Track View Controls

Track View contains a wide variety of tools for adjusting the values and times associated with keys. Many of these tools are beyond the scope of this book. This section covers some of the tools and controls that you are most likely to need while creating animations. Refer to the MAX documentation for tools not discussed here.

Filters

In even a simple scene, a full display of all the tracks in Track View can result in a display that is hundreds of pages long. The capability to filter the display to show only the portions that you are interested in is critical for efficient Track View use. Clicking on Filters displays the Filters dialog box shown in figure 14.40. Right-clicking on Filters displays the drop-down menu shown in figure 14.41. The options in this menu are the most frequently used options in the full Filters dialog.

Figure 14.40

By using the Filters dialog box in Track View, you can display only the information you need.

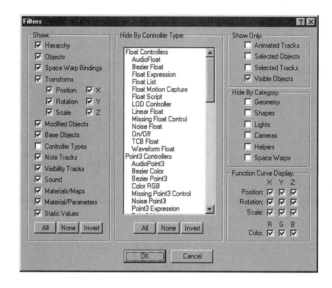

Figure 14.41

The Filters drop-down menu provides easy access to the most common filters.

The Show area of the Filters dialog box contains a list of checkboxes specifying how the hierarchical display will be formatted and which components will be displayed. In the Hide By Controller Type area, any controllers selected in the list are not displayed. The Show Only area filters items based on their animation, selection, and visibility states. The Hide By Category area filters objects based on their type. The Function Curve Display area filters which axes is displayed in Function Curves mode.

Adding Visibility Tracks

The Add Visibility Track button adds a new track to the selected object. This track controls the visibility of the object over time. When the track is added, it is automatically assigned an On/Off controller. When you add keys to the Visibility track, the keys set the visibility of the object to either off or on. When the time passes a key, the visibility of the object is set until another key or the end of the animation is reached.

The visibility of an object does not need to be either on or off. By assigning another controller to the Visibility track (such as a Bézier controller), you can achieve gradual visibility. The object is invisible at controller values of zero or less and then grows increasingly visible as the controller value approaches one. The object is fully visible at controller values of one or more.

When you assign a Visibility track to a parent object, the visibility of all children objects is similarly affected. If you do not want a child object to inherit the parent's visibility, right-click on the child object, select Properties from the pop-up menu, and turn off Inherit Visibility in the Rendering Control area of the Object Properties dialog box.

> **TIP**
>
> You can change the object properties for multiple objects by selecting the objects, right-clicking on one of the selected objects, and selecting Properties from the pop-up menu. Any changes made in the Object Properties dialog box are applied to all selected objects.

Out-of-Range Types

The Parameter Curve Out-of-Range Types (ORT) button displays the ORT dialog box shown in figure 14.42. The ORT dialog enables you to control how the animation of a selected track occurs outside the animated range you have defined. The default ORT is Constant, which uses the value at the beginning of the range for all frames before the range, and the value at the end of the range for all frames after the range.

Below each out-of-range type are two buttons. The one on the left represents what happens to the selected track before the animation enters the range in which you defined the animation. The button on the right defines what happens when the animation leaves the range you defined. You can select the left and right buttons in any combination of out-of-range types. For example, you could set the animation to be constant when entering the range and linear after leaving the range.

Figure 14.42

The Out-of-Range
types control how
the animation of a
track occurs
outside the
animated range of
the track.

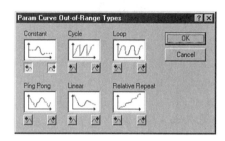

Copying and Pasting Time

You will often have a section of an animation defined for one object and want to copy that animation to another object, or to the same object except at a different time. This can be performed by using the Copy Time and Paste Time functions in Edit Time mode.

To copy a group of keys, enter Edit mode and select the track(s) you want to copy the keys from. In the Edit window, click at the start of the time range you want to copy and then drag the mouse to the end of the time range. Click on Copy Time to copy that block of time (and the enclosed keys in the selected tracks) to the Time Clipboard. To paste from the Time Clipboard, select the track(s) you want to paste to, click in the Edit window to define the insertion point (or click and drag to define a block of time), and then click on Paste Time. The Paste Time dialog box is displayed, asking whether you want to Paste Absolute or Paste Relative. If you choose Paste Absolute, the keys will be pasted with their original values. If you choose Paste Relative, MAX will subtract the track value at the insert point from the pasted keys' values and will adjust the value for any keys after the insertion range by the net change over the range being pasted. During the actual paste operation, the insertion range (if defined) is deleted, forming an insertion point, and then the Time Clipboard range is inserted at the insertion point. Any keys after the insertion point are pushed to the right by the size of the pasted block.

Copying and Pasting in the Hierarchy Tree Window

You can copy and paste controllers, objects, and modifiers in the Hierarchy Tree window. Generally, a copied item can only be pasted on a like item. The exception to this is that a modifier can be pasted on an object. If you are copying a controller, you can only paste to tracks that can accept that type of controller. You can, for example, paste a position controller to a position track, but not a rotation track.

To copy an item, select the item's name in the Hierarchy Tree window and click on Copy. To paste, select one or more compatible items (the targets) and click on Paste. The Paste dialog box is displayed, asking whether you want to paste as a Copy or as an Instance, and whether to also replace any instances of the targets that may exist.

Pulling It All Together

By using the different commands and modes of Track View and by using the appropriate animation controllers, you can easily build upon a simple animation to create a more detailed and lifelike animation. In the following exercise, you will use many of the tools in Track View in the creation of an animation.

THE BOUNCING BALL

1. Load **copy-key.max** from the accompanying CD. This scene consists of a ball sitting at the top of a flight of stairs. In this animation, you want the ball to bounce down the stairs and roll away on the floor.

2. Select the ball, advance to frame 15, and turn on the Animate button.

3. Move the ball so that it rests on the center of the first step down. Go to frame 5 and move the ball vertically so that the bottom of the ball is about one step's height above the top step.

4. Right-click on the ball, choose Properties from the pop-up menu, and turn on Trajectory. Click on OK.

5. Apply an XForm modifier to the ball. Choose Select and Squash in the MAX toolbar and choose Restrict to Y. Right-click on Select and Squash to display the Scale transform type-in. Shift+right-click on any of the spinners to set a scale key at this frame and close the transform type-in.

6. Go to frame 0 and squash the ball to about 80 percent along the Y axis.

7. Open Track View, right-click on the Filters button, and choose Animated Tracks Only from the pop-up menu. Right-click on the Objects track name and choose Expand All from the pop-up menu.

8. Select the key in frame 0 of the Ball/XForm/Gizmo/Scale track and clone the key to frame 15 by dragging the key while holding down the Shift key. Clone the scale key at frame 5 to frame 14. Select and delete the keys in the gizmo's Position track and collapse and expand the Gizmo tracks.

Drag the Time Slider back and forth, watching the motion and scaling of the ball. The ball is scaling between frames 6 and 14 when it should not be.

9. Right-click on the gizmo Scale key at frame 5. Click and hold on the the Out tangent type button and select the Step tangent type (third from the top).

10. Select the ball's Position track and the gizmo's Scale track. Click on Edit Time and, in the Edit window, drag the mouse from frame 0 to 15. Click on Copy Time.

11. Click at frame 15 in a track in the Edit window to define the insertion point and click on Paste Time. In the Paste Track dialog box, choose Paste Relative and click on OK. Figure 14.43 shows the Track View display at this point.

Figure 14.43

The Track View display after pasting the object Position and gizmo Scale tracks.

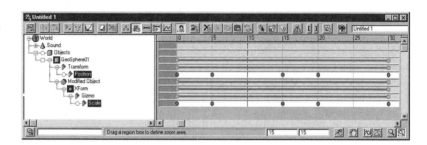

Drag the Time Slider back and forth, watching the motion of the ball. The motion of the ball as it hits the first step is definitely off.

12. Back in Track View, switch back to Edit Key mode and right-click on the key at frame 15 in the ball's Position track. Set the In tangent type to Fast (fourth from the top). Click on the small arrow pointing to the right next to the In tangent type button to set the Out tangent type to Fast. Use the right arrow button at the top of the dialog to advance to key number 5. Set the In and Out tangent types to Fast in the same manner as before.

Drag the Time Slider back and forth again. Much better. Figure 14.44 shows the ball's trajectory at this point.

13. Go back to Edit Time mode in Track View and select the time range of 15 to 30. With the Position and Scale tracks selected, click on Copy Time. Click at frame 30 to define the insertion point and click on Paste Time, Pasting Relative. Paste at frame 30 six more times. From the ball's trajectory in the viewport, you can see the ball bouncing down the stairs.

14. Select the ball if it is not currently selected. Go to the Motion command panel and click on Trajectories. Click on Sub-Object to enter Keys mode. Move the keys where the ball is hitting the steps or floor to line up the keys with the steps or floor. Move the key at the top of the last bounce so that it is a little bit above the floor. Click again on the Sub-Object button to exit Keys mode. Go to frame 160 and, with Animate on, move the ball right to the end of the floor. Figure 14.45 shows the trajectory of the ball at this point.

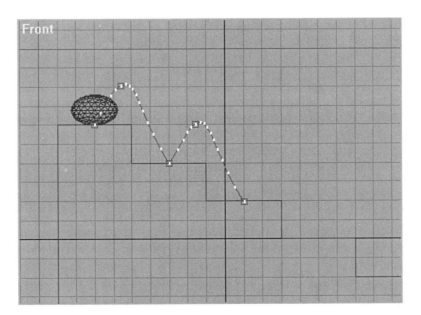

Figure 14.44

The ball's trajectory after adjusting the In and Out tangent types.

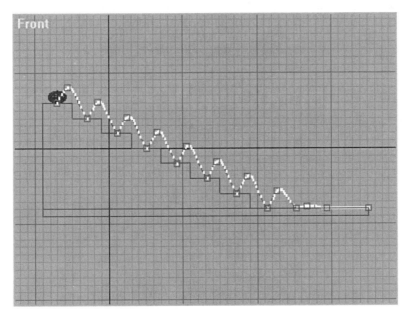

Figure 14.45

Align the keys to the steps and floor using Sub-Object Keys mode in the Motion/ Trajectories command panel.

15. We really don't want the ball to squash at the last animated frame. In the Edit Key mode of Track View, delete the gizmo Scale key at frame 135.

16. Click on Min/Max Toggle to show all four viewports, activate the Camera view, and play back the animation. The motion of the ball around frame 135 is a bit off. In Track View, right-click on the ball's position key at frame 135. Change the In and Out tangent type to Smooth, the first tangent type in the flyout. Click on the right arrow next to the Out tangent button to set the In tangent of the next key to Smooth. Play back the animation.

Everything looks pretty good, except it looks funny that the ball is not rotating.

17. Right-click on the ball and select Properties from the pop-up menu. Turn off Trajectory and click on OK.

18. Go to the Modify command panel and go down the Modifier stack to the GeoSphere. Add an XForm modifier. You want to rotate the ball before the scaling is performed on the ball, so the rotation XForm must be before the scale XForm in the stack.

19. In the viewports, you can see that the center of the gizmo is located at the base of the ball. In the Sub-Object list, select Center. Turn off Animate, click on Align in the MAX toolbar, and select the ball as the object to align to. Turn on all three Position options, set the Target Object to Center, and click on OK. Click on the Sub-Object button to turn off Sub-Object mode.

20. In Track View, right-click on Filters and turn off Animated Tracks Only. Scroll down the Hierarchy Tree until you find the XForm modifier directly above Object (GeoSphere) (see figure 14.46). Select the XForm's Gizmo Rotation track and click on Assign Controller. Select Euler XYZ from the Assign Rotation Controller dialog box and click OK. Expand the Rotation track branch.

Figure 14.46

The Track View Hierarchy Tree expanded to the Gizmo Position track of the Rotation XForm modifier.

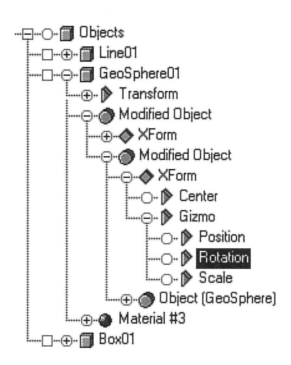

21. Select the Y Rotation track, click on Add Keys, and create a key at frames 0 and 80 for the Y Rotation track. Right-click on the Rotation key at frame 80 and set its value to 360.

22. Click on Parameter Curve Out-Of-Range Types and click on the arrow pointing to the right under Relative Repeat. Click on OK to exit the dialog box. Play the animation.

In this exercise, you have seen how the various animation tools in MAX work together to enable you to quickly go from a basic scene without any animation to the completed animated scene.

Conclusion

This chapter described the basic tools used for animating your scene. From this chapter you should have a basic understanding of the following tools and techniques:

♦ Creating Basic Keyframed Animations

♦ Working with Keys and Function Curves in Track View

♦ Using Key-based and Procedural Controllers

♦ Understanding Differences Between the Various Key-based Controller Types

Although you can create many animations by using just these basic tools, animating scenes with special requirements may be difficult with just these tools. The next chapters explore more advanced animation tools and techniques.

C H A P T E R 15

Exploring Other Animation Methods

This chapter focuses on advanced animation methods, with particular emphasis on using the following tools and techniques:

♦ Creating Object Hierarchies

♦ Adjusting Object Pivot Points

♦ Using Inverse Kinematics

♦ Using Space Warps

♦ Animating with Morphs

♦ Animating with Dynamics

♦ Animating with MAXScript

By the end of the chapter, you will have a good idea of how to create complicated animations and special effects by using these tools and techniques.

Creating Object Hierarchies

Chapter 14, "Exploring Basic Animation Methods," described how to animate single objects by moving, rotating, and scaling. At times, especially in character or mechanical animation, you want to animate an object by transforming it and have other objects repeat the same transformation. For example, if you animate the upper arm of a character, you want the lower arm, wrist, and hand to animate with the upper arm, as they would in real life. You can accomplish this in Track View by copying and pasting keys between tracks, but that process quickly becomes tedious.

The solution is to link one object to another and form a hierarchical chain. The linked object becomes the child, and the object it is linked to becomes the parent. When the parent object is transformed, the child object is also transformed, but if you transform the child, the parent is not transformed. This transfer of transforms from parent to child is called *forward kinematics*.

To link two objects together, you must use a selection tool called Select and Link. This tool and its sister tool, Select and Unlink, are on the main toolbar in figure 15.1.

Figure 15.1

The Select and Link and Select and Unlink buttons to link and unlink objects in a hierarchy.

To link an object as a child to another (parent) object, choose Select and Link. When you place the cursor over a selected object, it changes to the Make Link cursor. Click the object you want to be the child and drag to the object you want to be the parent. A line forms between the two, and the cursor changes to the Accept Link cursor. When you release the mouse button with the Accept Link cursor visible, both objects are highlighted for a moment and then return to normal. Although they look the same as they did before you linked them, the objects no longer act the same. When you move the parent now, the child moves with it.

Using this manner of linking, you can form a hierarchical tree that is very powerful for character animation. For example, you can link the hand of the character to a forearm, the forearm to an upper arm, and the upper arm to a torso object. Then, when you rotate the upper arm, the forearm and hand rotate with it.

The following exercise shows you how to link objects together quickly.

LINKING OBJECTS TOGETHER

1. Load the file **CH15A.MAX** from the accompanying CD. Figure 15.2 shows this file loaded in MAX.

2. Choose Select and Link, and click the ball at the end of the last arm.

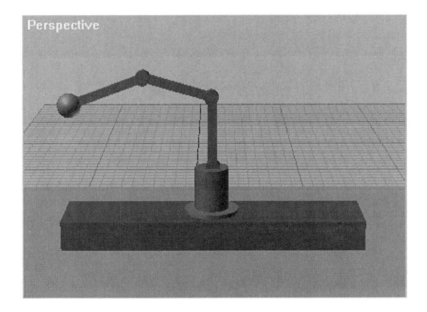

Figure 15.2

The exercise file in MAX before any adjustments.

3. Click and drag up to the first arm, and let go over the first arm. The ball and arm should highlight briefly to indicate they are linked.

4. Link the first arm to the first circular joint.

5. Link the first circular joint to the second arm.

6. Moving to the right and downward, continue linking each object to the next object.

7. Choose Select Object, Select by Name. At the bottom of the Select Object dialog box, turn on Display Subtree. As shown in figure 15.3, the Object list shows the object names listed from the parent down, with each child indented from its parent. Close Select by Name.

Figure 15.3

The Display
Subtree option in
the Select by
Name dialog box
shows the link
hierarchy.

8. In the Front viewport, select the first circular joint from the left and rotate it 45 degrees. Notice the way the rest of the arm responds.

9. Rotate the second joint –30 degrees. Notice that the rest of the arm (which is lower in the hierarchy chain) moves, but the objects higher in the hierarchy chain do not move.

10. Save the file as **CH15B.MAX** for use in a later exercise.

The transfer of motion from a parent object to its children, as shown in the previous exercise, is the basis of forward kinematics. By applying this type of animation with keyframes, and with some work, you can produce character animation.

Adjusting Object Pivot Points

While animating an object in MAX, you may need to rotate an object around a specific point, such as the center or one end. The point around which the object rotates and scales is called the object's *pivot point*. The point on a parent object around which its child objects are rotated and scaled is also called the *pivot point*. When an object is created in MAX, you generally should place the pivot point at either the center or the base of the object.

You can adjust an object's pivot point by selecting the child object and clicking on the Hierarchy command panel tab. On the Hierarchy command panel are three buttons that enable you to work with three different aspects of hierarchical relationships between objects. To adjust an object's pivot point, first select the Pivot button (see figure 15.4). In the Adjust Pivot rollout, you can adjust the location and orientation of an object's pivot point independently of the object's mesh, or vice versa, and you can apply a rotation or scaling effect on the pivot point that affects the position of any children.

♦ When the Affect Pivot Only button is selected, you can move or rotate the object's pivot point, and only the pivot point is adjusted (the object mesh and any child objects are not affected).

♦ When the Affect Object Only button is selected, you can move, rotate, or scale the object's mesh, and only the mesh is adjusted (the object's pivot point and any child objects are not affected).

♦ When the Affect Hierarchy Only button is selected, you can rotate or scale the position of any child objects with respect to the object's pivot point, but the object's mesh and pivot point are not affected.

Figure 15.4

The Hierarchy command panel, where you can adjust the Pivot, Inverse Kinematics (IK), and Link Info of the selected object.

When either the Affect Pivot Only button or the Affect Object Only button is selected, the Alignment area buttons are enabled. These buttons are shortcuts for placing or orienting the pivot point with respect to the object mesh or the world, or the object mesh with respect to the pivot point or the world.

The Reset Pivot button simply resets the object pivot to its original position and resets the orientation from when the object was created.

The commands in the Adjust Transform rollout are used primarily for linked hierarchies. When the Don't Affect Children button in the Move/Rotate/Scale area is selected, the object can be moved, rotated, or scaled, and any child objects will not inherit that particular transform. The Transform button in the Reset area aligns the pivot point orientation to the world orientation and does not affect the object's mesh or child objects. The Scale button sets the base scale value of an object to its current scale value and sets the current scale value to 100%.

The following exercise shows you how to use the Pivot options on the Hierarchy command panel.

ADJUSTING PIVOT POINTS

1. Load the file **CH15A.MAX** again. (If you are continuing from the last exercise, please reload the file from the accompanying CD.)

2. Select one of the arms of the object and rotate it a couple of degrees. Notice how it rotates around one end point.

3. Click the Hierarchy command panel tab.

4. Choose Affect Pivot Only. The Pivot icon appears as a tripod, as shown in figure 15.5.

Figure 15.5

The Pivot icon, with which you can adjust the pivot point's location and orientation.

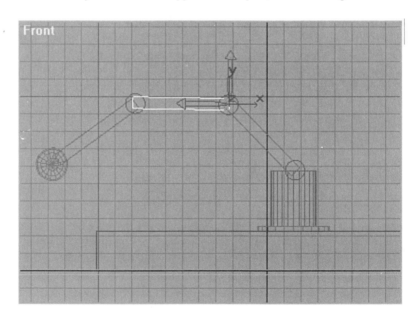

5. Choose Center to Object. The pivot point is centered on the object. Turn off Affect Pivot Only and rotate the object again. It now rotates around the pivot point.

6. Turn on Affect Pivot Only and drag the pivot point to a new location on the screen.

7. Again, turn off Affect Pivot Only and try to rotate the arm. It rotates around the pivot point.

8. Choose Affect Object Only. Move the arm to a new location. Notice how the arm moves and the pivot point does not. Again, if you try to rotate the object, it rotates around the pivot point.

9. Finally, with Affect Object Only on, choose Align to World in the Alignment area. The object mesh is now aligned to the world coordinate system.

Selecting the location of the pivot point for an object is critical when you are using forward or inverse kinematics. The orientation of the pivot point is also important when using rotational limits in inverse kinematics (described later in this chapter). The rotational limits are specified by using object local axes, which are the object's pivot point axes.

Controlling Child Inheritance

You can control which of the parent's transforms are passed to a child by selecting the child object and clicking the Link Info button Hierarchy command panel tab (see figure 15.6). In this panel, you can control which transforms can be directly applied to an object (the Locks rollout) and which transforms are inherited from the object's parent (the Inherit rollout).

Figure 15.6

The Link Info rollouts, where you can control which transforms of a parent object are passed on to the child.

In the Locks rollout, if you select any axis in the transform area, you cannot directly transform the selected object along that local axis. For example, if you have Move's Z axis checked, you can use Select and Move to move the object along its local X and Y axes but not its local Z axis. If the object is a child object and you move the parent object, the child object moves with the parent, no matter which locks are set.

Inherit, the second rollout, determines which transforms a child object inherits from the parent. For each selected axis in the transform area, the selected object inherits the parent's transform along that world axis. For example, if you have Move's X and Y axes cleared, the object moves up and down as its parent object moves but not side to side with the parent. If you were creating a Ferris wheel, you would want to attach the cars to the wheel as child objects so the cars would rotate as the wheel rotates. You would not want the cars to inherit any of the wheel's rotation, however, so you would clear all the axes for Rotate. Otherwise, the cars would rotate about their local axis along with the Ferris wheel and dump their passengers out.

Using Inverse Kinematics

There are two ways to create character or mechanical animation efficiently and effectively. The first is forward kinematics, which you have just seen. In forward kinematics, you animate a hierarchical chain by transforming parent objects and affecting child objects with that transform.

Inverse kinematics (IK) does just the opposite. Instead of transforming the parent, you transform the child—and the parent objects are affected all the way up through the chain. This is only part of IK's power. IK also enables you to place restrictions on how the joints work. In IK, you can use two types of restrictions: rotating and sliding. You can restrict the joints in any axis to any amount of rotation or to any distance, and by setting information such as joint precedence, damping, and so on, you can easily make the animation more lifelike.

The downside of IK is that you give up some control of the animation to the IK system by relying on the IK system to calculate certain keyframes and motion. The results are good in some cases but troublesome in others. Despite its downside, IK is extremely powerful for the creation of character and mechanical animation.

To use IK, you must first perform the linking operation used in forward kinematics. When linking, always start with the last object in the chain and work your way back to the parent object. Because it is inverse kinematics, the child objects affect the parent; therefore, the last object on the link chain should be a child object. After you have linked the objects, you can apply the IK parameters to the joints between the objects.

After the IK parameters have been set, you turn on inverse kinematics by choosing the IK button on the main toolbar (see figure 15.7). Then, whenever you manipulate an object that is part of an IK chain, the IK constraints are used. When the IK button is active, it turns blue. When the button is inactive, the chain acts as a normal hierarchical chain.

Figure 15.7

The Inverse Kinematics button turns MAX's interactive IK solver on and off.

You can do this with the Link Display rollout at the bottom of the Display command panel (see figure 15.8).

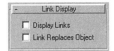

Figure 15.8

The Link Display rollout enables you to display the links between objects in a hierarchy.

The first option in this rollout, Display Links, draws a bone-like structure that represents the links for all selected objects. When the second option, Link Replaces Object, is enabled, the object is replaced by the link, which makes it easier to understand how the IK works. In figure 15.9, you can see the arm scene with both types of displays.

When the links are visible, you can select either the link object or the object you want to work with. When you transform one, the other is transformed also.

You can use dummy objects in your hierarchical chain to define joints or points **TIP** of rotation. Dummy objects, found on the Create command panel under Helpers, do not render, but add another link to the chain when necessary.

Figure 15.9

A mechanical arm, showing the links between objects in a hierarchy.

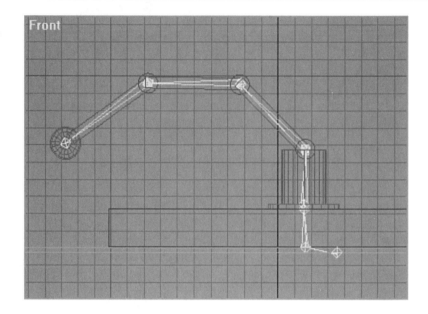

To adjust the IK parameters for an object, you first select the object and then click the IK button on the Hierarchy command panel. The resulting IK panel is shown in figure 15.10.

The five rollouts—Inverse Kinematics, Object Parameters, Auto Termination, Sliding Joints, and Rotational Joints—are described next, with their options.

The Inverse Kinematics rollout enables you to solve the motion for an IK chain attached to a follow object. A *follow object* is another object in the scene that has been animated. When you bind a portion of a kinematic chain to an object, that object becomes a follow object for the kinematic chain. Whenever an object in the kinematic chain is attached to a follow object, the motion of the follow object is translated into the kinematic chain. Solving the kinematic chain finds all the joint position and rotation keys necessary to make the animation occur correctly. The Inverse Kinematics rollout provides the following options:

♦ **Apply IK:** Solves the kinematic chain for follow objects.

♦ **Apply Only To Keys:** The IK solution is calculated only at the frames where keyframes exist for the follow objects.

♦ **Update Viewports:** Used for updating viewports as the IK solution is solved.

Figure 15.10

The IK rollouts specify the parameters to use for inverse kinematics.

♦ **Clear Keys:** Removes all keys from the kinematic chain prior to calculating the IK solution.

♦ **Start, End:** Enables you to define the range of time for which the solution is created.

In the Object Parameters rollout, you can define the objects in the chain and their precedence, bindings, and order. This rollout offers the following options:

♦ **Terminator:** Enables you to define the end of the IK chain by selecting one or more objects. After you have selected an object as a terminator, objects above the terminator in the chain are not affected when objects are moved beneath it.

- **Bind Position:** Enables you to bind the position of the selected object to the position of the follow object. Turning on the R button next to Bind Position maintains the selected object's position relative to the follow object. Turning it off moves the object to the follow object's position.

- **Bind Orientation:** Enables you to bind the orientation of the selected object to the orientation of the follow object. Turning on the R button next to Bind Orientation maintains the selected object's orientation relative to the follow object. Turning off the R button rotates the object to match the follow object's orientation.

- **Bind to Follow Object:** Binds the selected object to a follow object. Then, when you animate the follow object and click Apply IK, the IK chain is animated. Any other object can be used as a follow object, but dummy objects generally are used because they do not render.

- **Precedence:** Enables you to set the precedence of the object in the kinematic chain. *Precedence* defines an object's importance in the solution to the IK chain. The higher the Precedence value, the more important the object is.

- **Child–Parent:** Sets the precedence for the entire chain as child and then parent. When Child-Parent is selected, all child objects have a higher precedence than their parents.

- **Parent–Child:** Sets the precedence for the entire chain as parent and then child. When Parent-Child is selected, all parent objects have a higher precedence than their children.

- **Copy, Paste:** Enables you to copy and paste rotating and sliding joint parameters between objects.

- **Mirror Paste:** Use this when pasting constraints to mirror the constraint values.

In the Auto Termination rollout, you can specify whether to have interactive IK automatically terminated and, if so, how far up the chain you want the terminator.

The Sliding Joints rollout enables you to set the restrictions for sliding joints and to define how those joints act when IK is enabled. A sliding joint can move in any defined axis. If rotating joints are enabled, the joint can rotate as well as slide. By default, sliding joints are disabled and rotating joints are enabled. The Sliding Joints rollout offers the following options:

- **Active:** Defines whether the selected object can slide in the selected axis. The axis is defined by the parent coordinate system for the object.

♦ **Limited:** Enables you to limit the motion of the sliding joint.

♦ **Ease:** Enables the joint to resist movement or rotation as it nears the limits of its motion.

♦ **From, To:** Enables you to define the upper and lower limit of motion for the object in the selected axis.

♦ **Spring Back (check box):** When Spring Back is turned on, the spring force pulling the object back to the rest position gets stronger as the object moves farther from its rest position.

♦ **Spring Back (field):** Sets the rest position for the joint.

♦ **Spring Tension:** Sets the strength of the "spring."

♦ **Damping:** Enables you to dampen (diminish the strength of) the motion of the object, making it more resistant to IK forces. Values range from 0 to 1 (with 1 the highest damping force). You dampen the motion of an object to simulate real-world situations, such as inertia.

The Rotational Joints rollout enables you to set the restrictions for rotating joints and to define how those joints act when IK is enabled. The options on this menu are the same as those on the Sliding Joints menu, except that the To and From fields are measured as angles. Rotational joints are similar to your knee, elbow, and shoulder joints.

The following exercise shows you how to use IK to animate the arm scene in this chapter.

USING IK TO ANIMATE A SCENE

1. Load the file **CH15B.MAX** that you created earlier in this chapter. (If you did not complete the earlier exercise, load the file provided on the accompanying CD.)

2. Select one of the middle arms and rotate it quickly to see how it affects the rest of the object. As you can see, objects above and to the left of the selected arm also rotate. (This is forward kinematics.)

3. Choose Undo.

4. Select the entire mechanical arm, except the ground object, and click the Hierarchy command panel tab. Choose Child-Parent to set the joint precedence in this order.

5. Set the reference coordinate system to Parent.

6. Select the first circular joint on the left and move up the rollouts until you can see all the rotational joint parameters. Deactivate the X and Z axes and turn on Limited for the Y axis. Set the From value to 110 and the To value to –10. (If you use the spinners, you can see the joint move interactively, making it easier to define the limits.) Turn on Spring Back and set the Spring Back value to 74.

7. Select the next circular joint to the right. Deactivate the X and Z axes and turn on Limited for the Y axis. Set the From value to 75, the To value to –60, and the Spring Back value to 30. Turn on Spring Back.

8. Select the next circular joint to the right. Deactivate the X and Z axes and turn on Limited for the Y axis. Set the From value to -54, the To value to 0, and the Spring Back value to –45. Turn on Spring Back.

9. Select the large cylinder beneath the last circular joint. Deactivate the X and Y axes.

10. Select the base the arm sits on (object Box01). Deactivate rotation in all axes. Expand the Sliding Joint rollout, activate the sliding joint in the X axis, and turn on Limited, Ease, and Spring Back. Set From to –110, To to 110, and Damping to 0.5.

11. For each of the remaining objects in the scene, turn off all rotating and sliding joints.

12. Choose Select and Move, and move the ball on the end of the arm. Notice that only the ball moves (because it is a child object, with IK turned off). Choose Undo.

13. Turn on IK. Move the ball at the end of the arm again. Because IK is on, all the other arms now move correctly (as they would in real life). For correct animation, combine forward and inverse kinematic techniques.

The file as it should appear at this point is on the accompanying CD as **CH15C.MAX**; you can check your work against it, if you want.

To animate the arm, simply turn on the Animate button and begin setting position keys. The rest of the arm should now react appropriately and position itself correctly. Always create the animation by adjusting the position of the last object in the chain.

Another way to animate a kinematic chain, shown in the next set of steps, is to use a follow object.

1. Click the Create command panel tab and choose the Helpers button.

2. In the Front viewport, create a dummy to the left of and slightly below the sphere.

3. Set the animation slider to frame 100 and turn on Animate.

4. Move the dummy object vertically 170 units and turn off Animate.

5. Select the ball on the end of the mechanical arm. Click the Hierarchy command panel tab and choose Bind to Follow Object, Bind.

6. Click the ball, drag over to the dummy object, and let go when you see the cursor change. The Bind Position option is selected automatically. Click the R button next to Bind Position to make the bind relative.

7. Choose Apply IK.

Now, having created the animation and position keys for all objects in the IK chain, you can create a camera and a light and render the animation. The file **CH15C.AVI** on the accompanying CD shows the animation.

As seen in the previous example, using character animation is typically easier with inverse kinematics than with forward kinematics. If you use forward kinematics, you must work your way up the hierarchy, placing or rotating each individual object. As you work out toward the children, you may discover that a previous object wasn't positioned properly, requiring you to start over from that object. If you use inverse kinematics, you can simply place the child or follow objects, and the parents are automatically placed in the proper position.

Using the Bones System

In the previous sections, hierarchical chains were defined by creating a series of objects and then using Select and Link to link the objects together. An alternative method for creating a hierarchical chain is to use the MAX Bones system. In a Bones system, no actual geometry is created—the hierarchical links themselves are displayed in the viewports. You can link other objects to the hierarchical links, after which any animation of the Bones system is reflected in the linked objects.

In 3D Studio MAX, Release 1, the controller applied to each bone was the standard Position/Rotation/Scale (PRS) controller, with each controller only controlling the object it was applied to. Because the individual PRS controllers didn't know the state of the other controllers in the kinematic chain, it was necessary to use the Inverse Kinematics on/off toggle button and the Apply IK button to feed data to the individual PRS controllers for placing the objects in the right place at the right time. In MAX Release 2, an IK system controller has been added. In a system controller, a slave controller is applied to each object in the system, and a master controller is used to control the slave controllers. As a result, the interactions between multiple objects are handled by the master controller. This is exactly what is needed for IK, and the IK system controller is now the default controller for creating Bones systems.

When you use the IK system controller, the IK solution happens in real time and there is no need to use Apply IK to follow another object. To animate a Bones system by using the new IK system controller, you animate the position of special end effectors. An *end effector* is similar to a follow object, but it is created as part of the Bones system. When you create a Bones system, an end effector can be created automatically at the end of each kinematic chain. You can also create and animate end effectors at any level in the kinematic chain. Sliding and rotational joint restrictions are applied to individual portions of the kinematic chain, as described earlier. When you use the IK system controller, icons represent joint axes and any limits you have set. This direct feedback of the limit positions makes the limits easier to set.

Bones systems are created by selecting the Create command panel tab, clicking on Systems, and then clicking on the Bones button. The Bone Parameters rollout is displayed in figure 15.11. The IK Controller area contains the following options for creating a Bones system by using the new IK system controller.

♦ If Assign To Children is turned on, the IK controller is used while creating bones; if it is turned off, PRS controllers are assigned to each bone.

♦ If Assign To Root is turned on, the IK controller is assigned to the *root* (top bone in the chain); if it is turned off, a PRS controller is assigned to the root. In character animation, you will often want a PRS controller assigned to the root (allowing you to move the torso of the character) and the IK controller assigned to the rest of the character for animating the hands and feet positions.

♦ If Create End Effector is turned on, an end effector is created automatically at the end of each kinematic chain (the feet and hands, for example).

Figure 15.11

The Bone
Parameters
rollout, where you
create Bones
systems.

In the Auto Boning area, you can create a Bones system based on an existing hierarchical chain. For example, if you have a jointed character mesh already linked together (in which each body part is a separate object), you click Pick Root and then click the torso of your character. MAX then builds a Bones system with the same structure as your linked model. If the Auto Link option is turned on, MAX re-links the body parts to the appropriate bone after creating the Bones system. If Copy Joint Parameters is turned on, all joint parameters are copied from your model to the appropriate bone. If Match Alignment is on, the local axis of the bones is the same as for the matching body part.

USING THE IK SYSTEM CONTROLLER

1. Load file **CH15C.MAX** from the accompanying CD.

2. Click the Create command panel tab, click Systems, and then click the Bones button.

3. Click Pick Root, and then click the large base the arm sits on (object Box02). A Bones system is created to match the object hierarchy, as shown in figure 15.12. Right-click in the viewport to turn off Bones creation.

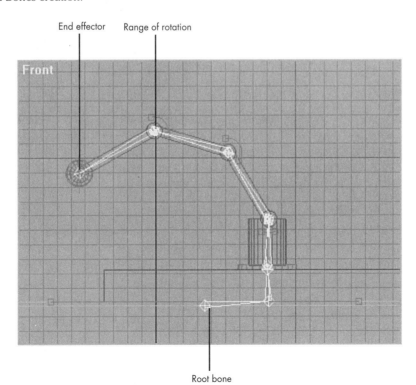

End effector   Range of rotation

Front

Root bone

Figure 15.12

The Bones structure created for a mechanical arm, using Auto Boning.

4. If the Inverse Kinematics button in the toolbar is activated, turn it off so that you can move or rotate the bones.

5. Because Create End Effector was on, an end effector was created at the end of the kinematic chain: the sphere. The end effector is shown as a blue + over the sphere. Advance to frame 100 and turn on Animate. Choose Select and Move. In the Front viewport, move the end effector up about 140 units. As the end effector is moved, the IK solution for the hierarchy is solved in real time.

6. Play back the animation. Note that the end effector and the sphere move in a straight line between the start and end positions.

7. In figure 15.12, you might have noticed the orange arcs located near the circular joints. These arcs represent the range of rotation for the joint. Select the link from the first to the second circular joint (counting from the left), as shown in figure 15.13.

Figure 15.13

The Bones link associated with the top rotational joint.

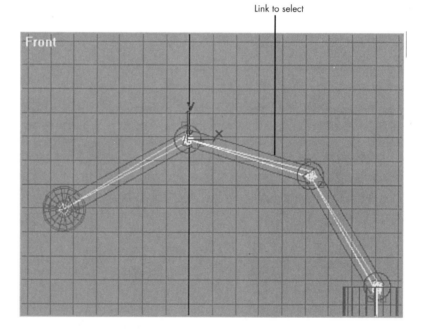

8. Click the Hierarchy command panel tab and drag the panel up to display the Rotational Joints rollout. Because Copy Joint Parameters was turned on, the Y-axis rotational constraints were copied to the bone. Adjust the From and To values to see how the range limit display changes.

9. Select the root bone, as shown in figure 15.13, and move it. Note that the base of the arm moves, but the end effector at the arm does not.

10. Click the Motion command panel tab and select the end effector. The IK system controller parameters are displayed, as shown in figure 15.14. In the IK Controller Parameters rollout, click Link in the End Effectors area and then click the root bone. Now select and move the root bone. The end-effector position remains constant relative to the root bone.

Figure 15.14

The IK Controller Parameters rollout in the Motion command panel specifies the parameters for an IK system controller.

This technique for linking end effectors to the root bone is useful for character animation, where the head and hand end effectors are linked to the root bone at the character's torso. When you move the root bone, the upper portion of the body moves, but the feet remain at their original location.

For more information on the IK system controller and its uses, refer to your MAX documentation and to New Rider's *Inside 3D Studio MAX 2.0 Volume III, Animation*.

Using Space Warps

A *space warp* is a nonrenderable object that affects other objects as they move through the space influenced by the space warp. Space warps act as force field generators, which can deform the mesh of other objects or apply force to objects and particles. For example, a space warp can pull or push particles as gravity does, or it can cause an object to explode. When you create a space warp, an icon for the warp appears in the scene. For an object to be affected by a space warp, you must bind the object to the warp by using the Bind to Space Warp tool in the main toolbar.

You create a space warp by choosing the Space Warp button in the Create command panel, selecting the appropriate space warp category from the category drop-down list, selecting the space warp type to create, and clicking (or clicking and dragging for some types) in a viewport.

To bind an object to a space warp, click Bind to Space Warp (see figure 15.15), click the object you want to bind, drag the cursor to the space warp, and let go. Both objects are highlighted briefly to indicate the acceptance of the binding. Multiple objects can be bound to the same space warp, and multiple space warps can be applied to the same object. When you bind an object to a space warp, the binding is applied at the top of the object modifier stack (see figure 15.16).

Figure 15.15

The Bind to Space Warp button to bind an object to a space warp.

Figure 15.16

The Ripple binding in the modifier stack for an object bound to a Ripple space warp.

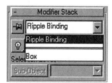

Space warps come in three categories: Geometric/Deformable, Particles & Dynamics, and Modifier-Based. Geometric/Deformable space warps deform the mesh of objects bound to them. Particle & Dynamics space warps apply forces to the individual particles in bound particle systems, and most can be used with Dynamics (described in the "Animating with Dynamics" section later in this chapter) to apply forces such as gravity and wind to objects. Instead of deforming the mesh of the object, these forces are applied to the entire object. Finally, Modifier-Based space warps are similar to Geometric/Deformable space warps in that they deform the mesh of objects bound to them.

Geometric/Deformable and Modifier-Based Space Warps

Figure 15.17 shows the Object Type rollout for the Geometric/Deformable space warp. Figure 15.18 shows the Object Type rollout for the Modifier-Based space warp. Except for the Bomb and Conform space warps, all Geometric/Deformable and Modifier-Based space warps duplicate object modifiers available in the Modify command panel. The parameters associated with these Geometric/Deformable and Modifier-Based space warps are the same as those for the corresponding modifiers and are described in Chapter 7, "Exploring Other Modeling Methods." The Conform space warp is a subset of the Conform compound object type, and its parameters have the same meanings as the parameters in the Conform object described in Chapter 4, "Basic Modeling Methods."

Figure 15.17

The types of Geometric/ Deformable space warps.

Figure 15.18

The types of Modifier-Based space warps.

For some of the Geometric/Deformable space warps (Ripple, Wave, and Conform), there is an additional area in the Parameters rollout called Display, which controls the detail or size of the Space Warp icon. The parameters in the Display area affect only the display and not the space warp's effect on objects.

For the Modifier-Based space warps, there is an additional rollout called Gizmo Parameters (see figure 15.19). When you apply the modifier these space warps are based on, the modifier gizmo is automatically sized to the bounding box of the object. Because Modifier-Based space warps are created independent of the objects, the size is set by the size of the space warp when it is created in the viewport. The Gizmo Parameters rollout provides spinners for adjusting the size of the space warp. The Gizmo Parameters rollout also includes a Decay spinner in the Deformation area. If you set the Decay spinner to 0, there is no decay and the space warp affects its bound objects regardless of their distance from the space warp. If you increase the decay, the effect on the bound objects falls off exponentially with distance.

Figure 15.19

*The Gizmo
Parameters rollout
for Modifier-Based
space warps.*

As mentioned earlier, when you bind an object to a space warp, the binding is placed at the top of the modifier stack. For the Ripple and Wave space warps, a Flexibility parameter is associated with this binding, which acts as a multiplier of the effect of the space warp on the object. Flexibility can be adjusted individually in each bound object's stack. Because this parameter belongs to each binding, it doesn't appear with the space warp parameters but is adjusted in the Modify command panel. To make this adjustment, you select the object and then select the binding in the object's modifier stack (see figure 15.20).

Figure 15.20

*The Flexibility
parameter in the
Ripple and Wave
space warp
bindings.*

In the following example, you will create a space warp and bind it to an object.

CREATING AND USING A RIPPLE SPACE WARP

1. In the Top viewport, create a box that is approximately 100 units by 100 units by 1 unit tall. Set the Length and Width segments to 20.

2. Click the Space Warp button and choose Ripple.

3. In the Top viewport, create a Ripple space warp by clicking to the side of the box and dragging out until the Ripple's Wave Length parameter is approximately 30. Release the mouse button and move the mouse up slightly to set Amplitude 1 and 2 to approximately 10.

4. Choose the Bind to Space Warp button and drag from the space warp to the box (or vice versa). Figure 15.21 shows the resulting object.

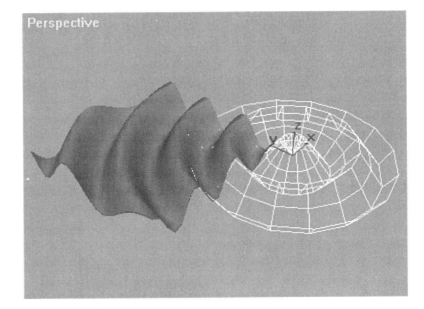

Figure 15.21

The effect of a Ripple space warp on an object.

5. Animate the properties of the space warp over time. To accomplish this, turn on the Animate button and adjust any parameter in the Ripple area at any frame you want.

6. Select the box and click the Modify command panel tab. Adjust the Flexibility value up and down to see the effect of this parameter on the box. This parameter can also be animated.

7. Move the box around in the viewport. As the relationship between the box and the Space Warp icon changes, the effect on the box changes.

For all the Geometric/Deformable space warps, the geometry of the mesh is affected by the relative position of the space warp to the objects. This is also true for the Modifier-Based space warps and several of the Particle space warps. For the Bomb space warp, the space warp's position acts as the center point of an explosion.

Bomb

The Bomb space warp is the only Geometric/Deformable space warp not based on a modifier or compound object. Bomb is used to explode one or more objects into their constituent faces (fragments). To be effective, the objects need to have enough faces to show the explosion effect well. The Bomb Parameters rollout is shown in figure 15.22.

Figure 15.22

The Bomb Parameters rollout for Bomb space warps.

To create a Bomb space warp, click anywhere in the scene. The location of the Bomb space warp is the location of the blast center (bound objects will be exploded away from or toward this point). Then use the Select and Bind tool to bind objects to the Bomb space warp. Only objects bound to the Bomb space warp will be affected by it.

In the Bomb Parameters rollout are three areas: Explosion, Fragment Size, and General. In the Explosion area, the Strength parameter specifies how strong the explosion will be. This value can be positive, which pushes the fragments away from the Bomb, or negative, which pulls the fragments toward the Bomb. The Spin parameter specifies how fast the fragments rotate. If Falloff On is turned on, the Falloff parameter specifies the radius of the explosion force. Objects beyond this radius are broken into fragments but are not affected by the explosion force. They are, however, affected by the Gravity parameter. If Falloff On is turned off, all object fragments are affected by the explosion force.

In the Fragment Size area, the Min and Max parameters specify the limits on the number of object faces to be included in each fragment. Each fragment becomes an element of the original object. Smoothing is retained across the faces of a fragment but is not retained across fragments.

In the General area, the Gravity parameter specifies the force of gravity on the fragments. This force is always applied along the world Z axis and can be either positive or negative. All fragments, including those outside the Falloff radius, are equally affected by gravity. The Chaos parameter adds random variation to the trajectory and spin of fragments after the explosion. The Detonation parameter specifies the time at which the bound objects are broken into fragments, and the explosion and gravity forces to be applied to the object fragments. The Seed parameter determines random number generators internal to Bomb, which select the faces and spin for each fragment. The Seed parameter is also used when applying chaos.

TIP

Use Particle Array (PArray), the Particle Bomb (PBomb) space warp, and the Gravity space warp together to produce a very effective explosion effect. The fragments created by the Bomb space warp do not interact with the scene, so you cannot have them bounce off the ground or other objects. If you use the deflector space warps, the fragments created by using Particle Array can bounce and break up into smaller particles. In addition, Particle Array can give the fragments thickness, which Bomb cannot do.

In the following example, you will see how to use the Bomb space warp to cause an object to explode. In a later exercise, you will use PArray and PBomb to blow up the same object, so you can see the differences in these two techniques.

USING THE BOMB SPACE WARP

1. Load file **CH15D.MAX** from the accompanying CD. The scene is based on the bowling alley you created in earlier chapters.

2. Advance to frame 0:0.21, just before the bowling ball hits the lead pin.

3. Create a Bomb space warp in the Top viewport, with the Bomb space-warp center next to the lead pin on the side where the bowling ball is located.

4. Using Select and Bind, bind the lead pin to the Bomb space warp. As seen in the Left viewport, fragments of the pin are already being shot up and away from the pin's position.

5. With the Bomb space warp selected, go to the Modify command panel and set Detonation to 0:0.21.

6. Advance to frame 0:0.22 to see the first frame of the detonation. The pieces of the pin are moving much too fast. Decrease Strength to 0.2. To stop the fragments from flying so high, set Gravity to 4.0. To make the fragments larger, set Min to 5 and Max to 20. To give the fragments some spin, set Spin to 1. Finally, to add some extra randomness, set Chaos to 0.5.

7. Play back the animation in the Camera viewport.

In this section you have seen how to use the Geometric/Deformable space warps to deform the meshes of objects. In the next section, you will explore the space warps used to effect particle motion.

Particle & Dynamics Space Warps

Figure 15.23 shows the Object Type rollout for the Particles & Dynamics space warps. All of these space warps can be applied to particle systems. The Gravity, Wind, Push, Motor, and PBomb can also be used with the Dynamics utility. Only the use of these space warps on particle systems will be discussed in this section.

Figure 15.23

The types of Particles & Dynamics space warps.

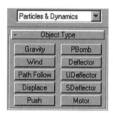

Wind

The Wind space warp is used in a particle system to create the appearance of blowing wind. To create Wind, click in the viewport to create the center of the space warp, and drag out to define the outer edge. The actual size of the Wind icon does not change its effect. The orientation of the icon does matter if the Planar option is chosen—the wind blows in the direction the arrow on the icon is pointing. To bind the Wind space warp to a particle system, use the Select and Bind tool.

Gravity

The Gravity space warp is a subset of Wind, containing only the Force area parameters. These parameters have the same definitions as for Wind.

Push

The Push space warp imposes a force on particles perpendicular to the Push icon. Unlike Gravity, a Push incorporates a feedback mechanism from the velocities of particles. As the particles approach the target speed, the force acting on them decreases until there is no force applied at the target speed.

Motor

The Motor space warp functions nearly the same as the Push space warp, but applies a rotational force rather than a linear force. All the parameters are identical to those in Push, except in the Strength Control area. In this area, instead of specifying a linear force and a target velocity, you specify a torque and target revolutions.

UDeflector, SDeflector, Deflector

The UDeflector, SDeflector, and Deflector space warps are used to detect collisions with deflectors and to bounce the particles off of the deflectors. The deflector in a UDeflector space warp is any geometric object you select. The deflector in an SDeflector is the Spherical icon of the space warp. The deflector in a Deflector is the Planar icon of the space warp. The parameters in Deflector are a subset of those in SDeflector, which in turn are a subset of those in UDeflector.

Displace

The Displace space warp, when applied to particle systems, applies variable forces on the particles, based on the bitmap or map applied to the Displace icon. From those areas of the icon where the bitmap or map has a low luminance value (the dark areas), no or low force is applied to the particle system. From those areas of the icon where the bitmap or map has a high luminance value (the light areas), a high force is applied to the particle system. The parameters associated with the Displace space warp are the same as those for the Displace modifier and are described in Chapter 7.

Path Follow

The Path Follow space warp is used to force particles to follow a spline. You can use the Taper parameters to control how fast the particles converge or diverge from the spline path as they move along it. You can use the Swirl parameters to control how fast the particles rotate around the path as they move along it. You can also control how fast the particles move along the path and whether they move at a constant speed.

PBomb

The PBomb space warp is used to blow particle systems apart. In the Blast Symmetry area of the PBomb Parameters rollout, you can set the blast force to be Spherical, Cylindrical, or Planar. With the Chaos parameter, you can add random forces to each particle. (The Chaos parameter value is used only if the Duration value is 0.)

In the previous example, you used the Bomb space warp to cause an object to explode. In this exercise, you will use PArray and PBomb to blow up the same object.

USING THE PBOMB SPACE WARP

1. Load file **CH15D.MAX** from the accompanying CD. The scene is based on the bowling alley you created in earlier chapters.

2. Advance to frame 0:0.21, just before the bowling ball hits the lead pin.

3. Create a PArray particle system in the Top view near the lead pin. In the PArray panel's Basic Parameters rollout, click Pick Object and select the lead pin as the object-based emitter. In the Viewport display area, turn on Mesh and set Percentage of Particles to 100.

4. In the Particle Generation rollout, set Speed to 0 and Life to 0:2.0.

5. In the Particle Type rollout, turn on Object Fragments in the Particle Types area. In the Object Fragment Controls area, turn on Number of Chunks. In the Mat'l Mapping and Source area, turn on Picked Emitter and then click Get Material From. In the Fragment Materials area, set Outside ID to 1 and Backside ID to 2.

6. Using Select by Name, select object Lane 2 Pin 0 (the lead pin) and hide it.

7. Create a PBomb space warp in the Top viewport, with the PBomb space warp centered next to the lead pin on the side where the bowling ball is located. Set Start Time to 0:0.22 and Duration to 0:0.0. Set Strength to 0.75 and Chaos to 25.

8. In the Left viewport, move the center of the PBomb space warp up about one-quarter the height of the bowling ball.

9. Using Select and Bind, bind the PArray particle system to the PBomb space warp.

10. In the Top viewport, create a Gravity space warp. Set Strength to 0. Turn on Animate. Then go to frame 0:0.20 and Shift+right-click the Strength spinner to set a key for Strength at the current key. Go to frame 0:0.21 and again Shift+right-click the Strength spinner. Go to Frame 0:0.22 and set Strength to 0.75. Turn off Animate and bind the Gravity space warp to the PArray particle system.

11. Create a UDeflector space warp. Click Pick Object and, using Select by Name, select Lane 2 as the object-based deflector. Set Bounce to 0.5. Bind the PArray particle system to UDeflector space warp.

12. Play back the animation in the Camera viewport.

The resulting MAX file is stored as **CH15E.MAX** on the accompanying CD for comparison.

As seen in the previous example, you can apply multiple, cumulative space warps to the particle systems. You can use the Path Follow space warp to route particles through your scene and use the deflector space warps to have the particles interact with objects in your scene.

Animating with Morphs

Morphing is the process of transforming one object into another over time. Many morphing effects were used in the movie *Terminator 2* to create the T-2000 Terminator made of liquid metal. In MAX you can easily morph between multiple objects, called morph targets. The object being created by the morphing is called the morph object.

There are two restrictions on the morph targets: all morph targets must have the same number of vertices, and the order of the vertices must match because as the morph is generated, MAX simply moves the vertices in the morph object to match the location of the same vertices in the morph targets. To illustrate the second restriction, if you have two face models with the same number of vertices but in a different order, a vertex on the nose of the first model might correspond to a vertex on the chin of the second model. Although MAX would enable you to morph between these morph targets, you would probably not be happy with the results. In practical application, one master object is created and copies of this object are made. The copies are then modified to form the morph targets, without creating or deleting vertices, thus ensuring the same number and order of vertices.

In 3D Studio MAX, Release 2, a new Morph controller was added. With the original Cubic Morph controller, each key represents a single morph target, so at the frame associated with a particular key, the morph object always looks exactly like that single morph target. With the Barycentric Morph controller introduced in Release 2, each key represents a series of weights for all morph targets; therefore, one barycentric key represents a morph object that is a blending of all morph targets. The Barycentric Morph controller is a superset of the Cubic Morph controller and is the default morph controller in Release 2. If you import scenes created in Release 1, they still use the Cubic Morph controller, but you can replace a Cubic Morph controller with a Barycentric Morph controller in Track View without a loss of data.

To create a morph, you first need to create each of the morph targets. Then, with one of the morph targets selected, you enter the Compound Objects object category in the Create command panel and click the Morph button. The Morph panel is shown in figure 15.24. The object selected when you click Morph is set as the first morph target. To add an additional morph target, select how the morph target is to be used

(Reference, Copy, Instance, or Move), click Pick Target to enter the pick mode, and then click each morph target. After selecting the morph targets, you can choose a morph target in the Morph Targets list and click Create Morph Key to create a key at the current frame. This key sets the influence of the selected morph target to 100% for the current frame.

Figure 15.24

The Morph compound object command panel, where you create the morph object and select morph targets.

In the Morph Target Name field, you can rename morph targets. You can delete a morph target by selecting the target in the Morph Targets list and clicking the Delete Morph Target key.

To adjust the influence of morph targets to other than 100%, you need to edit the morph keys in Track View. Figure 15.25 shows a Track View with a morph object. Figure 15.26 shows the Key Info dialog box for a Barycentric Morph controller key. The interpolation method for morph controller keys is a Tension/Continuity/Bias (TCB) controller. The top of the Key Info dialog box shows the parameters for the TCB interpolation parameters. These parameters are the same as the TCB controllers discussed in Chapter 14.

Below the TCB parameters is a list of morph targets, showing the percent influence each target has on the morph object. By selecting a target in this list, you can change its percent influence in the Percentage field. At the bottom of the dialog box is an option called Constrain to 100%. If this option is turned on as you adjust the influence percentage for one target, the influence percentage on the remaining targets changes to maintain a constant total influence percentage of 100%. It is recommended that you leave this option on, as total influence percentages other than 100 can scale the morph object up or down.

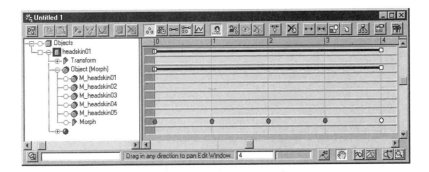

Figure 15.25

The Track View dialog box, showing the tracks for a Morph compound object.

Figure 15.26

The Track View Key Info dialog box for a Barycentric Morph controller key.

In the following exercise, you will use the Morph controller to perform facial animation of a character.

CREATING A MORPH OBJECT

1. Load file **CH15F.MAX** from the accompanying CD. This scene consists of five heads in various poses. A sixth head below the other five is a copy of the head furthest to the left.

2. Select the head at the bottom of the screen. In the Compound Objects object category in the Create command panel, click the Morph button.

3. Click Pick Target, and then select each of the right-most four heads.

4. Open Track View and expand the hierarchy to the Morph controller.

5. Right-click on the Morph controller key at frame 0.

6. Select one of the morph targets in the Key Info target list and change its percentage. Note that as you change the percentage, the morph object in the viewport updates to reflect the change.

In the previous exercise you saw how to deform the face based on several different morph targets. To model a complete character, you will usually use the Physique portion of Character Studio or use Bones Pro to deform the character mesh based on the underlying skeleton. It is usually easier to use the Morph controller below Physique or Bones Pro to perform detailed facial animation of a character.

Animating with Dynamics

The Dynamics utility is used to create animations that simulate real-world physics. Realistic object motion can be achieved based on the object's physical properties and the forces acting on the object. The Dynamics utility shipped with MAX is a rigid-body dynamics package. In rigid-body dynamics, an object's positions and rotations are calculated based on the forces acting on the object, but no deformation of the object occurs.

To perform a dynamic simulation, the following information must be specified:

♦ The objects included in the simulation

♦ The properties of the objects

♦ The object collisions to look for

♦ The external forces generated by space warps acting on the objects

♦ Any initial motion of the objects

To create a dynamic simulation, click the Utilities command panel tab and choose Dynamics. The Dynamics utility rollouts are shown in figure 15.27. To define a new simulation, choose New to initialize a new dynamic simulation. To specify a preexisting simulation, select the simulation name from the Simulation Name drop-down list.

Kinematic chains can be used in dynamic simulations; however, their use is beyond the scope of a Fundamentals book. For information on using kinematic chains in dynamic simulations, please refer to your MAX documentation.

Figure 15.27

The Dynamics rollouts, where you define the parameters for dynamic simulations.

Specifying Objects in a Dynamic Simulation

To specify the objects to include in the simulation, choose Edit Object List to display the Edit Object List dialog box shown in figure 15.28. Only objects included in the simulation will be considered in the dynamics solution. This includes stationary objects that other objects in the simulation can collide with.

Figure 15.28

The Edit Object List dialog box, where you define the objects to be included in a dynamic simulation.

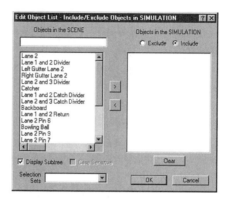

Specifying Dynamics Properties for Objects

To specify the properties for objects in the simulation, click Edit Object to display the Edit Object dialog box shown in figure 15.29. To specify the object for which you are defining properties, use the Object drop-down list at the top left corner of the dialog box. In the Misc Dynamic Controls area, you can turn on the Use Initial State option so the motion and rotation of the object at the start time of the simulation are taken into account. If the object is not moving, turn this option off. If you turn on This Object is Immovable, the object is not assigned any motion or rotation in the simulation. You want to turn this option on for solid, fixed objects such as walls and floors. By using the Move Pivot to Centroid button, you can move the object's pivot point to the mass center of the object. The method by which the center of mass for the object is calculated is based on the Calculate Properties Using option.

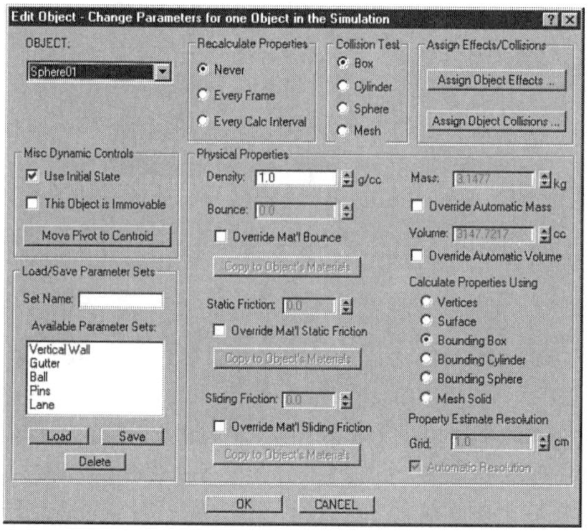

Figure 15.29

The Edit Object dialog box, where you define the dynamics properties for the objects in a dynamic simulation.

NOTE

If you plan to animate the rotation of an object outside the dynamic simulation time period, you should use Move Pivot to Centroid before animating the rotation. An object rotates around its pivot point, so if you first animate the rotation and then change the location of the pivot point, the way the object rotates will change.

The distribution of an object's mass around its center of mass affects how the object rotates. The classic example is an ice skater—if the skater is rotating and pulls her arms in, she rotates faster than when she extends her arms. The distribution of an object's mass can be calculated several ways in MAX, using the Calculate Properties Using option in the Physical Properties area. For objects other than simple boxes, spheres, and cylinders, you can calculate the center of mass by using one of the bounding methods, Vertices, Surface, or Mesh Solid (listed in order of increasing accuracy).

To place the object's pivot point at the center of mass, as described earlier, calculate the object's mass distribution during the simulation. How often the mass distribution is calculated during the simulation is specified in the Recalculate Properties area. Which option to use depends on whether the shape of the object is animated and, if so, how fast the shape is changing. If the shape of the object is not animated, choose the Never option. If the shape is changing slowly, choose the Every Frame option. If the shape is changing rapidly, choose Every Calc Interval.

In the Collision Test area, you specify the object boundaries used during collision detection. The choices are Box (the object's bounding box is used), Cylinder (the object's bounding cylinder is used), Sphere (the object's bounding sphere is used), and Mesh (the actual faces of the object are used). For the Cylinder method, the height axis of the cylinder is aligned with the object's local Z axis. The Mesh method is extremely calculation intensive and should only be used if the object's shape is complex or the results from other methods are inaccurate.

TIP

If you need to use the Mesh method on an object for collision detection, consider placing an Optimize modifier on the object. You can usually use a fairly high Face Threshold value to reduce the number of faces significantly while retaining the overall shape of the object. After solving the dynamic simulation, turn off or delete the Optimize modifier.

In the Physical Properties area, you specify the physical properties of an object. The Density parameter specifies the density of the object and is used to calculate the object's mass. The higher the mass of an object, the more resistant it is to changes in motion or rotation due to external forces (collisions and space warp forces). The Bounce parameter specifies how much an object will bounce after a collision. A ball made of lead, for example, would have a low Bounce value, and a rubber ball would have a high Bounce value. The Static Friction parameter specifies how hard it is to get a stationary object to move. The Sliding Friction parameter specifies how hard it is to keep a moving object in motion. To experience the difference between these two types of friction, press down on a table and push your hand along it. It takes more force to start your hand moving than to keep it moving.

The Mass parameter is typically calculated based on the object's density and volume. You can override the automatic calculation of Mass and specify a value, if you desire. Similarly, the Volume of an object is typically calculated based on the Density value and the Calculate Properties Using selection.

WARNING

If you calculate mass with Calculate Properties Using set to either Vertices or Surface, the internal volume of the object is not considered, resulting in a much lower calculated mass. You should not use the Vertices or Surface setting on objects for which collisions are being detected unless you override the automatic mass calculation. The motion resulting from a collision of two objects is dependent on the relative masses of the objects. If one object's mass is calculated by using Vertices or Surface, and the other's by using a bounding object or Mesh Solid, the relative masses of the objects will be incorrect and will result in incorrect motion after the collision.

The Bounce, Static Friction, and Sliding Friction values can be specified either in the Edit Object dialog box or in the object's material. It is usually easiest to use the values from the object's material if you have several identical objects with the same material (for example, pins in a bowling alley). For objects that are not the same, it is usually easiest to set the values in the Edit Object dialog box.

To set the property values in an object's material, open Material Editor and select the material. The bottom rollout for the Standard material type is the Dynamic Properties rollout, shown in figure 15.30. In this rollout, you can set the Bounce Coefficient, Static Friction, and Sliding Friction values, which will then be used for all objects that use the material. You can also set different property values for different object faces by using the Multi/Sub-object material type. In the same way that the individual materials are applied to object faces based on their material ID, the dynamic properties are applied to the matching faces.

Figure 15.30

The Material Editor Standard material type Dynamics Properties rollout.

Assigning Object Effects and Object Collisions

An *object effect* is a Particles & Dynamics space warp, such as Push or Gravity. You can assign effects to individual objects or to all objects, but not both. To assign effects to all objects, turn on Global Effect in the Effects area of the Dynamics rollout and click Assign Global Effects to display the Assign Global Effects dialog box shown in figure 15.31. All space warps in the scene that can be used for dynamics are displayed in the list of Effects in the Scene. You can select effects for inclusion or exclusion of all objects in the scene, in the same manner that objects were selected in the Edit Object List dialog box.

To assign effects on an object-by-object basis, turn on Effects by Object in the Effects area of the Dynamics rollout. In the Assign Effects/Collisions area of the Edit Object dialog box, click Assign Object Effects. This displays the Assign Object Effects dialog box, identical to the Assign Global Effects dialog box.

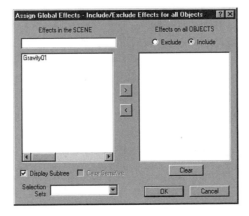

Figure 15.31

The Assign Global Effects dialog box, where you define the space warp forces to be applied to all objects in the dynamic simulation.

An additional effect that applies to all objects in the simulation is Air Resistance Density. Air resistance pushes against object faces pointing in the direction of the object's motion, causing an object to slow down or flutter. The higher the Density value, the more drag is applied to the objects in the simulation.

Because collision detection is CPU intensive, you need to specify which object collisions to detect. Much as you assigned effects to objects, you can globally specify a group of objects among which to detect collisions, or you can specify for each object certain objects to detect collisions with, but not both.

TIP If you have a lot of objects specified as immovable, assign collisions on an object-by-object basis. The dynamic simulation will be solved much faster.

Solving the Dynamic Simulation

After setting up the parameters necessary for the dynamic solution, actually solving the solution is easy—simply set the time range for the simulation and click the Solve button in the Dynamics rollout. The Dynamics utility calculates the motion of the objects at the first frame of the simulation and then steps through the time range, calculating the position and rotation of each object based on the object's previous motion, the forces applied by space warps, and the forces resulting from object collisions. Keys are generated for each object to store its position and rotation. Depending on the number of objects in the scene, the number of object collisions to detect, and the collision test methods, solving the dynamics solution can take anywhere from seconds to days.

If you are using collision detection in your simulation, you may find that objects are passing through one another. If this is the case, increase the Calc Intervals Per Frame, which specifies how many times per frame the object motions are solved. The higher this value is, the more accurate the simulation will be, but high values result in longer execution times. Finding the right number to use is a matter of experimentation; however, a value of 2 to 4 is usually a good starting point.

TIP If you know that a large number of objects aren't affected by the dynamics solution until near the end of the simulation time range, try to break the simulation into several parts. In each part, only include the objects for which you need to have the dynamics calculated.

In the following exercise, you will use the Dynamics utility to model a ball rolling down a bowling alley and hitting the pins.

CREATING A DYNAMIC SIMULATION

1. Load file **CH15G.MAX** from the accompanying CD. This scene is based on the bowling alley you created in earlier chapters and contains only the objects associated with the second lane of the bowling alley.

2. Create a Gravity space warp in the Top viewport.

3. Click the Utilities command panel tab, and then click Dynamics.

4. Choose Simulation Name, New.

5. Click Edit Object List. In the Objects in Scene list, select Lane 2 and Bowling Ball, and click the right arrow to include these two objects in the simulation. Click OK to close the dialog box.

6. Click Edit Object. In the Edit Object dialog box, choose Lane 2 from the Object drop-down list if it is not already the object shown. In Misc Dynamic Controls, turn on This Object is Immovable. Turn on Override Mat'l Bounce and set Bounce to 0. Turn on the overrides on both friction parameters and set each friction value to 0.02. In the Load/Save Parameter Sets area, type **Lane** into the Set Name field, and then click Save.

7. Choose Bowling Ball from the Object drop-down list. Turn on Override Mat'l Bounce and set Bounce to 0. Turn on the overrides on both friction parameters and set each friction value to 0.02. Set Density to 8. In Collision Test, turn on Mesh. In Physical Properties, choose Calculate Properties Using, Bounding Sphere. Type **Ball** into the Set Name field and click Save.

8. In the Assign Effects/Collisions area, click Assign Object Collisions, select Lane 2, and click the right arrow. Click OK to close the dialog box. Click OK again to close the Edit Object dialog box.

9. In the Dynamics rollout, turn on Global Effects and click Assign Global Effects. Turn on Exclude and click OK to close the dialog box. If you turn on Exclude without adding any effects to exclude, all the effects in the scene are applied to the object.

10. Set Start Time to 1 and Air Resistance to 100. Turn on Update Display w/Solve, and click Solve. This dynamics solution should only take about 10 to 30 seconds. When the solution is complete, advance the frame until the bowling ball intersects the first pin (this should be frame 16).

11. Click New to create a new simulation. Click Edit Object List, turn on Exclude, and click OK.

12. Click Edit Object. In the Edit Object dialog box, choose Lane 2 from the Object drop-down list if it is not already the object shown. Click Lane in the Available Parameter Sets, and then click Load.

13. In the Edit Object dialog box, choose Lane 1 and 2 Divider from the Object drop-down list. In Misc Dynamic Controls, turn on This Object is Immovable. Turn on Override Mat'l Bounce and set Bounce to 0. In the Load/Save Parameter Sets area, type **Vertical Wall** into the Set Name field, and then click Save.

14. Select Left Gutter Lane 2 from the Object drop-down list. Select Lane in the Available Parameter Sets, and click Load. In the Collision Test area, turn on Mesh. Type **Gutter** into the Set Name field, and then click Save.

15. Select Right Gutter Lane 2 from the Object drop-down list. Click Gutter in the Available Parameter Sets, and then click Load.

16. Select Bowling Ball from the Object drop-down list. Click Ball in the Available Parameter Sets, and then click Load. Click Assign Object Collisions, choose Exclude, and click OK to close the dialog box.

17. Select Lane 2 Pin 6 from the Object drop-down list. In Misc Dynamic Controls, turn off Use Initial State. In Collision Test, turn on Cylinder. In Physical Properties, set Density to 11.8 and set Calculate Properties Using to Mesh Solid. Under Property Estimation Resolution, turn off Automatic Resolution and set Grid to 1.0. Type **Pins** into the Set Name field, and then click Save.

18. In the Assign Effects/Collisions area, click Assign Object Collisions, choose Exclude, and click OK to close the dialog box. Turn on Move Pivot to Centroid and select the next pin from the Object drop-down list. When you select the next pin, the object properties are calculated for the pin and the pin's pivot point is moved to the pin's center of mass. When the dialog box shows the new pin, click Pins in the Available Parameter Sets, and then click Load.

19. Repeat step 18 for all the pins.

20. For each of the remaining objects in the simulation, load Vertical Wall to set the object parameters. These remaining objects are Lane 2 and 3 Divider, Catcher, Lane 1 and 2 Catch Divider, Lane 2 and 3 Catch Divider, Backboard, Lane 1 and 2 Return, Lane 2 and 3 Return, and Pit Wall. When you have set the parameters for these objects, click OK to close the Edit Object dialog box.

21. Open Material Editor and select the material applied to the pins. This material is Bowling Pin, shown in the sample slot as a white sphere with a red stripe. Open the Dynamics Properties rollout and set Bounce Coefficient to 0.3, Static Friction to 0.2, and Sliding Friction to 0.02. Close Material Editor.

22. In the Dynamics rollout, turn on Global Effects and click Assign Global Effects. Choose Exclude and click OK to close the dialog box.

23. Set Start Time to 15 (you want to start on the frame before the collision occurs) and set Calc Intervals Per Frame to 3. Set Air Resistance to 100. Turn on Update Display w/Solve, and click Solve. Due to the large number of object collisions involved in the simulation, the dynamics solution should take 2 to 3 hours to solve. When the solution is complete, play back the animation in the camera viewport.

24. Open Track View and expand the hierarchy tree to show the position track for Lane 2 Pin 0. Select the position key at frame 0 and right-click on it. In the Key Info dialog box, click and hold on the Out tangent type button and select the Step tangent type from the flyout. Close the Key Info and Track View dialog boxes. Switching to the Step tangent mode eliminates the

motion of the pin between the frame 0 and the first frame that the second simulation was solved for.

25. Save the file as **CH15H.MAX**.

The completed scene is included on the accompanying CD as file **CH15H.MAX**. If you run into problems, you can load this file and look at its settings.

As you can see in the preceding example, calculating the dynamics solution can take quite a long time if there are a lot of objects in the scene that can collide with one another. The key to working with dynamics is to experiment with the object parameters, using a subset of the objects in the simulation to determine which parameter values to use. When you are in the ballpark on these values, start adding new objects to the simulation and experimenting with their parameter values. Although it can take several hours or even a day to set up and solve the simulation, the alternative is to manually keyframe the animation, which can take several days and still not look totally realistic.

Animating with MAXScript

MAXScript is a complete programming language with which you can automate many aspects of MAX, including object creation and animation. MAXScript was designed specifically for MAX and provides access to the same internal functions in MAX used by plug-in developers.

With MAXScript, you can access nearly all the functions available in the user interface, as well as some functions not available in the interface. You can create all the object types available in the Create command panel, or you can create an Editable Mesh for defining the individual vertices and faces. You can apply modifiers to objects, link objects into hierarchies, create and assign materials, apply or change controllers on objects, create animation keys, and create custom controllers. You can even use MAXScript to link MAX to external programs; for example, you can link to a spreadsheet and use its data to control an animation in MAX.

MAXScript accommodates MAX-specific syntax, including wild-character path names for selecting objects in the object hierarchy and context prefixes for setting the animation state, time, and reference coordinate system. MAXScript also provides tools with which you can perform sophisticated programming tasks. Vector and matrix algebra are built in, enabling straightforward calculation of values to be used in an animation. MAXScript's use of collection sets enables you to perform operations easily on large groups of objects in a single statement.

MAXScript enables you to create custom rollouts in the Utilities command panel and to create modeless dialogs incorporating the standard MAX point-and-click user interface.

The details of MAXScript are well beyond the scope of a Fundamentals book. For more information on MAXScript and its uses, please refer to your MAX documentation.

Conclusion

MAX provides you with many advanced tools to assist you in creating animations that would be difficult or impossible to achieve by simply keyframing individual objects over time. From this chapter you should have a basic understanding of the following tools and techniques:

♦ Creation and Animation of Object Hierarchies

♦ Types of Space Warps and Their Effect on Objects and Particles

♦ Mesh Deformation, Using Morph Targets

♦ Setting up and Solving Dynamic Simulations

♦ A General Understanding of the Power of MAXScript

Although it may take some time to become proficient with these tools, you should consider this an investment in becoming a professional animator.

CHAPTER 16

Exploring Animation Rendering Methods

In MAX, rendering an animation is similar to rendering a still frame, except you are rendering multiple still frames and compiling them into an animation format. MAX allows you to render the animation from two different locations: the Render Scene dialog box and Video Post. Video Post, a special MAX dialog box in which you can perform image-editing and composite special effects, is discussed in Chapter 17, "Exploring Video Post Fundamentals."

This chapter focuses on rendering an animation from the Render Scene dialog box. In particular, this chapter focuses on the following topics:

- ◆ Animation Rendering Options

- ◆ Motion Blur

- ◆ Field Rendering

- ◆ Network Rendering

- ◆ Output Options

Animation Rendering Options

To render an animation, you start by activating the view you want to render. Then, choose the Render Scene button on the main toolbar, just as you would for a still frame. In the Render Scene dialog box (shown in figure 16.1), several settings apply to rendering animations. These include the time range, video color checking, motion blur, field rendering, and net rendering.

Figure 16.1

The Render Scene dialog box.

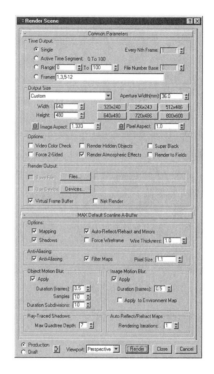

Animation is nothing more than the display of a sequence of images at a rate fast enough to give the illusion of motion. To achieve this effect, you have to render many still frames. In the Time Output area of the Render Scene dialog box, you define which frames you are going to render. You can render the active time segment, a specific range, or specific sets of frames.

Animations typically are rendered with the intent of outputting the animation to videotape. Unfortunately, videotape is not a great medium, because neither the NTSC or PAL video standard supports as wide a color range as MAX does. If you are rendering the animation with the intention of taking it to videotape, you should turn on the Video Color Check check box in the Options area of the Render Scene dialog box. This enables you to check the colors of each output image relative to acceptable color ranges for the videotape type (NTSC or PAL) you are recording to. You can define how Video Color Check is performed by choosing File, Preferences and clicking the Rendering tab in the Preference Settings dialog box (see figure 16.2).

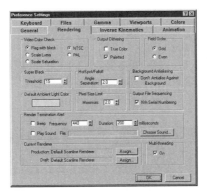

Figure 16.2

The Rendering tab of the Preference Settings dialog box.

In the Video Color Check area in the upper-left corner of the Rendering tab, you can determine how MAX handles the color checking. First, and most important, you should choose the video standard to which you are outputting. In the United States and Japan, it is NTSC. In other places, it may be NTSC or PAL—more than likely, it is PAL. Then you can determine how MAX should handle colors in your images that are not compatible with the standards.

The options found in the Video Color Check area are described in the following list:

♦ **Flag with Black:** When this option is enabled, each pixel that is out of the acceptable color range is colored black. You can adjust the materials or lighting so the material does not exceed acceptable color limits.

♦ **Scale Luma:** When this option is enabled, each pixel's luminance is scaled up or down until the color is within the acceptable range. If the pixel's color is already within the range, it is not scaled.

♦ **Scale Saturation:** When this option is enabled, each pixel's color saturation is scaled up or down until the color is within the acceptable range. If the pixel's color is already within the range, it is not scaled.

Very bright green colors fail video color checking. Even if a color passes video color checking, that does not mean the color will look good when viewed on a video monitor. All very bright colors tend to bleed when displayed on a video monitor, with bright red being the worst. When you design your colors in Material Editor, keep the saturation value of your colors at less than 200.

Motion Blur

If you look at a still frame from a movie or from a video, you will notice that the edges of moving objects are rather blurred along the direction of motion. This happens because the object is in one position when the shutter opens and in another when the shutter closes. The captured image is actually of the object in all its positions between the opening and closing of the shutter. You can use motion blur in MAX to approximate this effect. In a playback of animated sequences, motion blur provides a smoothness of motion that is not present if motion blur is not applied. Figure 16.3 shows a scene rendered without motion blur, and figure 16.4 shows the same scene rendered with motion blur.

Figure 16.3

A scene rendered without motion blur.

MAX supports three types of motion blur: Object, Scene, and Image. MAX performs Object motion blur by rendering multiple copies of selected objects within a single rendering. Scene motion blur is performed by rendering the scene multiple times and then compositing the resulting images. Image motion blur is performed by rendering the objects once and calculating a linear motion vector for each pixel, which is then blurred along its motion vector. Object and Image motion blur are performed either by using Render Scene or in Video Post. Scene motion blur can be performed only in Video Post and is described in Chapter 17.

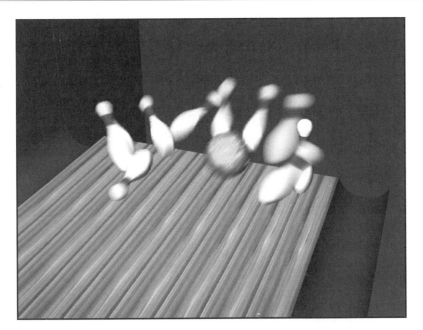

Figure 16.4

The same scene rendered with motion blur.

To perform motion blur on an object, you first need to turn on Motion Blur for the object. To do this, right-click on the object and select Properties from the pop-up menu to display the Object Properties dialog box shown in figure 16.5. In the Motion Blur area of this dialog box, you can specify whether to perform no motion blur, Object motion blur, or Image motion blur on the object. The Multiplier field for Image motion blur is described later in this section.

Figure 16.5

The Object Properties dialog box.

After you have turned on motion blur for one or more objects, you need to set the motion blur parameters in the Render Scene dialog box. In the MAX Default Scanline A-Buffer rollout, there are parameters for both Object and Image motion blur (see figure 16.6). For each type of motion blur, you need to click Apply so that type of motion blur will be calculated. Both motion blur areas also contain a Duration (frames) field, which specifies how much time to include in the motion blur around the frame being rendered. Think of this parameter as determining how long a camera's shutter would be open. This exposure time is centered around the frame. For example, if you are rendering frame 10 and set a Duration value of 1, the exposure period will be from frame 9.5 to 10.5. For a Duration value of 0.5, the exposure period will be 9.75 to 10.25. Typical Duration values are in the range of 0.3 to 0.5.

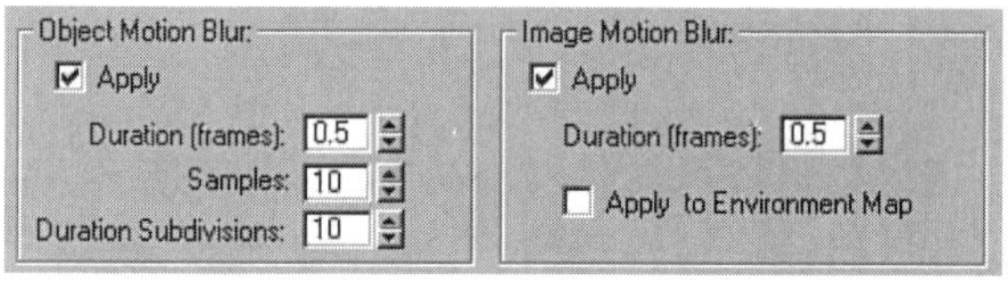

Figure 16.6

The Motion Blur areas of the Render Scene dialog box.

When using Object motion blur, there are two additional settings: Duration Subdivisions and Samples. The Duration Subdivisions parameter sets the number of copies of the object to render per frame. If this parameter is set to 3, one copy of the object will be rendered at the beginning of the exposure period, one at the middle, and one at the end. Figure 16.7 shows a scene rendered with Duration Subdivisions values of 3, 8, 12, and 16. Notice that as the Duration Subdivisions value increases, the number of copies increases, and the resulting motion blur looks smoother.

The Samples parameter controls how many times these copies are sampled in the final rendered image. It is best to think of Samples in terms of the percentage 100×(Samples/Duration Subdivisions). At 100%, all pixels from each copy of the object are included in the rendered image. At 50%, half of the pixels from each copy are included, resulting in dithering of the image. Typical Duration Subdivisions values are in the range of 10 to 16, with Samples set at 1 or 2 lower than the Duration Subdivisions value. Figure 16.8 shows a scene rendered with a Duration Subdivisions value of 12 and Samples values of 6, 8, 10, and 12. Notice that as the Samples value increases, each copy of the objects becomes more solid.

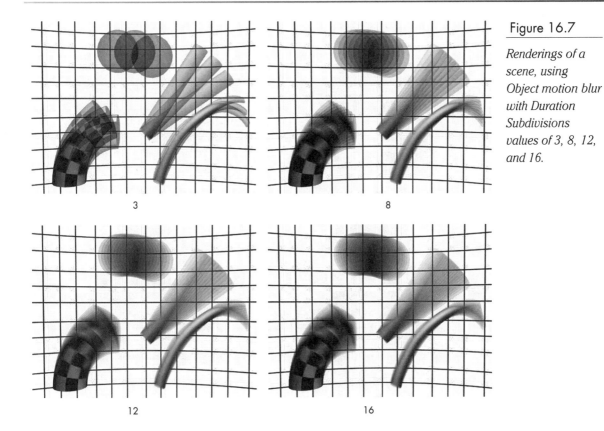

Figure 16.7

Renderings of a scene, using Object motion blur with Duration Subdivisions values of 3, 8, 12, and 16.

For Image motion blur, there are two additional settings: Multiplier in the Object Properties dialog box and Apply to Environment Map in the Render Scene dialog box. By using the Multiplier parameter, you can increase or decrease the amount of Image motion blur on an object-by-object basis. For example, with the Multiplier value set to 2, the object's "streak" is twice as long as when the Multiplier value remains at 1. The total length of an object's streak is a function of the Multiplier value and the Duration value. If the Apply to Environment Map option is turned on, environmental background images will also be blurred, based on the amount of camera motion. Figure 16.9 shows the same scene as in figure 16.8, rendered with Image motion blur.

Figure 16.8

Renderings of a scene, using Object motion blur with Samples values of 6, 8, 10, and 12.

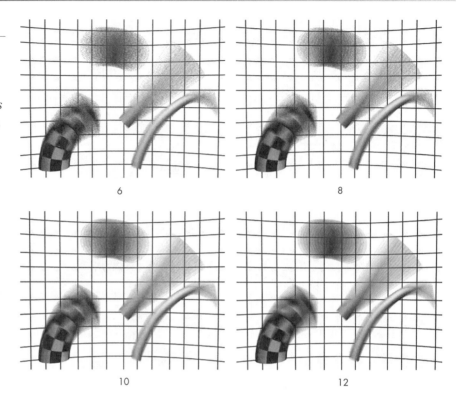

Figure 16.9

Rendering of a scene, using Image motion blur.

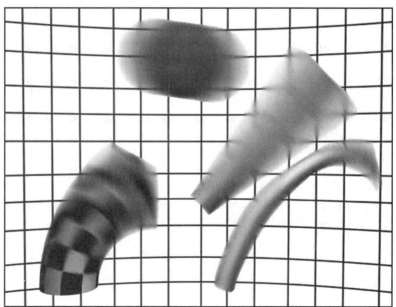

As explained previously, Image motion blur is performed by calculating a linear motion vector for each pixel and then blurring the pixel along its motion vector. The motion vectors are based on the difference in a pixel's position at a time slightly before the render time and its position at the render time. As a result, Image motion blur will not be accurate if the point on the object corresponding to a pixel is not moving in a straight line. Also, Image motion blur will not be accurate if the point on the object is not coming into the frame as it moves. This is most evident at frame 0, where typically there is no motion coming into the frame. Figure 16.10 shows an Object motion blur rendering in which the object is moving with a curvilinear trajectory. Figure 16.11 shows the same object rendered by using Image motion blur. Although Image motion blur is typically faster to perform than Scene or Object motion blur and usually looks better, the limitations of Image motion blur sometimes prevent its use.

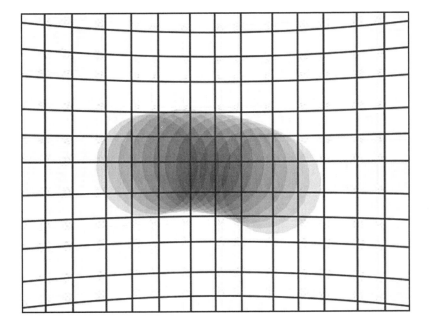

Figure 16.10

Rendering by using Object motion blur of an object moving with a curvilinear trajectory.

Animated object transforms, object deformations, and camera transforms are reflected when performing Object or Image motion blur. Animated environmental effects (including background images), camera parameters (such as FOV), and object materials are not reflected when performing Object or Image motion blur. Also, changes in the environmental background image due to camera transforms are not reflected when using Object motion blur, but can be when using Image motion blur.

Figure 16.11

Rendering by using Image motion blur of an object moving with a curvilinear trajectory.

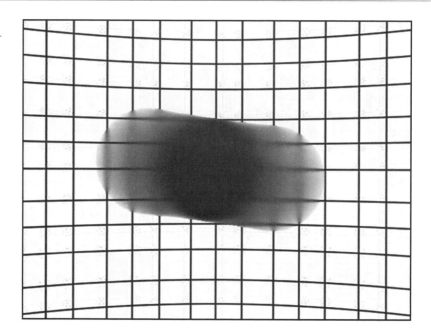

You should note that using motion blur can slow down the rendering process substantially and should be used only when necessary. Memory requirements depend on the number of faces in objects selected for Object motion blur and on the size of the output image for Image motion blur. For Object motion blur, additional memory is required for each copy of the object created. For Image motion blur, an additional 14 bytes per pixel are required. (For a 640x480 image, this means an additional 4.3 MB of memory.)

In the following exercise, you will render the bowling alley simulation created in Chapter 15, "Exploring Other Animation Methods." The scene will be rendered with no motion blur, Object motion blur, and Image motion blur to show you the differences in image quality and render time in a real-world example.

RENDERING AN ANIMATION

1. Load file **CH15H.MAX** from the accompanying CD. This scene contains the results of the dynamic simulation in the bowling alley.

2. Select the Camera03 viewport and click Render Scene. Select Range and set the range to frames 15 to 50 in the Time Output area. In Output size, select 320x240.

3. Choose Files and type an output file name of **SIM.AVI**.

4. Choose Setup, Cinepak Codec. Set the Compression Quality to 70. If Key Frame is turned off, turn it on and set it to 15 frames. Click OK to close the Video Compression dialog box. Then click OK again to close the Render Output File dialog box.

5. Now click Render to render the animation. When the rendering is complete, choose File, View File to view **SIM.AVI**.

6. In the Front viewport, select all the pins and the bowling ball. Right-click one of the selected objects and choose Properties from the pop-up menu. In the Object Properties dialog box, turn on Object in the Motion Blur area.

7. Select the Camera03 viewport and render the animation to file **SIM_OMB.AVI**. When the rendering is complete, view **SIM_OMB.AVI**.

8. Right-click on one of the selected objects and choose Properties from the pop-up menu. In the Object Properties dialog box, turn on Image in the Motion Blur area.

9. Select the Camera03 viewport and render the animation to file **SIM_IMB.AVI**. When the rendering is complete, view **SIM_OMB.AVI**.

When viewing the AVI files from the previous example, you can see that the use of motion blur makes the animation look much more realistic, but at a cost of increased rendering times. Rendering time was approximately three times longer when you used Object motion blur, but only about 10% longer when you used Image motion blur. In the previous example, the limitations of Image motion blur are not obvious while playing back the animation, so Image motion blur should be used in this case.

Field Rendering

The most important aspect of rendering an animation for video output is probably field rendering. Video output displays information in an *interlaced* manner. This means the video output first displays every other scanline of information and then repeats by displaying the scanlines it missed the first time. Most computer monitors are non-interlaced, so all scanlines are refreshed in order.

To get the smoothest motion in your animations when they are played back on a TV screen, you should always use field rendering. This causes MAX to render every other scanline of the frame and then to come back and render the scanlines it missed. When MAX renders the second set of scanlines, however, it moves forward in time in the animation by half a frame. Field-rendered images don't look as good as still frames because of this effect, but the motion on a videotape is excellent. Rendering to fields, of course, increases the overall processing time for the animation.

When you render to fields, you must determine which field of the frame is rendered first. You can render either odd or even fields first. You set this value in the Preference Settings dialog box under the Rendering tab, shown in figure 16.2. Before you decide which field order to use, you should match the order to the output device you are using. A DPS Perception Video Recorder (PVR), for example, can accept either order of field rendering; you just need to match the setting in MAX to the settings on the PVR. You should check the documentation on your output hardware or software to see which field order to use.

When you do field rendering, the playback of the animation changes slightly. Instead of referring to the playback speed as 30 frames per second, you say it plays back at 60 fields per second. Remember, each frame has two fields. When the documentation of a specific output device specifies 60 fields per second, this refers to the field-rendering playback speed.

Network Rendering

When rendering an animation, you can spend enormous amounts of time just waiting for the rendering of each frame to finish. It is not uncommon for rendering of an animation to take 2, 3, 5, 10, 20, or more days, depending on the complexity of the scene, the rendering options, and the overall number of frames. MAX offers two ways to decrease this amount of time. First, you can use multiple processors in a single system. Second, you can use network rendering.

In network rendering, a TCP/IP (Transmission Control Protocol/Internet Protocol) network is used to link a series of Windows NT or Windows 95 workstations together. As an animation submitted for network rendering is processed, the next frame of the animation is sent to the next available machine on the network for processing. A two-machine network cuts an animation's rendering time in half (if both machines are configured the same way), a three-machine- network cuts the time by three, and so on.

Large animation houses typically have rendering "farms" of ten or more machines strictly dedicated to rendering animations. After working on an animation at your workstation, you can test it by starting a network rendering and sending the animation out across the rendering farm.

NOTE　You can network-render by using multiple machines only when you are rendering to a sequence of bitmap files. You cannot use multiple machines to create an AVI or FLC animation file, because frames must be saved individually for these file formats. On a network rendering, depending on the configuration of the networked machines, you probably will not get the frames back in the correct order. To create AVI or FLC files, you must render on a single machine or compile the individual frames into an AVI or FLC equipped with Video Post or a nonlinear editing suite such as Adobe Premiere.

The four basic components to network rendering in MAX are described in the following list:

♦ **TCP/IP Networking:** TCP/IP is a common networking protocol used by a large variety of operating systems. This network protocol was chosen for MAX because it is so widely used. Because TCP/IP is the protocol for the Internet, you could, theoretically, do network rendering across the Internet; however, your NT workstation must have TCP/IP installed before you can do any network rendering. (Consult your NT documentation on how to set up TCP/IP.)

♦ **Manager:** Manager is a program that controls which animations are in the network queue, when they are processed, and which machines on the network will render which frames. For most end users, this process occurs transparently, because Manager is installed on only one machine on the network. The machine Manager runs on does not need to have MAX installed on it. The same machine can be used for running both Manager and Server.

♦ **Server:** Server is a program that queries Manager for the next frame of the animation to render. When Server receives the information, it launches MAX and renders the frame. When the frame has been rendered, Server notifies Manager that it is ready for another frame. Again, this process happens transparently. MAX needs to be installed on all machines running Server.

♦ **Queue Manager:** This stand-alone program is used to manage the network queue. You can manage the queue from any NT or Windows 95 workstation connected to your network and running TCP/IP. You can use Queue Manager to check the status of animations in the rendering queue, change their order, or delete them. MAX does not need to be installed on the machines Queue Manager is run on.

Configuring for Network Rendering

Before performing network rendering, you need to configure Manager on a single machine and Server on the networked machines. Both Manager and Server can be run on the same machine.

To configure Manager, open the MAX directory and double-click on Manager. A warning message is displayed, stating that Manager is not configured (see figure 16.12). Click OK. The 3D Studio MAX Network Manager Properties dialog box is displayed, as shown in figure 16.13. In the TCP/IP area of this dialog, the Manager and Server ports are defined. A TCP/IP port is used to distinguish between multiple destinations within a given computer. Unless you receive an error when running Manager or Server stating that a port is already in use, you should not change these port numbers. If you do change them, you will need to change them for all MAX Managers and Servers on your network.

Figure 16.12

The Network Manager "not configured" warning message.

Figure 16.13

The Network Manager Properties dialog box.

In the General area, the Wait for MAX to Load and Wait for MAX to Unload values specify how long Manager waits for a server to load after being given a frame to render or to unload after completing the render. If a server takes longer than the specified times, it is flagged as failed and no more frames are sent to it. Unless you are having problems with servers being flagged as failed, you should not adjust these values.

To finish the configuration, click OK. A subdirectory called Network is created off your MAX directory to store Manager's configuration parameters and network jobs. Manager closes automatically, and you need to double-click on the Manager icon to restart it.

To configure Server, open the MAX directory and double-click on Server. The same warning message as for Manager is displayed, stating that Server is not configured. Click OK. The 3D Studio MAX Network Server Properties dialog box is displayed, as shown in figure 16.14. In the TCP/IP area, the Manager and Server ports are defined—these must have the same values used for Manager. In the Manager Name or IP Address field, replace the text "maxserver" with the machine name or IP address of the machine running Manager.

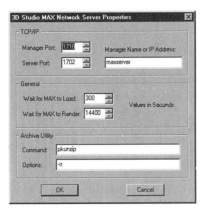

Figure 16.14

The Network Server Properties dialog box.

If you want to use the machine name and are running a small network that does not use the Domain Name System (DNS), edit the file called **HOSTS** in directory %systemroot%\system32\drivers\etc (where %systemroot% is the root directory of your Windows NT install). In this file, put the IP address of the Manager's machine name. An example line in this file would be:

192.125.100.101   Larry1

NOTE

In the General area, the Wait for MAX to Load and Wait for MAX to Render values specify how long Server sends messages back to the manager saying MAX has loaded or how long Server waits for MAX to render the current frame. If MAX takes longer than one of these times, the server is flagged as failed and no more frames are sent. Unless you are having problems with servers being flagged as failed, you should not adjust these values.

In the Archive Utility area, the de-archive program name and any extensions are specified. When you submit a network rendering job with Include Maps turned on, MAX creates an archive file, using the program specified in File, Preferences, Files (see figure 16.2). This archive file contains the MAX scene and any bitmap files used in the scene. The Archive Utility program specified in the Server configuration must be capable of de-archiving the file created by the archiving program.

The default archive and de-archive programs are PKZIP and PKUNZIP. These are 16-bit DOS programs and do not support long file names. SZipW and WinZip are 32-bit archiving programs compatible with MAX. Check the Kinetix forum on CompuServe or the Kinetix support Web site (www.ktx.com/3dsmaxr2) for these or other archive programs.

WARNING

To finish the configuration, click OK. A subdirectory called Network is created off of your MAX directory to store Server's configuration parameters and network jobs. Server closes automatically, and you need to double-click on the Server icon to restart it.

WARNING

You must authorize MAX on all network server machines before running it. Otherwise, after MAX loads, a message box appears asking you to authorize it (see figure 16.15). Authorizing MAX on every machine, of course, does not mean you have to purchase a copy of MAX for each machine; however, you have to attach the MAX dongle to the network render station temporarily and run the Authorize 3DS MAX program on the machine. See the MAX documentation for performing a Compact install of MAX on the server machines.

Figure 16.15

*The MAX
authorization
warning message.*

Preparing a Net Rendering Job

After Manager and Server are up and running, you can network-render by using MAX. Before you start to network-render, make sure all machines you want to use in the network are set up and turned on. (This instruction might sound silly, but you don't want to come into work some morning only to find your previous night's rendering stalled by a downed computer.)

To perform a network rendering job, load a scene and choose Render Scene from the MAX toolbar to access the Render Scene dialog box. In the dialog box, set any options, the time range, the output size, and the output file path and name.

When you specify the output file path in MAX, that file path is passed as text to each server and resolved at each server based on its disk configuration. If you specify a file path such as c:\outfiles\, each rendering computer stores output files to what it sees as c:\outfiles\. In our example, c: will most likely be a drive on the server, so the output files will be stored locally at each rendering computer. You then have to gather the output files together manually where you want them.

Rather than storing the output locally, most people want to save the rendered files to a network drive. In many network rendering farms, a drive array may be set up to handle the enormous amount of data that can be generated during network rendering. Typically, you will pick the machine with the largest hard drive and save all the files to that machine. This is especially true if you are using a PVR, because you will want to save files directly to the PVR.

There are two ways of storing to a network drive. The easiest way is to map a common network drive to the same drive letter when you configure Server at each machine. A good network drive letter is N: (for Network), but you can use any free drive letter you want. (Refer to your NT documentation for more information on setting up network connections and shared drives.) When you specify the output file path in MAX, set the drive letter to this common drive letter. Because this drive letter points to the same drive on all the networked computers, all the output files will be placed in the same location.

Another way to output to a network drive is to specify the output path in MAX by using the Universal Naming Convention (UNC). UNC names begin with a double backslash and do not include a drive letter. This is the convention:

\\machine_name\directory\subdirectory\filename

You can either type the UNC name into the File name field or click the Network button in the Render Output File dialog box shown in figure 16.16. (To display the Render Output File dialog box, choose Files in the Render Scene dialog box.) If you click on Network, NT's Map Network Drive dialog box is displayed, as shown in figure 16.17. In this dialog box, you can select the machine, drive, and path where you want to store the output files. After you select these, the Drives field in the Render Output File dialog box points to this machine and path by its UNC name. At this point, type the output file name in the File name field.

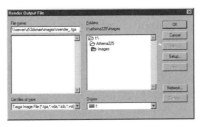

Figure 16.16

The Render Output File dialog box, which uses a UNC path name.

TIP

To prevent the selected machine and path from being mapped as a drive, open the Drive drop-down list and select None from the bottom of the list (see figure 16.18).

Figure 16.17

The Map Network Drive dialog box.

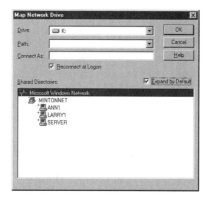

Figure 16.18

The (none) drive option will not map the selected drive to a drive letter.

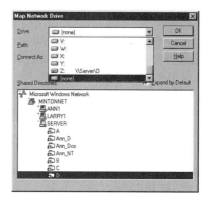

To simplify network rendering, it is best to use UNC names whenever possible within a 3DS MAX scene, even if the directory is on the local machine.

Submitting a Net Rendering Job

After you have set your rendering options and specified the output file path and name, turn on the Net Render check box in the Render Output area and choose the Render button. At this point, the Network Job Assignment dialog box is displayed, as shown in figure 16.19. You use this dialog box to submit the network rendering job to the queue.

Under Job Name, give the animation a job name. All job names in the queue must be unique. To increment the Job Name quickly, click the + button.

Within the Settings area, you can choose to submit the **.MAX** file and all bitmap files by using the Include Maps check box. When Include Maps is turned on, the **.MAX** file and all bitmap files are placed in an archive file. The program used to create the archive file is specified in the Archive System area in File, Preferences, Files. You must use an archive program compatible with the de-archive program used by the servers (see the "Network Rendering" section earlier in this chapter). If Include Maps is turned off, you need to ensure that all servers have access to the directory where the bitmaps are located. The easiest way to accomplish this is to establish a directory on a network drive to contain the bitmap files, and then point to this directory by using File, Configure Paths, Bitmaps when installing each server. The common bitmap drive and path can be specified as a mapped drive or by using its UNC name, just as you specified a UNC name for the Render Output file path name earlier.

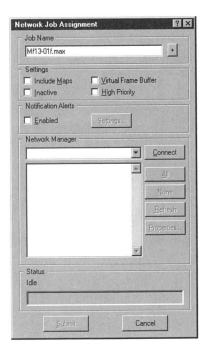

Figure 16.19

The Network Job Assignment dialog box.

The other options in the Settings area are Inactive, Virtual Frame Buffer, and High Priority. If Inactive is turned on, the job is submitted but not rendered until released by Queue Manager (see the following section, "Using Queue Manager"). If Virtual Frame Buffer is turned on, the Virtual Frame Buffer is displayed on the rendering computer as the scene is being rendered. If High Priority is turned on, the job is placed in the network rendering queue above any jobs whose High Priority option is not turned on.

In the Notification Alerts area, you turn on Notification and indicate under what conditions you want to be notified. A sample Notify program is provided with MAX that plays a tune when a render is completed or a failure has occurred. You can create your own Notify program to perform other functions, such as sending e-mail or calling a pager number to let you know the machine wants you back at the office.

In the Network Manager area, if no Manager has been previously used, or if a new Manager is to be used, click the blank field of the drop-down list and type in the name or IP address of the Manager machine. Then choose Connect to connect to the Manager machine.

A list of servers appears in the list window of the dialog box. Select the machines you want to render the animation. Machines with green dots are available and yellow dots indicate machines that are present but rendering another job. Red dots indicate machines that are present but flagged as failed. Grays indicate machines that were previously defined but are no longer present. When you select a machine, an arrow appears over the dot, as shown in figure 16.20.

Figure 16.20

The Network Job Assignment dialog box, showing the job assigned to both servers.

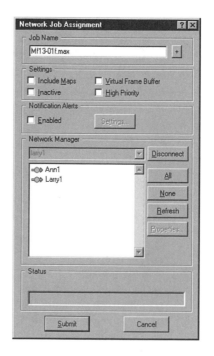

If you are not sure about the configuration of a Server machine, select it and choose the Properties button. Figure 16.21 shows the resulting Server Properties dialog box.

Choose Submit to submit the job to the network. The job is placed at the end of the queue and processed when it is at the top of the queue.

Figure 16.21

The Server Properties dialog box.

Using Queue Manager

After you start the animation on the network, you can use Queue Manager to monitor the activity of the network rendering. With Queue Manager, you can activate and deactivate jobs, check on the status of jobs, and re-order jobs in the queue. Queue Manager is a separate utility you can run on any machine connected to the network with TCP/IP, including via dial-up networking. Figure 16.22 shows the Queue Manager interface.

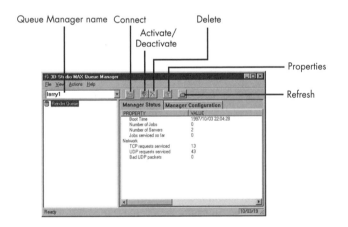

Figure 16.22

The 3D Studio MAX Queue Manager, where you can control the network rendering queue.

Again, you have to enter the name or IP address of the Manager machine and click the Connect button, located to the right of the Manager IP drop-down list. After you do this, you will see each network job listed on the left of the Queue Manager in the Job Queue list. If you select a job and expand its view, you can see all the Server machines that are working on it. Figure 16.23 shows the Queue Manager with a completed job and a rendering job listed.

Figure 16.23

The Queue Manager with one completed and one running job.

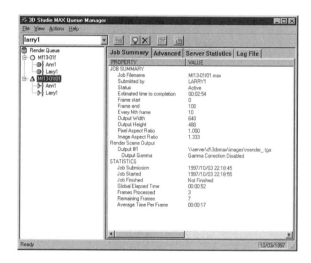

Any jobs that are active and rendering are shown with a green triangle next to them. Any jobs that are active but not yet rendering are shown with a black triangle. Any jobs that are inactive are shown with a gray cube. Any jobs that are completed are shown with an aqua sphere. Any failed jobs appear with a red triangle.

Any servers that are active and rendering the job are shown with a green triangle next to them. Any servers that are active but not assigned to the job are shown with a dotted square. Any servers that aren't assigned to the job are shown with a gray cube. Any failed servers appear with a red cube.

On the right of the Queue Manager is the Status Display. Different tabbed panels are available in the Status Display, depending on what is selected in the Job Queue. If the Render Queue is selected, the panels show Manager statistics and machine configuration. If a job is selected, the job status, render properties, and server statistics are shown. You can also display a log file for the job. If a server is selected, the status and machine properties of the server are shown. You can also display a log file for the server.

You can activate or deactivate a job at any time by selecting the job and clicking on the Activate/Deactivate icon or choosing Queue Manager's Actions, Activate/Deactivate or by right-clicking the job and selecting Activate/Deactivate from the pop-up menu.

You can stop a server machine from rendering a job at any time by selecting the server and clicking the Delete button or choosing Actions, Delete, or by right-clicking the server name and selecting Delete from the pop-up menu.

In the same manner, you can also delete a job from the Job Queue. To delete the entire queue, choose Actions, Delete Entire Queue.

Jobs are rendered from the top of the Job Queue down. You can click and drag the jobs within the queue to change their execution order.

Finally, you can use Queue Manager to assign times of the day when a server will be available for network rendering. To do so, select the server and choose the Properties button from the toolbar. Figure 16.24 shows the resulting Server Properties dialog box.

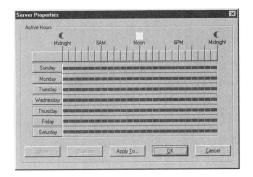

Figure 16.24

The Queue Manager Server Properties dialog box.

To set the times when a server is active or inactive, click and drag across a time slot. Time slots are broken down into hour increments. To select all the hours in a day, click on the day's name. After you highlight a time slot, choose Allow or Disallow. If you choose the Allow button, the time slot turns green. If you choose the Disallow button, the time slot turns red. When the time slots are blue, the server is always available. Figure 16.25 shows a server setting that disables network rendering during working hours.

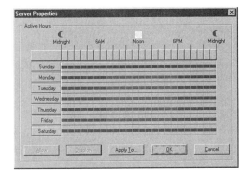

Figure 16.25

Server properties for working hours disallowance.

After you set the times, choose the Apply To button. A list of active servers then appears in the Apply Server Properties dialog box, as shown in figure 16.26. Select the servers you want to apply the schedule to, and click OK.

Figure 16.26

The Apply Server Properties dialog box.

Generally speaking, you do not have to set server properties, because machines to which you will be network-rendering are dedicated to that purpose. But having the capability to schedule network renderings in this manner can be useful.

Network rendering is a powerful capability of MAX, but it sometimes gets fouled up. If this happens, restart all machines, including the Manager machines. The network rendering will take up where it left off.

Running Manager and Server as Services

In the above discussions of Manager and Server, these programs were run as normal programs in Desktop mode. You can also run Manager and Server as Windows NT services. A service is started when you boot NT, even before you log in as a user. Services run in the background and are not visible to users. Installing Manager and/ or Server as services allows background rendering and is convenient, but it does have its downside. The main problem with running as a service is that, if there is a problem, you won't see any error or warning messages. It therefore is critical that you use Manager and Server in Desktop mode for a period of time until you are sure your configuration is stable.

Another issue is that services normally run in what is called the *system account*. This account is restricted to accessing drives on only the local machine. A problem occurs when you want to save files to a network drive. When MAX is run under the system account, it cannot write any information to the network drive due to a user rights error. To solve this problem, you must set up the service to work with a specific account under NT, with network connection rights specifically devoted to network rendering.

For information on running Manager and Server as services and creating a new account for these services, see "Network Rendering, Installing Network Services Under Windows NT," in MAX's online reference manual.

Output Options

The last thing to look at when it comes to rendering animations is your output options. Animations can be output to a variety of file formats and hardware devices. The most common formats and hardware devices are described in the following list:

♦ **Individual Bitmap Files:** Animations can be rendered to individual bitmap files such as TARGA, TIF, and GIF. These files are numbered corresponding to their order in the animation. Use the *N*th serial numbering option if you choose this method often. This method is the most common and works great with network rendering.

♦ **AVI Files:** Microsoft's Audio Video Interleaved format is a digital video format you can play back by using the Media Player. This format is popular for preview animations or distribution on CD-ROM. You cannot use it with network rendering.

♦ **FLC Files:** You cannot use Autodesk's proprietary online animation format with network rendering.

♦ **Accom WSD Device:** This specialized device records 30 or 60 seconds of uncompressed animation with the best quality possible. This device uses a special driver in MAX. You access it by choosing Devices instead of Files in the Render Scene dialog box.

♦ **Perception Video Recorder (PVR):** This device uses individual bitmaps and records them to a proprietary animation format on a dedicated hard drive that can be played back at 30 or 60 fields per second.

♦ **Other:** You can use many other devices with MAX to compile and play back animations. You can use, for example, MPEG cards, other MJPEG cards, and software such as Adobe Premiere or Speed Razor.

Animations are often rendered to individual bitmap files, even if that is not the desired final format. You can then use MAX's Video Post, or an external program, to compile the individual bitmaps in the final format. Because most of the other formats perform compression on the images as they are saved, this separates the rendering step (which can be a significant investment in time) from the compilation of the images in the final format. This also allows you to more easily correct any flaws in the animation without worrying about the possible image degradation due to decompressing and recompressing the images stored in the final format.

Conclusion

Rendering an animation correctly with the correct options is essential to good animation productivity. MAX provides you with many tools, including powerful network rendering, to increase your power and reduce the time necessary to render animations. This chapter discussed the following:

♦ Motion Blur

♦ Field Rendering

♦ Configuring for a Network Rendering

♦ Output Options

Up to this point, you have been limited to the visual special effects provided by environmental effects. The next chapter deals with special effects performed on rendered images by using Video Post.

C H A P T E R 17

Exploring Video Post Fundamentals

Up to this point, you have seen many basic features of 3D Studio MAX from modeling to rendering to animation. The last feature to take a look at is the Video Post, which is used to apply special effects to various parts of a scene. A Lens Flare from a bright light is an example of a Video Post effect. This chapter focuses on how to make use of the Video Post features of 3D Studio MAX. In particular, this chapter focuses on the following:

♦ What Is the Video Post

♦ Working with Video Post

♦ Working with Image Filters

♦ Working with Compositors

♦ Working with Optical Effects

What Is the Video Post

The Video Post (or VP) is a post-production special effects suite. Through VP, you can apply image filters or composite images together. This is accomplished through the use of a timeline and a Video Post queue, as shown in figure 17.1.

Figure 17.1

The Video Post dialog box showing an empty queue and timeline. By adding events to the queue, you can create special effects.

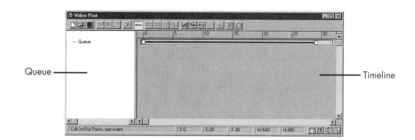

Queue

Timeline

Video Post is essentially a post-production routine. In other words, when MAX finishes rendering an image, it hands the image to Video Post, along with other pertinent data such as Z-Buffer data or Object Channel data. Video Post then processes the image using a wide variety of filters or compositors. Video Post is similar to using filters in Photoshop to adjust an image. As a matter of fact, most Photoshop filters (as long as the filter is a 32-bit filter) can be used inside of the Video Post as image filters.

Video Post filters can apply special effects, such as blurs, highlights, or glows to specific parts of your scene. This is accomplished through some of the extra data that is passed to the Video Post from MAX. This data includes the Geometry Buffer and the Material Effects Channel. The geometry buffer (called G-Buffer) is used to assign an ID number to a specific object. Then this number can be used to apply filters to that specific object. The Material Effects Channel works the same way, but at a material level instead of an object level. Figure 17.2 shows you an example of a scene without Video Post effects. Figure 17.3 shows the same scene after applying a few Video Post effects.

As you can see from figures 17.2 and 17.3, Video Post is a powerful image processing program that can be used to add that little extra bit of realism and flare to a scene to make it stand out from others.

Figure 17.2

A scene without any Video Post effects.

Figure 17.3

The same scene after applying a few Video Post effects. Notice how much different the scene looks with Video Post in use.

When using Video Post, all scenes are set up and rendered from Video Post, instead of using the Render Scene command, and the same controls in Video Post are within Render Scene, so this should not present any problems. If you do not render from Video Post, no Video Post effects will appear in the scene.

Working with Video Post

The Video Post Module of 3D Studio Max is accessed by selecting Render, Video Post. The dialog box shown in figure 17.1 appears. This dialog box is the heart of the Video Post system. The VP dialog box is broken down into three sections: a toolbar, the VP Queue, and the VP Timeline.

The Video Post Queue

VP is based on a queue analogy in which you add events to the queue. These events are then processed in the order in which you entered them. You will almost always have at least three events in the queue when rendering in the Video Post. The first event is a scene event, which tells Video Post which view you want to render and with what parameters. Then, you will have at least one filter or compositing event that processes the image after rendering. (Often you will have more than one filter or compositor.) The last event is always an output event so that you can save the file in any format that is supported by MAX.

NOTE   Although you will often use Video Post at render time, you can substitute an input file event instead of the Scene event to process a series of still images that have already been created.

To add a Scene event to the Video Post, select the Add Scene Event button on the VP toolbar. You are then prompted with the Add Scene Event dialog box where you can select the view and set the Rendering Options, which are defined by the currently selected rendering engine. You can also set the length of time for the VP queue if you wish. The length of time is given in frames in VP.

After you have added a Scene event to the VP queue, you add one or more filters or compositors to the queue. This can be accomplished in two different ways. First, you can select the Scene event and add the filter directly on top of the event, which creates a hierarchy, as shown in figure 17.4. The second is to add the filter event directly after the Scene event, as shown in figure 17.5. You must choose one method or the other depending upon the type of filter you use. The Starfield filter, for example, requires the first one, whereas all of the Lens Effects filters require the second.

Figure 17.4

The Video Post queue with a hierarchical filter setup. Here, the filter is applied directly to the Scene event.

Figure 17.5

The Video Post queue with a linear filter setup. Here, the filter is applied in the order of the VP queue.

A compositor, on the other hand, is a filter that combines two images into a single image by compositing one image over the top of the other. To make use of a compositor filter, you must have at least two input events in the queue. Usually these two events are a Scene event and an image input event. Then, by selecting both queue events, you can apply the compositor filters.

Filters and compositors are applied by selecting the appropriate button on the VP toolbar. This brings up the Add Image Filter Event (or Add Image Layer Event) dialog box, which is shown in figure 17.6.

Figure 17.6

The Add Image Filter Event dialog box, where you can select the filter, setup, and parameters associated with that filter.

Each filter that you add to the VP queue can be given its own name. You can have multiple glow filters applied to your image, for example. Instead of seeing multiple Lens Effect Glow entries, you could rename them with more specific titles, such as Outdoor Light Glow or Car Headlight Flare.

Then you have a drop-down list where you can select the filter that you want to apply. MAX ships with 13 filters that you can choose from. Many of the plug-ins for MAX are also Video Post filters and appear in this list when loaded. After you select a filter type, you can choose the Setup button to set up the parameters associated with the filter. Some filters have no parameters at all and others have several hundred. Figure 17.7 shows you the setup parameters for the Lens Effects filter, which is one of the most complex filters available but is easy to use.

Figure 17.7

The Lens Effects Flare setup dialog box. Notice how much control you have over the various features of the Lens Effects filter.

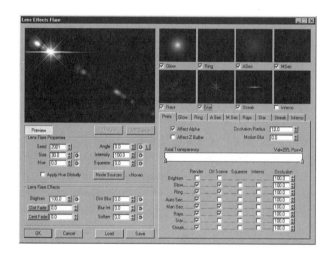

After you set up the parameters associated with the filter or compositor, you can choose OK to return to the Add Image Filter Event dialog box. Then choose OK to return to Video Post.

The Video Post Timeline

After an event is added to the queue, this event has an associated timeline, which defines in time where this filter is active. When an event is unselected, the timeline is blue; when an event is selected, the timeline is red. Each timeline entry has a start point and an end point that can be adjusted by simply clicking the start or end and dragging it along the timeline to adjust its position. If you need to adjust the timeline to a position that is not visible in the VP dialog box, you can use the View control buttons in the lower right of the dialog box to control the view. All of this should be familiar because the actual workings of VP are very similar to Track View.

After the input, filters, and output events are set in the VP queue, you can select the Execute Sequence button from the toolbar to render the queue. Figure 17.8 shows the dialog box that appears when you choose Execute Sequence.

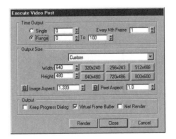

Figure 17.8

The Execute Video Post dialog box, where you can set the output size, range, and a few other parameters.

When the queue is selected, MAX processes the VP queue frame by frame, using the VP queue order that you defined.

VP queue sequences can be saved and loaded into other scenes at any time. The first three buttons on the VP toolbar can start new queues, load existing ones, or save them. Saved queues have a *.VPX extension.

Working with Image Filters

An Image filter is a processing algorithm that modifies a 2D image in some way. Examples of an Image filter are blur, contrast, fade, glows, highlights, and lens flares. Many of these effects can be applied in other packages such as Photoshop, but applying them in VP is much easier.

Some Image filters can process an entire image, whereas others only process specific objects or work at specific depths in a scene. The Z Focus filter, for example, can blur objects behind other ones, making the image look as though it was filmed through a camera with a relatively low F-stop setting, allowing a slower shutter speed.

The control of where Video Post filters work is handled through three different mechanisms in MAX: the Geometry Buffer, the Material Effects Channel, and the Z-Buffer.

The G-Buffer ID of an object is controlled by selecting the object and accessing the Object Properties dialog box. Here you will find a G-Buffer spinner that can be adjusted to set a specific G-Buffer number for use in Video Post. You can then set a Video Post filter to work only with objects that have a particular G-Buffer number.

The Material Effects Channel number is set in the Material Editor by selecting the Material Effects Button at the bottom of the preview window. These numbers work just like the G-Buffer but are limited to materials instead of objects. So if you have an object with Multi-Sub/Object materials applied, you can set the filter to affect only one of those materials if you want. Sometimes the Material Effects Channel is referred to as the Material ID, which is different from the Multi/Sub-Object Material ID number. Material IDs in the Material Editor are limited to 16, thus limiting the number of VP effects you can use.

The last method of selecting objects for use in VP is the Z-Buffer. The Z-Buffer is simply the distance that an object is from the camera. This information is automatically transferred to VP by MAX, so you do not have to do anything other than set the Z-Buffer settings in the Image filter, if it supports such an option.

NOTE Almost all Video Post filter parameters can be animated through Track View. To accomplish this, you need to open Track View and adjust the animation after you have added the Video Post filter to the VP queue.

The following exercise shows how to apply a Starfield background as a Video Post filter to the background of a nighttime scene of a water fountain. (The water has been removed from the scene for the sake of speed).

APPLYING A STARFIELD IMAGE FILTER TO A SCENE

1. Load the file **MF17-01.MAX** from the accompanying CD (see figure 17.9).

2. Select Render, Video Post to access Video Post.

3. Choose Add Scene Event.

4. Select the Camera view as the view and choose OK. You may want to check the Render options. They are set for optimal image quality.

5. Choose OK to return to VP.

6. Select the Camera entry in the VP queue.

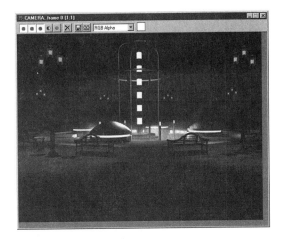

Figure 17.9

The Water Fountain scene before adding the Starfield background.

7. Choose Add Image Filter Event.

8. Select Starfield from the drop-down list to select the Image filter you want to use.

9. Choose Setup. This displays the Starfield setup dialog box.

10. Set the Dimmest Star setting to 40. Set the Count spinner to 20000 and Compositing to Background.

11. Choose OK to return to Add Image Filter Event. Then choose OK to return to VP.

12. Choose Execute Sequence.

13. Set the Time Output to Single and the size to 640x480. Make sure Virtual Frame Buffer is checked and choose Render. The image is rendered as shown in figure 17.10. Compare it to the image in figure 17.9.

The files in this chapter take a substantial amount of time to render. To speed this up, you can turn off the ray-traced materials in the Copper and Water materials and turn off shadows in the rendering options.

NOTE

The park benches and street lamps in the water fountain scene have been provided by Nsight Studios (www.nserve.com/nsight) from their Model collection.

NOTE

Figure 17.10

The Water Fountain scene after adding a Starfield background. Notice how the added context adds realism to the scene.

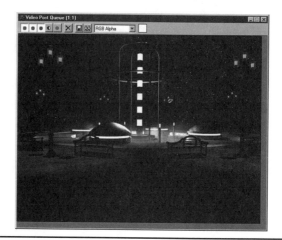

As you can see from the last exercise, setting up a simple Video Post queue is not that difficult. Many filters in VP do not provide previews, however, so many times the only way to see the effect is to render the scene. (Most of the Lens Effects filters do provide their own previews.)

NOTE If you have Photoshop or Premiere, you can use many of the 32-bit plug-ins from these programs as Image filters, providing you with an almost limitless number of choices and effects that you can create.

Filters are a powerful method of adding many optical effects to MAX scenes that could not otherwise be generated. Another option is to use Video Post to composite two or more image sources into a final image.

Working with Compositing Events

Compositing filters are different from Image filters because compositing filters are used to combine two or more images into a single image. Usually this is done by making use of the alpha channel of one or more of the images that are being composited.

The alpha channel is an extra 8 bits of image data (making the image 32 bits) that represents 256 levels of transparency in an image. Images that have alpha channels are usually generated by a program such as MAX. This transparency data can then be used to composite the image over the top of another. This type of compositing is useful any time you want to composite a rendering over a still image or series of still images and have the images blend together well.

You can accomplish a similar task by using the Environmental controls and applying a bitmap as the background. You will find, however, that VP compositing filters are a little more accurate when it comes to transparent or small, thin objects that are difficult to composite.

The following exercise shows how to use VP to composite the fountain scene over a sunset. The fountain scene has been modified slightly to match the sunset image.

COMPOSITING A SUNSET INTO A SCENE

1. Load the file **MF17-02.MAX** from the accompanying CD. This is the water fountain adjusted to match the sunset.

2. Select Render, Video Post.

3. Select Add Image Input Event.

4. Choose Files and select the **Sunset92.tga** file from the CD.

5. Choose OK to return to the VP.

6. Choose Add Scene Event. Add the Camera view to the Queue.

7. Select both the Input and Camera events. (You can do this by holding down the Ctrl key and clicking each entry.)

8. Choose Add Image Layer Event.

9. Select Alpha Compositor and choose OK.

10. Choose Execute Sequence and render the first frame to 640 x 480. Figure 17.11 shows the resulting image.

Figure 17.11

The water fountain scene composited against a sunset.

Just like Image filters, compositors are easy to set up and use. Just make sure, if you want to composite existing images over others, that they have alpha channels.

NOTE If you have Adobe Premiere 4.2 for Windows, you can use many of the Premiere transitions and filters inside of Video Post, which provides you with much of the power of Premiere, without having to actually use it. These transitions and filters provide you with many special effects.

Working with Optical Effects

One of the new features of MAX 2 that gives Video Post so much power is the optical effects package that provides lens effects. Being so used to viewing the world through a camera lens, you have probably become used to seeing many effects that are only present when using a camera lens. A lens flare, for example, occurs when you have a bright light in front of the camera. The flare is simply a result of light bending off the camera lens. In real life, without a camera lens, flares don't really exist, but we are so used to seeing them that many scenes don't look quite right without them.

Other optical effects such as Z Focus are necessary to make scenes look more realistic by blurring objects at various depths in the scene or focusing attention on a specific part of a scene. MAX 2 has four filters that handle four different optical effects: Lens Flares, Glows, Highlights, and Z Focus. The flare and glow modules are touched on here; the others are left up to you to explore on your own.

Lens Flares

A lens flare is a common optical effect seen in many movies and commercials. A lens flare occurs when a bright light source at any angle causes reflections in the camera lens. The result is a bright spot with smaller glowing spots crossing over the image. Most of the time, lens flares are seen when the sun or other bright sources of light are in the image.

The MAX Lens Flare filter provides complete control over each and every part of a lens flare. As a matter of fact, the Lens Flare filter is composed of six different parts: Glow, Ring, Auto Secondaries, Manual Secondaries, Star Streak, and Inferno effects.

When you set up the Lens Flare, the first thing to do is select the Node source, or the source of the lens flare. Generally, this is a light object but can be any object in MAX. The Node Source button spawns a Select By Name dialog box where you can select the source.

After you have selected the Node source, turn on the Preview and VP Queue buttons. A sample version of the scene in the VP queue is rendered and the flare is applied. Be careful; scenes that take a long time to render can take a few minutes to appear in the preview. When the preview is generated, you can use the Update button to update the preview. Most of the time, the preview updates after you have changed a parameter automatically.

The Preview windows in the Lens Effects modules are excellent help, but they unfortunately render the entire scene to show the VP queue preview. This can be rather time-consuming. To help alleviate this problem, hide all objects in the scene, except the objects to which you are going to apply the effect.

 TIP

To the right of the main preview window you will find the individual preview windows for each part of the lens flare. Each preview window has its own check box, which enables or disables that particular preview. Then, all you have to do is set the various flare properties.

First, you should set the lens flare size, which is given as a percentage of the overall image size. Usually, a size of 20 or 30 is sufficient to generate a good lens flare. Other properties include the angle, hue, brightness, and squeeze. Squeeze produces anamorphic squeezing when unusually large aspect ratios are used during rendering. A film resolution rendering, for example, is usually a 2.35 to 1 aspect ratio and the lens flare can be squeezed to match this.

After the general properties are set, you can use the Preferences tab in the lower-right of the dialog box to set whether or not each part of the lens flare is rendered. The Offscene column of check boxes determines whether portions of a lens flare appear when the source is not visible or off the screen. In real life, the flare effects appear even when the source is not onscreen. Each option can also optionally be squeezed according to the settings under Lens Flare Properties. Each part of a flare can also have an Inferno or fractal noise effect applied as well. Lastly, you can set the occlusion for objects, which is used when the flare source goes behind an object in the scene to correctly hide the flare.

Then you simply set each portion of the lens flare, such as the glow or star, as you see fit. Use the smaller preview windows to refine each part and the main preview window to see the result.

Glows

The Glows portion of the lens effects package is heavily used in many instances. Glow applies a glow around any object by its G-Buffer setting, Material ID, Color, Z-Buffer depth, Surface Normal angle, or other parameters. The glow routine is essentially the same as the glow portion of the lens flare but can be applied separately.

Glows can have Inferno effects applied as well as occlusion. Also, as with the Lens Flare module, you have a preview window that you can use to view the scene with the Glows applied and before rendering.

The following exercise shows how to apply a few glows to the water fountain scene that you worked on earlier. These glows are centered around the lights in the scene, which would normally have an aura around them at night.

ADDING GLOWS TO THE WATER FOUNTAIN

1. Load the file **MF17-03.MAX** from the accompanying CD.

2. Hide all the objects in the scene, except for the lampposts.

3. Open Video Post. You will see the Camera event with a Starfield applied.

4. Choose Add Image Filter event.

5. Select Lens Effects Glow and choose OK.

6. Double-click the Lens Effects Glow entry in the Queue and then choose Setup. (You must add the Glow event before entering setup to view the preview correctly.)

7. Turn on Preview and VP Queue. It takes a few seconds for the preview to appear.

8. Set the Source to Material ID and the spinner to 2. You should see the Preview update almost immediately.

9. Go to the Preferences tab and set the Size spinner to 5. Figure 17.12 shows the resulting preview.

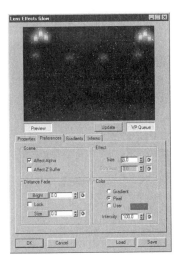

Figure 17.12

The Glow preview after applying a glow to the lamppost lights. Notice how much more realistic the scene appears.

10. Choose OK to return to the Video Post queue.

11. Hide the Light Post objects and unhide the Tower Light01 object.

12. Unhighlight any entries in the queue and choose Add Image Filter event. Add another Glow, choose OK, and return back to the setup.

13. Enable the Preview and VP Queue buttons.

14. Set the Object (G-Buffer) ID to 3.

15. Under the Preferences tab, set the size to 30. Figure 17.13 shows the preview at this point.

16. Choose OK to return to the Video Post.

17. Unhide all objects and choose Execute Sequence to see the final results.

18. Save the file as **MF17-03b.MAX**.

Figure 17.13

The Glow module with a preview showing the glow around the Tower Lights.

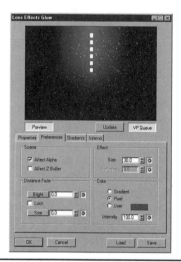

As you can see from the previous exercise, using the Glow module is not difficult at all. After the G-Buffer or Material Effects Channel is set up, you can apply the glow and use the preview to see exactly what is going on as you make changes to the glow parameters.

Conclusion

Video Post is essentially a special effects package that enables you to perform some basic non-linear editing and image filtering, all of which is controllable. This chapter focused on how to make use of the 3D Studio MAX Video Post. In particular, you learned about:

♦ How to Post Process Images

♦ How to Composite Two Images Together

♦ How to Add Optical Effects to a Scene

Now you have reached the end of your journey into the fundamentals of 3D Studio MAX 2. Remember, this is just a starting point, and there is much more to learn. As a matter of fact, with a product such as MAX 2, you will never stop learning!

G L O S S A R Y

Many of the terms in MAX may be unfamiliar to you. The following is a list of the most common terms and their definitions.

3D Acceleration   Video hardware enhancements that dramatically speed up the display of 3D Scenes. MAX 2.0 supports cards that support OpenGL 1.1, Heidi, or Direct3D (Under 95 or NT 5.0).

3D Digitizer   A mechanical arm with sensors that determines the physical position of a key point on an object and creates a 3D version based on that data.

3D Object Library   Stock 3D objects in a variety of different formats and resolutions, as an alternative to modeling.

3D Paint Software   Software program or plug-in that enables you to paint texture maps or materials directly onto the surface of an object.

Align   A command that brings object surfaces flush with each other or centers multiple objects along one or more axes.

Alpha Channel   An optional layer of image data that provides an extra 8 bits of information about transparency. The alpha channel is used as a mask for compositing one image over another.

Ambient Color   The hue an object reflects if it isn't directly illuminated by a light source. Ambient color is intended to be representative of the color of the light reflecting off the objects in a scene, but only radiosity can truly accomplish this.

Ambient Light   In theory, the cumulative effect of all the light bouncing off all the objects in an area. Generally set as a global value that illuminates all objects in the scene equally.

Angle of Incidence   The angle at which a light ray strikes a surface and is reflected into the viewer's eyes.

Animated Texture   A video or animation file used instead of still images as a texture map, causing the texture on an object to change over time when the scene is rendered.

Animation   In 3D Graphics, the modification of any kind of object, light, material, or camera by moving or changing it over time. The creation of action or movement with inanimate objects.

Animation Controller   Any of a number of different methods for creating or modifying animation keyframes or object behavior. Controllers include: TCB, Bézier, audio, noise, and expression.

Anti-aliasing   A method of softening the rough edges of an image by adding or modifying pixels near the stair-stepping points. These create a blend between the object and background colors.

Array   A matrix or pattern of objects extrapolated from a single object or group of objects. Usually found as radial or linear arrays, but can also be three-dimensional.

Aspect Ratio   The relationship between width and height of an image, expressed as a decimal ratio. Aspect Ratio is calculated by dividing the width by height, for example, an image 4" by 3" would have an aspect ratio of 1.3333.

Atmospheric Effects   Camera- or light-dependent effects such as fog or volume lights that are added to a scene.

Attach   A command that allows separate elements to be joined into one object.

Attenuation   The decay of light over distance from the original light source, used to simulate light over long distances.

Axis   An imaginary line in 3D space that defines a direction. The standard axes used in 3D programs are called X, Y, and Z.

Backface Cull   The removal of faces from the backside of an object in a viewport. Culling results in more realistic, less confusing views of scenes.

Bank   The rotation (or roll) that an object or camera may perform when it moves through a curve in a path. This simulates the results of centrifugal force on a real-world object as it executes a turn.

Bend   A modifier that deforms an object by applying torsion around the selected axis.

Bevel   A flat transitional plane located between two other planes, usually set at an angle that is half the difference between the two.

Bézier Spline   A type of spline where the control points always exist on the resulting curve. Extending out from the control points are tangent points, which allow the curve to be modified without moving the control points.

Bias   In a TCB animation controller, the bias adjusts the location of maximum extreme point (or peak) of the motion path or control curve in relation to the keyframe.

Bitmap   A term referring to an image encoded as a series of dots or pixels. TIF, Targa, JPEG, and Gif are examples of bitmap file formats.

Blinn   A shading method that provides smoothing and specular highlights that are not quite as bright as Phong highlights. Named after its inventor Jim Blinn.

Bluescreen   A blue background that serves as a stage for actors. The blue can be removed after filming and replaced with a different background. Costumes and props shot on a bluescreen stage cannot contain blue or purple pigments, because the compositing process would cause any blue or purple elements to become transparent. An alternative is a greenscreen, which allows blue and purple objects, but no green ones.

Bones Deformation　A technique of animating an object (usually a character) by defining and animating an internal skeleton that automatically deforms the surrounding mesh. Character Studio and Bones Pro are two plug-ins that perform this function.

Boolean Operation　A set of commands that adds, subtracts, or joins one object to or from another, commonly used to reshape or "drill holes" in objects.

Bounding Box　A stand-in in the shape of a box that has the same overall dimensions as the object. Bounding boxes replace mesh intensive objects during movement or other translations, so that the system won't be bogged down redrawing a large amount of mesh.

Box Coordinates　A type of mapping coordinate system well-suited to rectangular objects, which applies the image coordinates from six different directions, one for each surface on the object.

Bump Map　A grayscale image that varies the apparent surface roughness of an object by manipulating the normals.

Camera　In 3D Graphics, an object that is used to simulate viewing a scene like a real-world camera. In general, these objects have controls similar to cameras, such as FOV, Lens Length, and others.

Camera Target　The point in 3D space that a camera is looking at, which is indicated by a small box attached to the camera object.

Center Point　The geometric center of an object, the center of the coordinate system, or the center of a selection set.

Chain　A series of linked objects using the hierarchical parent-child relationship but extending it by additional generations to grandchild, great-grandchild, and so forth.

Chamfer　See Bevel.

Channel　An individual attribute of a material that can accept images, or be set to affect the appearance of the object to which they are applied. Typical channels include Diffuse, Bump, Opacity, Shininess, and Self-Illumination.

Character Animation　The process of imbuing objects not only with movement but with personality. Virtually any object can take on personality if character animation techniques are applied to it.

Child　An object linked to another that is closer to the beginning of the hierarchical tree (its parent).

Chroma　The color of an object determined by the frequency of the light emitted from or reflected by the object.

Chroma Key　A process that electronically removes a solid color (usually blue or green) and allows it to be replaced with another image. Often used to composite virtual characters into virtual environments. In some cases, a video "super black" signal is used instead of a visible color.

Clipping Plane   Also known as the viewing plane. A user-definable cut-off point that makes everything on the camera's side of it invisible during rendering.

Clone   A method of copying an object in MAX. Objects can be cloned as copies, instances, or references.

Closed Shape   A shape that has an inside and an outside, separated from each other by an edge.

CMYK   Cyan Magenta Yellow blacK. The different colors of ink in the four-color printing process that are applied as tiny dot patterns to form full-color images.

Codec   Compressor Decompressor. Any one of a number of different methods for compressing video and playing it back. Digital video file formats such as AVI and Quicktime are designed to accept plug-in compression technologies in the form of codecs.

Color   The hue of an object, determined by the frequency of the light emitted by the object. In computer graphics, color is determined by the combination of Hue, Saturation, and Value in the HSV color model, or Red, Green, and Blue color levels in the RGB color model.

Color Depth   The amount of data used to display a single pixel in an image, expressed in bits. For example, an 8-bit image contains 256 colors or levels of gray.

Color Temperature   A value, in degrees Kelvin, that is used to differentiate between near-white and spectrums of light.

Compositing   The process of combining different elements into a single scene. This may refer to combining still photos or bluescreen video with computer graphics backgrounds, or be applied to any process in which separate images are combined together.

Compositor   A video post filter type that is used to perform compositing within MAX. Compositors require two input events in the Video Post queue to function correctly.

Compression Rate   The speed at which digital video data is encoded for playback, defined in kilobytes per second (KB/s) For the movies to playback properly, the target system must be capable of pulling the movie data off the storage medium and displaying it at that speed.

Constraint   A restriction placed on the movement of an object in IK, in order to force it to behave like a physical joint.

Continuity   In a TCB controller, continuity adjusts how tangent the path is to the control point. In filmmaking, it is the process of maintaining a smooth flow of consistency in props, costumes, action, and direction from shot to shot in a scene.

Control Vertices   (CVs) Control points that exert a magnet-like influence on the flexible surface of a patch, NURBS spline, or NURBS surface, stretching and tugging it in one direction or another.

Coordinate System   Two or three sets of numbers that use a grid-based system to identify a given point in space.

Crossing   A method of selecting objects with a region, circle, or polygon. All objects within or touching the region are selected.

Cylindrical Coordinates   A mapping coordinate system that wraps the image around one of the object's axes until it meets itself, like the label on a soup can.

Decal   An image that can be scaled and moved around on an object independently of any other texture mapping.

Default Lighting   The startup lighting in MAX, which enables the user to begin rendering without having to define a light source. This is two omni lights in MAX.

Deform Fit   A type of deform modifier for a loft object that enables you to define the shape of an object using an X-axis outline, a Y-axis outline, and one or more cross sections.

Degradation   The reduction of geometry detail, based on viewport playback speed. When the minimum playback speed is compromised, the shading level of the viewport is reduced to restore the speed.

Depth of Field   The portion of an image that is properly focused. In photography, depth of field is controlled by the aperture setting. In 3D Graphics, depth of field is normally infinite but can be controlled through the use of Video Post image filters.

Detach   An operation that disconnects an element of a larger object, separating it into two objects. The opposite of attach.

Diffuse Color   The hue assigned to an object. This is the color that is reflected when the object is illuminated by a direct lighting source.

Diffuse Map   A mapping channel used to change the object's color from the color defined by the color settings, usually a pattern or image.

Digital Retouching   The process of using 2D paint programs to modify photographic stills or movies.

Digitizing   The process of transforming images, objects, or sounds into a digital form that the computer can manipulate.

Directional Light   Also called a distant light. A virtual illumination source for simulating far away light sources such as the sun. It projects light along one axis only, and all the light rays (and hence, shadows) are parallel.

Displacement Map   Also known as a deformation map. A grayscale image applied to an object that actually distorts the mesh, deforming it according to the gray value. Often used to create Terrain models.

Dolly   In filmmaking, a wheeled platform that a camera is mounted on, and the process of moving the camera around on the floor during the shot. In 3D, it means a camera movement made toward or away from the subject.

Dongle   A hardware key, which is a physical device plugged into the parallel port of a computer.

Double-Sided Object   An object with normals on both sides of the object's faces, allowing it to be seen from any viewpoint, even inside.

DPI Dots per Inch   Resolution expressed in the number of dots or pixels that the medium can display in one inch. 300 dpi is a common laser printer output resolution.

Dummy Object　An object that does not render, so it can be used as an invisible component of a chain or as a reference point for establishing remote axes of rotation.

Dynamics　A system used to simulate real-world physics such as gravity, friction, and collisions in a computer animation. For example, a bowling ball striking bowling pins is a great dynamics simulation.

Ease From　A keyframe parameter that controls the acceleration of the object or event as it leaves the keyframe.

Ease To　A keyframe parameter that controls the acceleration of the object or event as it enters the keyframe.

Edge　The visible line between two vertices that form a face.

Emitter　A simple polygonal shape that acts as a point of origin for particles in a particle system.

Environment　The backgrounds and/or atmospheric effects that are present in a scene.

Exclude　A feature that enables listed objects to be unaffected by the selected light source.

Export　Saving a file in a cross program or cross-platform format, such as DXF.

Extrude/Extrusion　The process of pushing a 2D shape into the third dimension by giving it a Z-axis depth.

Face　The area enclosed by the edges of a polygon, forming a three- or four-sided surface.

Face Extrusion　A process that takes a selected face or faces and extrudes them in or out from their current positions.

Face Mapping　An image mapping type that tries to conform the image to individual faces on an object.

Falloff　The portion or range of a light source that is at a reduced or 0 intensity setting. Also, a set of transparency options that sets how much more or less transparent an object is at its edges.

Field of View (FOV)　The angle, in degrees, that encompasses everything that can be seen through a lens or virtual camera viewport.

Field Rendering　Output option that renders images in the same way that a television displays them: in two alternating passes, one with every odd scanline rendered, the other with every even line. Compare with frame rendering.

File Format　The manner in which data is organized in a computer file. Common image file formats include BMP, PICT, and TGA. Popular 3D file formats include 3DS, DXF, and OBJ.

Fillet　Also called a radius edge. An arcing transition between two planes or lines.

Filter　A video post routine that applies image-processing techniques to the final rendering.

First Vertex　The vertex in a shape that is used for orientation during skinning operations. Usually the one that was created first but it can be any vertex assigned as such.

Flat Shading A display or rendering mode that shows off the surface and color of the objects in a faceted manner, because the polygons aren't smoothed.

Focal Length The distance in millimeters from the center of the lens to the image it forms of the subject (assumed to be an infinite distance in front of the lens). Short focal lengths will result in wide angle images, while long ones are used for tele-photo shots.

Forward Kinematics The default method of animating linked objects, in which the movement of the parent object affects all the offspring down the chain.

Frame In filmmaking or animation, a single still image that is part of a sequence. Also, the visible portion of a scene when viewed through a camera or viewport.

Frame Rate The speed at which film, video, or animated images are displayed, in frames per second (FPS).

Frame Rendering The default output option that renders the entire image. Compare with field rendering.

Freeze A command that leave an object visible in a scene, but prevents it from being selected or changed.

Function Curve A graphical way of displaying object transformations or other animatable parameters.

G-Buffer Also called a geometry channel. A number assigned to an object so it can be referred to or selected in video post filters.

Gamma In a computer display, refers to the overall brightness of the screen. Also, a measure of brightness for all output technologies as a way of predicting their appearance when the image is viewed on a color display.

Geometry General term for 3D objects.

Ghosting A viewport display option that displays ghost images of animated objects before and after the current frame, so you can see where the object came from and where it is going in the animation.

Gizmo A helper object that is used to apply various modifier effects to an object. For example, the gizmo is used to determine the location, scale, and orientation of mapping coordinates.

Glow A video post effect that creates a soft halo of light around selected objects or materials.

Grid Cross-hatched lines visible in the viewport and used like graph paper for determining scale when creating objects.

Group A command that enables the user to select a related collection of objects and then temporarily combine them into a whole.

Helper An object that is used in conjunction with other commands to create certain effects. A dummy object is an example of a helper object.

Hidden Line A display or rendering mode that draws the edges of an object as in a wireframe display, but only ones that would be visible if the object were opaque.

Hide A command that makes an object invisible.

History   A record of all modifiers and settings applied to an object. Also known as the Stack.

Hotspot   The portion or range of a light source that is at the full intensity setting.

HSV   Hue Saturation Value. A color selection interface used in MAX that enables the user to adjust the hue (chroma), saturation (intensity), and value (brightness) to select a color.

Import   Loading a file saved in a cross-program or cross-platform format, such as DXF.

Include   A light source option that enables the user to select a list of objects that the specified light will affect. All other objects in the scene are ignored.

Instance   A type of duplicate of an object, light source, map, animation controller, or camera in which changes to one are adopted by all.

Intensity   A measure of the brightness of a light source.

Inverse Kinematics (IK)   Method of controlling linked objects by moving the far end of the hierarchical chain, which then causes the rest of the chain to conform.

Keyframe   A user defined point where an animation event takes place. MAX then tweens the events from keyframe to keyframe.

Lathe   Process of spinning a 2D shape around an axis, extruding it in small steps as it is rotated.

Lens Flare   The pattern of bright circles and rays that is seen when you point a camera lens at the sun or other bright light source.

Link   A hierarchical connection between two objects.

Local Coordinates   Coordinate system that uses the object itself as the basis for the axes.

Map   A bitmapped image, either scanned or painted, that gives a material unique qualities that aren't available by simply varying surface attributes.

Mapping   The process of developing and assigned material attributes to an object.

Mapping Coordinates   A set of coordinates that specify the location, orientation, and scale of any texture applied to an object.

Mask   A black-and-white or grayscale element that is used to prevent certain areas of an image from being affected by a process.

Material   The encompassing term for all the different images and settings that are assigned to an object's surface.

Mesh   Slang term for a 3D object or scene, called that because it resembles a wire mesh sculpture.

Mesh Optimization   The process of reducing the density of a mesh object by combining closely aligned faces.

Metal   A rendering mode that simulates the specular highlights and surface characteristics of polished metal surfaces.

Mirror   A transform that reverses an objects or copies a reversed version of it along a specified axis.

Modifier A routine that is applied to an object to modify its appearance or properties.

Morph Animated 2D or 3D technique that makes one image or form smoothly transform into another.

Motion Blur The smearing of an image or object when the subject or camera is in motion.

Motion Path A spline that represents the path of an object, used for reference when making adjustments to the animation.

Multiplier A light source setting that increases the intensity of the light past the RGB setting limits.

Named Selection Set A set of objects that are referred to by a single name so they may easily be selected in the future.

Network Rendering The process of rendering individual frames of an animation on different machines across a network.

Noise Random variations applied to materials, colors, or animation parameters to give a more natural look or motion.

Normal Imaginary marker that protrudes from a polygon face and indicates which side of the polygon is visible and what direction its facing.

NTSC American video standard, which is 29.97 frames per second.

NURBS Uniform Rational B-Splines. A type of spline that has control points that reside on or away from the resulting curve. Curves can be used to form surfaces, which are also controllable with control points.

Objects A term referring to individual meshes in a scene that have a single name.

Opacity The degree to which light rays cannot penetrate an object.

Opacity Map A grayscale image loaded into a material's opacity channel that makes the object's surface appear to vary from opaque to transparent.

Operand An object or shape being used in a Boolean Operation.

Origin Point The center point of the cyberspace universe, where the central axes meet. Identified by the coordinates 0,0,0.

Output The stage in 3D production where a file, photographic slide, or section of video tape or other media is used to store the image or animation.

Overshoot A technique that turns a spotlight into a point light, but shadows are only cast in the areas defined by the hotspot and falloff regions.

PAL The European Video Standard.

Palette The full set of colors used or available for use in an image. Usually refers to images with 256 colors or less.

Pan A side-to-side rotation of a camera around its vertical axis.

Parametric Modeling Modeling system in which objects retain their base geometry information and can be modified at almost any point by varying the parameters that define them.

Parent In a chain of linked objects, the object that is closer to the base of the hierarchy than the other object attached to it (its child).

Partial Lathe   A lathe operation in which the cross-sectional shape is not revolved a full 360 degrees.

Particle System   An animation system that enables the user to generate and control the behavior of a vast number of tiny objects. Used to simulate natural effects such as water, fire, sparks, or bubbles.

Patch Modeler   A modeling system that uses a network of control points to define and modify the shape of the patch, which is usually a lattice of either splines or polygons.

Phong Rendering   A rendering method that retains the smoothness of Gouraud shading, but adds specular highlights for more realism.

Pivot Point   User defined rotational center of an object, often the same as where the three local axes meet.

Pixel   PI(X)cture Element. The smallest unit of graphics that a video adapter generates, usually about the size of a pinpoint. Pixels can be nearly any color, depending upon the capabilities of the adapter.

Pixel Size   A render time setting that controls the oversampling of pixels, smoothing lines and producing better images.

Planar Coordinates   A type of mapping coordinate system well-suited to flat objects. It applies a set of rectangular image coordinates from a single direction.

Plug-in   An add-on feature that works within MAX. Plug-ins are popular for adding new capabilities to products without generating a new version of the software.

Point   In 3D space, the smallest area that it is possible to "occupy" is called a point. Each point is defined by a unique set of three numbers, called coordinates.

Polygon   A closed shape with three or more sides.

Polygonal Modeling   The basic type of 3D modeling, in which all objects are defined as groups of polygons.

Polyline   A line with more than one segment (at least three vertices).

Post Production Effects   Also known as video post effects. In MAX, this refers to transitions, color manipulations, or special effects applied to frames of an animation after it has been rendered.

Preview   An output mode that creates a fast-rendering test animation or a display mode that generates a simplified version of the scene in real-time.

Primitive   Any of a number of basic 3D geometric forms, including cubes, spheres, cones, cylinders, and so forth.

Procedural Object   An object generated by a mathematical formula, such as a procedural texture.

Procedural Texture   A type of texture that is mathematically defined, which can be used to simulate wood, marble, and other materials but usually doesn't look as realistic as scanned textures.

Quad   A four-sided polygon commonly used in 3D programs.

Radiosity   The property that states that light reflecting off an object goes on to illuminate other objects as well. Also, a rendering method that takes into account the color and shape of all surfaces in the scene when calculating illumination level, and produces images of a near photographic quality.

Raytracing   A rendering method where the color and value of each pixel on the screen is calculated by casting an imaginary ray backward from the viewer's perspective into the model, to determine what light and surface factors are influencing it. This is implemented as a material in MAX.

Real-time   The immediate processing of input data and graphics, so that any changes result in near-instantaneous adjustments to the image.

Reference   Similar to an instance, a duplicate of an object where changes to the original affect all references, but changes to the references are independent.

Reference Coordinate System   The coordinate system around which transforms are performed. This is user-selectable such as world, screen, or local coordinates.

Reflection Map   An image or process used to create an environment for a reflective object in order to roughly simulate the effects of raytracing on reflective objects.

Refraction   The bending of light waves that occurs when they move through different types of materials.

Refraction Mapping   A material option used as a means of simulating the effects of light refraction in programs that don't offer raytracing.

Refresh Rate   The number of time per second that the screen image is repainted on the monitor, measured in cycles per second or Hertz (HZ).

Rendering   The process wherein the computer interprets all the object and light data and creates a finished image from the viewport you have selected. The resulting image may be either a still or a frame in an animation sequence.

RGB   Red-Green-Blue. The three primary colors in the additive (direct light) color model. Computer monitors vary the brightness levels of red, green, and blue pixels in order to create the gamut of displayable colors.

Roll   To rotate a camera around its viewing axis, making the scene appear to spin.

Rotate   A transform that spins an object around the selected axis.

Rotoscoping   The process of adding film or video to animation, either as a finished element or for use as a reference for the animated characters.

Safe Frame   A defined area of a frame that will not appear cropped when viewed on a television. Appears as a box outline in the selected viewport.

Saturation   Also called intensity. The measure of how concentrated a color appears to be. A fully saturated red, for example, cannot be any more red than it is, whereas a red with a low saturation begins to turn gray.

Scale   A transformation that adjusts the size of an object. Also, the mathematical relationship between the size of a subject in reality and the size of its representation on paper is 1/4"=1'-0".

Scanline Rendering   Typical rendering method used by MAX. Renders the image as a series of horizontal lines.

Scripting   The process of programming specific actions into the MAX system. Usually used when you need added functionality or find yourself repeating the same set of commands over and over again.

Segment   A step or division in an object, similar to the way a building is divided into floors.

Self-Illumination   A material channel or control that adjusts the degree to which an object appears to be lit from within.

Self-Illumination Map   A grayscale image loaded into the material's self-illumination channel that creates the impression that some portions of the object are lit from within.

Shadow Map Size   A setting that adjusts the amount of memory that the system can use to create a given shadow map. The larger the map, the more refined and detailed it will be.

Shadow Mapping   A method of creating shadows in a scanline renderer that works by creating a grayscale texture map based on the lighting and mesh in the scene, and then applies it to the objects at render time.

Shape   A collection of one or more splines combined together to form a single object.

Shininess   The overall reflective nature of the object, in other words, its glossiness.

Shininess Map   A grayscale image loaded into the material's shininess channel that varies the reflectivity of the surface. Used to make portions of an object dull or shiny.

Skew   A transform that forces one side of an object in one direction along the selected axis, and the other side in the opposite direction.

SMPTE   Society of Motion Picture and Television Engineers. In video and 3D graphics, a time format consisting of minutes, seconds, and frames (57:31:12 would be 57 minutes, 31 seconds, and 12 frames).

Snap   A feature that causes the cursor to snap from one position to another according to user-defined grid spacing, or in reaction to various portions of an object such as vertices, edges, or center points.

Snapshot   Creates a copy of an object at a specific point in time or converts a procedural object to a mesh object.

Space Warp   A 3D effect that affects only objects that are bound to the warp and are within the influence field of the warp. A bomb explosion is an example.

Specular Color   The hue of any highlights that appears on an object at Phong rendering levels or higher. Specular color is also affected by the shininess setting, or mapping, and by the color of the lights.

Specular Highlight   The bright reflections of light on glossy objects in Phong rendering levels or higher.

Specular Map   An image loaded into the specular channel that varies the color and intensity of the specular highlights of the surface. Useful for creating the effect of prismatic or metal flake surfaces.

Spherical Coordinates   A mapping coordinate system that wraps the image around the object in a cylindrical manner, and then pinches the top and bottom closed to surround it.

Spline   A line usually curved that's defined by control points. Bézier, B-Spline, and NURBS are common types of splines.

Spotlight   A directional light source that radiates light from a single point out into a user-defined cone or pyramid.

Squash and Stretch   Modified scale operations that treat the object as though it has volume. Squashing an object makes it spread out around the edges, while stretching it makes the object get thin in the middle.

Stack   A live history of changes made to an object. You may, at any time, go back in the stack and make adjustments to any modifiers. This makes MAX a parametric modeling system.

Steps   The number of additional vertices generated between control points on a spline or predefined vertices on a poly.

Storyboarding   The process of visualizing a film or animation by breaking it down into a sequence of sketches that illustrate the key movements in the scene.

Strokes   A method of accessing commands in MAX by using simple mouse movements while holding down the middle mouse button.

Sub-Objects   Smaller elements that combine together to form a larger object. For example, vertices, faces, and edges are sub-objects of mesh geometry.

Surface Approximation   A method for approximating NURBS and Patch surfaces with triangles for rendering purposes. More accurate approximations result in better renderings, but with longer render times due to larger face counts.

Surface Attribute   A basic material setting such as color, shininess, or opacity that affects all parts of an object equally.

Tangent Point   Also called a weight. The portion of a spline control system that acts like a magnet to attract the spline in its direction.

Taper   A transform that compresses and/or expands an object along the selected axis.

Target   A positioning aid that enables the user to see where a camera or light is pointed from any viewport.

TCB Controller   Tension/Continuity/Bias controller. One of the most common methods of providing control over the keyframe control points.

Teeter   A type of loft deformation that enables the cross-section to be rotated around the X and/or Y axes perpendicular to the path.

Tension   In a TCB controller, the amount of curvature that the keyframe allows in the path before and after the keyframe.

Tessellation   The process of increasing the number of faces in a selected area by subdividing existing faces.

Texture Map   A bitmapped image, either scanned or painted, that gives a material unique qualities that aren't available by simply varying the surface attributes.

Tiling   The technique of repeating an image to cover a larger area.

Timeline   A graph-like interface for viewing and manipulating animation events.

Trajectory   The motion path for an object that already has animation applied to it.

Transform   A general term for an operation that alters the position, size, or shape of an object. Typical transforms include move, scale, and rotate.

Triangle   A three-sided polygon, the basic polygonal shape used in MAX.

Tweening   Process in which MAX takes control of how the object is transformed or blended between keyframes.

Twist   A transform that wrings an object around the selected axis.

UV or UVW Mapping   UV or UVW coordinates look similar to the XY image coordinate system, but they conform to the mesh, no matter how it bends or twists. UVW coordinates are used for mesh objects, and shifting them allows very precise repositioning of maps on an object.

Value   The lightness or darkness of a color (tinting or shading).

Vertex (Vertices)   A single point in space through which parts of an object pass.

Video Post   A post-production routine where you can filter, combine, or composite various events, scenes, and images.

Video Safe Colors   Colors that fit into the luminance and saturation limits for television broadcast. Colors outside this range blur and distort the video signal.

VP Event   A placeholder for scene views, input images, filters, compositors, or output operations in VP.

VP Queue   The order in which video post events are processed.

View Coordinates   A coordinate system that uses the viewport as the basis for the X, Y, and Z axes. The axes remain the same no matter how the user's perspective on the 3D scene changes.

Viewing Plane   A plane surrounding the viewpoint at a perpendicular angle. It is an imaginary flat panel that defines the limits of the user's field of view.

Viewpoint   A position in or around cyberspace that represents the viewer's current location.

Viewport   A window that looks into 3D space.

Virtual Memory   The use of hard drive space as temporary storage when the computer system runs low on RAM.

Volumetric Light   A type of light source with an adjustable 3D volume that can simulate the behavior of natural light in an atmosphere.

VRML   Virtual Reality Modeling Language. A web browser technology that enables the user to explore simple 3D environments online.

Weight   See Tangent Point or Control Vertices (CVs).

Weld   An operation that combines the overlapping vertices of shapes or objects together.

Window   A method of selecting objects, similar to crossing. But here, objects must reside completely within the bounding region to be selected.

Wireframe   A display or rendering mode that draws objects using lines to represent the polygon edges, which makes the object resemble a sculpture made of wire mesh.

World Coordinate   The fundamental coordinate system of 3D space, which is unchanged by the user's viewpoint.

X Axis   Typically the horizontal or width axis, running left and right.

XY Coordinates   The normal coordinate system for 2D images and shapes. The X axis runs horizontally and the Y axis vertically.

Y Axis   Usually the vertical or height axis, extending up and down.

Z Axis   The axis normally associated with depth, which runs forward and back.

I N D E X

G

H

Inside 3D Studio MAX 2 Volume I

by Doug Barnard, Paul Kakert, et al

The definitive resource for 3D Studio MAX users! This industry favorite will take you beyond the documentation to explain professional concepts, behind-the-scenes information, and advanced techniques that will enable you to master this powerful program. A must-have for your 3D Studio MAX library!

ISBN: 1-56205-857-6 $59.99 USA/$84.95 CAN   CD

Inside 3D Studio MAX 2 Volume II: Modeling and Materials

by Ted Boardman and Jeremy Hubble

Using real-world examples and expert advice from experienced 3D Studio MAX professionals, you'll explore various modeling techniques: from technical modeling for engineering visualization, to architectural modeling and rendering, to modeling for the Web, to character modeling. Detailed examples show you how to create man-made textures, natural materials, special effects, and animated materials.

ISBN: 1-56205-864-9 $59.99 USA/$84.95 CAN   CD

Inside 3D Studio MAX 2 Volume III: Animation

by George Maestri, Angela Jones, et al

Expanded to go beyond the basics of animation, this title goes in-depth on how to create professional-level animations. Real-world, detailed tutorials illustrate techniques used by animation experts from gaming, design, and film works.

ISBN: 1-56205-865-7 $59.99 USA/$84.95 CAN   CD   

Digital Character Animation

by George Maestri

Add the spark of life to your computer-generated animations! Animation expert George Maestri provides you with all the essential information needed to create convincing CG characters in 2D and 3D. The full-color presentation and step-by-step tutorials make this nonsoftware-specific book a must for every animator library.

ISBN: 1-56205-559-3 $55.00 USA/$77.95 CAN   CD

For more information or to purchase a title, please visit your local bookstore or call 1-800-653-6156.

New Riders

REGISTRATION CARD

3D Studio Max 2 Fundamentals

Name _____ Title _____

Company_____ Type of business _____

Address _____

City/State/ZIP _____

Have you used these types of books before? ☐ yes ☐ no

If yes, which ones? _____

_____

How many computer books do you purchase each year? ☐ 1–5 ☐ 6 or more

How did you learn about this book? _____

Where did you purchase this book? _____

Which applications do you currently use? _____

_____

Which computer magazines do you subscribe to? _____

_____

What trade shows do you attend? _____

_____

Comments: _____

_____

_____

Would you like to be placed on our preferred mailing list? ☐ yes ☐ no

---

☐ **I would like to see my name in print!** You may use my name and quote me in future New Riders products and promotions. My daytime phone number is: _____

New Riders Publishing   201 West 103rd Street ◆ Indianapolis, Indiana 46290 USA

Fax to **317-581-3550**

Fold Here

BUSINESS REPLY MAIL

FIRST-CLASS MAIL PERMIT NO. 9918 INDIANAPOLIS IN

POSTAGE WILL BE PAID BY THE ADDRESSEE

**NEW RIDERS PUBLISHING
201 W 103RD ST
INDIANAPOLIS IN 46290-9058**

MACMILLAN COMPUTER PUBLISHING USA

A VIACOM COMPANY

Technical ---- Support:

If you need assistance with the information provided by Macmillan
Computer Publishing, please access the information available on our web
site at **http://www.mcp.com/feedback**. Our most Frequently Asked
Questions are answered there. If you do not find the answers to your
questions on our web site, you may contact Macmillan User Services at
(317) 581-3833 or email us at **support@mcp.com**.